CONTEMPORARY YOUTH CULTURE

CONTEMPORARY YOUTH CULTURE

An International Encyclopedia

Volume 2

Edited by Shirley Steinberg, Priya Parmar, and Birgit Richard
Christine Quail, Assistant Editor

GREENWOOD PRESS
Westport, Connecticut • London

Library of Congress Cataloging-in-Publication Data

Contemporary youth culture : An international encyclopedia / edited by Shirley
Steinberg, Priya Parmar, and Birgit Richard ; Christine Quail, assistant editor.
    p. cm.
  Includes bibliographical references and index.
    ISBN 0-313-32716-5 (set : alk. paper) — ISBN 0-313-33728-4 (v. 1 : alk. paper) —
ISBN 0-313-33729-2 (v. 2 : alk. paper)   1. Youth—Social conditions—21st
century—Encylopedias. 2.Youth—Social life and customs—21st century—
Encylopedias. 3. Popular culture—Encylopedias. 4. Subculture—Encylopedias.
I. Steinberg, Shirley R., 1952– II. Parmar, Priya. III. Richard, Birgit.

   HQ796.C8154   2006
   305.23509′045—dc22   2005025482

British Library Cataloguing in Publication Data is available.

Library of Congress Catalog Card Number: 2005025482
ISBN: 0–313–32716–5 (set)
    0–313–33728–4 (vol. I)
    0–313–33729–2 (vol. II)

First published in 2006

Greenwood Press, 88 Post Road West, Westport, CT 06881
An imprint of Greenwood Publishing Group, Inc.
www.greenwood.com

Printed in the United States of America

The paper used in this book complies with the
Permanent Paper Standard issued by the National
Information Standards Organization (Z39.48–1984).

10 9 8 7 6 5 4 3 2 1

All photos by Christine M. Quail, PhD
SUNY Oneonta

In celebration of a most amazing young woman,
Shiri Berg, you lived your youth to the fullest
Shirley

To Mayah, my love and future
Priya

To my darling Heinz-Hermann with hugz
Birgit

Contents

Contents

Volume 1

Contents

Poetry and Lyrics

Preface

WHY STUDY YOUTH CULTURE?

Shirley R. Steinberg

The notion of youth as we know it has not existed very long in historical time. Such an understanding is central to the conversation about contemporary youth and the forces that shape and reshape what has been called youth in the early twenty-first century. Youth does not float in some timeless and placeless space, above and beyond the influence of historical and social forces. Like any other human dynamic, youth is shaped by macrosocial forces such as ideology. Although individual response to such forces may be unique and self-directed, it is not simply free to operate outside the boundaries drawn by such social influences.

Thus, we posit that youth is a social construction, and based on this assertion we set out to examine the forces that are presently constructing it. Many times, scholarly observations of youth have been content to leave the definition of youth uncontested and separate from larger social forces. Thus, over the last few decades, youth has been viewed as "non-social" or "pre-social," more the province of developmental psychologists with their universalizing descriptions of its "normal" phase. Such academic approaches, although pursued with good intentions, have not served the interests of youth and those who seek to help them. By undermining an appreciation of the diversity and complexity of youth, such viewpoints have often equated difference with deficiency, and sociocultural construction with the natural. The complicated nature of youth, youth study, youth psychology, social work for youth, and adolescent and youth education demands more rigorous forms of analysis. A new era of youth has been emerging since the end of the Second World War, noticed by relatively few people who make their living studying or caring for youth. Although scholars are putting more time into the study of youth, it is still not part of the mainstream discourse of most youth-related fields of study and practice. This shift has been shaped in part by the development of new information technologies and the so-called information explosion resulting from them. Information technologies are not the only factors reshaping youth, but they are very significant in this process. Because of this significance, it was argued that those with the financial resources to deploy such technologies have played an exaggerated role in reconstructing youth. This, of course, is why it is essential to study corporate ideologies and influences vis-à-vis youth culture. Because of the profound changes initiated by a variety of social, economic, political, and cultural forces, many analysts maintain that we can no longer make sense of youth by using traditional assumptions about its nature. Even though youth differs profoundly around the world, we can begin to discern some common trends in industrialized and to some degree in industrializing societies. With increasing numbers of one-parent families, the neo-liberal withdrawal of government from social responsibility for the welfare of children and youth, the transformation of the role of women in society, and increased access to information via new information technologies, the world of children and youth has profoundly changed over the last couple of generations.

In respect to changes in access to information it can be argued that young people now in the era of the new (postmodern?) youth possess huge amounts of information about topics traditionally viewed as the province of adults. Some scholars have argued that youth often have more information than adults in these domains because of the time many have to access TV, radio, the Internet, music, and other media. One of the traditional ways suggested to differentiate between youth and adults has involved knowledge of the world. In light of recent changes in information access it is safe to conclude that traditional distinctions between youth and adulthood may no longer be relevant.

Such factors not only change the way we categorize youth and adulthood but change the nature of the relationship between them. Such changes hold profound consequences for parenting, teaching, social service casework, youth psychological counseling, and other youth-related fields. In the context of parenting, evidence indicates that many youth have gained more influence in the life of the family. In such families negotiation, engagement, and more open and egalitarian forms of interaction have replaced authoritarian, hierarchical parent-child relationships. One can identify this loss of traditional forms of parental control in families operating in a variety of social and cultural contexts.

In a new private space created by youth, young adults use their access to information and media productions to negotiate their own culture, albeit within the ideological confines of the productions to which they are privy. Acting on this prerogative youth find it increasingly difficult to return to the status of passive and dependent entities that the iconography of innocence demands. This conflict, the empowerment and new agency that many youth sense in the context of the new youth versus the confinement and call for higher degrees of parental, educational, and social authority of the ideology of innocence, has placed many children and youth in confusing and conflicting social situations. The types of efficacy and self-direction they experience, for example, outside of school creates personal styles and modes of deportment that directly clash with the expectations of them possessed by numerous educators. The outcome of such interactions is not surprising, as the self-assured, adult-like countenance of particular youth is perceived by educators as insolent and disrespectful.

In conversations with youth and educators the recipe for conflict is apparent. Concurrently, this same recipe for conflict is present in the interactions of parents and youth in the social context created by the new adolescence.

When this social context is juxtaposed with the tendency of Western societies, U.S. society in particular, to view youth as economically useless, we begin to understand the sense of confusion and frustration felt by many young people. While the labor market demands that they delay their entry into the workforce to a later and later age, youth are seduced by the material desires of a consumption-based view of selfhood and educated by an information environment that opens the secret knowledge of adulthood to them far earlier in their lives than previously considered appropriate.

Thus, youth in this new social context receive conflicting signals about their role in society, about what it means to be adolescents. In the literature on youth in the early twenty-first century we are beginning to observe debates about the future economic role of young men and women. Those who embrace the innocence paradigm advocate the protection of youth from economic participation. Those who celebrate the changes leading to the empowerment of youth discuss the reemergence of the useful young person. Do not confuse this latter position with a lack of concern for the abuse of youth through the horrors of child and young adult labor. With both parents working outside the home, many argue, new domestic responsibilities may fall to children and youth that will further change their social role in the family. Recognizing this shift, advertisers are already beginning to advertise home appliances and food in young people's magazines.

In the new adolescence the distinction between the lived worlds of adults and youth begins to blur. Certainly youth and adulthood are not one and the same; however, the experiences of adults and youth are more similar now than they were before. Even the materials and artifacts of childhood play in the late years of the twentieth and first years of the twenty-first centuries come from the same informational networks that adults use in their vocational lives. Corporate producers, marketers, and advertisers, recognizing these dynamics before other social agents, have reduced the prior target market segmentations based on chronological age to only two (1) very young children and (2) all other youth. Abandoning divisions suggested by developmental psychology, such business operatives realize how blurred age categorization has become.

It is important to note that despite this blurring of the lines that separate youth and adulthood, youth has not simply collapsed into adulthood. Indeed, the new youth, the contemporary youth, seems to distinguish itself from adulthood on the basis of an affective oppositional stance in relation to it.

In this encyclopedia, this concept of oppositionality provides a central insight into the ways that contemporary youth have manifested their differences.

Why indeed, call this an encyclopedia? If we had been given infinite time and resources, we still could not have included every important issue, concept, behavior, and culture of youth. In fact, we had trouble finishing this encyclopedia, even with this large set of entries. We did not intend to exclude any youth, nor were we able to include every youth. What we did was to survey what scholars in the area of youth studies deemed interesting to youth in this time and in North America. We hope that along with researchers and parents, that students, youth themselves, will enjoy and use this collection. And we want to add to it. We invite all readers who believe they have additional information or new entries to contact us at the email address at the end of this preface. We intend to keep our study of youth culture contemporary, and that means we will continually update our work. As we have found as we study youth, what is *in* today, is most certainly *out* tomorrow.

Unlike a traditional encyclopedia, we have included entries that are not entirely scholarly. Some of the pieces are autobiographical, some are poetic, and some are created to be a reference. The authors are experts and participants in the cultures they describe, and are engaged in the act of studying contemporary youth and the many cultures and subcultures that are included in that study. We organized the entries conceptually, in that we chose the sections and order in a way we hoped would make sense to the reader.

The Encyclopedia of Contemporary Youth Culture is organized in five sections. As we organized the volumes, we were determined to create sections that reflected what was important to youth (**Sections Two, Three,** and **Four**). We surrounded those sections with **Sections One** and **Five**. **Section One: Studying Youth Culture** sets the tone for the reader to inquire into the reasons for the study of youth culture as a discipline and area of interest. Authors discuss youth in general, as a culture and as a cultural group. They place youth within the larger population and designate youth as an essential demographic group. Authors also discuss the globalization of youth cultures, and different concerns, issues, and problems that youth face. In **Section Five: Teaching and Learning In and Out of School** we present essays that discuss the education of youth, both within and out of formal school settings. By placing this section at the end, we hope that it presents pedagogical choices for teachers and students to continue creating a curriculum that is driven for youth and with youth.

Section Two: Media Culture and Youth addresses the culture that drives the youth of the twenty-first century. Constantly changing, media has exploded in to a world that is interpreted by youth entirely differently than by adults. Driven by MTV, clubbing, music, video, advertising, television, video games, Manga and Anime, instant messaging, cellular phones, the World Wide Web, Disney, and the relentless kinderculture of adolescence, today's youth are experts on the operation and purposes of media. Unlike adults, youth are immediately drawn to media and know how to operate, consume, and disseminate it. Largely North American, European, and Japanese in origin, youth media literacy has become the predominant theme in understanding contemporary youth. Unfortunately, many school curriculums are determined to avoid or ignore youth media culture, isolating students and reinforcing their belief that adults really are *out of it*.

Section Three: Youth Identities and Subcultures looks at ways in which youth have created their own self and group expression. Identity has played an essential role in the development of young men and women through every generation. Identity seems to be that which an adolescent insists on having and yet, something which she or he continually searches for. Even though the essays are titled with the major theme of the piece, each essay seems to blend the essentials of youth culture: music, physical looks, sexuality, fashion, sports, and dating/dance activities. This section looks at both the whimsical and serious parts of youth identity, and places adolescents within a chosen identity or culture. From the early influences of the Teddy Boys to the sex bracelets of today's middle and high schools students, identity must be considered in order to consider youth.

Section Four: Politics and Youth Activism is the most unusual section in an encyclopedia of this type. To so many, the construct of youth is negative, a *stage* in which to get through quickly, and a group that must be controlled and kept busy. In this section we examine the amazing accomplishments and organizations that youth have created and promoted in order to achieve identity, social justice, and awareness. How proud we felt as editors, to create a section that proclaimed the majesty and brilliance of groups of young men and women who refuse to allow corporate or governmental preferences to dictate their lives. In an era that has become increasingly tense at the global level, we celebrate the youth who have insisted on taking their futures by storm, and creating realities that will usher in a better world. We do not attempt to judge youth, nor to particularly identify with each movement. In taking the words of The Who's *My Generation* to heart, we "don't try to dig what they (we) all say." Celebration is not appropriation, nor critique, we present youth culture as we see it, hear it, and feel it.

The three editors of this book come to this project from strong youth cultures of our own. As the oldest, I (Shirley) have been fighting the fact that I am not still eighteen years old. While being a teenager was hard, really hard, (remembering the Vietnam War, the draft, and battling conservative parents), I also watched the Beatles' first performance on *The Ed Sullivan*

Show, saw *Buffalo Springfield* on stage in 1965, and never woke up in the morning without the sounds of KHJ Los Angeles beating through my brain. Rock and roll was the formation of my consciousness. My clothing, language, and thoughts revolved around it. As a person from the sixties, I am continually shocked that I am not *still* that teenager. Remnants appear when our "kids" (all over 23) insist that I turn down the music, that they find it deafening. I like that…it means I still have *it.*

Birgit is the curator of an amazing archive of youth culture in Frankfurt, Germany. Interestingly, she may be one of the only curators of a museum that uses many of her own things as artifacts. Self-described as a sort of Goth punk in the eighties, Birgit wears the piercings and hair that remind us all of where her heart lies. I recall a favorite day with Birgit as I climbed through the archives and she would grab a piece of clothing or pointed black boots and tell me where she wore them and the color of her hair that day. She took her culture seriously, and it became her life's study.

Priya comes from the post-MTV culture. Raised in Central Pennsylvania, she grew up listening to mainstream rock, pop, and hip hop; yet it was hip hop that raised her consciousness. As a teenager she felt she connected to the messages that the music sent. An East Indian by ethnicity, the small, white, rural town in which she lived created a marginalized persona who didn't have a peer group with whom she could identify. Hip hop became an escape for her and created a voice. Priya now grounds her scholarship and pedagogy in hip hop, and that which gave her a voice as a teenager now has helped her establish her work as a writer and teacher.

We present this encyclopedia to you, not as a complete work, or a definitive set that defines all youth culture, but as a work in progress, much like contemporary youth culture is itself. We relish our lives as former youth, and we celebrate the lives of the youth of today. Our hope is that readers will both identify and understand young men and women, and that this encyclopedia will encourage the field of youth studies to flourish and grow; and, most importantly, we invite youth to participate in this study and conversation.

We thank the contributors of *The Encyclopedia of Contemporary Youth Culture.*

We have been privileged to work with a global spectrum of writers who regard the study of youth as a passion. We have placed selections of spoken word poetry throughout the encyclopedia, written by gifted high school students. We cannot thank you all enough for giving part of yourselves to the success of this encyclopedia.

Shirley R. Steinberg

Please write us with suggestions, questions, or continued conversations at: nycresearch@aol.com

Section Three

YOUTH IDENTITIES
AND SUBCULTURES

A Traitor to My Heritage

Elizabeth Bonilla

A traitor to my heritage!
A traitor to my heritage is this statement true?
Mixed with African American, Dominican and Puerto Rican yet
still a full-blown American and Cherokee Indian, Plus a woman.
Cherokee Indian is in my past family, a slave
My grandmother.
Someone I don't know but follow her every footstep
She is my ancestor.
I resemble her appearance,
White or tan, people say
Straight yet curly
Different hair, race
Dominican the meringue, and bacatha
Music flows
Spanish heritage is all I know
Puerto Rican that's all me
Salsa, la Plena, dancing
Spanish parties
Arroz con pollo, guandules, red beans
Fried chicken, black eyed peas
Macaroni and cheese
African American
Yes my grandfather
Yes see he is as black as me
In attitude, intelligence, and all knowledge
They say that because of my color life would be easy
I find that they need some knowledge and realization
And
As a woman you need some certification
Some back round of mind needed to see how we are eligible in
this male society
Women of color don't you understand that we get no credit in our
native lands
We are traitors to our heritage
We are defined as mutts
Sorry but not me
I'm of mixed heritage and proud to be

ALTERNATIVE GIRL CULTURE

Birgit Richard

YOUTH CULTURES

Youth cultures are international, global communities of style, which have developed across all linguistic and geographical barriers since the postwar period. An essential aspect, before digital media were used, is the integration of members of a style, which develops because of the same musical preferences. This has always existed and is as invisible as the usage of digital media. A community of style is constituted over long distances, first by print media, then by television. On the basis of studying the position of women in real youth cultures such as punk, gothic, and techno and house, it is necessary to consider how cultural spheres change by new opportunities for communication.

In contemporary youth cultures girls and young women still stick to their role as users. Only very rarely are they stylistical programmers of a scene, especially when it comes to its core constituent, the music.

GIRLS AND WOMEN IN REAL YOUTH CULTURES

The relationship between fashion and feminism can be characterized as changeable, perhaps even stormy. After all, a hostile relationship in the beginning developed into a rather friendly, sometimes even emphatic one.

A paradigmatic change in feminist reception in the 1980s leads to a new assessment of fashion. Thus, the opportunities for the development of girls in youth cultures have to be newly assessed as well; clothes and fashion are an essential area of representation. The initial condemnation of fashion as an economic instrument for the realization of male fantasies of power now turns into excitement about a supporting instrument to shape one's own identity.

Today, the topos of masquerade or "drag" is cherished as a means of producing a sexual identity. Graw, however, points to the inclusion of fashion in the economic machinery. Since it is possible to attach fashion to stereotypes, it is not only a heavenly repertory, which unconditionally puts the means for visual self-realization and for a free playing around with masquerades at the disposal of women.

Shaved heads, except for a ridge between brow and neck, domestos-pants, spider-web blouses and Dracula capes, Sesame Street chains, and

"Heidi" plaits as components of three different images of style have to be put into the context of visual shaping of the self. This selection dissociates women in youth cultures from an adult culture. From punk and gothic girls to girlies of the techno/house scene, the images of style created transform resistance into a hyper-conformism to contemporary stereotypical role models, which can easily be misunderstood. Young women look for the niche of fashion that is up-to-date and unoccupied: punks simultaneously choose the aggressive "unfeminine" with military clothes or the "dirty style" of sex-shops in the 1970s. In the 1980s the gothics adopted the romantic-melancholic fashion of a fragile Victorian femininity. In the 1990s the girlies adopted infantility to obtain freedom for female experiments with their body and constructions of identity.

Punk is supposed to be the climax of the emancipation of female adolescents; developments thereafter—the contemporary girl cultures in particular —of which the "girlie" is one facet, are considered to be conformist and hardly autonomous. Of course the extreme forms of punk women show the clearest deviation and manifestations of protest. Today, rebellion has to be more subtle. The failure of a 1980s punk revival, with punk accessories and emblems (punk typography, Union Jack T-shirts, studs, and pink hues), was bound to happen, because these stylistic expressions and the form of protest they embody is not socially relevant at the moment.

Images of women have to be put into the context of styles changing in general, which are no longer aggressively rebellious. The aesthetic processes of bricolage have changed; they became more inconspicuous and difficult to decipher. This is opposed by criticism from a tendency of the "old school feminism," which does not try to analyze the ambiguity of symbols by asking for differences, but rejects this form of masquerade as unclear and unauthentic. This demonstrates the inability to differentiate between questioning clichés and stereotypes and their conformist perpetuation. The subtle aesthetic differences are not recognized as being subversive.

FEMALE PUNKS

Originally there was no linguistic difference between male and female punks, since the scene could do without. This provoked the media in creating silly expressions like "punkette" in England and "punkerin" in Germany. The desperate search for a female term expresses the fear that in these youth cultures a different relationship between the sexes might be shown than it is in ordinary social life. The punks exist since the mid-1970s and in Germany they are a subcultural evergreen with a constant number of "followers" and "detractors." The critical and rebellious impetus disappeared and in contemporary styles is becoming transformed. The musical and aesthetic forms of punk became quite common.

Punk has a hedonistic image of the body, which requires the release of energy, for example, in Pogo, a dance consisting of jumping, shooting up, and jostling. In an archaic and ritual manner the body is perceived to be shapeable (a lot of earrings and tattoos), its vulnerability is picked out as a central theme. The visual aggressiveness, triggered by the accessories, is a threatening posture, which demands distancing. In a fight, items like chains or earrings offer an ideal area for attack. Structurally, punk is no belligerent, male style. In contrast to skinheads its construction allows for the inclusion of girls on equal footing.

> Women have risen here in the Punk scene alongside men, this is not a male event, where women have found their little place . . . but women have chances, they can develop, if they want. When women are more up to it than men, they can show it here. . . . We have started together as Punks, not as blokes and women.

The sexes are first visually mixed. Male punks can wear skirts or similar items of clothing, like bondage-pants with flaps and make-up, female punks wear army or work boots, extremely short, dyed hair, or a shaved head leaving only a ridge between brow and neck. They reject bourgeois concepts of orderliness and cleanliness, the clothes are torn and dirty from living on the streets.

Women are no longer embroidering elements for rock-superstars, but form their own bands and play all instruments. They have pushed into the male territory of rock music. Famous punk women and female punk bands include Siouxsie and the Banshees, Raincoats, Ostro 430, Ätztussis, Mania D., Liliput and X-Mal Deutschland and women of 1970 punk.

> We are different to a lot of women we know. But then we're different from a lot of guys we know too. . . . We happen to be four of the strongest people we ever met. We haven't met any guys who are stronger. That's why there are no guys in the group. It wasn't planned as an all-girl group. We just didn't know anyone better.

The lyrics of female punks explicitly express, among other things, the sexual desires of women. They take what they want, if necessary, with physical violence. They describe men like men usually describe women, taxingly, scrutinizingly. This aggressive component is revived by the riot grrls in particular. "I want to f*** you like a dog/take you home and make you like it."

In a kind of female live-cell therapy for the ossified punk, feminist punk bands, loosely linked, like Bikini Kill or Bratmobile at the beginning of the 1990s, resist the male dominance in the punk scene and announce the "Revolution Girl Style Now!" They celebrate their own festivals, like the Pussystock Festival in New York City, and launch new female fanzines like Girl

Germs or Satan Wears a Bra. Female punks, and subsequently the riot grrls, make Cixous' demand come true:

> She should start saying something, and not let them tell her, she had nothing to say.

A lot of female punks reject the conventional forms of love and sexuality. Boredom and disgust opposite the clean, inhibited bourgeois sexuality and sex as a consumer good, a mass product of pornographic fantasies, are expressed by posturing of both sexes with articles from sex-shops. Punks do not wear this kind of clothes because men explicitly want them to, but because they are essentially inspired by stylistic protagonists of the scene like Vivienne Westwood.

Today, when the demonstration of any kind of sexuality is fairly common, punk has long lost its provocative power. However, the self-determined rejection of all traditional ideals of female beauty is still provocative. Behavior like spitting on sidewalks, fights, and Pogo is still not widely accepted in women and a logical consequence of spare-time spent in public places. Military clothes like heavy army boots combined with skirts help to temporarily break up traditional role models. They are the practical demonstration of a different, autonomous role for women. A lot of the male punks appreciate the described behavior and are not afraid of it:

> The girls among us were totally independent . . . they were absolutely brilliant, I found them really amazing, they radiated a complete self-assurance.

The female punks developed an independent aesthetics and expressed their sexuality, which contained a rebellious element against traditional sexual role models: male stylization (getting equal with men like, for example, the skingirls) and stressing the different quality of women. Temporarily, the punk woman rejects the assumption to be "a man minus the chance to present yourself as a man = a normal woman."

The attempt by punk-women to show toughness led to harsh consequences in public. This is demonstrated in comments such as "Just look at how you look like, do you have to dress that way, you b****, you slut," or, "The way you look, your face should be shot apart with acid." A woman willingly and obviously evading the stress going along with cosmetics and beauty is supposed to be a slut. At the times of punk this singular image of being different is turned into a positive icon. The riot grrls later started a broader reinterpretation of the negative connotations, which in the 1990s turned this stigma into a positive icon of identity for women of black and white youth cultures. When the term "b****" appears in the title of an album of one of the most influential hip hop producers and vocalists, Missy Elliot, then, in her fight against stereotypes within the black community, she uses the same strategy they use to dissociate themselves from the white culture, calling themselves "nigger." By breaking out of the sexual role model the woman feels her sexual identity, her self-image slipping away:

> I don't feel as a whole. I feel like someone torn apart, ripped open . . . having lost my frame of reference.

Thus, punk should not be misunderstood as a heaven of equal opportunities for women; it is an inconsistent phenomenon. Nevertheless, against the background of other youth cultures like skins, psychos, teds, heavy metal freaks, hip hop, still mostly dominated by males, punk women were able to develop bases for an inclusion on equal footing.

FEMALE GOTHS

The subculture of the goth, in the field of music called "dark wave," started in Britain in the early 1980s and derived from the gloomy, resigned side of punk and punk. The goths took the "gothic novels" of the romantic period as a point of reference, which can be deduced from the English expression "gothic punk." They also like to call themselves "the blacks." This self-labeling is not completely unproblematic, so in the 1990s the not totally serious Gothcode 1.1. (resembling a program with updates, www.asta.unisb.de/schuetz/astogothcode.html) is supposed to make it easier to get in touch with other "blacks" on the Internet. The opposite number can decipher from codes to what category another gothic assigns himself or herself. There is, for example, the "Jammergoth." Life is a permanent existential crisis—you simultaneously weigh what is more unsettling, the expanding conflict in Bosnia, the transitoriness of things. There is also the "shy goth: please, don't look at me. . . . I hope they are not talking to me." Other manifestations are the muntergoth, grantelgruftie, sarkigoth, der-goth-der-nur-noch-dahinvegetiert (German terms expressing different kinds of character and philosophies of life).

Color is still of essential importance for this youth culture. Black is a symbol of the inevitable death and all that is negative. "The blacks" also use the traditional symbolism of the evil and the devil. The attractive combination of the color black and uncovered skin, the contrast between pale faces, black make-up and clothes, has its roots in the aesthetics of the preferred characters of the gothic novels of the romantic period. One of the ideals of beauty there is the pale, white, female body, covered in black. The goths put the color black, under normal circumstances intended for the temporary phase of mourning, into a context of ordinary situations and apply it to all situations in life. The color black is contrasted by silver metal studs and ornaments on accessories and clothes. In the 1980s, we find the pointed, tightly tailored buckled shoe, recalling the pointed shoes of the outgoing middle ages, and death's-head or bat buckles.

271

It is typical for the gothics of that time that all clothes are worn loosely and droopy. In the beginning, women wore long skirts and dresses, men often wide Turkish pants. The detached attitude toward their own body can be verified by wide capes, wraps, scarves, Dracula-capes, monks' habits, and cassocks. In contrast to punk, a more distinct separation of the sexes is postulated, which means that women especially dress within the framework of conventional clothes for women. Some male gothics break the barrier between the sexes by wearing droopy clothes and make-up on their faces.

The goths have nothing to do with the actively aggressive principle of torn clothes and the aesthetics of ugliness and poverty of punk. They style themselves as aristocratic, "beautiful" angels of death, corresponding to historical ideals of beauty. Thus, the preferred materials in the 1980s are soft, traditional, and natural fabrics like lace, velvet or silk, and less frequently leather, patent-leather, or rubber, somewhat detached from notions of romantic eroticism.

In the 1980s an unusual hairdo like the "plate" (also called flat anti-tank mine or plate skull) played an important role for men. At this time, women preferred black, long uncombed hair, which was extremely backcombed and supposed to be reminiscent of the tangled hair of witches. In addition, we saw a special way of putting on make-up, often used by both sexes: black eye shadow, lipstick and nail varnish counteract a chalky white face. This "dead" way of putting on make-up, "painting to death" or "walking around dead" as the goths call it, anticipates the fate of the future dead and expresses solidarity with the dead.

The most important symbolic principle, always appearing again in clothes and accessories, is the attempt to represent a dead body or a walking dead, living in a twilight world. The clothes goths wear in everyday-life represent the permanent celebration of death and mourning.

In the 1990s, the female goths deal more offensively with sexuality. Now, there is not only a fragile femininity, needing protection, but also a clear aggressive trend, albeit tending more toward self-injuring. The figure of a morbid, luxurious vamp develops, wearing patent leather and leather. The romantic accessories of the style reminiscent of witches are no longer relevant. Thus, the style undergoes a modernization, clearly shown by using all up-to-date infrastructures like gothic events, flyers, and DJs.

THE GIRLIE IN THE TECHNO AND HOUSE SCENE

Remember the days when women were women and girls were under 21?

The term "girlie" has rather negative connotations. It is supposed to be a heavy blow against feminism, a silly escape from becoming an adult, and an expression of fear of sex in the age of AIDS. The "girlie" is suspected of promoting stereotypical images, such as the image of Lolita for the satisfaction of pedophile fantasies or the image of the dependent, easily seducible, naive girl, projected in incarnations of the commercial girlie, for example, the singer Blümchen. The problem with the girlie-image is that it does not refer to an independent style of youth culture, but can be found anywhere; it is a common feature of all styles. The girlie is difficult to define and should rather be considered an aesthetical process.

It is difficult to demonstrate the irony of this female image in its stylization to an extremely young girl. "Riot grrl" Courtney Love with her frivolous "kinderwhore" style is above suspicion when it comes to the affirmation of pedophilic images and their ironical distortion. All important female figures, which have developed since the 1980s, describe themselves as "girl." It is not "riot woman," it is "riot grrl" and this choice of terms is meaningful. The girl embodies a freshness not yet characterized by patriarchal structures. "Riot women" does not make any sense, because a "woman" carries connotations of a fixed image and few opportunities for development.

The girlie image is also an expression of an infantility quite common in society and supposed to give relief from the burdens of ordinary life. The reference to childhood shows the deliberate stylistic dissociation from the adult world.

The girlie as a female image developed from the techno and house scene and has a special function there. There, girlie means an offensive retreat from the images of femininity for adult women, non-acceptance, and circumvention of female images on offer. In the techno and house scene, the rejection of growing older and the cultivation of a shrill, infantile taste form the basis for an unprejudiced community life and the comfort of all in the large surrogate family of an event.

In the club and event scene the infantile image of the 1960s with big heads and childish eyes and body (Twiggy) is revived and described with expressions such as "girlie," "cutie," and "babe." "Heidi" plaits, hair slides, the miniaturization of accessories such as backpacks, toys (water pistols), and sweets (tablets of lemonade powder on necklaces) are an important stylistic element. The infantile look is comprehensive; even drugs, such as ecstasy pills, get a childish face marked with smileys, Fred Flintstone, dinosaurs, or dolphins.

The original "girlie" image of the techno and house scene creates a narcissistic, but not an anti-feminist, social climate. It is not really regressive, but gives shelter to girls and young women in a mixed youth culture.

> At the beginning in particular, I was delighted by the fact that I didn't feel observed when I was dancing . . . no one looks at me, no one makes obvious advances. You have more freedom to do what you want, I don't have to think about whether I'm dancing in a sexy way and make the bloke behind me randy.

The biographical importance of carefree and undisturbed dancing indicates the meaning of this freedom. Analogous to the "girlies," in the 1990s the "sex-positive-feminists," who approve of sex and men, also suffer from the prejudice of "anti-feminism." Naomi Wolf, bell hooks, and the cybersex-apologist Lisa Palac in particular represent a stylish "babe feminism," whose basic level corresponds to the girlie image on other levels. Women and girls in particular symbolize an autonomous and innocent handling of their bodies by using the original girlie concept of a pre-adolescent and pre-sexual outfit. They show that sexual attraction is not the objective of the partial exposure. By assigning themselves to an infantile category, they show their desire to be left alone. It also bears witness to the totally narcissistic ecstatic experience of their own body as an auto-erotic experience, which does not require assurance from the male side, but which is not relinquished either. Shaking off the term "woman" indicates the dissociation from the obligations of an overly sexualized society, in which the number of images of violence has long since been outstripped by the number of images of sex. All re-definitions in this area would be taken over and in turn became commercially available images of deviation. A difference can only be formed by going back to childhood. By indicating this barrier, girlies convey to men the signal of inviolability. These also wear large necklaces with wooden pearls and, as a fun-guerilla armed with brightly painted pumpguns, delight themselves in a childish squirting of water from their water-guns. By reverting to infantile elements, men can do without macho poses for the purpose of being sexually impressive and may try to deal playfully and naturally with the other sex. Male physical images tend to a visual crossing of borders towards the opposite sex, to androgyny. The physical auto-erotic self-experience in dance also functions as a surrogate for sex. Other physical concepts, such as the gay and fetish cultures, are integrated into the techno and house scene. Fashion softens up the hardened structures of gender-constructions, even though the androgynous forms often only serve the purpose of aesthetical differentiation.

> Cross-dressing is about gender confusion. Cross-dressing is about the power of women . . . is about the emergence of gay identity.

Men rarely are true cross-dressers, transvestites, or drag queens, in the sense that the style of fashion becomes a way of life, an attitude. Poofy postures and coquettish flirtation with bisexuality become a fashion phenomenon. The decisive fact, however, is that in the laboratory of techno events or house clubs the visual experiments of redecorating the body, the "feminization of youth" is possible at all. Only in its manifestation of the "girlie look" is women's clothing an independent image of the style; there is no form for the female raver. Many other elements are transformed copies of men's clothing, like training clothes, and shoes with heels. Female crossings of borders toward the male gender can also be observed in transformed sportswear, bulky shoes, and the adoption of gay dance-gestures. The change in male physical images and experiences was largely inspired by the cultural practice of the gay, black minority culture in the United States, which came to Europe via the early English acid house scene and house clubs in the 1990s.

The plushy and kitschy interiors of house clubs, taking the form of gold and brocade and a preference for sweet devotional objects, are essentially inspired by the means of shaping travesty, the artificial-ecstatic exaggeration of the "feminine." The roots of this aesthetics are found in gay subculture, their ecstatic adoration of the ample House Diven, representing a combination of female, physical presence, and the mythical pursuit of love and fulfillment as a secularization of the gospel tradition.

The exaggerated gay hyper-poses of the feminine in the manner of "vogueing" (the term derives from the *Vogue* magazine in the film *Paris Burning*) are now the standard for female and male motions in the techno and house scene.

The "infantile" protest runs through the whole youth culture, from riot grrls to the techno scene. In each instance, the aesthetic-stylistic protest becomes more exaggerated and grotesque, until it culminates in the "cartoon style" of the girlie-image. "And feminist zines like Bust, Cupsize, and Roller Derby thrive by raging against the patriarchy in baby T-shirts." Thus, the girlie has to be assigned to the category of strategies of female masquerade.

A COMPARISON OF FEMALE IMAGES OF REPRESENTATION

It's cute to be an angry young woman; it's trendy to be an angry young woman.

Extreme rebellion and an easily assigned visual protest with the proclamation of total feminine difference is in danger today of becoming a new trademark like it is represented by the riot grrls. Today, the emphasis on differences leads to tailor-made segments of the market, where all types of women can be provided for. The other social strategy of neutralization consists of assigning a niche with little or at least rather restricted chances of follow-up, as it is found in the operational system of the arts.

A basic requirement for the free development of independent female forms of style deriving from the analysis of real youth cultures is the androgynous nature of the physical image of men. Furthermore, the principle of "drag" and masquerade has to be applicable in both directions. For punk, the essential quality is the unisex-character of the range of styles; there are less explicitly male or female items of clothing.

Androgyny can also be proved in a segment of gothic culture, albeit less in the field of music, which leans towards EBM and Industrial Music. The girlie of the techno and house scene also has androgynous features: she is very sporty, putting emphasis on workouts, and is the dialectic counterpart to the physical image defined by the gay scene and "drag." If we want to adhere to the definition of "drag" developed by Judith Butler, who considers it to be a model for the blueprint of a gender which lacks an original, we find in this strategy a multiplication of the feminine, a loop.

This stylistic process is an indication of the possibility to conquer up-to-date places in society for the development of networks. In the close social interdependence of youth cultures and society lies the danger of, but also the chance for, a subtle change.

The total detachment from mixed party crowds, the ghettoization in pure girl cultures, and the preference for the "tomboy," (the male-female rock star as the true protagonist of female rebellion) do not lead to liberation, since they are questioning the feminine physical images' chances for a follow-up. It does not make any sense to compete with male toughness in music, as is done, for example, by L7 with their "muscular work ethic, no pain, no gain," who can be assigned to the category of "female machisma." The cross-dressing strategy of the techno and house scene, interpreted as an expression of stylistic queerness, besides an exposure of the weak construction of visual norms of gender, also points to processes determined by technology and media, like the popular gender-switching or -bending on the Internet.

Resource

www.asta.unisb.de/schuetz/astogothcode.html

EATING DISORDERS AND SEXUALITY

Ellen Essick

The similarities between the mentalities of anorexia nervosa, bulimia, and sexual repression among young women are undeniable. Young women starve their bodies until they can no longer resist both physical and sexual hungers. But the guilt associated with indulging becomes overwhelming and purging and punishment ensues. Both biological and sexual hungers are natural. However the messages sent to young women by their culture are that neither of these hungers are normal and, in fact, are immoral and inexcusable. As a result, educators, medical professionals, nutritionists, and therapists spend countless hours attempting to treat or prevent the eating disorder while ignoring the elephant of sexuality and sexual desire hanging out in the living room. Young women must feel comfortable in their own bodies as well as with their own sexuality in order to address issues of eating disorders.

Although the incidence of eating disorders has fluctuated over time, one statistic has remained constant: eating disorders continue to affect women at disproportional rates. Ninety percent of those individuals affected by eating disorders are women, 85 percent of American women diet chronically, and 75 percent feel humiliated by their body size and shape Women are killing themselves to fit into a tight culturally determined box defining their appearance and self-esteem and women, particularly those with eating disorders, literally kill themselves to fight a battle that they are destined to lose. Eating disorders have the highest death rate of any mental illness. The mortality rate associated with anorexia nervosa is twelve times higher than the death rate of all causes of death for females fifteen to twenty-five years old. Twenty percent of people suffering from anorexia will prematurely die from complications related to their eating disorder, including suicide and heart problems. Anorexia is the third most common chronic illness among adolescents, and 95 percent of those who have eating disorders are between the ages of twelve and twenty-five. In addition, eating disorders have the highest mortality rate of any psychiatric diagnosis.

Every day thousands of young women wake up, step on a scale and from that moment on plan a day dictated by an arbitrary number revealed on that scale. They make decisions concerning what they will eat, what they will wear, and the duration of their exercise programs. Some will also make decisions that will even more significantly affect their physical and emotional health. Decisions such as how many calories to consume, how many laxatives will be necessary, how to find the time necessary to exercise obsessively and how to purge without anyone knowing are all decisions that begin to take hold and control the lives of many of these young women. This obsessive way of living becomes time consuming and even physically debilitating for many women. In order to truly address the causes and successfully treat and prevent eating disorders we must explore the cultural expectations of women both physically and sexually.

From the moment a girl is born, the cultural expectations based upon her gender are impressed upon her. She is taught that sacrifice for the sake of others is part of her role in life. She learns that being accepted by others is necessary at all costs. "Be a good girl." "Follow the rules." "Be nice." "Don't fight." "Get along." "Be smart." "Don't be too smart." "Be pretty." "Be thin." These are just a few of the messages—which sometimes even contradict themselves—that girls hear from very early ages. What are the messages that we send to girls throughout their lives that have perpetuated the ideas of women as "nice girls" with "perfect bodies" that are prevalent in our society today? These definitions of womanhood are not part of women at birth. Biological differences exist between men and women at birth, but this is where biology ends and society creates the unrealistic image of women that is so detrimental both physically and emotionally to women today. Understanding and accepting one's sexuality in a society that expects women to be heterosexual and pure can be quite challenging as well as frightening for many women. Women are expected to be virginal, thin, pretty, and heterosexual.

A young woman learns early in life that different sets of behaviors are required of her by others, including other females around her, in order to remain feminine. Anything different earns her any number of negative labels from masculine to lesbian to slut. If she is very young and refuses to follow the expected norms she gets a slight reprieve and is labeled a "tomboy" by those around her. This is only for a short time, however, as she must soon begin following the "appropriate path." Attached to these physical and behavioral requirements are moral imperatives providing reinforcement for "keeping women in line." The guilt often attached to this morality ensures that women will not only continue to strive for an unrealistic body ideal, but will be guilt ridden for not reaching what is also seen as a moral ideal. A young woman's sense of pride and self are destroyed as she attempts to attain these unrealistic moral standards. Similarly moral standards are relayed to women about any possible sexual behavior. Exploring one's own sexuality means breaking an implied moral code of sexual abstinence. Since the same message is not often sent to males, women begin to realize and struggle with this double standard. Men don't have to be virgins but their sexual partner certainly should be one. The conflicting messages heard by many women can become overwhelming. It becomes an impossible task for many women to know where they fit into this confusing picture. They want to be seen as feminine yet in order to be successful in many arenas they must behave in direct opposition to this "feminine standard."

Women remain in an endless state of ambivalence as they are reminded of the different meanings attached to sexual desire. Feminist writer Naomi Wolf often discusses the mixed messages sent to women with regard to their own sexual behavior and desire. The woman who is sexually conservative is considered a prude but the woman who allows herself to fully experience her sexual being is labeled a slut. Even the recent television series *Sex and the City*, well known for the sexual explorations of its characters, gave in to the social expectations of the "good girl" image as its run came to an end. Each of the major characters moved toward a more traditional view of sexuality for their futures. In a recent television interview, Sarah Jessica Parker commented that if the show had not ended at that time the women would have run the risk of being labeled sluts instead of women enjoying the full potential of their sexuality. It is evident that many women receive sexuality education from very early ages throughout a variety of settings, including family, friends, home, and school. They learn sexual anatomy and physiology, menstruation, and the consequences of unprotected sexual intercourse. However, there is rarely any mention of sexual desire, pleasure, or any discussion of sexuality outside of traditional heterosexuality. Over time, what it means to be a woman has been constructed in such a way as to eliminate the acknowledgment of desire totally from the discussion of sexuality. Women are to perform sexually, behave appropriately, and maintain all standards of feminine behavior.

Free advertising for soda from graffiti artists

In addition, denying or suppressing sexual appetite keeps one's moral status intact. For decades women have received messages reinforcing the need for restraint and caution with sexuality in order to remain pure for their partner in a traditional heterosexual world. Our society has an enormous investment in keeping women thin as well as sexually pure through the use of guilt. For many women bodily restraint and denial of hunger becomes the metaphor for sexual restraint and suppressing the sexual appetite. Eating disorders have become a bodily response to the cultural restraints put on a woman's body and sexuality. Today for many women body desires and body image have become enmeshed and a focus on body image shadows most thoughts and discussions of desire. It is much easier to talk about food, exercise, and body weight than about fears regarding sexuality. The messages that women are to be desirable while expressing no desire of their own are heard loud and clear as evidenced by the bodies and the body image of many women. Women starve their bodies to meet society's expectation of sexy but are constantly reminded not to act on any sexual feelings of their own.

Today, young women often starve in an attempt to meet an unrealistic media portrayed image. Femininity, defined by the weak, fragile, docile body, has become the parameter by which young women begin their quest to have the perfect body and become the "perfect woman." No matter how much effort women put into the quest for this perfection through starving, exercising, or purging, the requirements can never be met. If they are unable to restrain and give in to the food, they often feel guilty for their lack of will power. Sexually, women often behave the same way, abstaining from sex, but later feeling guilty if they give in to their sexual desires. In order to address eating disorders, we must be willing to address not only individual issues of sexuality and comfort with one's own body but we must also begin to help young women recognize the unrealistic and degrading images of women as sexual beings and the same society's expectation that women will in fact refrain from embracing their own sexuality.

Note

Statistical information regarding eating disorders was taken from the Renfrew Center Web Site. Renfrew compiled this information using a variety of current resources for data on eating disorders. Individual references for statistical data can be viewed at www.therenfrewcenter.org.

Resources

Bloom, C., Gitter, A., Gutwill, S., & Zaphirolpoulos, L. (1994). *Eating problems: A feminist psychoanalytic treatment model.* New York: Basic Books.

Wolf, N. (1997). *Promiscuities.* New York: Random House.

Wooley, S. (Ed.). (1994). *Feminist perspectives on eating disorders.* New York: Guilford Press.

Exploring the Culture of "Sluthood" among Adolescents

Wendy Walter-Bailey and Jesse Goodman

"Slut" may be defined as a female adolescent who becomes the victim of a rumor regarding her supposed "promiscuous sexual activity," which is used to marginalize and ostracize her from her peers.

HISTORY

The perception of women who are sexually active as deviant, unclean, and untrustworthy has a long history in the Western cultural tradition. For example, the Old Testament is filled with stories of women who are condemned due to their sexuality. Starting with Eve eating from the tree of knowledge (some might suggest it was the tree of carnal knowledge), the Old and New Testaments, along with the Koran, routinely condemn women who are sexually active. During the Middle Ages, one can find numerous tales of women who were identified as witches and burned at the stake as a result of their presumed sexual activities, among other things. "Hussy," "tramp," and "harlot," as well as "slut," are just a few of the many terms that have been used throughout Western history to marginalize young women.

Women's sexuality began to appear with increasing regularity in post–World War II Western societies, and Kinsey's *Sexual Behavior of the Human Female* uprooted the myth of asexual young women. Nonetheless, "bad" (sexually active) female adolescents lived in fear of being "found out" and thus becoming "fallen women." Although the pejorative attitudes toward women's sexuality greatly dissipated during the 1960s' "sexual revolution," many social and educational observers note that in every part of our nation, adolescent girls are regularly victimized by rumors and innuendoes related to their supposed sexual activities. As we discuss later, the possibility of being called a "slut" is still a form of marginalization that is very much part of our schools and culture. Its resilience led Leora Tanenbaum in her book, *Slut!*, to suggest that this ignoble identity might very well be considered a Jungian archetype. If "slut" is an archetype, it is likely that this form of oppression among adolescents will continue for many decades to come. As a result, it is necessary for educators to first confront their own attitudes toward sexuality, understand the nature of this phenomenon, and also explore some ideas of what to do about it.

"EARNING" THE SLUT LABEL

Why do kids call each other sluts? There are several reasons. Rumors are spread about girls who refuse conformance to the rules of sexuality, in that they act too casual or flaunt their sexuality rather than acting passively demure or virginal. Girls who flirt too heavily, blossom too early, or dress too scantily are singled out as loose and easy. More often than not, rumors are spread by other girls with the intention of ruining the reputation of the targeted female. In one such case an unfortunate schoolgirl who is envied by her peers because of her attractiveness might find herself alienated and alone after destructive reports are circulated inferring that she is a slut. This victim may be less sexual than the girls who initiate the gossip; however, the rumor mill is relentless and powerful. In another case a girl might find herself on the receiving end of the slut epitaph if she flirts with a boy who is desired by one of her peers, or is perhaps the boyfriend of another female. Far worse is when one girl "steals" the boyfriend of another by making out, or going out on a date. When teen girls participate in these behaviors they, more often than not, find themselves as targets of revenge and their reputations will be slandered. Since females feel vindicated by lashing out and hurting other female peers, labeling a girl a slut not only ensures that she will be forced to remain in the margins of school culture, but it also guarantees that she will suffer personal pain.

Yet another common victim of vicious sexual rumors is the girl who is the outsider, or, as Rachel Simmons terms it, the "odd girl out." Because labeling others is a widespread practice among adolescents, those students who do not conform to the mainstream youth culture earn a negative label. The adolescent need to categorize, label, and injure others is met when the girl, who is already disconnected from the mainstream, is called a slut to let her know that she is outside the boundaries of "appropriate" and popular youth culture. As Naomi Wolf suggests in *Promiscuities*, girls, adolescents, young women, and women all risk being labeled a slut if they are somehow sexually "out of line." Not obeying the cultural rules of appropriate sexual behavior is directly related to the pain and punishment endured by females of all ages. There is no space for a female to be sexually expressive based on her desire or the pleasure she might derive from being sexual. The social mores imposed on girls and women surrounding female sexuality are rigid and confining, and those who dare to step outside the lines are punished and made to suffer.

THE PAIN OF SLUTHOOD

The humiliation girls endure when they are labeled sexually deviant by their peers is immense. Some teenagers' experience is so devastating that they must move to a new school or new town in order to escape the hurtful comments and scornful gazes. As Leora Tanenbaum's *Slut!* affirms, girls are more injured by the negative commentary from other girls than they are from boys. Frustrated and alone, these ostracized young women often resort to self-destructive behaviors such as drug and alcohol abuse, eating disorders, self-mutilation, academic withdrawal, or risky sexual conduct. These girls live their adolescent lives on the outer realms of school culture, lonely, and miserable knowing that at any moment they could be publicly humiliated by any number of their peers. Because this vicious cycle of rumor spreading and reputation destroying behavior is so common among female youth, teachers often do not recognize it as sexual harassment; however this is perhaps one of the most destructive forms of sexual aggravation these girls experience.

The stories of young women who suffered through adolescence as a "slut" are limitless. The pain that these girls tolerated as teenagers carries well into adulthood. Perhaps one of the most ironic results of this marginalization is that often these victims blame themselves. This blame and self-loathing creates a sense of powerlessness and a lack of trust in others. These are not easy feelings to overcome even if the rumors about them are false (which they often are). This overwhelming self-deprecation frequently inhibits the marginalized teenager from trusting her instincts, thus she is unable to develop healthy relationships. In some cases, this perceived lack of agency and voice in relationships leads to girls becoming victims of sexual assault (i.e., date rape) or other forms of abuse and harassment. Because they feel powerless, these same girls, if in an intimate relationship, might fear losing the "love" of the male if they insist on his use of a condom, or fear that false rumors will spread about their planning to have sex; thus unprotected sex becomes a common event. Rape or sexual assault is endured by the adolescents labeled as "sexually deviant" because they see themselves as guilty or deserving of such abuse. Victims of date rape are afraid to tell their parents, peers, or authorities. Who will believe a girl who is a "slut"? Young men (or older) are in a position to take advantage of these young women and the victims assume they have no recourse (no voice, no choice, no agency). What girls perceive is anger from the perpetrator, or from others with whom they confide, thus self-blame for a sexual experience they did not choose becomes the standard. Date rape continues to go unreported by such young women as they fear that the ramifications of confessing what happened will be far worse than the emotional pain they, perhaps unknowingly, will carry with them the rest of their lives. Although many young women overcome their experience of sexual marginalization and become stronger in spite of it, the pain they experience during their lives as young adults could be lessened by reexamining the current sex education curriculum in schools.

COMPREHENSIVE SEX EDUCATION

Unfortunately, sex education curriculum in most schools throughout the United States is severely restricted to biological reproduction, and perhaps a brief mention of birth control devices and sexually transmitted diseases. Given the sexual duplicity that adolescents face in our society (e.g., being bombarded with sexual images in popular culture, but told not to engage in sexual activity), conventional sex education curricula is woefully inadequate. A comprehensive sex education curriculum would include a much wider range of topics than typically found in most schools. First it would encourage male and female students to ask questions well beyond reproduction, STDs, and puberty. No question an adolescent has should be seen as inappropriate, and an anonymous system for asking difficult questions (such as about abortion, transvestites, masturbation, or incest) is ideal. Second, a comprehensive sex education would include not just learning about body parts and functions, but also focus on students' self-image of their bodies, efforts in our culture to determine beauty, and, most importantly, helping young people develop a genuine appreciation of and nurturing responsibility for their bodies.

Finally, a comprehensive sex education would include an exploration of the dynamics of sexual relationships. Communication between potential sexual partners is critical. The complexity of saying "no," for example, is of special value. Often adolescents who are engaged in sexual activity assume that silence is the same as someone agreeing to what is happening when this is not always the case. Adolescents need to learn how to speak to each other about their sexual behavior. Exploring the idea of informed consent raises issues of intoxication and other substance use, and circumstances that might make it difficult for young people to make sexual decisions. These topics might also lead to an examination of sexual desire, arousal, and orgasm; definitions of sex (e.g., kissing, petting, and intercourse); peer pressure to be sexual; date rape; teen pregnancy; and power (e.g., who in the relationship makes most decisions, do both individuals listen to the concerns of the other).

Clearly, teachers need to be more than just well informed. Teachers should study and become knowledgeable about and aware of adolescent social stratifications in general—sexual and otherwise. While maintaining their authority, they need to create an environment in which students feel comfortable and nurtured enough to explore difficult issues, and one that allows disagreements without personal attacks. The study of sex in adolescence is ideally taught as a process of mutually constructive experiences among students and between students and their teacher.

Resources

Books

Hersch, P. (1998). *A tribe apart: A journey into the heart of American adolescence.* New York: Ballantine Books.

Hine, T. (1999). *The rise and fall of the American teenager.* New York: HarperCollins.

Orenstein, P. (1994). *Schoolgirls: Young women, self esteem, and the confidence gap.* New York: Doubleday.

Simmons, R. (2002). *Odd girl out: The hidden culture of aggression in girls.* Orlando, FL: Harcourt.

Tanenbaum, L. (2000). *Slut!: Growing up female with a bad reputation.* New York: HarperCollins.

White, E. (2002). *Fast girls: Teenage tribes and the myth of the slut.* New York: Scribner Press.

Wolf, N. (1997). *Promiscuities: The secret struggle for womanhood.* New York: Fawcett Books.

Wurtzel, E. (1998). *Bitch: In praise of difficult women.* New York: Anchor Books.

Article

Goodman, J. (1991). Redirecting sexuality education for young adolescents. *Curriculum and Teaching,* 6 (1), 12–22.

QUEER PUNK

Bart Vautour

"Not gay as in happy, but queer as in f*** you." It is difficult to trace a genealogy of queer punk, also known as queercore. We do know that queer punk came out of the late 1980s and early 1990s, but there are ongoing disputes about just where and how it arose as a viable subculture. One of the main aspects of queer punk's rise in visibility has been the disappearance of the explosive "straight" punk scene of the 1980s and 1990s. This straight scene has largely disintegrated or been incorporated into mainstream media culture. Corresponding to this, contemporary representations of gay or lesbian communities are steeped in stereotypical notions of feminized men and masculinized women. As these communities become more and more visible, they cater more and more to mainstream (straight) viewers and mirror so-called "normal" relationships. Queer punk aims to throw the incorporation of both punk and queer by mainstream society into crisis. Punk and queer have come together to continue pushing the boundaries that they once disrupted by separate means.

Queer punks were not accepted by either conventional gay communities—because they were punks—or conventional hardcore communities—because they were queer. It is hard to believe that either of these cultural formations can be spoken of as conventional. Believe it. In recent years both of these categories have come to mean something quite different in the eyes of mainstream culture. Before, both queers and punks were thought of as threatening to the very social fabric of civilized society. Punks fought against the middle-class establishment and queers threatened the very ideals laid out in the notion of family values. Now, punk has been incorporated and marketed specifically to middle-class white youth. Queer, like punk, has lost its oppositional edge and most visibly signifies men with good fashion sense whose job it is to teach the average straight person how to dress. More specifically, what have been the major changes in the representations of either queer or punk? When considering queer punk as a youth culture, we have to begin with an understanding of the two cultures from which queer punk emerged while it has, at the same time, called them into question: punk culture and queer culture.

The disillusionment with the mainstream queer scene can be summed-up by saying that there has never been a viable mainstream "queer" scene. Rather, in mainstream culture there has been a "gay" scene. In recent years an increasingly visible lesbian scene has emerged and carved out some spaces for itself in the male dominated gay communities or "ghettos." Some commentators believe that the emergence of a viable and visible lesbian scene in mainstream culture has been as equally isolationist as the gay scene with which it struggled for space.

The word "queer" has been reclaimed from being a pejorative term and is used as a badge of difference. As an emerging generation is increasingly turned off and pissed off about the orthodoxies of being "gay" or "lesbian," "queer" is emerging as the choice umbrella term for living non-heteronormative lives. Heteronormative is the term used to point toward cultural practices that have been heretofore reserved for "normal" straight people. The best example, in this case, might be marriage. In other words, the self-proclaimed gay movement has largely been a middle-class phenomenon, or at least aimed at gaining the status and rights enjoyed by middle-class heterosexuals within society.

As gay and lesbian cultures formed and worked to carve out spaces in cities, in legal systems, and in media, the oppositional character of their lives and identities have become more acceptable and tolerable. In other words, the oppositional character is not so oppositional any longer. Now, it would seem that this general and widespread acceptance has its costs. Gay and lesbian people had to be highly politically mobilized in order to win this space. They had to pick their battles. So we saw gay men mobilize to win space but only managed to do so while marginalizing women with whom allegiance could have been made. But lesbian women, too, continued to work hard to carve out spaces in the wake of the general success of the gay male population. In doing so, it would seem that transgendered, transitioning, two-spirited, and nonexclusive folk were, at least for a while, left out of consideration. For example, many female-identified people have been left to fend for themselves within exclusively female communities that, while fighting for legitimacy for their own life practices, tend to be quite hostile to anyone who does not fit the mould or identity that they have created, justified, and consolidated. This has materialized explicitly in the common practice of turning female-identified people who are in crisis away from women's shelters.

The disillusionment that accompanies the current punk scene is perhaps easier to understand. Punk was political. The products of punk culture emerged to signify the politics of the movement. Now, the products—stuff like bondage gear, ripped clothing, and loud angry music—are so everyday that they no longer signify the politics of punk alone. That is not to say that they do not carry on a residual message but that these products, as signs, are no longer able to guarantee specific meanings. How did this happen? The de-politicizing of punk came about through a sort of incorporation. Punk was incorporated, or brought into other ways of being circulated, by mainstream media and fashion industries. So, the products of punk culture were taken over by powerful industries and turned into consumer products as opposed to political products.

Needless to say, queer punk, being a politically minded project, has developed complicated critiques of both the mainstream acceptance of same-sex relationships and the incorporation of punk signifiers into mainstream fashion and music cultures. These punked queer bodies have been able to utilize some of the old methods of punk to put the uniforms and conventions of the gay/lesbian scene into crisis. When punk first emerged the uniform was an important part of the signifying practice. This signifying practice or style was offered in direct confrontation with middle-class codes of dress, presentable attire, cleanliness, and a general clean-cut look. The punk aesthetic was evidence of working class youth's disdain for upward mobility and middle class posturing. Now, some thirty years later, the uniform of punk no longer carries the confrontational character in majority culture, but it does carry the confrontational character into the mainstream gay culture. Instead of confronting codes of dress, presentable attire, cleanliness, and a general clean-cut look in middle-class cultures, the punk uniform now works to confront those stereotypes in queer culture.

Most queercore politics are driven by a vast impulse for survival—the politics are about celebrating outsider status, rejecting the moral majority's insular meanings of what is right and natural. Consequently, queer punks have built their own networks, with their own zines, music, and events.

Some of the early queer punk zines are as follows: *JDs, Bimbox, Thing, Homocore, Chainsaw,* and *Fertile LaToyah Jackson. JDs,* which began in 1986, often featured G. B. Jones's intelligent graphics and photos as well as Bruce La Bruce's coarse and confrontational writing. *Fertile LaToyah Jackson* was the brainchild of the famous Vaginal "Cream" Davis. Because of the nature of Do-It-Yourself (DIY) fanzine culture, many of these zines are difficult to access in print form. The above zines (or commentary on these zines) or other queer punk zines often turn-up with some searching in hyperspace.

Bruce LaBruce is a key figure in the queercore movement. LaBruce has been active in Toronto, Canada, for many years

Graffiti establishes identities

producing fanzines. With his first widely recognized film, *No Skin Off My A***, LaBruce became known internationally for his work in the queercore movement.

Another film of note is *QUEERCORE (a punk-u-mentary)* by Scott Treleaven. This documentary displays some of the foremost characters of the anti-establishment queer punk scene in North America. This film comes complete with a queercore soundtrack.

In terms of music, queer punk is not really set apart from conventional punk sound. The difference lies in its lyrics exploring themes of injustice, oppression, same-sex, and multiple-sex attraction. Musically speaking, God Is My Co-Pilot, Pansy Division, and Team Dresch are among the better-known queercore bands. Other bands that could be considered important to the queercore movement are Double Zero, Fifth Column from Toronto, and Cheesecake from Boston, Los Crudos, Tribe 8, Aryan Disgrace, Mukilteo Fairies, and The Butchies.

Something called "riot grrrl" started to take off around the same time as queercore. Riot grrrl is best characterized as a feminist movement started in the punk scene and personified chiefly by bands like Bikini Kill and Brat mobile. The members of this movement were sick of the seeming spread of the sexist punk scene. Kathleen Hanna, the founder of Bikini Kill has moved on to create Le Tigre, an extension of the riot grrrl music of the nineties with the added bonus of electronic sound samples. The group also adds multimedia and performance art elements to their live shows.

Another interesting note is that the queer punk scene does not seem to be as built-up in Europe as it is in North America. One possible explanation for this is that punk zine exchanges are stronger in the United States and Canada, and it was through this network that queer punks started organizing.

Another possible explanation could be found in the fact that the European hardcore/punk scene has long-established links to anarchist youth organizations that tend to be more queer positive.

The idea of a queercore movement is still theoretical for many young people who do not have the safe spaces or access to resources to be able to participate in the way people in big cities are able to participate. Even if queercore scenes are not in every community, young people can create their own environment by surrounding themselves with its products in various forms. The best resource for finding more information about queer punk or queercore is by far in hyperspace. Increasingly, hyperspace is a place to create and maintain queercore communities for young people who do not have easy access to a viable and safe queer punk scene.

Resources

Books

Arnold, G. (1998). *Kiss this: Punk in the present tense.* New York: St. Martin's Press.

Kirsch, M. H. (2000). *Queer theory and social change.* London: Routledge.

LeBlanc, L. (2001). *Pretty in punk: Girls' gender resistance in a boys' subculture.* New Brunswick, NJ: Rutgers University Press.

Sabin, R. (1999). *Punk rock: So what? The cultural legacy of punk.* London: Routledge.

Warner, M. (Ed.). (1993). *Fear of a queer planet: Queer politics and social theory.* Minneapolis: University of Minnesota Press.

Articles

Cooper, D. (1992, June 30). Queercore. *The Village Voice*, 31–33.

Fenster, M. (1993). Queer punk fanzines: Identity, community, and the articulation of homosexuality and hardcore. *Journal of Communication Inquiry,* 17 (1), 73–94.

Hsu, B. (1991). Spew: The queer punk convention. *Postmodern Culture,* 2 (1).

THE METROSEXUAL AND YOUTH CULTURE

Rodney E. Lippard

Author Mark Simpson first identified the metrosexual and coined the term in an article dated from 1994. Although the term continued to be used in Mr. Simpson's region of the world, the United Kingdom, it was not until almost a decade later that it became a part of the American media lexicon and thereby a part of the American popular culture vernacular. What spawned the most current interest in this word and topic was another article by Simpson about David Beckham, the captain of England's soccer team, in the online journal Salon.com titled "Meet the Metrosexual." In this article, Simpson defines the metrosexual: "The typical metrosexual is a young man with money to spend, living in or within easy reach of a metropolis—because that's where all the best shops, clubs, gyms and hairdressers are. He might be officially gay, straight or bisexual, but this is utterly immaterial because he has clearly taken himself as his own love object and pleasure as his sexual preference." Given the latter part of this definition, it is hard to distinguish between a metrosexual and a narcissist; however, in the American popular culture vernacular, the term has come to mean a man who is clearly heterosexual but who exhibits traits and behaviors that have come to be stereotypically identified with gay men. In other words, the metrosexual is a heterosexually identified male who enjoys what one may refer to as the finer things in life (i.e., shopping for clothes, using grooming products, the arts, fine foods, and wine) and who is concerned with his outward appearance.

Also, although Simpson's definition locates the metrosexual within the proximity of a metropolis, in fact the metrosexual can now be found in almost any current setting. The spread of metrosexuals seems to coincide with the phenomenal media sensation and popularity of the Bravo television series *Queer Eye for the Straight Guy*, in which five self-identified gay men, known as the Fab Five, surprise a willing heterosexual male who allows them to make him over into what is supposed to be a more pleasing version of himself in order to make him more appealing to his respective female significant other. Each of the five gay men is representative of an area of the metrosexual's concern: clothing, grooming, decorating, food and wine, and culture. With the seemingly overnight success of this sleeper, there was a rise in the awareness of the metrosexual in American culture. At the present time, metrosexual is seen more as a label than an identity. In other words, one may not identify himself as being metrosexual; however, if someone were to label him as metrosexual he would probably not deny it. This, however, may be changing. In the irreverent cartoon series *South Park*, episode 708 had almost every heterosexual male citizen declaring his metrosexuality. The change may also be evidenced in the fact that the American Dialect Society voted metrosexual as the word of the year for 2003. There are at least two possible outcomes to the parody of the metrosexual idea in the *South Park* episode and what could possibly be seen as overexposure to the word coming from the American Dialect Society: the concept will be embraced and men will start identifying as metrosexual, or, and maybe more likely, it will become a passing fad and men will want to disassociate themselves from the term. Only time will tell if this concept remains or becomes a footnote in history. At the time of this writing, a new term is already in place, retrosexual, to define "a man who spends as little time and money as possible on his appearance and lifestyle" and thus, the backlash has begun.

Although elements of the metrosexual have been identified in the past, it is the blending of these elements in combination with youth culture that makes the metrosexual a unique identity in the present. In the past, there have been examples of men who took an extreme pleasure in the way they looked—fops and dandies are a couple of examples of such. However, given the time period in which these men lived and were identified, there was either no question about their sexuality because sexuality was not a topic of polite conversation, or, given the stereotype surrounding gay men, these men were presumed to be homosexual. Mr. Simpson in his definition of metrosexual claims that the metrosexual's sexuality is unimportant, but that it could be seen as a form of narcissism. However, it appears clear that the popular culture definition of metrosexual places high emphasis on the fact that the metrosexual is a heterosexual man, thereby separating this identity from those prior.

In the past there have also been men who have redefined masculinity as being men who are in touch with their feelings. To some feminist critics, this has been seen as the result of feminist politics and as presenting a "softer" man; however, again it is the combination of this redefined masculinity with the other aspects of the metrosexual that make the metrosexual a unique label. Therefore, the metrosexual label can be seen as giving men, especially young men, a way of being in which they are able to enjoy what is typically seen as feminine traits, and also traits that are stereotypically associated with gay men, while maintaining their masculinity in the form of their heterosexuality. This redefinition allows young men to be more in touch with themselves and their feelings, but it also defines masculinity as if it was synonymous with heterosexuality.

It should come as no surprise, especially in a consumer capitalist culture such as American popular culture, that those who are most interested in the metrosexual label are those in the area of advertising and marketing, as it creates a new niche market. One of the defining concepts around the metrosexual is that of "product." Mostly, this term "product" has to do with lotions and gels that are used on the hair or body; however, the term can be broadened to represent clothing, food and drink, entertainment venues, and, to some extent, cultural events where one goes to be seen. Marketing and advertising have always been focused on selling desire, and in the past with men this desire was usually about women and wealth, and achievement of desire came in the form of a rugged individualism that was usually obtained through beer and cars, and sometimes tools. With the metrosexual a new venue of marketing opened that included cosmetic products, clothing, fine food, and wine, to name a few. This advertising to the metrosexual is predicated on the assumption that this market niche has expendable income; therefore, this advertising is aimed at a particular socioeconomic class of man.

A final component of the metrosexual is how the metrosexual identity is negotiated through youth culture. In a culture so obsessed with youth, namely American popular culture, the metrosexual is both defined by and defines youth culture. Combining the consumer culture with a youth-obsessed culture has resulted in an array of products that are aimed at men who are trying to maintain or regain their youth. In some ways, the promise of eternal youth is also the promise of the metrosexual; in other words, if one buys the products and subscribes to the identity of the metrosexual along with the accoutrements that go with the identity, then one will be forever young. However, in the circular fashion that is popular culture, the identity of the metrosexual has an influence on youth culture in that it creates the parameters to which a certain group of young men have to subscribe. So while the metrosexual identity promotes certain products that are marketed to make a man feel and appear young and exciting, it is because one has these different types of products that one is a metrosexual.

The metrosexual identity is one that is problematic at best. Viewed in a certain way, the metrosexual can be seen as paying homage to gay men in that it celebrates traits that are stereotypically associated with gay men; however, viewed another way, the metrosexual has co-opted these traits while also objectifying gay men but by maintaining his heterosexual identity he does not suffer the stigma that is still a part of being a gay man in the current society. The metrosexual identity could be viewed as a redefinition of masculinity; however, by equating heterosexuality with masculinity it negates the masculinity of gay men. Finally, because the metrosexual is based on consumption of products, it is clear that advertising and marketing agencies expect the metrosexual to have a certain amount of expendable income. This limits this identity to a certain class of people, thus ignoring other classes. It could also be noted that the metrosexual identity seems to appeal and be applied to white men for the most part, thereby excluding other races and ethnicities. It will be interesting to witness in the coming years whether this identity is one that is embraced by the public at large or whether it will become only a punch line in the jokes of comedians.

Resources

American Dialect Society. (n.d.). Words of the Year. Retrieved September 23, 2004 from http://www.americandialect.org/woty.html#2003

Salon.com. (2002). Meet the Metrosexual. Retrieved September 18, 2005 from http://www.salon.com/ent/feature/2002/07/22/metrosexual

Wikipedia: The Free Encyclopedia. (2004). Metrosexual. Retrieved September 22, 2004 from http://en.wikipedia.org/wiki/Metrosexual

The Word Spy. (2004). Metrosexual. Retrieved September 22, 2004 from http://www.wordspy.com/words/metrosexual.asp

———. (2004). Retrosexual. Retrieved October 5, 2004 from http://www.wordspy.com/words/retrosexual.asp

TEDDY BOYS

Heinz-Hermann Krüger

Between the years 1956 and 1958, riots broke out after rock 'n' roll movies or concerts in Dortmund, Germany, and also in every second West German city. These violent acts moved the negative image of the so-called Teddy Boys into the public sphere. Most of the fifteen- through twenty-year-olds involved were juvenile blue-collar workers and apprentices. Although between 5 and 10 percent of all adolescents of the fifties took part in riots of the Teddy Boys, they created the most sensation during the years 1956–1958, evidenced by heavy debate among the German public and widespread media coverage. At that time, science, which had depicted an image of a well-adapted, capacity- and career-oriented generation of the young, now focused on several studies dealing with the Teddy Boys phenomenon. Even the Lower House of the German Parliament held a debate about the rioting adolescents in 1956.

But the story of the Teddy Boys during the postwar time started earlier. Even during the beginning of the fifties, predominantly male adolescents in groups had been conspicuously seen in the metropolis wearing eccentric clothes, standing at certain street corners, and forming hordes that bothered passers-by or demolished public parks.

ABOUT THE HISTORY

The phenomenon of the Teddy Boys is not only typical of the fifties. The historical origin of juvenile gangs such as the "Blasen" in Munich or the "Schlurfe" in Vienna can be traced back to war and prewar times. Together with the "Meute" in Leipzig and the "Pirates of the Edelweiss" in West Germany, those groups belonged to young workers who opposed the representatives of the NS-regime with nonconforming behavior and their marked subcultural style. For example, the members of the "Blasen" in Munich had long hair and wore wide pants and colored pullovers. Alternatively, the members of the "Pirates of the Edelweiss" wore checked shirts, dark short pants, and white hosieries, and they referred to the tradition of the German Youth Movement with their songs while hiking. The juvenile groups differed not only in clothes, headdress, and songs, but each was also backed by a coherent leader: the adjustment of the dominated conception of arrangements of the NS-regime and the official spare-time offers of the HJ. The young workers responded to the repression of the NS with militancy and preparedness to physical confrontation. The older generation of workers did not adjust as well, but returned sooner to their own everyday culture based on their experiences prior to 1933 and the persecution of the Nazis.

THE GANGS OF THE TEDDY BOYS

The Party of the Social Democrats (SPD) and the trade unions confined themselves to activities of the welfare state in Germany. Although attempts to politically reorganize certain worker milieus were finished during the postwar time around the middle of the fifties, the political situation and the social-cultural milieu of the working class could not been described as a civic process of "new normality," or an enhancement of the standard of life. Remains of the common worker culture still existed during the fifties, despite the dissolving of homogenous proletarian social milieus based on fascism and war. These remaining elements of the common worker culture manifested themselves in an unbuttoned style seen in the workplace and in the neighborhood and represented the masculine pride of physical work and their solidarity with each other.

Composed predominantly of young, male workers, the Teddy Boy gangs held relics of the worker's everyday life culture depending on their age. These relics showed up in the group's hierarchical structure, demonstration of the superiority of their physical strengths, and also their solidarity—all elements adopted from their families and particular working-life culture. The following verbal narratives are from interviews with former Teddy Boys that I conducted in 1983. Ludwig M. described the hierarchy:

> We hadn't fixed a statute. But there was a structure. First, there was the gang leader, the chief, he always was justified. Nothing else was there afterwards, and then there was the deputy. . . . Within our groups, brutality was not too strong, probably because we have known each other since childhood. Was the president, who was the strongest, was always all right. And somebody who did not do as he was told got a box on the ears or a hook on the chin or blows with the chain over his back. There was also another coherence, cause we worked altogether in mining. We saw each other every day, and we should have to trust on our colleagues underground.

Although, Ludwig M. and most of the other members of this Teddy Boy gang from Dortmund worked in mining like their fathers and grandfathers, they could not have gotten the ethos of their work and profession from the older workers. The older workers expected obedience, hard work, and humor from the younger workers, but only offered them subordination and monotonous work during their training workshop. Ludwig M. shared the mining work ethos:

> And in Eving at that time, it was in common that everybody had to be an apprentice of mining at the shaft "Minister Stein." At that time, I remember how we started at the mine with 350 apprentices, and there was no work for us. Day by day, we had to beat out wire straight, and

if the wire was straight, we have shown it to the foreman. Then, he humped it again, and we had to bend it straight again. This went on together for days. As apprentice in the mining working at the tread-mill was the worst one. Every half year, every apprentice had to work at the treadmill for one month. There, we had to pick the stones out of the coal. This was a hard work, a monotonous one and for idiots.

Because of this brainless job, the young Teddy Boys tried to balance their frustrations through action and experiences in their spare time. They used the public street sphere and developed their own activities. They populated the public places and parks, because they did not have enough freedom in their confined homes or at official leisure-time centers, as they exist today:

And because we had so much spare time, we have said to the boys, okay, let's build up a gang. We called ourselves the "Fright of the Fauster Street," cause we lived in Fauster Street. If we were together in the gang, we felt strong. If we sat in the park at a place called "Pilz," then other adults went along other places. We only got orders at home and at work, but we have been somebody at least. We just used to get together and roar around and bowl.

The activities of these gangs were directed out, so that their own neighborhoods were defended against foreign Teddy Boy gangs: "Every street had such a gang. And no one should have come too close then. This was their beat, their territory." Their activities were addressed especially in contrast to the heavy demands of the authority of the adults. According to Ludwig M.,

I remember, the construction of Evinger Street was finished and there stood a steamroller. And on Saturday evening as we got together there and we have seen the steamroller, we went to it with 15 guys. We started the steamroller by accident and we drove therewith along Eving Street until a garden party. It took one hour until the police came. We haven't done any harm. We have driven very carefully. But the demonstration and the whole crack thereby. Because of this happening, the gang is captured by the police and ascertained juridical at the first time.

With the conquest of territories, formation of gangs, and their happenstance criminality, the Teddy Boy youth in the fifties referred to their experiences as children during the postwar time. The half legal activities of burgling coals or collecting nonferrous metal, were tolerated as emergency cases in the first few years of the postwar time, but in the mid-fifties they were prosecuted.

During this time, the activities of the Teddy Boy gangs shifted from the worker's living areas to downtown. Like the motorized "James Dean Club" in Dortmund, these gangs drove mopeds in hordes across the city and, with disregard for the rules of the road, provoked with all of the state's authority. According to Werner K.,

> And as we drove together, and we started already with 30 or 40 mopeds, you have to imagine that this was like a delirium if the hounds were together. And we had have tons of fun. At the traffic lights we stopped at green, and if it was red we drove ahead with fabulous ructions. If 40 bikes open the throttle, plus we have hooted and honked too, we felt very shocking, then this is worse than a delirium.

ROCK 'N' ROLL AND REBELLION

After the movie *Rock around the Clock* at the end of 1956, the downtowns of the West German metropolis became a central field of action not only for members of the Teddy Boy gangs but also for the other juvenile sympathizers. Liselotte H. described the effect of the movie:

> We have first gone to Bill Haley's movie *Rock around the Clock*, this was so great, absolutely fantastic. And then in Gelsenkirchen on Bahnhofstreet, I don't remember how many we were. Everybody who saw the movie and afterwards there were so many people who joined the company and demonstrated together. We used slogans like: "We need Rock 'n' Roll."

The rebellion of the Teddy Boys was spontaneous and situation-related. Everybody met at street corners and public places after seeing a rock 'n' roll movie or by hearing the spread of the rumors. There often were conflicts with the police because of smashed windows, Christmas garlands hanging around, damaged trashcans, or destroyed commercial pictures. The activities of the Teddy Boys were not based on theoretical or argumentative ideas of social criticism and social change. Instead, the ideas were diffused by the sense of discomfort constituted by the riots and chosen targets of the provocation.

Marginally, the movement contained some elements based on the tradition of juvenile gangs of the 1930s and 1940s such as having long hair and colored pullovers, or singing hiking songs like those sung during the riots in Duisburg. The stylistic adoption of American culture was pivotal since 1955 with additions such as jeans, petticoats, leather jackets, shoestring-ties, and Elvis headdress, all accessories and symbols of the American movie and fashion industry.

The youth observed these influences and changed their stylistic effects. The Teddy Boys especially used jeans to identify themselves. Once used as working pants, blue jeans worn skintight interposed not only a feeling for their own bodies, but accentuated their sleek, swaying way of walking. The Teddy Boys consciously created a distance between their own style and the style of adult's more proper attire. Ludwig M. reflects on the conflicts about skintight pants and Elvis-headdress that he had with his parents: "And these pants had been so tight, and the adults had some bell-bottomed trousers . . . If we walked out at age 16 and 17, our hair was dressed and pomaded with Brisk and such stuff. Because of this, I got in trouble at home."

Oriented to the style of rock 'n' roll girls during her youth, it was much more difficult at Liselotte H.'s home: "Once I wore my hair very short like Elvis, parting it at the back of my head and my neck was always shaved correctly, very short, the ears clear, the quiff in front of the face. . . . Furthermore, I liked wearing bobby socks and pants. As my father saw me he really striped off my clothes. A decent girl doesn't look this way, he said."

The inspiration of rock 'n' roll, expanded itself into physical activities, hooting and flouting at concerts, a dance style that belonged to the new elements of the Teddy Boys. The music and the dance of rock 'n' roll infused a new atmosphere into their bodies. Rock 'n' roll was an expression of the feeling of being alive, to which adults responded irritably: "It started at home with trouble, if Bill Haley played in the radio. I couldn't have been sitting restful at breakfast then. Sometimes I got some slaps round my face, right and left, and the radio was switched off. Other songs like Caprifisher were okay, but not rock 'n' roll. This was switched off," said Liselotte H. "For the adults, we only had been chaotic people because we've danced rock 'n' roll and this wasn't decent," said Susanne O.

With its accentuated corporality and obvious sexual overtones, rock 'n' roll was borne as a provocation for the older generation because it was a breach of female grace and male knighthood. Rock 'n' roll brought into question norms based on traditional ethics of the Protestant such as thriftiness, hard work, and the renunciation of libido. In general, rock 'n' roll did not change the traditional gender roles (e.g., the man still asked for the dance, led the woman through the dance, and produced the sensational loops). But it set up the possibility of expressing indirectly the sexual needs of the young, especially the girls. With it, the young could defy the chaste decency of the prudish republic during this time. At most 1–2 percent of girls in the whole generation participated in this group life, and ultimately the Teddy Boys reflected a considerable resistance in the historical context of the fifties. The everyday interactions of the Teddy Boys were embossed by masculine norms like protecting girlfriends, preparing for physical confrontation, and driving mopeds. The girls had to elude the strong control of their parents in order to secretly join in the Teddy Boy activities, according to Liesotte H.:

And if they slept I crept out of the house, very quiet I took the keys. At six o'clock I needed to wake up my parents. At five o'clock I got home, and I pretended that I had slept.

In addition to the risks of being disobedient, the girls' participation in the group life posed a risk of moral contempt. The movement of the Teddy Boys in the fifties differed fundamentally from the preceding youth movement with its stylistic orientation to the newly established youth-related industries of music, movies, and fashion.

As a new generation, the members of the Teddy Boy's subculture were not only composed of one social class like the "Pirates of the Edelweiss," who were derived from the working class or the "Swinging Youth," which was a movement of the upper and middle class. From 1956 until 1958, the middle class youth took part increasingly in the street fights of the Teddy Boys because they had had similar experiences in their everyday life within society. This generation's model of the Teddy Boys comprised the different classes linked by their similar experiences of rock 'n' roll music and the collective riots that ensued.

"THE CRACKLING PETTICOAT IS SNAZZY"—THE NEW TYPE OF TEENAGER

The movement broke up gradually by the end of the fifties as the protest-oriented life style of the Teddy Boys gradually increased in popularity. At this time, the spare free market increased and aimed at the juvenile consumer. It commercialized the subcultural style attributes of the young and monopolized them by offering brands from the fashion industry. The Teddy Boys were involuntary trendsetters of a first phase of modernization, which resulted in a new teenager oriented industry. In the meantime, petticoats could be bought in every general store as popular fashionable accessories. Astrid N. shared, "In the fifties I tested different styles. With ponytail, tight waist—snazzy, with a crackling petticoat."

After losing its expressiveness and wildness, rock 'n' roll developed into a shallow and defused form, and was offered by dancing schools as an acknowledged social dance behind the waltz and foxtrot. The aggressive and rebellious songs of Elvis Presley, Chuck Berry, or Little Richard were relieved by songs of Peter Kraus ("Sugar, Sugar Baby") or Ted Herold ("Wonderful, How You Kiss Today").

At this point, the history of the Teddy Boy gangs and clubs branched out in several directions. After integrating their commercial elements and prosecuting their inappropriate elements, most of the Teddy Boy gangs disintegrated at the end of the fifties. Some clubs managed to cross into the sixties. Their mopeds developed into motorbikes, their leather jackets into uniforms. The Teddy Boys developed into a new identity, as rockers in another subculture.

THE IMPORTANCE OF IDOLS IN ADOLESCENCE

Birgit Richard and Heinz-Hermann Krüger

The orientation by idols, or role-models, is typical for the youth stage. However, the term "idol" is not often used, because it sounds pregnant and pathetic, similar to the term "hero." Instead, synonymous terms such as "cult," "model," or "star" are in more frequent use. "Idol" is etymologically derived from the Greek word *eidolon,* which can have ambiguous meanings such as figure, image, illusion, idol, graven image, or false ideal. The roots of this word indicate the inseparable connection of idol and pictorial representation.

The visual presence of the modern idol is mediated through technological pictures, such as photography and TV images. Modern media renders idols eternally reproducible. However, the idol may not remain in an immaterial—for example, musical—form. Rather it must be transformable, the immaterial picture has to be captured on a material carrier.

Among young people, artists, writers, scientists, or politicians generally do not achieve cult status. Instead, their idols come for the most part from the area of leisure and popular culture. With the production of pop stars and movie heroes, the film and pop music industry is the traditional center of idol construction, especially since the 1950s. However, the palette of idols has broadened continuously since that time. Besides youthful movie-idols (like River Phoenix or Johnny Depp) there are now also highly popular sports idols (basketball: Dennis Rodman, Charles Barkley; soccer: Lars Ricken, David Beckham; swimming: Franzi von Almsick); cartoon and video game heroes (SuperMario); heroes from TV series (for example *Baywatch* star Pamela Anderson); and the numerous hosts from music channels such as MTV. Sports idols appeal to different age groups, from the school child up to the adult. Comic heroes and cartoon figures can be assigned to childhood when the admired idols and role models still come mostly from the concrete personal environments such as family and neighborhood. With the beginning of adolescence, however, media idols increasingly gain importance.

During the youth stage, the orientation by idols turns into a particularly significant experience. Young people experience the end of their childhood as a break with the familiar. But the finality of that break bears also the expectation of widening new horizons. Childlike love objects get relieved and replaced by the intense admiration of a beloved idol. Thus, in the search for one's own positioning in the world, idolatry—the admiration of a star's image—can support the process of becoming more independent from family bonds.

There is a self-determined space emerging through the admiration of idols in which adults usually do not intervene, because they consider juvenile dreaming a temporary stage of infantile behavior. The development of self-determined and imaginative forms of gaining knowledge and compiling everything associated with the star adds to the creation of one's own cosmos beyond the comprehension of adults. So the construction of an idol is a good way to distinguish oneself clearly from the adult world. Usually parents cannot understand the hysterical admiration of stars; though idols played an important role in their own youth, and they still tend to show similarly irrational admiration, for example, for new car models.

The older a person is the more the existence of an emulated idol gets denied; however, individual persons with an exemplary function still exist. Through new media such as music channels, even people between thirty and forty years of age can admire the idols of their youth for a longer period of time. But obviously their idols differ a lot from the idols admired by the current young generation. The admiration of a famous person and the construction of a fantasy relationship to him or her are expressions of erotic desires and a form of sublimated sexuality. The admiration of a dream boy (a member of a boy group) or a dream woman (like silicone wonder Pamela Anderson) leads to the creation of erotic fantasy worlds. Although compared to male fans, female fans tend to focus less on direct sexual contact with the idol. Nevertheless, idols generally can help in defining a new relationship with one's own body.

The star becomes meaningful insofar as he or she presents a role model for the construction of one's own identity, that corresponds with the idol for example in behavior or dress style. However, as a model for a youthful life-style an idol presents just a surface that can be imitated. In spite of all efforts by modern media to present idols as naturally and everyday-like as possible, we never see more than surfaces.

Actually, a star's abilities and talents (in case of sports idols, for example) are less important than the admiration of his or her appearance and style. Therefore, personal style (expressed in tattoos or hair style) increasingly gains in importance even among sports idols (for example, Dennis Rodman). "Style" makes the star stand out from the team. Social privileges and aggressive assertiveness are among the features of male stars that particularly impress fans of the same sex. Clichés like "the stars get all the girls" or smashed hotel rooms are an expression of these privileges that the stars are often more than willing to redeem.

By that, fans get the impression that stars are granted everything that they themselves do not have. So the idol is adored and desired. He is good looking and has an immaculate body that perfectly corresponds with the actual beauty ideal. For this reason the admiration of an idol can also serve to increase a feeling of an otherwise lacking self-confidence. It can distract, however, from one's own abilities, which, compared to the adored idol, are perceived as less valuable.

Rebellious idols who openly provoke are more exceptional. They are allowed to do a lot of things that are usually denied to "normal" adolescents, though, within an open space that society assigns to them. Therefore, idols play a similar role as artists: As with the artist, deviant behavior is almost demanded and expected by society. But nonetheless, deviant behavior is restricted through specific boundaries.

YOUTH IDOLS IN THE HISTORICAL CHANGE

Each subculture, and, respectively, any musical style, has its own idols. The admiration of idols connects young people with international fan communities where they can share their secret wishes and fantasies. Especially since the postwar time, pop icons exist increasingly in a process of globalization or internationalization. And American models in particular have been of growing importance to the West European youth since that time. In the 1950s there was nobody as close to the spirit of male and female teenagers as James Dean, whom his fans trustingly called Jimmy: "And this was the time when it happened with James Dean. He had just died, and was such an idol. He played his own life. He played only once, he was somebody who showed what's really going on. That impressed us a lot."

Most of the young could deeply understand his convincingly shown despair, resignation, and deep sadness about the adult world, who so much ignored his emotional life . His rebellious behavior and at least momentary fearlessness, coupled with an impressive ability to also show his weakness, was perceived as highly encouraging. Especially when faced with the ignorance, correctness, and rites of order held up by their parents, who, however properly, fell asleep with a full fridge and perfect front garden.

Another type of a rebellious idol of the fifties is embodied by Marlon Brando. In the movie *The Wild One* he acts as Johnny, a young guy who has enough of the whole fuss one has to do just to earn some money. Instead he prefers to drive around aimlessly with his gang on their motorbikes. Johnny expresses a character who aggressively rejects the adult culture that is determined by conformity and a rigid work morality that is typical of the 1950s.

Idols point to the direction of the youth's protest and distinction against the parental generation. Brando and Dean embody, both in their own way, a protest against the authority-focused, anti-emotional, body-hostile adult world of the 1950s. Whereas James Dean expressed this protest with a more introverted, sensitive and slightly vulnerable sensuality, Marlon Brando and his gang, clad in black leather, expressed a rather crude manliness, which symbolized an aggressive readiness to assert their own youthful needs and desires against the will of their parents—if necessary even with violence.

An idol of the late sixties following the rebellious attitude embodied by Marlon Brando is Jim Morrison, poet and singer of The Doors. His early death caused by drug addiction promoted his cult status. Today his fans still make a pilgrimage to his grave in Paris. Jim Morrison is not a tragic and fragile idol like James Dean, but a rabble-rouser who also provoked because of his openly experienced sexuality.

The 1970s are particularly represented by the furious rebellion of punk, a movement that brusquely refused all stars, idols, and superbands such as Pink Floyd. Negating any exemplary function of inaccessible pop icons ought to rouse the youth from their lethargy and motivate them to creative and autonomous activity. The production of three-chord songs turned everybody into a potential star. The slogans are "no more heroes anymore" (Stranglers) and "kill your idols" (Sonic Youth). Nonetheless, because of his spectacular death through overdose and the story around the murder of his girlfriend, Nancy Spungen, somebody rose to stardom with punk: Sid Vicious, bass player of the most famous and in the beginning most provocative punk band, The Sex Pistols. He is the tragic and at the same time rebellious idol of this scene.

The idols of the gothic scene, who were arising from the darker side of punk during the 1980s, were most of all those who committed suicide because of their grief and deep melancholy. Therefore, persons dealing with death, isolation, and loneliness in their melancholic music were predestined to become idols. The intense occupation with death is based on a particular attitude toward life, determined by a feeling of loneliness and isolation, a lack of friends, love, and communication, as well as problems with school, identity, and disappointed love. The admiration for gothic punk is still particularly concentrated on Ian Curtis who was the singer for the band Joy Division. He committed suicide because of a disappointed love: "Joy Division is really . . . really something special, you know . . . honest, I find them honest . . . particularly the singer . . . because . . . one can say perhaps he was just sick, however, somehow there is more behind that . . . some, some of the songs show . . . that he committed . . . you see, it is the consequence of that, what he had sung on the records, this was in consequence followed by his suicide."

The sympathy for the fate of these tragic idols helps in overcoming a person's own situation, in which suicide is out of the question, since it would be admitting of failure in one's own life.

In contrast, within the vibrant dance movement of techno and house, tragic idols like that are still rather unknown. Since the mid-1980s, the aftermath of punk, the techno and house scene is at pains to establish another musical style without idols. Beginning with electronically produced music, this movement is complemented by the pop art ideal to make music like a machine. This ideal ought to serve to concentrate on music, without any identifiable persons distracting from that. The goal is a "no star" anonymity. The pioneers coming from Detroit, like Juan Atkins, call themselves Cybotron or Model 500. According to Blake Baxter's description of the origin of this musical direction, the only thing that is important is the project: working with music machines and coming together with people and wavelengths. Still, in the 1990s a lot of DJs produced their music under changing project names, which allowed them to produce different musical styles (for example the man behind Dr. Rockit, Wistmountain, and Herbert is Englishman Matthew Herbert). Musicians are no longer fixed to one specific musical style, so they can undermine the expectations of the audience, which always demands that new tracks should sound like the old ones.

DJs are originally an integral component of parties and events, but not their center or star. Nevertheless, techno and house cannot avoid completely the process of idol construction. Actually, to insiders of the scene, the mysterious character of project names adds to the appeal of tracking their idols and the project names that they use for new releases: "Together with the DJs emerged also a piece of your own identity along with techno because everywhere there were DJs that you knew. You'd been in the same school with them, and suddenly they are something like a star, they are accessible and have the same background. That imparts identity. Finally someone from next door becomes famous."

The idol whom one admires comes from one's own environment, is approachable and accessible. But despite that, due to the popularity of techno, the figure of the DJ turns into a myth and replaces the desire of becoming a rock star. Some of the American house music legends, who never wanted to be idols and who are still rather common, non-privileged club DJs in America, turned into stars in Europe, where they were also correspondingly marketed (for example Frankie Knuckles, Jeff Mills).

IDOLS AND MARKETING—ACTUAL TRENDS

The inaccessible greats of this scene, though initially not planning to become superstars, are contrasted by the local DJs, who play records to an audience familiar to them. Depending on the cooperation of DJs, this more local orientation can be transformed by the typical mechanism of the rock business: The DJ plays his records rather unnoticed in a small club, but on some night his abilities get discovered and he gets big success, eventually finding himself listed in the Mayday line up.

The lack of big names at the beginning of this movement caused some disorientation among the various industries; however, not so among the kids. As a commercialized mass movement techno without idols is unthinkable. Stars are essential to the selling of music and new products in the arising market. Without corresponding front figures music products are not marketable. In this way the DJs themselves turn into a kind of brand through which event sponsors can sell a lot of other products, too.

To be able to advance new ways of dancing and hearing emotionally, the style needs identification figures, and international techno legends such as Derrick May or Kevin Saunderson are very suitable for this. "The Kids want to see their heroes, therefore DJs have to travel." Actually, techno journals such as Front Page, despite its innovative graphics and layout, construct traditional identification figures in a conventional style: They show the classic subjects of music journalism, such as the presentation of "stars" in interviews and photographs of DJs.

Marusha turned into a cheerful identification figure for female and male techno fans. She is uncomplicated and always in a good mood. Actually, her former occupation as shoe vendor repeats the classic American myth of the dishwasher who becomes the big star. For female fans Marusha has become one of the most important identification figures. She is part of the 10 percent of female DJs, a token woman DJ, who can be marketed so broadly. She incorporates female fans into the style, and in some cases she encourages them to reach for the turntables themselves.

The reason there have hardly been any female idols in the techno scene since its expansion into a mass movement is that there is a lot of money and power involved. And since the beginning, female DJs have had the stigma that women basically cannot play records, therefore they are no serious competition to male DJs. Thus women only rarely get a chance at the turntables.

Viola: "It's a pity that also in the techno scene especially the men are active: The girls dance to the boy's DJ-tunes. As a DJane I am still an exotic girl."

Since female DJs have this exotic status in the scene, they are only conditionally marketable. They do not correspond with the standard idol of the scene: The male DJ is admired by male techno fans because of his mixing technique. However, in the case of a female DJ, the male audience is only interested in her appearance, not in her talent for sampling and mixing.

Thus, Marusha is a pop icon as of the 1970s and 1980s. Like all stars she circulates through pictorial images so that her fans can share her and get the feeling of possessing a piece of their admired idol. Star marketing and merchandising are based on this pictoriality. Marusha is represented in the classic media for the circulation of teenage idols: The German teenage magazine Bravo has existed since the 1960s and is complemented by additional journals such as Sport Bravo and Bravo Girl, as well as a Bravo-Hits compilation and Bravo TV. Whoever is backed up with Bravo's exclusive star reportage, such as Kelly Family, can be sure of unlimited admiration.

The idol is in the center of pop idolatry, that is, the admiration of pop images. Teenagers build altars in their rooms which serve the cult of their admired stars. The images of the star, in the form of posters, buttons, postcards, and T-shirts spread and multiply in the rooms of fans. Thus, by decorating their walls with various shreds of pictures showing the admired person, the fans literally create projection screens for their own fantasies and desires.

Furthermore, the media constructs different stars for male and female recipients. Boy bands are a special marketing phenomenon of the 1990s; the best-known examples are *East 17* and *Take That*. These boy bands, with their styled bodies, were specifically composed as cloned compilations for girls in puberty: Athletic bodies, acrobatic dance and stage shows, an individual style for each member, representing the whole range of hair colors, are all in order to appeal to as many different types of girls as possible.

However, "boy bands" is only a new name for what had been understood as teenie-bopper groups in the 1970s, exemplified by *The Bay City Rollers*. An entire corporate identity was created around these bands (like "Scott's in target checks") in order to sell scarves, T-shirts, and other merchandising products. The quantity of these groups has increased since that time. Their medial image is made up from pseudo-intimacies that emphasize the normality of the star. Boy groups serve the confirmation of traditional values, and they demand a traditional and conventional behavior from their feminine fans. Even if they demonstrate risky tricks on stage, like the *Backstreet Boys*, boy groups are not at all rebellious. Likewise, the *Kelly Family* even fulfills several functions of idol construction: That is, female fan hysteria (girls admiring Paddy and Angelo) without showing unambiguous "f*** me"-posters, as is common among female *Take That* fans.

Linus, 16: The music is simply great. Unfortunately that's very rare today. In fact, every rapper can pack up and go home.

Stella, 13: They are so different! . . . The whole family sticks together.

Tanja, 12: I got a small plush-tiger for Joey. I like Joey, he's like a big brother for me.

The *Kelly Family*, maliciously called "the singing rags," represents an intact extended family in a protected, clean, and drug-free world. However, at the same time their life on the houseboat in Cologne also has something adventurous and unusual. Their nice and non-aggressive songs turn them into idols that address several generations, from the teenager up to the grandparents. Beyond that, they also cover different sorts of desires: They present a variety of boys and girls to fall in love with. The *Kelly Family* manages to combine the traditional, even rural, with apparently modern elements. Their palette of traditional folk songs is broadened by the use of electronic instruments such as the e-guitar. This suggests a certain progressiveness and openness to modern influences, even though the songs remain in the folk genre. The *Kelly Family* embodies an old patriarchal family ideal and traditional values held up by the strong leadership of their father. The *Kelly Family* clarifies the polarity of star worlds; they represent the ideal of pure and clean stars while the rest of the pop business is succumbing to the thrill of drug excesses.

Likewise among sports idols the polarization of stars into good and bad is obvious, even though the bad boys are among the most wanted men. Compared to the particularly good and fair players, the players that—beyond their talent—behave also in a particularly striking or aggressive and rebellious way (soccer: Cantonar, Gascoigne, basketball: Rodman, O'Neill, Barkley) are the ones who will become idols. And they are also the ones who will be specifically supported by companies such as Nike, whose marketing strategies build upon identifiable characters. Those players become idols, who beyond their talent can show off a particular style and shine with strong personalites in spite of their subordination to a team.

The young soccer player Lars Ricken is in contrast a rather adept sport idol. Parallel to his soccer career he passed his school-leaving exam to later study business management. Swimmer Franzi von Almsick and tennis star Boris Becker are further examples. Their interest centers on their athletic abilities and its marketing, showing that personal style is less important to these idols.

FROM THE TRAGIC HERO TO THE "POST-HUMAN" STAR: AN ATTEMPT TOWARD AN IDOL-TYPOLOGY

Since the 1950s there have been recurring patterns to which one can assign each new idol. Three traditional types of young people's idols can be found to have existed—with modifications—basically since the postwar era:

Type 1: The tragic idol, who stands for failing at the requirements of the purposeful, rational adult world. The decline of individuality can end in suicide. In the case of the tragic idol, the admitted failure that is being destroyed by the world and daily existence turns into cult. The myth "live fast, die young" can be traced from James Dean to Kurt Cobain of Nirvana, from Sid Vicious to River Phoenix.

Type 2: The conservative idol stands for conformity and a fast rise into the adult world and the contact with adult values. These idols present themselves as the ones that have made it. They are performance-oriented sports idols (such as Lars Reckon), or represent themselves, such as the members of boy groups, with luxurious cars. In this case medial presentation puts the emphasis particularly on the idol's normal daily life.

Type 3: The rebellious idol is characterized by the aimless and aggressive rebelling against norms and taboos. Precursors and analogies can be seen in the artist and the dandy, who lives his life regardless of sanctions (such as Marlon Brando or Jim Morrison).

Type 4 is a rather new phenomenon: Settled in the contemporary arena of music and pop stars, this is the cloned "post-human" idol, as exemplified by Michael Jackson and Madonna. These stars show split, multiple, and artificially produced identities and bodies. The post-human star and his image are no longer produced by the music business alone, but the star self-constructs him or herself, or at least participates actively in the construction of an image.

The construct of an unapproachable, divine, and fragile femininity, as with Marilyn Monroe, has disappeared. Instead, artificiality is dominating, a play with gender, masquerade, and crossdressing, as vividly demonstrated by stars such as Madonna and Dennis Rodman. They serve to expose identity constructions among the stars.

Thus, the idols of the 1990s and beyond are multiple coded idols. One can idolize them simply because of their appearance or admire them because of their virtuous performance and play with media patterns. In contrast to the post-human and rebellious idols, since the 1950s the conservative and tragic idols have been fairly constant, preserving rather traditional values. They show no subversive character, but confirm the existing conditions, under which they are easily transferable into commodities.

REMIX CULTURE

Bart Vautour

Remix culture challenges the accepted ways of producing cultural products. Remix is a pastiche or collage that reappropriates corporate modes of production in an attempt to question and rework the way meanings are regulated. The use of "re-" asserts both a performative context that imitates, mirrors, and reflects, as well as a different sort of presentation that undermines the notion of a "true" reproduction. Today's youth are living in a remix culture: a culture that is participating in "the changing same"; a culture renewing, manipulating, and modifying already mediated and mixed cultural material; a culture jamming. The way some music is made in our current moment is no different. Although the main metaphor used to explain remix culture is music, remix culture has spread to other realms of youth production as well.

What exactly does remix culture confront? To begin with, originality has been one of the main legitimizing concepts in the production of Western music. "Western" is an inadequate term that points toward musical production that is historically grounded in larger late-capitalist formations of cultural production. Indeed, it would seem that the three main pillars of the dominant musical paradigm or convention are originality, individuality, and copyright.

Originality and the "individual voice" have become the central criteria for the way people are supposed to create new cultural products or texts. These criteria serve to make (sonic) writings objects that can be legally owned; in other words, (sonic) writing may be regarded as intellectual property and placed under copyright. For example, when we hear a Beatles song performed by other musicians, the Lennon/McCartney duo are still the important people, while the accomplishments of the musicians playing or the technical support persons are not given any attention. Another interesting shift that has historically occurred in the Western musical paradigm is that the authority of sonic writing has shifted because of technology. The authority and copyright once rested in the score (musical notations represented in a twelve-tone system on paper) and not the performance. This was because the performance would necessarily produce variations depending on the musicians playing. With the advent of hi-fi digital sampling (as opposed to lo-fi analogue recording) the textual authority has shifted from the written score to the digital representation of ones and zeros.

When we hear Western music—at the site of reception—we are hearing both the represented ones and zeros (binary code) and narration of specific musical conventions. When we are hearing a narration; we are specifically listening to the telling of a sonically articulated cultural event or events.

Remix culture aims at telling a different story. People who participate in remix culture are not concerned with the rule of individual voice or the legal issues involved in copyright. Rather, the practitioners of remix act like scavengers to make art and music with found objects. The found objects, in this case, could be the songs and sounds that have already been made by other people. Remixed music is often illegal or unauthorized. The corporate producers of music do not much like people using the music that they own because they do not earn any money from remixed music, unless, of course, they are the ones who are doing the remixing. In the case of big companies remixing music and sounds that they already own, the remix is not illegal.

An important distinction that we must make is between the practice of mainstream remix and a more underground and political remix. Mainstream remix is actually just about remake. Mainstream or corporate musical production succeeds by endlessly putting out repackaged material that does not do much other than redistribute the old in a new guise. Corporate music relies upon uniform beats and chord progressions embedded within contemporary conceptions of music. This type of music thinks innovation is the way to find *innovative* ways of maintaining the status quo and making more money. Often, the artists do not actually make much money on this sort of remake. Instead, big music distribution companies make the lion's share of the profit.

While remix culture is explicitly not about mainstream capitalist culture, it is crucial to make a distinction between underground or sub-cultural formations and the mainstream appropriations of those formations. Should we consider Puff Daddy's sampling of Sting an oppositional remix? How did "Grammy Rap" become *Grammy* Rap?

Rap and hip hop were, and still are, oppositional black ways of making music that were neither born in art galleries, drawing rooms of the rich, nor the studios of the music industry. Remix culture came out of clubs, out of "houses" and off the street, and out of the labor of DJs and hip hop MCs. The problem is that mainstream capitalist culture has silenced some of the oppositional force that hip hop produced when it first started. Hip hop has changed many times and will continue to change. While some of the changes have tried to keep the oppositional force—sometimes crossing boundaries of nationality, ethnicity, race, class, gender, and tradition—others have stopped questioning the issues that were central to early rap and hip hop musicians. Mainstream hip hop has also stopped producing in the same way, opting instead to conform to the musical conventions that hip hop and its black urban practitioners were responding to and confronting at in the time and place where it began.

Just as mainstream capitalist culture has spread Grammy Rap globally, the megaproduction of depoliticized hip hop culture has also sent along a trace of the oppositional origins of the remix: a non-incorporated residual element. In other words, corporate agendas cannot quite get a tight grip on this type of music because of the way it is often made.

Remix culture asserts that the remix is an overt challenge to accepted capitalist musical paradigms and conventions. But how exactly does remix confront mainstream ways of making music? The practice of remixing undermines the dominant musical paradigm because it draws upon exact replicas of already established and articulated music, coded into ones and zeros due to digital technology, to recreate and narrate a different cultural reality. Before digital technology it was impossible to replicate the exact sonic textures of music but now we are able to reproduce exact replicas of the music and play it over and over again without changing anything sonically. As a result, now, the foremost location of difference—the signifiers that create variation in performance—is the context in which it is played. Remix throws the normal listening practice of concentrating on "who wrote it?" into crisis.

Who is remixing music and what are they doing to the music that makes it remix and not just the same thing over and over again? The main practitioners of remix are today's youth. They are the DJs and computer-kids that have found ways to technologically change and modify music. For example, they sometimes speed up the music or slow down the music. They can mix songs together or just sample a few lines from a given song and put it to a different beat. The possibilities are endless when it comes to remixing electronic music.

Most importantly, today's youth have taken control over where and how music can be played and shared. Whether it is about playing this remixed music at clubs or about sharing different mixes globally over the Internet, today's youth are distributing music in historically unprecedented ways. Today's youth have found interesting ways to turn their consumption into production and then make it available to a public sphere.

In spite of the fact that, at this globalized moment, corporate industries consider youth to be consummate consumers, this marketing strategy cannot account for the diverse and unique ways in which today's global youth *produce*, or rearticulate their acts of consumption *as a process of production*. In the case of music, global youth have taken the products of the Western musical paradigm—with help from the increasing spread of technological literacy—and appropriated and reconfigured how these products sound and get publicly circulated. This is a version of hybridity that allows today's youth to exist within the larger corporate order while wielding a certain mode of productive *dis*order. It is the resistance to this dominant way of producing cultural products like music that becomes important in exploring remix culture.

As noted above, there are ways other than music through which young people around the globe are taking things that they are supposed to quietly consume and reproducing them in new and oppositional ways. For example, skateboarders utilize public and corporate space in ways that the builders and architects never imagined. Culture Jamming could be thought of as another example. Guerrilla Radio or Pirate Radio is another illustration of youth taking over networks and corporate products and remixing the conventional uses of advertising and marketing. The possibilities for remix abound.

Resources
Books

Attali, J. (1996). *Noise: The political economy of music*. Trans. B. Massumi. Minneapolis: University of Minnesota Press.

Born, G., & Hesmondhalgh, D. (Eds.). (2000). *Western music and its others: Difference, representation, and appropriation in music*. Berkeley, CA: University of California Press.

Klein, N. (2000). *No logo: Taking aim at the brand bullies*. Toronto: Vintage.

Miller, P. D. (2004). *Rhythm science*. Cambridge, MA: MIT Press.

Muggleton, D., & Weinzierl, R. (Eds.). (2003). *The post-subcultures reader*. Oxford: Berg.

Neal, M. A., & Forman, M. (Eds.). (2004). *That's the joint: The hip hop studies reader*. New York: Routledge.

Shapiro, P. (Ed.). (2000). *Modulations: A history of electronic music: Throbbing words on sound*. New York: Caipirinha Productions.

Articles

Boisvert, A. (2003). On bricolage: Assembling culture with whatever comes to hand. *HorizonZero: Digital Art and Culture in Canada*, 8, [online]. Retrieved September 18, 2005 from http//www.horizonzero.ca/textsite/remix

Schutze, B. (2003). Samples from the heap: Notes on recycling the detritus of a remix culture. *HorizonZero: Digital Art and Culture in Canada*, 8, [online]. Retrieved September 18, 2005 from http//www.horizonzero.ca/textsite/remix

INDUSTRIAL CULTURE

Birgit Richard

Our tune is the crying of the machines. Our music is the roaring of engines. Our sounds are the final rearing. We are dancing the downfall, to be able to live.

[Unsere Melodie ist das Schreien der Maschinen. Unsere Musik ist das Brüllen der Motoren. Unsere Klänge das letzte Aufbäumen. Wir tanzen den Untergang, um zu leben.]

—Einstürzende Neubauten

"Industrial culture" designates a special trend in music, which has its roots in punk. Monte Cazazza, with his sentence "Industrial music for industrial people," christens the whole musical trend, plus an independent label. The music, developed in England, attempts to musically express the gloomy situation in English industrial towns.[1] The designation "Industrial culture" also contains a conspicuous ironic touch, since, at that stage of its development, Britain was going through a recession. The crumbling Industrial Age is not invoked for nostalgic reasons, but rather a former industrial society is reflected, which undergoes a fundamental change. Industrial also considers itself to be a reaction to the beginning of mediazation, to the influence of the media and its dependence on and entanglement with power. This entry will outline elements of Industrial culture. See "Industrial Bands" for a discussion of key artists in this genre.

Punk's concentration on the theory of the situationists inspired the new Industrial trend to focus on dealing with the depression of a society ruled by economic interests. Industrial culture radicalizes the ideas of punk with full knowledge of the mechanisms of provocation in the arts.

The Industrial scene is no adolescent subculture in the original sense, since most of its members are of a postadolescent age. It is a subculture developed from the extreme fringes of the arts; it is not a clearly identifiable, expressively public style. Industrial commutes between a subculture and the arts. The interdisciplinary approach of Industrial combines the music with technology, science, literature, and the arts. The emphasis of this subcultural style lies on the music, around which the various aesthetic and literary media, which underline and expand the intention of the music in the sense of a comprehensive work of art, then assemble. In their music, many Industrial bands attempt to realize Brion Gysin's cut-up theory, which characterizes William

Burroughs' literary style in particular. Burroughs cuts up audiotapes of various recordings into the smallest fragments, just to reassemble them arbitrarily. He describes weapons and technologies of war games.[2] The cut-up collage uses time-axis-manipulation, which means that, for example, tones are shifted downward by a semitone when recorded, just to be shifted upward when played. The cut becomes independent; it is no longer embellishment or correction, but becomes a stylistic means of music and art.[3]

Some of the most important protagonists in Industrial music are Throbbing Gristle, Chris and Cosey, Coil, Psychic TV, plus Cabaret Voltaire, Test Department, Monte Cazazza, SPK, and Einstürzende Neubauten. Industrial music is predominantly characterized by the unusual instrumentation. Steel hammer mechanisms; tools and machines like drill, flex, and pneumatic hammer; materials like stone, metal, and plastics; or synthetically produced noises are used as instruments. In addition, these groups use formerly anti-musical elements, such as various tapes with industrial sounds and sounds from everyday life, which are used in a manner reminiscent of a collage. Sound collages are created that represent a section of the background noise of an industrial society.[4] This kind of music closes a gap punk had left open.

The prevailing themes are death, illness, war, and crime. The functional principles of and the growths of cancer in a disease-stricken society are laid bare. Industrial culture bands try to comprehend and trace the patterns of how the decaying industrial landscape affects people's souls. Thus, in their lyrics and on their record covers they predominately deal with a perverted human behavior, whose development they put down to the conditions in a highly mechanized society in an accusing fashion. They develop a great interest in the cases of mass or ritual murderers, such as, Charles Manson, the child-murderess Mary Bell, the couple Ian Brady and Myra Hindley; this interest often is interpreted as an approval of murder and violence. However, this is about the presentation of the worst, omitted aspects of society—areas even omitted by the media or reported on in a very particular way. These special cases of violent crime are, so to speak, the great tales of the scene. They deal with hardcore sex, military experiments on humans and animals, venereal diseases, and misshapings of the human body, with pathology (the band SPK in particular), and with insanity, thus with the aspects of society pushed into an area invisible to the public.

To impress the structures of society and its failings on the audience, almost all involved in the Industrial culture scene use media such as slides, super-8 films, videos, photographs, or special light effects. Music and images merge into a multimedia performance. At the time, the multimedia notion was so new in music that the electronic equipment necessary for the generation of noises had to be built by the members of the scene themselves. Therefore, the scene's own production of the records of Industrial bands became necessary as well. Traditional studios were both unwilling and unable to produce the unusual sounds in an adequate fashion.

Additionally, from the beginning, it is of major importance to quite a number of members of the Industrial scene to develop their own structures for the dissemination of their ideas. They founded their own record labels (e.g., Industrial Records by Throbbing Gristle or the Factory Label) and video labels (Double Vision by Cabaret Voltaire). The bands follow-up on the efforts of punk to produce music and videos on their own, so that at no time do they lose control over their products.

Another Industrial objective is the attempt to expose the manipulative structures of the media in an information society by carrying certain strategies of manipulation to extremes, thereby bringing them to the public's attention. This objective is also pursued by publications of the scene, such as "Industrial News" by Throbbing Gristle. The cut-up techniques of Industrial bands, at the end of the 1970s an innovation that reaches only a very small audience, in the 1990s are processed for a mass audience: sampling has become the new basis of music.[5]

INDUSTRIAL CULTURE AS THE TRANSFERENCE OF ARTISTIC AVANT-GARDE INTO ADOLESCENT SUBCULTURE

To prove a direct historical connection between subcultures and avant-garde is a difficult undertaking. The developments of artistic avant-garde trends and adolescent subcultures occur separately, if we disregard a number of cross-links between 1900 and 1960. Their temporary symbiosis and interlocking can be explained by a process of intellectual activities or artistic production becoming ordinary, the development of an independent adolescent phase in life, and a change in its social importance. The decisive factor for popularity of a bohemian attitude in adolescent subcultures, formerly reserved for the artistic avant-garde, is the postulate of overcoming the separation of art and everyday life. Artistic means of expression, such as the combination of visual and acoustic sensorial stimuli, become very important for the upheaval of purposes in life and consciousness of a mass bohemian culture at the end of the 1960s. Youth movements such as the Dutch Provos obtain their forms from happenings, the French students movement from the Strasbourg branch of the "Situationist International," the German extraparliamentary opposition from the group "SPUR." The hippies are the first adolescent mass movement that derives directly from the expansion of the bohemian, avant-garde, Beat generation. This historically unique symbiosis of the artistic bohemian world and adolescent mass culture is made possible by its dissemination through the media. This convergence has the effect that with the disappearance of the artistic avant-garde the bohemian world becomes a subculture in its own right and does away with itself in everyday-life by a spread of the bohemian attitude through the masses.

Industrial culture made close connections to artistic avant-garde movements quite noticeable. At the end of the 1960s, Industrial developed from an artistic environment and became a culture in which cultural and subcultural forms are inseparably linked.[6] It is therefore necessary to draw some sketches of certain trends in action art—a designation which here shall comprise happening, event, Fluxus, Nouveau Realistes, concept art, actionism, body art, and performance[7]—which inspire the subculture.

Action art is a modern phenomenon. Their boundless experimentation with basic qualities of art follows the tradition of futurists, dadaists, and surrealists. Action art is multidimensional, breaks down traditional borders between genres, and involves new media. The authenticity of life shall be introduced into the arts. In contrast to the initiators of action art, dadaists, and futurists, the main tendency in action art is not so aggressive and not full of malicious criticism and provocation. This aggressive trend in action art is continued by Industrial. It shall be proved that youth culture becomes the place where obsolete forms of avant-garde art are preserved in the Underground culture of music.

The first hallmark of both Industrial and action art is multimediality, indirectly contained in the following elements. As we have seen in the chapters above, all Industrial groups experiment with acoustic stimuli and anti-musical elements. There have been drums for phonographs with, for example, noises of steamrollers, ship bells, and from ordinary life since 1898, making music part of the acoustic ambience of everyday life. In the area of the arts, Marinetti's onomatopeic poem "Zang Tumb Tumb" from 1914, thus futuristic noise-music, marks the beginning of this development.[8] Luigi Russolo uses noises from ordinary life, suchas sounds of trams in motion, misfiring of cars, and the raucous bawling of crowds for his compositions. Furthermore, he constructs motorized instruments for the generation of noises, the so-called "Intonarumori".

From 1918 on, the Russian poets Gastev and Mayakowski give concerts for factory sirens and other noises: The most famous example was performed in the port of Baku in 1922. The instrumentarium consists of factory sirens, foghorns of ships, machine-gun salvos, two batallions of artillery, and the noises of thousands of members of the audience.[9]

Here we can see the roots of Industrial culture, which is a comparable phenomenon when it comes to the generation of noises and also directly refers to the influence of the futurists, though without sharing their positivist euphoria about progress and technology. The Industrial culture scene represents the decaying inner life of an industrial machinery still shining only on the outside.

In the 1960s, this noise-music is taken up by John Cage. Silence and remaining silent are introduced as new elements, as is the dadaistic principle of coincidence. Further parallels on the level of music can be found in the Fluxus concerts, for example, in Nam Jun Paik's "Opera Sexotronique," performed in 1966. We should also mention the De-Collage music of Vostell, which creates a noise scenery by using instruments unspecific to music.[10]

The use of robots, flesh-machine-installations, and technical equipment, predominantly found in SRL, has its theoretical origin in concepts of the futurists, who set upon breaking up the insurmountable hostility between human flesh and the metal of engines. Later, in particular the destructive force of machines is picked out as a central theme. Wolf Vostell arranges collisions between a car and a train. Direct parallels to the performances of SRL can be found in the "Homage to New York" in 1960, in which a self-destructing machine, weather balloons, and smoke bombs are set on stage.[11] Another example are the "Metametics" by Jean Tinguely. He processes garbage and used and discarded objects of modern technology and is thus also a precursor to Trans High Tech Design. The "Metametics" are without function, their obsolescence is built-in. The meaningless destroys itself. Thus they are, in a technical sense, counterproductive anti-machines. Tinguely's machines are supposed to inspire playing with them. They are a combination of threatening-destructive and comical effects. This comical variant is missing from SRL; their machinery appears absurd and scary. In the 1980s, Tinguely formed assemblies such as "Das Atelier des Künstlers von 1985" or "Die Hexen oder Schneewittchen und die sieben Zwerge" (1985), which, through the combination of parts of machines, animal skulls,[12] and furs, show a marked resemblance to performances of SRL. The combination of corroding iron (i.e. dying and dissolving metal) and skulls creates an aesthetics of agony. Here, dead matter also seems to be reanimated, it starts to move again. The material is worthless without an engine; to Tinguely their stoppage means death. He deals with the intense preoccupation with death to make the latter look ridiculous and to partly deterrorize it. Industrial, on the other hand, attempts to increase the terror to draw attention to it. The absurd combination of dead biological matter with metal shows that technology can "revive" dead matter, which only leads to absurd excesses, which no longer have anything to do with the former life of the matter now dead. Another example for parallels between Industrial and the Fluxus movement is the robot, for example Nam Jun Paik's remote-controlled Robot KT 678. The most extreme example is the amputation-robot by the Canadian John Faré, which he built with the cybernetician Golni Czervath. As further contemporary parallels we should call to mind the Unnatural Bodies by Jim Whiting and the cybernetic pets by Nicolas Baginsky.

Another connecting strand is the use of the individual body in a sadomasochist manner, its ritual destruction or injuring. The Industrial scene is closely connected with the manifestations of the Viennese action art. COUM's extreme actions do not differ very sharply from actions by Günther Brus or Otto Mühls. The willingness for self-injuring, which can also be found with Valie Export and Gina Pane, can only be found on the fringes of action art.[13] The aggressive character can only be detected in early happenings. Otto Mühl and Hermann Nitsch introduce injuries and death as metaphors. The provocation culminates in self-destructive acts by

Günther Brus and Rudolf Schwarzkogler, who use their own bodies. Brus wants to turn the body into a painting by body-specific means, as in "Zer-reißprobe," in which his blood is used as paint by cutting into the skin. Schwarzkogler in his stage-managed photographs presents the injured body and death as action. This is also the tradition of the self-mutilations in the early actions by Wolfgang Flatz, who, for example, has a fist scratched onto his back or becomes the target of darts, or in his dismantlings ("Demontagen") lets himself be swung between two steel sheets as a human tongue (e.g., "Stahlglocke").

The culmination of the gruesome self-destruction is reached with the action by the Canadian John Charles Faré ("Dying is an art like everything else"),[14] who in 1968 executed the amputation of individual extremities with the help of two assistants and two robots, fixed to the operating table. The body-parts are replaced by metal or plastic imitations. Suicide in installments takes place in a sequence of actions, lit by the spotlights of the robots. The end is constituted by self-decapitation. In the beginning, Industrial culture exercised physical self-injury in reality; however, it later acquired techniques to simulate injuries.

The demands on the recipient are common to both Industrial and action art. The provocation of an orgies-mysteries-theater is only for a very short time able to affect a society that ghoulishly relishes murder on television, but backs away from naked bodies and excrements. The shock tactics of the Industrial scene are more subtle, since in addition they directly address the perception mechanisms of the audience.

It was the objective of the action artists to provoke intense, spontaneous reactions from the audience. The provokingly destructive, sometimes even brutal attitude of the action artists toward their audience turn some actions into a kind of torture. Nam Jun Paik throws eggs on his audience, and Peter Weibel and Valie Export whip down from stage and throw balls of barbed wire into the audience. The Fluxus-artists design environments and instal-lations that scare the viewer. Wolf Vostell's happening "Dogs and Chinese pp," an after-happening, in which a dark, totally overheated room could only be entered in bathing clothes and the exhibits had to be illuminated with torches,[15] is an example worth mentioning.

If we take Nitsch's definition of a happening as a basis—an event effect-ing chaos, movement, upheaval, and an intense experience—the perfor-mances of the Industrial bands can definitely be considered happenings.

The principles that action art and Industrial culture have in common are therefore multi-mediality, noise-art and anti-musical elements, the use of robots and machines, use of the body culminating in self-destruction and shock-tactics directed against the audience.

Notes

1   Vale, V., & Juno, A. (Eds.). (1986). Industrial Culture Handbook. Research Issue # 6/7, p. 10f. San Francisco (below shortened to InCuHa).

Cazazza refers to a sentence by Andy Warhol from 1977, the first idea for the name of the label was Factory.

2   A description of the environment of Industrial bands: "The terrace opposite stops short in the grey air, thick with moisture, revealing vistas of factorys, tower blicks, endless tightly patterned semi's . . . hills in the distance. Sometimes the factorys work at night—the noise can be heard in the house, filtering through dreams: dull, percussive, hynotic." (Intro to an interview with Cabaret Voltaire, Search & Destroy, June 78); John Savage: Introduction. In: InCuHa, op.cit., p. 4

3   This technique breaks up power by the means of a positive feedback, an endless loop. Kittler, F. A. (1986). *Film, Grammophon, Typewriter* (p. 169). Berlin.

4   ibid., p. 171

5   Genesis P. Orridge: "When we finished that first record, we went outside and we suddenly heard trains going past, and little workshops under the railway arches, and the lathes going, and electric saws, and we suddenly thought, "We haven't actually created anything at all, we've just taken it subconsciously and re-created it." InCuHa. op.cit., p. 11.
   Thus, meanwhile the musical approach of a band like Cabaret Voltaire is obsolete. Their experimental, electronic music is supported by self-produced videos and slides. Both the music and its visualization are determinded by the mysterious combination of contradicting fragments of reality. Cabaret Voltaire call themselves "modern primitives," because they focus on rhythm.

6   The direct reworking of artistic influences can predominantly be found among the protagonists of the English (original) subcultures, who very often attended art schools and impart their knowledge of various artistic means of expression e.g. on Punk or Wave.

7   Lischka, G. J. (1988). Performance und Performance Art. In *Kunstforum International*, Band 96, 65–193. Performance Art starts with the futurists and is spread with the development of the media. Lischka designates the Situationist International as her first theoretics. We should bear in mind that the roots of Punk are also found in this movement. Performance crystallizes from Happening, Event, Fluxus and Actionism.

8   Telephoning, hammering and the orders of a Turkish general, artillery- and machine-gun fire are supposed to represent the siege of Adrianopel. Almhofer. op.cit., p. 21.

9   Henri, A. (1974). Total Art. *Environments, Happenings and Performance* (p. 15). London.

10 Vostell uses the noises of construction-engines, pneumatic hammers, cars or noises of the destruction of objects: an excavator crushes radiograms and radios with an iron bowl or in his environments ordinary noises (fragments of glass on the floor) are distorted by electronic amplification. Schilling. op.cit., p. 121.

11 See also Tinguely's "Study for an End of the World No. 2", taking place in the Nevada desert in 1962, dominated by machines and explosions. Henri. op.cit., p. 172.

12 Animal skulls, human skulls appear only once. The death performed is not supposed to refer entirely to the fate of humans.

13 Scheiß-Aktion von Günther Brus (1967). Irrwisch. In O. Mühl. *The Death of Sharon Tate* (1969). Gina Pane's self-injuries shall illustrate the hopeless position of women. Schilling. op.cit., pp. 169, 162. Other Body Artists, like Vito Acconi, bite themselves in to the upper arm and trace the impressions with ink (action in 1970). The Canadian Chris Burden crawls through fragments of glass and gets shot at. A Japanese artist in his action "life" jumped out of the window. The most contemporary examples of extensive self-mutilation of women are the cosmetic operations performances by Orlan.

14 The actions always took place on Fridays at 8.30 pm. The first operation, a lobotomy, was carried out in Kopenhagen in June 1964. On 17 September 1968 Farè turns up in the Isaacs Gallery in Toronto to get his right hand amputated. Beforehand, Farès body is fitted with small microphones, which transmit his pulse and breathing frequency in a distorted fashion. The hand gets amputated and preserved in a jar. From former actions, he already lacks a thumb, two fingers, eight toes, one eye, both testicles and several shreds of skin. Craig, T. (1972, November). John Fare you well. *Studio International*, 949, Band 184, 160.

15 You. Happening in a swimming pool filled with yellow, blue, red sacks of color and bones of oxens. People were lying on top of each other in the blood of an ìoxen-lungs-trampolineî, squirting color onto each other. There is a yellow tennis-court, a bicycle with an exploding color television set and parachutes. Signal bombs create orange-colored smoke, the participants wear gas-masks. Cf. also "In Ulm, um Ulm und um Ulm herum" von 1964. Alan Kaprow concludes a happening by driving the participants from a wooden box with a mower.

INDUSTRIAL BANDS

Birgit Richard

Industrial culture is discussed in the previous entry. This entry will further illustrate the unusualness of industrial music and performances, with an overview of several key Industrial bands that are part of the Industrial culture movement.

BOYD RICE

Boyd Rice creates music reminiscent of collages (spiced up, for example, with scraps of noise from recordings of the suicides of the sect of Jim Jones in Jonestown, Guyana). His musical performances with a self-constructed ventilator-guitar, which makes an extreme volume possible, are supplemented by other aggressive acts such as glaring light, which mercilessly shines into the audience's faces. He creates noise affecting the body. Another self-constructed instrument of Boyd Rice is an organ, whose pipes consist of cow-lung, -windpipe, and -larynx, connected to an air compressor.

MONTE CAZAZZA

One of the most extreme protagonists and initiators of the Industrial trend, besides Throbbing Gristle, is Monte Cazazza. He deals with the worst human desires and behaviors, using a large variety of media, photographs, collage, film, music, and performance to present his extreme topics. Which topics these might be can be deduced from his request list: "Self defense, Magic, Psychic Phenomena, Dream Imagery, Pornography, Survivalism, Weapons, Hypnosis, Murder and Death Rites, Religious and other Cults, Terrorism, Electronic Devices, Animal and Human Experimentation, Ecological and Corporate Disasters and Accidents, Subliminal and Psychological Methods of Control (e.g., subliminal advertising), Chem Germ Warfare, Medical Mutations." This list is amended by a preference for pornographic films; an interest in people such as Gary Gilmore and Aleister Crowley; and an interest in mass psychology, polygraphs, the Jonestown People's Temple or the Baader Meinhof Group. Monte Cazazza also predominantly deals with the stages of technological development in various areas, for example, with military experiments on the destruction of objects by vibrations of particular frequencies. He observes military experiments such as measuring the movements of the pupils, which give information on whether someone is telling the truth and how they react on the influences of certain images. It is of major importance for him to find out, where and how these technologies are used for the manipulation of humans in civilian life. People such as Monte Cazazza, who, owing to the topics they pick, are regarded as sick perverts, attempt to provide specific information on areas society does not want to know anything about.

EINSTÜRZENDEN NEUBAUTEN

A German group, which might be called an Industrial band with their own style, is the Einstürzenden Neubauten. Their name is supposed to mean old objects, meanings, buildings, and musical trends get replaced by new ones. The end of progress is reached, when things do not grow older any longer, but are destroyed at the moment of creation. The band uses

Walter Benjamin's "destructive character" as their basis. Their instruments are self-constructed steel hammer mechanisms made of pipes, T-beams, steel springs, chains, steel slabs, cans, building site equipment, pneumatic hammers, welding equipment—in short, everything you can get from scrap yards, building sites, and garbage dumps. Meanwhile their legendary rehearsal room could be found in the base of a motorway bridge, where they created noises to go with the permanently vibrating concrete. Einstürzende Neubauten set to music the emptiness and hopelessness of metropolitan life in Berlin. They are the reflection of the ugly sides of towns, with which, however, they identify themselves, which is rather typical of all other Industrial protagonists as well.

Since they started, the Neubauten have always caused an uproar. For example, when they visited the Dachau concentration camp, their short-cropped hair and their pajama tops made them resemble the victims of concentration camps, which was quite macabre. In the ICA in London they drill through the stage-floor with drills and pneumatic hammers, in posh discotheques in New York they scare off the trendy audience with burning rubber tires. The Neubauten present industrial labor as a sound experience and a performance: "no music, rather: noise. The modern tune is noisy. Only metal will survive." ("keine Musik, besser: Krach. Die moderne Melodie ist Krach. Nur Metall überlebt.")Musical examples are "primitive" music and music by dilettantes. The Einstürzenden Neubauten do not regret downfall and destruction, the bloody holocaust that everyone else is terror-stricken by:

> There's war in the cities, and that's all right by us. . . . There's not much time left until the final collapse, our odysseys destroy cities and nocturnal wanderings raze them to the ground. . . . For me, these are the last days, it's the apocalypse, definitely. We'll have another three or four years, then it's over. No discussion. Downfall means downfall.

They welcome destruction, physical decay, violent death with cynical, malicious joy.

The tendency to use strange names can also be found in the song titles of the Neubauten: *Abfackeln* (burn down), *Kollaps* (collapse), *Mit Schmerzen hören* (to hear it under pain), *Hirnsäge* (brainsaw), *Abstieg* (decline), *Zerfall* (decay), *Tanz Debil* (feeble-minded dance).

Meanwhile, the Einstürzenden Neubauten have become the main advertising feature for German avant-garde-music. They performed, for example, on the documenta 7 and have written musical scores for the theater (Andi, Zadek; Hamlet Maschine, Heiner Müller) and for a ballet.

The Einstürzenden Neubauten also show an interest in the physical effects of music.

Thus, all Industrial bands have extreme, unusual performances, images, and music in common, physically and psychologically almost unbearable for the audience. The experience of strategies of manipulation in the military and in the media and the examination of processes of perception are realized in the music and in performances on stage. All groups have subliminals on the visual and auditory level in common, images, words, light effects, which are only perceived unconsciously, but get a foothold in the brain like a virus and affect behavior. Kittler's assertion, rock concerts and discos are the rehearsal of circumventing barriers of perception, can only be partially applied to Industrial bands, since they would like to see their concerts understood as the attempt to increase the awareness of opportunities for manipulation by the entertainment industry.

The concerts are supposed to offer extraordinary, synaesthetical experiences, not only a distraction from ordinary life. There are great physical demands on the members of the audience, in some cases they are aggressively attacked. The experience they undergo affect the body or are supposed to uncover the unconscious, which also shows parallels to action art.

In contrast to the down-to-earth street style of punk, Industrial culture is heavily charged with theoretical approaches. It is dealing with literature, philosophy, medicine, law studies, and the natural sciences. The Industrial culture scene's approach to problems in society can be considered as a subcultural form of "studies." The example of the group Throbbing Gristle, who, in a nonscientific/theoretical manner, rather early on revealed the meaning of what later will be called information society, shall demonstrate the multiple activities of an Industrial band that developed from a cultural context.

FROM COUM TO THROBBING GRISTLE

Some of the Industrial groups directly derive from action art. The group Throbbing Gristle with Genesis P. Orridge (his real name is Neil Andrew Megson) and Cosey Fanni Tutti developed from the performance group "COUM-Transmission" (founded in 1969).[1] The efforts to shock can also be put down to the cultural context and notions of the late 1960s. COUM wants to break down the barriers between art and ordinary life and recreate the magical power art exercises in primitive tribal communities. The best-known performance by COUM was the "Prostitute" exhibition in the ICA in London in October 1976, where, alongside exhibits like, for example, used tampons, jars with maggots, whips, chains, blood-stained clothes, and nude pictures of the stripper Cosey as part of popular culture, paintings and sculptures of the group were also shown. This exhibition created a scandal, which was even debated in Parliament. COUM performances are no longer allowed to take place; the exhibits are censored. COUM presents another form of the orgies-mysteries-theatre of the Vienna action artist Hermann Nitsch. Many activities can be perceived as direct parallels to the Viennese action artists. COUM also carry their action to the extreme of masochist self-mutilation. No provocation is left out: They throw up, give themselves enema, and perform sexual acts on stage. Genesis P. Orridge gets tied to a cross, with torches in his hands that burn his palms. These are orgies in blood, vomit, urine and semen. Typically, COUM's symbol of transmission is the image of a limp penis after orgasm, which went along with the motto "We guarantee disappointment."[2]

The intention to revert to ordinary culture from the context of the arts and to address the man on the

CBGB is considered the birthplace of punk.

street induces COUM to turn to music. They want to break up the restrictions of a galleries-orientated business in the arts. COUM becomes the group Throbbing Gristle (TG) (1976–1981), which is rather inclined to music. It deals with topics like torture, cults, concentration camps and the behavior of the wardens, watchdog-training, stories of uniforms and insignia, images of sex and death, Aleister Crowley, unusual crimes—especially those committed by children or psychopaths, venereal diseases, and forensic pathology. TG is fascinated by relics of the industrial era, by its architecture, at a time when nobody ever thought about having these buildings preserved as historical monuments. Throbbing Gristle often take their audience to the limits of what is psychologically and physically bearable by the unusual noises arising from a recreation and direct assimilation of the noises of an industrial and military environment. This is, for example, demonstrated by the title "Weapontraining," which reproduces noises of various weapon systems.

Another unsettling factor for the audience is the extreme film material. Thus, the audience often reacts very aggressively: at a performance in the SO 36 in Berlin 1982, the audience silences the PA by pouring in beer, because the combination of film—TG show their incredibly cruel castration video—and the unusual frequencies of the Industrial music becomes psychologically and physically unbearable.

Throbbing Gristle are the consistent display of a particular lifestyle, which consists of questioning and rejecting social values. Their philosophy is simply to be open-minded, to recognize all individual opportunities you have and not to suppress anything. TG apply the shock tactics of the art business to their whole lifestyle. The objective is to find out something about social conditions and environments of gruesome murders, suicides or mass psychoses. Thus, they always spend their holidays at places where extraordinary crimes were committed: in Los Angeles, 10050 Cielo Drive, where Sharon Tate was murdered, or on the Spahn Ranch, where the Manson family lived. In an interview, Genesis P. Orridge tries to explain what these visits are all about: "You could see how people could really get into a trip that became more and more kind of a fantasy life. . . . A lot of people hate us. The NMA hate us, they were outraged that I went to Poland and saw the death camps."(Genesis)

On an LP cover (subtitle: Music from the Death Factory), the band creates an Industrial Records signet, which for two years nobody pays any attention to, until Genesis reveals that this is by no means an image of a normal factory, but one of one of the ovens in Auschwitz. TG expose the neutrality of a picture and simultaneously show the worthlessness of an image without accompanying information in the mass media. In addition, TG demonstrate, how easily a misinformation can manipulate people. The group wants to illustrate that information is the basic value in our postindustrial society: power lies with those who have the monopoly on information and those who are able to deal with it. Genesis: "When I told them about Auschwitz, the picture was suddenly outrageous, so it actually changed physically before their eyes by them being fed that one extra line of information. I find that disturbing."

TG want to expose the concentration of power of those who are well-placed at the sources of information. "We're interested in information, we're not interested in music as such. And we believe that the whole battlefield, if there is one in the human situation, it is about information."Everything is fascinating—what society does not want to see, what is reserved for specialists like doctors, but still publicly accessible, like disease, decay, or death. Genesis P. Orridge, for example, starts corresponding with Monte Cazazza and sends him dead animals via mail or assembles "mutants" from animal carcasses. He is looking for beauty in these processes of decay and thinks, that the putatively ugly and marginalized can aesthetically be alluring as well.[3]

TG is often reproached for a one-sided preoccupation with crime. Their interest in the dark sides of human behavior can be put down to the suppression by society of antisocial and "evil" human impulses and behavior, which then in some human beings erupt even more violently. They also introduce primitive rites into the music, which are also supposed to replace the role of ceremonies of shamans and witch-doctors in a progressive and mechanized society. TG achieve a strange combination of rituals and an artistic production, which uses industrial-technological means.

MARC PAULINE AND SURVIVAL RESEARCH LABORATORIES

"Taking equipment and remanufacturing it, turning it against its engineer's better wishes. Making things out of it, it was never intended to do"

Marc Pauline and the Survival Research Laboratories (SRL) are a team of mechanics, who build machines for plain destruction from technical components and scrap of various areas like the military and agriculture—another reference to all technological material having arisen from the military that fight each other in multimedia performances and destroy themselves and their environment.[4]

Fixed parts of each performance are, beside the main actors, the machines of steel, various materials such as window frames with glass or telephone booths and torn, festering heads, cast of plastic, with human features. The monumental image-material, which can be found on various vehicles, such as framed photographs, showing images from horror films or of assassinations, plays a special role here. Huge screens in various forms[5] drive through the scenery and fall victim to the merciless iconoclasm of the machines.

The SRL instrumentalize these media for their purposes, and the media images are not the only victims of their "War on information." These material victims of the machines are all kinds of animal carcasses, either mummified (like in Mummy go round, where several mummified animals are hung into a merry-go-round) or fresh from the butcher, like cows, sheep, chicken or pigeons. The mummified animals are mechanized by fitting in steel rods. The carcasses become organic robots, such as the "Rabot," a mechanized dead hare.[6] In addition, we find moving, absurd meat skewers with pieces of meat and robots with rotating animal-heads. Hare—or pig—halves are torn apart, cows immersed into boiling yogurt baths.

The scenery providing the background for this machine-theatre of cruelties contains allusions to the architecture of the town in which the performance takes place. Building fronts, houses in motion, small shacks, glasshouses, and churches are reminiscent of human dwellings. They cannot provide protection against the raging machines. The scenery, a modern realization of an apocalyptic inferno, though limited in space and time, is shrouded in smoke clouds and glaring light, liquids are sprayed around, all possible objects set ablaze by flame-throwers, for example, freight cars in motion (Amsterdam). SRL create the image of a modern descent into hell, which they produce with great delight: "One way to reach complete freedom from the restraints of civilization, is to burn civilization down, then you're free of it."[7]

Besides the deafening noise of non-muffled machines, the squeaking of steel hinges and the roaring of engines, a collage of sounds plays an important role: screams, whimpering, noises of animals, film scores. Soundtrack scraps of horror films are distorted and sampled, condensed into an atmosphere of violence, threat, and anguish. SRL start with the development of standing machines. Later, all machines and flying objects are remote-controlled, the process since the end of the 1980s coordinated by computers. Meanwhile, SRL have developed a standard range of particular machines. Among the main actors continually appearing again, the stars of the machine-theatre, which can always be rebuilt and equipped with additional, destructive functions, we find: "The Legs Machine," a walking steel column; the "Screw Machine," difficult to steer, with an installed flame-thrower and a harrow for an engine shaft; "The Big Arm," being able to pick holes in concrete; the "Rotary Mouth," with counter-flanging cogwheels; and the "Inch Worm" with long, spiked grippers. They permanently develop new martial machines from "lost property." Thus, within fifteen years, huge moving skulls with moveable jaws, gigantic flails, a machine with quadrangular wheels (finally achieving squaring the circle), robotized maulers, eight-legged walking spider-robots, a ballistic missile-car, a small battle-robot, clumsily handling its BB-gun and knife, a kind of steamroller with two interlocking spiked rollers and a huge steel-grit robot, throwing flames. The preferred motion of the various extremities of the machines is the blind, destructive rotation.

Above all, SRL prefer to use military equipment: helicopters,[8] lasers, catapults, flame-throwers[9], ballistic missiles and ballistic missile launch-pads are self-constructed. Dynamite, explosives, and time-bombs are brought to explosion. The arsenal of weapons used comprises guns, from simple cannons, laser-guns, small ballistic missiles launched from catapults, self-constructed ten-barreled rifles made of stainless steel to triple-A guns. "I hope that the neighborhood didn't catch fire. These were military flares, man. This was no joke."[10] As illustrated, SRL vividly illustrate the use and purpose of weapons as media: guns fire sheets of paper with slogans requiring the audience to contravene all social values: "SELF INTEREST IS YOUR ONLY INTEREST ACT ACCORDINGLY; THE WEAKNESS IN OTHERS IS YOUR ONLY POWER; COVER YOUR VICE WITH DECEITFUL LABELS; CALL THE TRUTH AN INSULT TO AVOID ACCEPTING IT AS A FACT; APPEAL TO HUMAN GREED AND GULLIBILITY FOR YOUR OWN SICK PURPOSES; DO ANYTHING WRONG TO GET PUBLIC APPROVAL; DEMAND UNEARNED REWARDS; RADIATE INFLUENCES OF DESPAIR AND DEFEAT WHEREVER YOU GO."[11]

For every performance, an individual choreography is drawn up, depending on the acting machines and robot-actors.[12] The machines dance (the "Legs Machine" in particular), their motions are seemingly ineffective and unspecific to machines. Nevertheless, their motions are "in character" and can almost be called natural. They crawl, jump, and run through the scenery apparently self-propelled.

Pauline: "The machines were totally at ease in the world we create for them and I felt like that everything they did was completely natural."

Heckert: "They suddenly start to take on a life of their own and they do things that somehow relied on intelligence that goes far beyond."[13]

These dinosaurs of the industrial age appear to be alive; their specific independent existence turns them into steely descendants of a new species.

The machines give a rather foolish impression, despite their uninhibited destructive rage, as if they destroyed unintentionally. In its clumsiness, there is a certain infantile innocence contained in the brute force the machine exerts on organic and inorganic matter.

The machines are always the only survivors in the scenery created for them. The organic life forms, represented by carcasses and robots with plastic heads, do not stand a chance against the violence of the machines. Like weak-willed dolls, they are grabbed, they jiggle, get squashed, crushed, ground, or burnt. The robots with human heads appear especially pitiful; they crawl and pull along their crippled extremities. The performances illustrate the inevitability of the destruction by the machines of all that is alive. Thus, these performances differ sharply from those that take place in a framework of action art or happenings: SRL push humans away from the centre, machines dominate the action.[14] SRL demonstrate that the natural environment falls victim to a merciless machinery.

> Pauline: "I hated Hippies. Hippies were for peace, and I wasn't for peace, I was for death and destruction."

> Heckert: "Rain screws everything up . . . rain slows down all working pro-cess. . . . Let's face it, rain is good for trees and I'm not a tree." [15]

They identify themselves with the destructive force of their machine-creatures. Animals and humans, with their socially decisive image-products, are destroyed by the machines: "I thought it's like a symbol of like the new death, or like modern death." [16]

In addition, SRL very often use the skull motif as a traditional symbol of death. The historical symbol is rendered into steel and brought to life, gets animated: moving skulls, snatching steel-sets of teeth and bunches of plastic-skulls can be found in every performance. Death, grabbing and snatching, does not remain stuck on a symbolic level, it is intervening directly.

Besides, SRL offer a droll walk through the history of weapon technology, from the antique catapult to ballistic missiles. The presentation of the evolution of destructive weaponry illustrates that the weapon systems, continuously getting replaced in a pointless arms race, eventually destroy everyone equally. SRL predominantly use technological "junk," the military discards in increasingly short intervals. They use "technical corpses" and create a kind of zombie from military garbage. Thus, SRL are an example for the direct "misuse of army equipment "to create a parallel situation to society as we see it . . . with the raderick that makes no sense at all but is very force ride, the whole idea of uncovering lies with tricks and illusions . . . is just becoming a magic trick, just a magic show." [17]

Pauline does not call himself an artist.[18] He is an extreme performer of the machine age, processing technical information in particular. He simulates war on a small scale, an apparently raging machine runs amok. It demonstrates its meaninglessness and, in the confrontation with organic and inorganic matter, its scary destructive force. The chaos of houses in motion, low-flying missiles, mechanical arms surfacing from oil baths, sound collages, noise, screams, animal noises, fire and mechanical pieces of equipment with mummified animals squirting liquids, conveys the feeling of being involved in battle on a battle-field. SRL work with material and noises directly associated with war to demonstrate its absurdity in an exemplary way. The audience cannot escape; they are shot at and threatened by the machinery.

> When the "shockwave" kind of hits you in the face and you know that you are hit with something and even if you really understand how it works, it's not gonna make it any less surprising or any less of an affront to your personal dare that you have between you and the world.

The machines SRL use are not inhibited by any mufflers. No filter stops the poisonous exhaust gases and oil-residues of the engines. The machines represent the unmasked original condition of machines. The audience has to endure the noise and the stench. The machines are grabbing for the audience or are suddenly driving towards them. SRL play with the audience's fear and create a sense of relief to have got out of this war of machines rather unscathed, since instead of the audience animal victims and plastic-proxies are supposed to suffer.

> The cat there is just basically a vehicle for my tank, to show what a real victim is all like, going down, kicking and screaming all the way. Well, it's grabbed by the tank, wiggles and tries to get away. . . . What else can we do, we flamed it, right? [19]

The audience is supposed to feel as bad as possible, a state automatically setting in because of the noise, stench, and the attacks by machines. The outward appearance of these machines has nothing to do with high-tech or micro-electronic war equipment. Although they are controlled by technology of ultimate modernity, the machines themselves are quite the opposite of non-transparent black boxes. They have to be endured by all senses. They are representatives of war and their destructive force can still be experienced directly. Physically, the audience might catch a tiny little sense of what war actually means.

> The audience were kind of victims, they're thought of being sacrificed. [20]

By the drastic means of the performance, the mercilessness of war becomes sensorially comprehensible. The merciless machinery of destruction consists of various incarnations of the harrow in Kafka's penal colony. The technological junk becomes imprinted into surroundings and artificial bodies. This gives rise to the impression of gladiator fights of the machines of various powers on a rather limited territory. The stage-managed war scenario of the SRL is more realistic than the immaterial, stage-managed images of war in the media. For a process of developing an awareness of these phenomena it is much more efficient, since no intellectual distancing is possible.[21] SRL use the means of war and its effects to confront the issue of war.

With these highly mechanized, artistically extreme actions and their radical statements, SRL move on the fringes of an arts system that are rarely paid any attention to and overlap with adolescent subculture. The origin of SRL and of the protagonists of the Industrial scene clearly derives from the avant-garde trends in the arts of the 1960s.

Notes

1   Besides, the members could be assigned to the Mail Art scene zuzuordnen. Genesis P. Orridge is convicted for his 1979 obscene Mail Art postcards, which show, for example Buckingham Palace with a backside. Genesis is also convicted for a postcard showing Réné Magrittes Time Transfixed from 1939 zeigt. Walker, J. A. (1987). Cross-overs. *Art into pop, pop into art* (p.131). London.

2   Vale, V. & Juno, A. (Eds.). (1982). *William S. Burroughs, Throbbing Gristle, Brion Gysin*. Research # 4/5, 71. San Francisco.

3   In San Francisco, Monte Cazazza belonged to the New Bay Area Dadaisten, a Neo-Dada movement, which he had to leave rather soon because of his radicalism.
    The fascination with death even shows when TG describes the meaning of flowers: Genesis: "Flowers are always supposed to be nice, but they're usually associated with bad news like deaths and illnesses and people having arguments and trying to make people like them again." Sleazy: "The best thing to do to flowers is hang them upside down. If you hang them upside down then they dry in the condition that they were when you hung them, so they remain preserved, even though they're dead." Research # 4/5. op.cit., p. 79.

4   Stockcart or "Monstercar" races, which take place in the USA, are certainly sources of inpiration, too.

5   Partly, they are mechanized, like the image of the assassination of the Japanese prime minister by a rightwing student: a hand with a mechanical knife surfaces from the picture, stabs into the picture, blood circulates. Image screens, which show distorted pictures from a film by Fritz Lang, are torn apart by a liquids-spitting, spiked missile (Fort Mason Performance).

6   The carcasses are cut to the right size with a chain-saw. They are then fitted with mechanical steel-joints and brought to life by a robot-construction. This is predominantly done in collaboration with Monte Cazazza.

7   Marc Pauline in the video *The will to provoke*

8   This helicopter was able to release explosives in various target-directions with a bomb release gear. It had a gripper with which he could grab objects and crush them, its landing gear were spikes. Marc Pauline gets the components for the helicopter from discarded military stocks. InCuHa. op.cit., p. 31.

9   The components for the machines are mostly stolen. With the flame-thrower you can break glass, the hand-held flame-thrower has a range of twenty-five feet.

10 Marc Pauline in the video *A scenic harvest from the kingdom of pain*

11 Video *Virtues of negative fascination*

12 Performances: "Unfortunate Spectacle of Violent Self-Destruction," "Food for machines" (1979); "A cruel and relentless plot to pervert the flesh of beasts to unholy uses" (1982); "Machine Sex" (1979); "Assured Destructive Capability" (1979); "Useless Mechanical Activity" (1980); "Pearl Habour Day" (1980); Scenes of tomorrow's battlefields, "A fiery presentation of dangerous and disturbing stunt phenomena" (1981); Amsterdam, 17 July 1988: A PLAN for social improvement BASED ON ARCHIEVING COMPLETE FREEDOM FROM THE RESTRAINTS OF CIVILISATION. Afterwards, Kraakers set houses ablaze with self-constructed flame-throwers.
    In Europe SRL-Performances could be seen in Kopenhagen, and in 1992 in Graz.

13 Video *The will to provoke*, Marc Pauline and Matthew Heckert

14 With SRL machines have apparently taken over, like in the film *Terminator*.

15 Mark Pauline: InCuHa. op.cit., p. 37. Heckert in the video *The will to provoke*

16 Marc Pauline in the video *Virtues of negative fascination*

17 Marc Pauline in the video *Virtues of negative fascination*

18 For inspiration, he reads in particular Burroughs and Pynchon.

19 Marc Pauline in the video *The will to provoke*

20 Matthew Heckert, video *Virtues of negative fascination*

21 The impossibility to be detached from the performance by considering it as an artistic event is the reason for the negative reception in Europe. In Amsterdam, a civic group is formed immediately. While people in the USA find the performances entertaining, SRL in Europe are abused as as weapon-fetishists and war-mongers. The performance for the Steirische Herbst in Graz 1992 in a priggish reception of the critics ("how can you approve of such a performance in the face of Yugoslavia") was regarded as unsuitable, as politically incorrect.

Resource

Pauline, M., & Heckert, M. (Directors). (1988). *The Will to Provoke: An Account of Fantastic Schemes for Initiating Social Improvement* [VHS]. Survival Research Laboratories (Distributor). Burbank, CA: DefAmerican Visuals, Inc. C. 1989.

REGGAE

Olaf Karnik

"Reggae gone international," announced Ranking Toyan in 1981. The Jamaican toaster commented on the international success of Jamaican pop music. He also referred to the development that reggae had already been produced in Great Britain (Aswad, Steel Pulse, Linton Kwesi Johnson, ein Steel Pulse zuviel), the United States (Johnny Nash, Wackie's, Clocktower, etc.), and Africa (Alpha Blondy). This feedback was hardly surprising. The Rastas had always glorified Africa (Ethiopia) as their homeland, and the United States (Miami, New York) has always served as an emigration country for those who could afford it, not to mention America's role as a musical source of inspiration. With American R&B of the 1960s, and particularly the soul of the "Impressions" from Chicago, there was an enormous influence on the creation of the musical parameters of rock steady and reggae. Jamaican music had received its strongest feedback in the country of its former colonizers. This includes Bob Marley's global breakthrough in the 1970s, supported by Chris Blackwell's Island Records. It further entails the various British record labels (Trojan, Pama/Jet Star, Greensleeves, Virgin, etc.) licensing and promoting Jamaican reggae internationally as well as the archetypal reggae DJ David Rodigan. To sum up, the Jamaica–Great Britain axis is fundamental to reggae's popularity.

MIX-UP

In the 1950s, the first emigrants from the Caribbean entered the United Kingdom. Here they criticized the new living conditions with calypso songs such as Lord Kitchener's *London Is the Place for Me*. These observations caused an initially slow but growing interdependence among sound cultures. In fact, ska, rock steady, reggae, and later dancehall and ragga, furnished information for exile Jamaicans and their British kids about Jamaica. These styles equally inspired independent productions in Great Britain and proved attractive to white kids from the working- and middle-class. Without ska and rock steady, "skinhead reggae" would be unthinkable. No UB 40 or Simply Red would exist without roots reggae. In turn, without the British Orchestra, we would not witness any Trojan releases spiced up with violin arrangements or reggae cover versions of white pop music.

Over the years, Jamaican music culture has inevitably evolved into hybrids. Furthermore, the adaptation to the existing audio-social environment has been complex and multifaceted. Subgenres such as Lovers Rock and Linton Kwesi Johnson's dub poetry emerged. Adrian Sherwood's and Dennis Bovell's experimental productions came onto the scene. Finally, the 1990s witnessed the continuation of Jamaican Dub traditions in British Digital Dub (regardless of the low standing that Dub enjoyed in Jamaica at that time). These developments derived from Great Britain's reggae context. Often, mingled production and reception conditions among Whites and Blacks accompanied these trends.

At the latest since the 1970s, reggae has provided key impulses for British pop music. First, punk bands such as The Clash or The Ruts released reggae songs. Second, reggae's influence is visible in the ska revival of The Specials, Selector, and Madness. Third, reggae informed new wave acts such as Public Image Ltd., The Slits, and The Flying Lizards, and Mark Stewart & The Mafia. After all, reggae inspired Adrian Sherwood's On-U-Sound, Massive Attack's and Smith & Mighty's Bristol Sound as well as entire genres such as Raggamuffin, Jungle, Drum & Bass, TripHop, and 2Step. In fact, all these strands of British pop music have tremendously benefited from Offbeat, bass sequences, and the sound-mixing pioneers. In this context, however, the wide range of models for identity construction is more significant. This spectrum offers a socialization with reggae in Great Britain. Regardless of the form, it causes subjectivations referring to societal roots.

SUNSHINE REGGAE AT THE FIRE DEPARTMENT

In the United Kingdom, reggae is anchored in elements that have shaped British culture(s). This cultural embeddedness is the key difference to reggae's situation in Germany. Here, reggae's popularity is hardly rooted in a former exile culture. Likewise, Germany cannot look back upon a notable record of reggae productions. It is particularly difficult to name five German pop bands of the 1970s and 1980s incorporating reggae elements into their sound-architectures. Consequently, reggae always lacked originality and sounded exotistic. Selected adaptations of the Nina Hagen Band, BAP, and ska songs during the time of the Neue Deutsche Welle (New German Wave) indicate this secondhand nature. And in no other country did the

Danish band Laid Back's stupid disco hit "Sunshine Reggae" probably yield worse consequences for the understanding of this music and culture. This song simply associates reggae with Bacardi-feeling, summer parties, and drinking songs.

Reggae has always been a reception-phenomenon in Germany, for example. As such, it is particularly easy not to take this music seriously. Today, Stefan Raab is thus still capable of continuing the tradition of successful reggae parodies dating back to Mike Krüger's and Thomas Gottschalk's performances in the early eighties.

Reggae dancehall only emerged in Germany within the context of hip hop, ragga, and jungle in the early and mid-1990s.[1] These styles founded a school of historical adaptation. This school still exists today with producers and fans actualizing different reggae eras simultaneously.

Styles, codes, sound systems, and DJ techniques—performing in Patois, or in German, dreadlocks or baldhead, or none of this—all this had to be learned first, then tested, and finally configured culturally with painstaking difficulty. In this context, the smooth cultural-mimetic adaptation process (one-to-one) proved to be most successful and internationally most compatible. This development, however, could not occur without numerous semantic rejections, as the following example shall illustrate: in the fall of 2002 in Cologne, a poster advertised a Gentleman concert with the slogan "Unity Is Strength." Obviously, this line raises the question of what kind of unity is implied here? Who does this statement address? And how political is this motto nowadays? Do not the military, corporations, George W. Bush, Islamic and Christian fundamentalists and Nazis equally demand "Unity" (even so for completely different reasons) as compared to Jamaican and American Ghetto people striving for integration? "Unity Is Strength" thus counts as a de-contextualized phrase. Yet, it is semantically enriched with the flavor of existential urgency. This degenerating slogan leads middle-class German reggae fans to confess to two truths: (1) To share the same taste in music, to possess a profound knowledge about reggae, and to celebrate this taste and knowledge ritually; (2) The illusion to actually possess a reggae culture analog to Jamaica or England.

Except for rare single recordings (e.g., Chicken George), notable reggae productions, renowned sound systems (Silly Walks, Pow Wow, etc.) as well as labels (Germaican Records) and distributors specializing in reggae have only emerged since the mid-1990s in Germany. Regarding production aesthetics, we can roughly distinguish between releases for the international and domestic market. Gentleman and the production team Silly Walks Movement, for example, have approached Jamaican standards more closely. This way, they manage to gain international attention. Jan Delay & The Sam Ragga Band, Seeed, and D-flame, however, predominantly perform for the German-speaking reggae and pop market. Meanwhile, Patrice has abandoned reggae conventions. Now he articulates himself in the internationally mainstream code of the singer/songwriter individualism. Contrary to Patrice, the Berlin producers of Rhythm & Sound focus on blending dub and techno. And their amalgam fashions a very own definition of reggae as hybrid.

AUTHENTICITY AND IDENTITY

Tilman Otto, alias Gentleman, the biggest star in the German-speaking reggae scene, has disagreed with labeling the necessarily hybrid nature of a reggae socialization in Germany "authentic." The Cologne singjay (i.e., vocalists who mix singing and toasting) has delved into an over-affirmation of Jamaican culture. During numerous longer trips to Jamaica, he has even acquired the Patois dialect. On the one hand, he performs in Patois his commendable anti-hatred messages as well as his songs of praise for Jah, the Rasta God. These songs are packed into simple pop formulas: "Jah ina yuh life, everything is nice" is Jah in your life, everything is nice. On the other hand, reports state that he also speaks Patois with his German band members while touring. Obviously, this is not meant to be funny but has to be understood as a comprehensive process of a new identity-formation. The album's title already alludes to this process: while faithful Rastas have always possessed Jah, Gentleman is—for the moment—only on the path to him.[2]

With respect to a comprehensive "authentic lifestyle," this self-conditioning has to cover daily life as well. And success seems to show Gentleman is right. Indeed, "Journey to Jah" entered the Top-20 album charts in 2002. Furthermore, Gentleman performed at numerous international festivals, and the Jamaican Dancehall scene treated him with respect and recognition. There are a number of key elements for this success. The album features guest appearances by stars such as Bounty Killer, Luciano, Morgan Heritage, Capleton, Junior Kelly, and Jack Radics. Moreover, top acts such as Bobby Digital, Black Scorpio, and Richie Stevens produced more than half of the songs. Yet, "Journey to Jah" is more, it is a hit package at Marley level. And definitely one of Four Music's best releases ever, the label that counts Die Fantastischen Vier, Thomas D, Afrob, Freundeskreis and Joy Denalande as its clients. Therefore, Gentleman's critics prefer to outline his skills (singing style, song quality). Doubtless, he possesses these abilities. So this is the "good show-argument." But would it occur to someone to praise Marley's skills?

ASSIMILATION IN REVERSED DIRECTIONS

From a European perspective, Gentleman's efforts for authenticity may, on the one hand, appear dubious. On the other hand, it must be stressed that production conditions have fundamentally changed since Marley's death. Nowadays, only few Jamaicans are confessing Rastafarians. Upholding reggae's musical legacy is no longer a natural phenomenon in Jamaica, and almost half of all Dancehall releases consist of productions following American Hip Hop and R&B. Parallel is the battle for survival has intensified in Jamaica's Ghettos. Among the youth, violence is omnipresent, and homicides cover the daily agenda. This development implies consequences for the symbolic debate on the societal conditions within the dancehall. Results include harsher hatred-tirades against opponents and countless songs (the so-called "Batty Boy-Tunes") discriminating against homosexuals. Gentleman's love and peace messages have also to be viewed in light of these developments.[3] Indeed, his songs equally address the Jamaican public and position themselves within the value-rivalry between opinion leaders such as Bounty Killer, Elephant Man, Capleton, and Beenie Man. Interestingly, Gentleman's voice is accepted even though he does not even come from Jamaica.

His credibility rests on the perfect mastery of the symbolic codes inherent within the Dancehall culture. Only on that condition he is capable of focussing on the relevant issues. Contrary to the 1970s, when reggae gained world fame, cultural assimilation nowadays runs into reversed directions. It moves from the first world to the third world. Earlier, Bob Marley's world fame witnessed a refinement of his sound via production techniques tailored for the rock market. Yet today, Gentleman has to sound as original as possible. Skin color, origin, and social milieu are no longer relevant for authenticity. Instead, devotion to the cause has evolved as the essential ingredient. This authenticity type is no longer rooted in traditional elements once marking "identity." Now it rests on mimetic qualities, that is, the desire to completely merge with and the talent to adopt a cause.

UP IN MY ROOM—AFRO-GERMAN INDIVIDUALISM

The Afro-German Patrice, however, craves for a separation of genre-conventions. Although three years ago, his debut album "Ancient Spirit" was celebrated as an example of free-spirited "author-reggae," the twenty-three-year-old Hamburg resident has almost completely abandoned the genre with his programmatically-entitled album "How Do You Call It?" Although large parts were produced in Jamaica, reggae elements are hard to find, or only come across as "Vibe." Since everybody is into reggae he wants to focus on something different, Patrice explained in an interview with the German daily "taz."[4] Likewise, he stressed that his African roots are more important to him. Ultimately, he has never really felt comfortable within the reggae scene, and has always been slightly concerned about the tendency of imitating Jamaicans there.

Next to reggae, Patrice blends hip hop, rock, soul, blues, and funk elements into a superb black pop synthesis of good songs and grooves, catchy refrains and lyrical texts, in a way as if black music's fragmentation into single branches had never existed. So, Patrice reminds of Prince or Stevie Wonder in past decades, performers who embodied this classic individualism of great stars creating black pop music for all people. Produced on a high level and for an international market, Patrice therefore re-cultivates a proven authenticity-type: the individual that is shaped by various influences, and accepts cultural hybridity as a precondition for its own productivity. Europe is familiar with this pattern. Henceforth, Patrice's album already sounds like a timeless classic at first listening. There is a sense of clarity about it almost leading to boredom. Contrary to Gentleman, who urgently targets the diffuse mass of ghetto people and voluntary authenticity-seekers, Patrice's music communicates intimacy and addresses the listener as an isolated individual. This is precisely the flaw of "How Do You Call It?"

SPEAK FOREIGN LANGUAGES IN YOUR OWN COUNTRY

Jan Delay & The Sam Ragga Band represent a typical example of a German reggae-socialization via hip hop. While Jan Delay invented the pseudonym Jan Delay to release a German roots reggae album ("Searching for the Jan Soul Rebels"), Eißfeldt, who usually plays hip hop with Absolute Beginner, changed style and code. More than ever, his singsong is marked by mumbling and moaning. Words are connected French-style, vocals are stretched, consonants swallowed, syllables stressed differently, and whole sentences squeezed or extended due to reggae conventions. All this occurs with an ease and naturalness one hardly suspects when dealing with the German language. Here, language is designed to sound different. The meaning or "attitude" of the texts manifests itself in an aesthetic-sensual manner, and other things can be heard. In 1970s rock music, performers such as Rio Reiser and very occasionally Udo Lindenberg managed to create such an experience.

With his phonetic transformations Jan Delay does not walk alone through Germany's reggae halls today. Earlier, Max of Freundeskreis had accomplished another conversion with "Halt dich an deiner Liebe fest" ("Stick to Your Love"). Newcomers such as Nosliw are capable of twisting their tongues, too. You can compare these new articulations with, for example, the rolling "r" of bands such as Rammstein whose groaning language reminds of speeches by Goebbels and Hitler. Consequently, it is logical to include phonetic practice ("style") as a category of political and politicizing expressions in pop music. This is one of Delay's goals as regards content. He strives to realize these aims on different levels as the following three examples show. First, Delay voices statements such as "Ich möchte mich nicht in Köpfen befinden, zusammen mit Gedanken, die unter Einfluss vom Axel-Springer-Verlag entstanden" ("I do not want to be inside heads with thoughts that emerged under the influence of Axel Springer Publishers"). Second, in the clip for "Alles ist vergiftet" ("All Is Poisoned") you can watch VIPs' and politicians' heads on animated figures in an apocalyptic entertainment scenario. Third, he released pieces such as "An die Bürger von Konsolien" ("To the Citizens of Consolien") and www.hitler.de.

Jan Delay does not lack critical observations or ironic comments on the societal or youth-cultural situation in Germany: together with The Sam Ragga Band, he scored a trendy reggae hit in late 2002/early 2003, aptly entitled "Die Zeit steht still" ("Time Stands Still"). Did not classic roots reggae in Jamaica equally function, namely to reflect on and criticize societal conditions?

Employing 1970s roots reggae to describe current and local societal conditions forms a new aesthetics. This new aesthetics lacks authenticity, and The Sam Ragga Band is aware that "hard core reggae fans" bemoan this loss. In an interview with Intro, Marc Wilkes justifies this approach by stating that we are all reggae fans. But we absorb this influence and try to merge it with our own experiences. We do not want to imitate Jamaican stuff, we do not want to sound like King Tubby or Bob Marley. In Germany, many attempt to create a distinct Jamaican Swing. White middle-class kids toasting Patois-style, this is ridiculous. We speak a different language, we live in a different society. That's what we process. Jan once labeled this style "Karl May-reggae."

In the summer of 2002 on Gentleman's Web site (journeytojah.com), where you can read his fans' email input, Jan Delay was thus characterized as the guy from Hamburg "who wants to f*** up *our reggae*." This lack of humor is hardly surprising in a milieu where people desperately aim to establish a reggae-identity of utmost authenticity, an identity solely rooted in a reception-relationship. Gentleman may serve as the exception here since he lived on Jamaica. As a producer and exchange culture is establishing itself in Germany, a balancing process between reggae-cultural norms and creative space has slowly begun: "Germaica" is still under construction. Another indication is that female reggae artists have so far lacked profile.[5] Either way, Jan Delay & The Sam Ragga Band have taken into account reggae's previous reception-reality in Germany. They do not pretend as if "Sunshine Reggae" and "Red Red Wine" had never existed. Instead, they aim to make the best out of the negative consequences and remaining misunderstandings. Ultimately, their music enables you to dance and laugh.

KING IN MY EMPIRE—PRODUCER STATUS

Eventually, producer teams such as the Silly Walks Movement from Hamburg or Rhythm & Sound from Berlin are in a better position than performers as they take fewer chances. Yet all the more, they are in a stronger position to influence what is regarded as "official" or "abnormal." In the fall of 2002, Silly Walks Movement, which is also active as a DJ-team resp. Sound System, released a Various Artists hit compilation entitled "Songs of Melody." This album unites everybody since it ranges from Buccaneer to Natural Black, and from Jamaica to Afro-Germans such as Patrice and Max of Freundeskreis. It also features Gentleman AND Jan Delay. At least, female artists Tanya Stephens, Ce'Cile and Pam Hall are represented on "Songs of Melody." Whether the performers sing in Patois, English, German, or even in Spanish does not really matter because the songs just flow. Due to modern roots sound and production skills, the little clash of cultures over reggae has been resolved. And some of the riddims are likely to gain attention.

Rhythm & Sound, aka Mark Ernestus and Moritz von Oswald, offer the most sophisticated production skills in the business. Nonetheless, Rhythm & Sound's simple-wrapped 10- and 12-inch records, with or without guest singers such as Paul St. Hilaire, Cornell Campbell, The Chosen Brothers (aka Lloyd "Bukllwackie" Barnes), and Claudette Barnes from Love Joys, do not exert much influence in Germany's reggae scene. Again, "hard core reggae fans" criticize the lack of authenticity in Rhythm & Sound's musical language. Techno and electronic music as well as space-opening dub techniques and bass sequences clearly shape the sound. Up-and-down dynamics typical for reggae and dancehall may indeed be missing. However, since their beginnings in the mid-1990s, Rhythm & Sound have created nothing less than an entire new groove formula. This formula synthesizes techno's and reggae's essential and repetitive structures. As Ernestus and von Oswald have employed dub-typical sound deconstructions for reconfiguring the material as well, vocals are now located above a track.

Meanwhile, many imitators have attempted to follow Rhythm & Sound's globally unique example. Yet, despite their profound knowledge of reggae—ranging from production techniques and resources to label and cover aesthetics and the vinyl's quality and formats—they remain outsiders. They have not released anything but sublimely pulsating music. Neither have they have given any interviews nor are there any photos. Seemingly, this is the only way to work undisturbed. In addition, they engage in comprehensive re-releases from the Wackie catalog, created by Lloyd "Bullwackie" Barnes, who emigrated from Jamaica to New York in the late 1970s. Besides, they run their own re-release label "Basic Replay," designed for rare reggae productions. Therewith, Rhythm & Sound mark their own historical fix points. Together, Wackie's, Rhythm & Sound, and the obscure productions with analogous rhythm machines transform old formats into new riddims, as the attentive listener may notice. These riddims stand in the tradition of reggae. In fact, it does not always have to be Real Rock Riddim.

Rhythm & Sound's "Vibe" contains as many traces of life as a Central European city. There is a gray sky, some flowers, drumming bass emanating from a cellar of a former factory plant, cerebral moments of sound. What kind of reggae would be more authentic here? And then there is something floating within the sound, often labeled spirituality. Maybe it is not there but is evoked in the listener's mind via the music's spatial depth and time-span silence. The record starts spinning . . . hissing . . . the music gently paves its way into the listener's ears and then marches on evenly and stoic. Over time, an exalted, metaphysical atmosphere pervades the room. This atmosphere brings forth a radical break with everyday life. Quality time can be felt, a new sound zone of complete reflection is created, you are in tune with yourself: standing on a mountain with open arms, being Jah.

Note: This article was first published in Testcard, No. 12: Left-wing Myths (Mainz: Ventil, 2003).

Notes

1 One of the few exceptions with a predominantly regional stance is Hans Soellner's project Bayerman Vibration as it has been active at least since 1990. How to value this blend of Rasta-aesthetics, sound left-wing-anarchic Hippie culture, and Bavarian dialect is another (hemp) story, and cannot be explained here due to space limitations.

2 From the total identification with Reggae follows the affirmation of the Rastafarianism religion, i.e. the belief in Haile Selassie. Haile Selassie is the Black Ethiopian King who the Rastas selected as Jah.
Reggae's spiritual impetus thus did not cause Gentleman to believe in Christ, which would correspond with his culture group. Instead he converts to Rastafarianism. For Gentleman, this is not a simple act of will but a slow adaptation-process, as the album's title *Journey to Jah* may indicate.

3 Nevertheless, it needs to be mentioned that Rastafarianism does not belong to the most progressive religions—even though it took on a major role during the time when Jamaica became independent in 1962, and during the political debates between right-wing conservatives (under Edward Seaga) and Michael Manley's democratic socialism. In the 1970s, Roots Reggae and Rastas sympathized with Manley's emancipatory policies. In turn, Manley attempted to instrumentalize Reggae for his aims, for example, in 1972 when he used Delroy Wilson's "Better Must Come" as his political message. Not least does the connection between Reggae and left-wing resp. left-opposition politics date back to this 1970s tradition. Ulli Güldner further stresses that people are completely mistaken when labeling Rastafarianism as a religion free of homophobic tendencies even while preaching Love & Peace. See his analysis in Riddim, 04/02, Dez/Jan/Feb 2003, pp. 41–44, Köln 2002.

4 *taz*, 19 October 2002.

5 Contrary to Soul and R&B yet similar to HipHop, female artists only hold a minor role in the Macho-dominated Reggae business. Nonetheless, some women are present in the scene: Marcia Griffiths, Susan Cadogan, Lady Saw, Patra, Binta Breeze, Rita Marley, Althea & Donna, the Love Joys, etc. Although in comparison, there are not any popular female performers, women are active in DJ-teams (e.g. Beez Sound) or act as spokes(wo)men of the scene, for example Ellen Köhling who holds a chief editor position at *Riddim*, the lead journal for German Reggae and Dancehall.

EMO MUSIC AND YOUTH CULTURE

Brian Bailey

Emo, short for "emotional music," is an evolving and complex American youth subculture that listens to a specific genre of music, which is characterized by feelings of vulnerability and a willingness to express heartfelt confessions about adolescence. Emo music draws from various genres of contemporary music including rock, rap, punk, indie, pop, and heavy metal by artists such as Finch, Taking Back Sunday, Atmosphere, Slug, Coheed and Cambria, Snow Patrol, and Dash Board Confessional. The behaviors, attitudes, and values expressed through the music involve emotionally turbulent themes often associated with adolescence such as despair, nostalgia, heartbreak, hope, and self-loathing. Although these themes are not new to contemporary music, the various and sometimes conflicting social practices associated with Emo subculture contain valuable insights into what it means to be an adolescent today. For many youth, Emo subculture facilitates identity formation, social interactions, and emotional involvement. It is a place where many adolescents share their experiences about the world and express their feelings about life through music. Perhaps educators need to take notice of this cultural movement, in order to learn how their students are dealing with the difficult business of growing up in today's world.

Emo, like many other music-centered cultural movements is difficult to define and even more difficult to narrow down to one all-encompassing narrative. The grunge, new wave, punk, mod, gangsta rap, and hippie movements from prior decades carried different meanings for different people both inside and outside the music subculture. This is also the case for Emo in that meanings seem to evolve, replicate, and recombine so that Emo, which seemingly started as a somewhat "agreed-upon" collective subculture, has in fact become a highly contested set of meanings and collective practices. To some, it appears to be a cathartic experience through a genuinely outward release of painful emotions coupled with a sense of grace, self-pity, and hope. For others, it means rejecting the music industry hegemony for a DIY (do-it-yourself) lifestyle and following a band that seems like "your own little secret." For many kids, it means behaving in a way that respects people's feelings, and to others, it means striving to look like their favorite emo band's lead singer while singing along at a concert. Unfortunately, for some participants in this music culture, the outward expression of feelings makes them a target for ridicule by peers and adults that find Emo melodramatic and trite.

What generally seems to be agreed upon is the origin of Emo music. In the 1980s, Washington, D.C. became a hot bed for the Emo scene, spawning groups such as Minor Threat with its leader Ian Mackaye and Rites of Spring featuring Guy Picciotto. The music emerged from punk rock roots to include themes such as rebellion, disdain for authority, and rejection of the mainstream music industry and culture. What made Emo separate from punk and hardcore rock was the move away from angry songs of rebellion to more hear-felt introspective reflections by the artists. These pioneers of Emo were still rebellious but expressed their angst in a sensitive way through songs about self-loathing, dejection, and personal turmoil.

The Emo movement grew to other areas of the country to include bands with small, local, yet loyal followings like Seattle's Sunny Day Real Estate; however, somewhere along the way (some say it was in 1999 when Vagrant Records signed the Emo band Jawbreaker), the record industry took notice. This is where defining Emo subculture gets elusive. Like many other aspects of youth culture, the music and its associated practices and themes were appropriated for profit and turned into a product for mass consumption. Before long, Emo bands such as Dashboard Confessional and Weezer appeared on the cover of *Rolling Stone*, on the radio, and in the buzz bins of MTV. The slippery part of describing Emo lies in the contradiction that was inherently created when Emo started appearing in mainstream media outlets. The newfound popularity threatened the original intentions of Emo music participants, which focused on genuine feelings, grassroots sentiments, and a rejection of mainstream music through independent record labels and small, local music venues. As a result, Emo developed into a space of tension between independent authenticity and corporate mass media.

As Emo music worked its way into the popular media channels, it no longer appealed to many of the original participants. Hence, the evolution of Emo subculture split into two groups within the subculture: The first could be labeled as "Emo Independents"; those that reject the mainstream bands and styles associated with Emo. The other group is often known as the "Emo mainstream"; the fragment of the subculture that embraces Emo despite its growing popularity and subsequent corporate product. These two groups are by no means definitive or absolute. In fact, most people probably fit somewhere in between these two categories and possibly within more than one group at the same time. At best, it is a messy distinction full of gaping contradictions. It is, however, one way of making sense out of what Emo means to the people that engage in the subculture.

Emo "independents" are the kids that get psyched because they make up a small group of early insiders and take great pride in being "in the know" about an emerging new Emo band. Much like people that follow punk music, they revel in alienation from the popular and seek out the unpopular. Emo "independents" are participants in the subculture that are loyal to the original intentions associated with the mid-eighties Emo scene in Washington, DC. They see Emo as a means for independence from the corporate dominated music industry. They love the raw emotion that comes from real expressions on issues that unite human beings and often create their own forms of Emo through their bands and zines. For these people, Emo was once pure, subsequently ruined by the corporate music industry, and is now dead. They are still committed to independent music by seeking out bands that have yet to sign with a major corporate record label, yet they do not like what Emo has become and have chosen to move on or reject the "Emo" label altogether. They oppose the multinational corporations who dominate the music industry thus offering fewer and fewer choices for artistic expression. Emo "independents" make extraordinary efforts to reject the music industry by supporting Independent record labels, DIY operations, and locally owned music venues and radio stations.

In an apparent contradiction to the Emo purist circle of participants, there are those in Emo culture that enjoy everything that Emo represents and associate strongly with bands that have been labeled Emo even if it is through popular channels. These participants are the second wave adapters in the subculture and are often known as the "Emo kids." They are mostly white, suburban, high school and college kids that dress alike, watch MTV's TRL, and attend mainstream Emo concerts like Dashboard Confessional, The Get Up Kids, and New Found Glory. It should be noted that some (especially Emo "independents") might tend to look down at this subcategory of Emo culture as "sell-outs" and "wannabees."

Dashboard Confessional is the most popular of the bands that "Emo kids" follow, and their music is characterized by songs (sometimes called screamo) that alternate between whispering and screaming intimate reflections. Often, Dashboard Confessional lyrics are about a relationship that has gone bad and the singer is trying to come to terms with the emotional fallout. The band has a section of their Web site called the Dashboard Confessional Community where fans can send blog (Web log) entries for posting. This is one of the spaces in the subculture where "Emo kids" can interact with a social group of insiders centered on the music and lyrics of their favorite band. While the Dashboard Confessional Community may be a marketing strategy for Vagrant Records, it represents a genuine place for youth interaction in that they are relating their own lives to the themes of Dashboard Confessional's songs. Evident in this community are some of the difficult feelings that often accompany adolescence and an openness to share these emotions with other fans of Dashboard Confessional, much in the same way the band does through their songs like "Rapid Hope Loss" or "As Lovers Go." This is part of the "slippery nature" of Emo. Dashboard Confessional is the site of separation for many in the rift in Emo culture. The Emo "independents" see

Dashboard Confessional as an insincere bastardization of their subculture and its sentiments due to their mainstream, corporate status on MTV, whereas Emo "mainstreamers" see Dashboard Confessional as a talented band (and community) that provides enjoyment and authentically addresses a difficult time in life. The distinction between the Emo "independents" and "mainstreamers" are important as we consider youth culture. It is indicative of the way in which music subcultures initiate, evolve, and are experienced by youth. It reminds us that we cannot place a single definition on youth culture. It also exemplifies an all-too-common phenomenon in our society whereby corporate interests seek to colonize youth culture.

There may be aspects of Emo that are relevant and important for educators. As literacy studies expand our definitions of text and what it means to be literate in today's world, we might be wise to take notice of Emo music and other popular texts that permeate youth culture. The overt, genuine, manner of dealing with inner feelings in Emo has implications for learning, especially for teaching adolescents. Unfortunately, many forms of school learning ignore the emotional nature of knowledge in favor of logical, factual content. This is exemplified by the mounting pressure placed on students to perform on standardized tests and the stress that goes with applying for acceptance into elite colleges.

Educators might also learn from the ways in which popular music convey contradictory messages about dealing with emotions. Take, for example, the rapper Marshall Mathers, aka Eminem, with his revelations of genuine feelings of emotional trauma through his lyrics one minute and then sarcastic lines about "b****es" and "beat downs" the next. This may indicate to adolescents that the best way to deal with emotions is to keep them inside, to react with violence, or to make a sarcastic joke about them. Perhaps schools could learn from Emo and incorporate these texts into curriculum as a way of helping students with the affective nature of knowledge and life. Perhaps a discourse in school centered on genuine feelings and emotions could address student violence in a world where Columbine-like shootings seem to be more and more prevalent. There is a convincing body of literature that makes claims for more "emotional intelligence" in schooling and Emo may be a bridge for making a connection between affect and intellect.

Another reason to consider the importance of Emo in teen's lives is related to motivation towards schooling. Many educators are concerned with how increased pressure to perform in school has led to an overwhelming percentage of students that are bored, stressed-out, and all together disengaged in their own intellectual development. Often, school curriculum is disconnected from some of the students' interests. Emo may have the ability to engage students in exploring their feelings and dealing with emotions because it relates so well to their inherent interests about relationships. Perhaps school leaders and teachers could learn from Emo music about how to engage students in exploring school related activities. For example, students might be more likely to engage in Shakespearean literature, like *Romeo and Juliet*, if the teacher were able to contextualize the experience in Emo music. It is possible that Emo subculture presents an opportunity to help students connect their personal narratives and out of school literacies with school-based literacies. By coupling contemporary culture with school culture, many students may feel more connected to the curriculum in school, thus more likely to see it as important and interesting. Many social psychologists and education researchers believe that it's imperative to learning to have students that engage in literature or other school related topics because they find it personally interesting. While it is important not to colonize youth culture for educational purposes, Emo might be one way to engage students in school while seeing the world from a youth perspective.

Resources

Books

Cooper, A. (2002). *Coloring outside the lines: A punk rock memoir.* Elgin, TX: Rowdy's Press.

Gaines, D. (1990). *Teenage wasteland: Suburbia's dead end kids.* Chicago: The University of Chicago Press.

Greenwald, A. (2003). *Nothing feels good: Punk rock, teenagers, and emo.* New York: St. Martin's Griffin.

Hebdige, D. (1979). *Subculture: The meaning of style.* London: Routledge.

Kincheloe, J. L., Slattery, P., & Steinberg, S. R. (2000). *Contextualizing teaching.* New York: Longman.

Resh, J. (2001). *Amped: Notes from a go-nowhere punk band.* Chicago: Viper Press.

———. (2003). *A misfit's manifesto: The spiritual journey of a rock and roll heart.* New York: Villard.

Steinberg, S. R., & Kincheloe, J. L. (1997). *Kinderculture: The corporate construction of childhood.* Boulder, CO: Westwood.

Articles

Dolby, N. (2003). Popular culture and Democratic practice. *Harvard Educational Review,* 73 (3), 258–284.

Greenwald, A. (2003). The crying game. *Spin Magazine,* 19 (3), 70–76.

Identity

Christine Subryan

When you look in the mirror,
who do you see?
Do you see the person you want to be?
Or do you see the person you're told to be?
Who determines your identity?
Is it you or society?
Do you tell yourself
that you're an achiever and the future?
Or do you leave it to society to say,
"You're a loser?"
Who's the only person that really knows you?
Nobody but you.
So don't leave it to society to define you
Take charge of your life
And be the best you can be
You create you
You create your identity.

DISCOS: FROM LIBERATION TO COMMODIFICATION OF PLEASURE

Elena Duque

The creation and development of the disco is closely linked with sexual freedom, female emancipation, as well as the creation of a new youth culture. In fact, today, "club culture" is a term that refers to a particular lifestyle that young people engage in that is connected to the discos. Discos have allowed women the freedom to dance, given that they had to wait until men asked them to dance. Through disco music, now they can dance "alone." Also, discos are spaces that leave room for greater aesthetic freedom. Women can dress provocatively without having to adapt to protocols that are characteristic of other spaces where they are forbidden to wear certain clothes and makeup. In relation to sexual freedom, discos have been organized to promote relationships through the establishment of spaces such as "the privé." In this sense, the evolution of the discos, on many occasions, has been carried out commercially. What once was a space where young women and men could establish relationships freely, away from a watchful eye and the repression of the morals of the time, on many occasions, it has turned into an instrumentalization of pleasure where sex is nothing more than advertisement and a consumer good. The market has converted the freedom of establishing affective and sexual relationships into the "sexual consumption" of people as objects. Female sexual liberation has been (and continues to be) subject to much manipulation by the market, guiding women toward becoming a sexual object as well as a consumer of pleasure instead of allowing her to create her own sexuality.

THE DISCO AS A SPACE OF LIBERATION AND THE CREATION OF A NEW CULTURE

The appearance of discos can be placed in relation to the French resistance against the Nazi occupation. There were nightclubs of Paris where American jazz artists use to play until they were forbidden by the Nazis in 1940. Due to this persecution they were forced to reorganize clandestinely in basements and change from live music to recorded music, which gave rise to the name *Le Discotheque*. Discos have also had great importance during more idealistic and utopian times, like the sixties and seventies, and have declined in more pessimistic historical moments, like during the spread of postmodernism in the eighties.

In Spain, for instance, the first discos appeared in the sixties coinciding with utopian social movements, the spread of feminism, the onset of the crisis in the patriarchal family, the change in women's fashion—with the advent of the miniskirt and bikini—and the sexual revolution. The explosion of discos in the seventies, the enormous fame of some, like Studio 54 in New York, and the appearance of the DJ cabin in the movie *Saturday Night Fever* came about with the end of the dictatorship years in Spain, and during a decade of utopian struggles. Throughout the eighties, many of the utopian ideals of the sixties and seventies were rejected, devaluing universal principles and common struggles, dismantling hopes and dreams. Similarly, there was a backlash against the earlier fashion, which included discos, and their aesthetics such as bell-bottoms and platform shoes. With the fall of the Berlin wall and the onset of the nineties there is a return to some ideals from the sixties and seventies. In this sense, that very year (1989) one of the most significant techno music festivals was initiated in Berlin, the *Love Parade*, which continues to be celebrated annually.

A space for youth liberation, discos have been a catalyst for the evolution of a youth culture, which today is called the "club culture." This form of youth life is associated with going to discos, and implies certain attitudes and forms of behavior.

DISCOS AS A SPACE FOR FEMALE LIBERATION AND SEXUAL LIBERATION

If we look at the liberation that discos have represented for young people it becomes evident that they have contributed enormously to women's emancipation and to sexual liberation. Its antecedents, "public dances," have generally been spaces of freedom for women, where they have been able to dance in public, make themselves up, feel attractive, and definitely feel freer even while these dances were regulated by strict norms. Discos provide a step further for women to be in public and at the same time "hidden" from most of society, "in public" and "alone" with other women and men of their generation without being under the watchful gaze of family members or guardians.

These spaces have frequently been closely related with the establishment of affective and sexual relationships, especially ones that are illicit or prohibited by the social norms of the time. They do favor engaging in relationships with dynamics that are considered to be inappropriate in other contexts

Women's freedom in the discos is no longer as differentiated from that attained in other spheres, but continues to provide them with more leeway when it comes to dressing, moving and expressing themselves through dance. Women have to be more cautious in their way of dress in other spaces, because it might be too "low-cut" for going to work, too "short" for going to a family gathering, too "tight" for the first date, and so forth. In discos they do not have these kinds of limitations. However, this fact does not provide absolute freedom, since there are certain aesthetics that young women do not choose, they must follow to "fit," feel attractive or succeed, which generate at the same time all sorts of perceptions toward their bodies.

"CLUB CULTURE" IN A CAPITALIST AND CONSUMER SOCIETY

Regardless of their connection to women's sexual emancipation, discos are spaces for leisure time in a capitalist society, and as such, they are highly connected with consumerism. The "club culture" is a youth culture and is also a business. Many young people become "hooked on" it in a consumerist sense, keen on dressing in the latest fashion, being the most popular in their group, having the most success with the girls and boys, and so forth. The "culture club" opens up a whole world of advertisements, music, fashion and aesthetics. Participating in this culture is related to the consumption of goods such as music, clothing, and various accessories. This turns the "club culture" into a business, which sells people a way to be included to it through consumerist leisure time.

MANIPULATED FEMALE SEXUAL LIBERATION AND THE COMMODITIZATION OF PLEASURE

Historically female sexuality has frequently been repressed and monopolized by patriarchal interests. It has been reduced to reproduction, suppressed, pursued, and demanded on other occasions. Some clear examples of this are the so-called "sacred prostitution" or the *droit de seigneur* in the Middle Ages, and sexual offenses for which women could be judged throughout history. At the same time, the education of women has also produced and reproduced this same type of manipulation. However, the feminist movement has had an enormous impact on female sexual liberation, denouncing oppression and seeking alternatives.

All processes of liberation need to be undertaken through deep reflection and dialogue in order to assure that it does not become another form of oppression hidden behind a liberatory discourse. Within different spheres, the attempts to become free from oppression have, on occasion, turned into obligations to partake in everything that was formerly forbidden, without reflecting on whether this really means having the capacity to choose freely. Without a doubt, female sexual freedom has been justly defended and many things have been gained over the years. However, there is still way to go, particularly because it continues to be manipulated in many ways. Some women, traditionally obligated to reach marriage as virgins have seen how at times liberation, far from allowing them to decide at long last, has instead meant having to engage in sexual relationships that they may not wanted. Liberation has been manipulated on many occasions, not allowing women to be free at last to decide their sexuality, instead, once again being told what they have to do.

False liberation led many to seek relationships in order to feel included in the sexual revolution, or to do things without thinking about whether they actually wanted to engage in them. In this way, the quest for sexual freedom, at times, was approached by adopting the hegemonic model of masculinity, or that of the *womanizer*. (This term refers to a man that "loves and leaves them," who bases his pleasure on chasing. Once he has made the conquest, the excitement of the chase fades and so does the value of the "prey." Once he gets her, he looks down on her because "she's easy.") At times, it has been these types of relationships, of "using and discarding," that have characterized some women's claim to equality. But we must ask ourselves, why does gaining sexual rights have to be linked with male chauvinist attitudes? Does equality really mean turning the tables?

Sexist Advertisements

The manipulation of feminine sexuality and how discos commodify it, favors the use of sexist advertisements for commercial benefit. From free entries for women, to the promotion of discos as opportunities for "picking up," sexuality becomes an advertisement. In fact, what is being sold is perpetuating the manipulation of female sexuality.

I would like to pay special attention to the *go-gos*, who were already present in the early discos of Paris. The objectification of women and their conversion to sexual objects does not originate in discos, but is present in them. At times, waitresses dress provocatively as an aesthetic commitment to be in style and make the disco attractive, but it also has an instrumental aim. If we look at the go-gos, the issue becomes more complicated if we want to attribute the label of sexual objects to them, since representing the objectification of the woman depends on the context she is in, and also on how she dresses, how she moves, and so forth. They can reproduce the most conservative stereotypes about women and men and generate sexist comments from observers while they can also express the victories in relation to our bodies and lives; we do not want to minimize the use of go-gos as a sexist advertisement.

Critiques about "Liberated" Women

We have already identified how some women on occasion imitate the masculine behavior of *womanizer*, "using and discarding" people in relationships. In this way, some women and adolescent girls establish instrumental relationships in discos, feeling "liberated" since they think they are acting "just like men." Nevertheless, reality shows us that this perspective is erroneous; first, because not all men act this way, and second, because when a woman imitates this hegemonic masculine model she is not valued, she is looked down upon, and she is not seen as "equal" to a man but "easy." Far from representing sexual freedom, women acting as "liberated" by adopting these types of behaviors socialize themselves into unequal relationships of domination and oppression. Through the "womanizer" model, freedom and liberation is misunderstood. Freedom is not about the number of relationships, but about the possibility to choose whether a woman wants to have one, three, or fifty relationships. Freedom is also about the possibility to choose who they want to have relationships with.

Obviously, it is sexist to criticize a woman for establishing the same types of relationships that men are praised for. However, we have to ask ourselves, should feminists fight and defend a sexual freedom valuing women who imitate a masculine model built on misunderstanding of what freedom is? Today, more and more women reject men's false liberation and define alternatives to these conservative and unequal forms of relationships.

The Commodification of Pleasure

Discos have been organized to favor relationships as part of the commercial strategy, and many relationships that take place in the disco are not free but the result of a commodification of pleasure. When people began to dance alone, they created musical spaces for slow dances. "Slow dancing" was a way to turn back to "the old days," explicitly marking the moment to approach the person that one chooses. This situation could feel uncomfortable, since stopping the music to start the slow dances seemed more instrumental. Also, the bars and tables, in the first discos, were spaces that provided opportunities to approach someone, but there is a physical space directly related with relationships in discos: "the privé." This is a clearly marked space which is always far from the main dance floor and the entire clamor; it is characterized by dimmer lights and comfortable seats where people go once they have made an encounter in another part of the disco. "To accept" having a relationship in a disco does not necessarily imply going to the privé, and "accepting" to go to the privé does not necessarily mean engaging in some form of sexual practice, but some people can assume it does. The sexual freedom to have relationships in discos becomes instrumentalized when the disco goes from being a space that allows people to act freely, to determining when and where relationships should be engaged.

In addition to the mercantilization that the organization of the disco promotes, what occurs within the very relationships is even more problematic. The freedom to establish a relationship in discos without pre-established norms has been greatly reduced to establishing relationships focused on "picking up." These relationships are mainly characterized by an instrumentality. That is to say, in such encounters people use others as objects; there is no intent of demonstrating feelings and there is often a lack of respect and disdain as well. The "pick up" relationship is considered both by people who do not go out with this aim, as well as many who do, as relationships lacking in feeling.

At the same time, the "pick up" becomes the accumulation of conquests as in collecting objects. In this way, sexual liberation is often understood (or misunderstood) as how to engage in the greatest number of sexual relationships while "using and discarding" people like objects. But there is no questioning of whether these relationships are freely chosen or imposed through the capitalization of pleasure in these contexts. How did we arrive at confusing freedom to decide about our sexuality without external impositions, with the obligation to maintain the greatest number of instrumental relationships possible?

We must free ourselves from this commodification of pleasure in order to be able to decide freely about our sexuality. Who cares about the number of relationships we engage in? What does the number and variety of sexual practices we engage in matter? Who cares if we have one, many, or none? Who cares if they occur simultaneously or not? What is important is that we decide freely about our sexuality, sharing our intimacy with whom we want. It is not about someone telling us when and how, or labelling us as liberal or repressed depending on the relationships we have, nor about using people or being used by others as objects, or goods to be consumed. Of course, the commodification of pleasure does not only occur in discos, if that were the case it would be much easier to put an end to. It permeates much of our surroundings in our daily lives. We cannot allow sexual freedom, our sexuality and our pleasure, to be converted into something that we cannot enjoy and decide upon freely. We have to recover our sexual liberty, freeing ourselves from using people as consumer goods. We must also reclaim discos as spaces of sexual freedom, since that is precisely their origin.

TECHNO AND HOUSE CULTURES

Birgit Richard

The techno and house subculture in Germany marks a turning point in the history of youth cultures. The post-punk era was characterized by a patchwork of fragmented subcultures clearly alien to each other. But for the first time, in the middle of the 1990s, a pure dance style became a mass movement assimilating nearly two million youngsters and post-adolescents into a common culture. The so-called "rave nation" is a heterogeneous subculture with similar leisure and consuming habits. The most striking aspect of that development is that the scene became a mass movement in just the two years between 1993 and 1995.

Within current German youth cultures, techno represents an extraordinary phenomenon because it changed the shape, aesthetics, and traditional structures of contemporary youth cultures. As a powerful subcultural style it introduced a package of new visuals based on the possibilities of desktop and electronic publishing and computer graphics and animation, with an immediate effect on general aesthetics and products of society. It is the first subculture that uses and exploits all computer-generated forms of the digital age, and it has already led to an explosion in the aesthetic fields of symbols, signets, and designs. Technodesigners develop new ideas in the arbiters typographics (like Designer´s Republic), techno magazines become avant-garde layout, and techno clubwear and streetwear styles rise into the haute couture. New products like energy drinks change the form and contents of tin cans.

Furthermore, techno is a self-reflective style, specializing in the production of its own images and representations (photos and video), and it is a self-conscious style able to use the same methods as the media in the reproduction of its characteristic elements. Most important is the change of status of music, like disco music of the seventies, showing that music for pure dancing fun retains its qualities.

TECHNO AND HOUSE STYLE IN GERMANY

What made techno so popular in Germany is the fact that it offers different musical styles ranging from the extreme, fast hardcore (as distinguished from the British understanding of hardcore) or "gabber," to the soft and psychedelic (ambient, goa, and tribal music). The musical platform is completely electronically produced, which allows a producer to create a variety of new musical elements quickly with no time to fragment into various discrete substyles. This electronic substance can generate every possible characteristic of popular music even while the music conveys an electronic expression for nearly every mood, as in the words of Minister of House's "Mister Fingers" (1989): "I am, you see, the creator and this is my house. And in my house there is only house music. You may be Black, you may be white, you may be Jew or gentile. It doesn´t make a difference in our house."

From the moment the party begins, social differences like class, age, gender, color, profession, political opinion, or sexual preference—the forming factors for a personal identity in everyday life—are eradicated by the unifying factor of the music and its rhythm. Communication problems disappear; different people enjoy meeting each other. The intense experience of partying with others and the common goal of a peaceful party unites young people. The rave represents a counter-scenario to the feeling of isolation in the fragmented and atomized societies of the Western Hemisphere. The virtual rave place becomes a timeless, de-localized and de-realized artificial zone like the computer-generated artificial worlds. The ideals of the rave nation, love, peace, and unity, gain significance in the virtual room of the rave event. After the weekend the daily routines reestablish all the differences. Then the rave community becomes fractured again, splitting into two main parts: the users (dancers) and the elite (DJs and producers).

Moreover, if the "regular" ravers try to enter the spheres of production, they encounter a strong line of distinction drawn by the producing elites, who have developed a coded language based on the knowledge of the recorded material they handle. For a nonprofessional it is nearly impossible to develop a personal style of music reception because of the large number of records. So someone must prestructure the material for the home listeners and dancers. This is what the DJs do, by for example, presenting their playlists.

Techno aesthetics include a wide range of symbolic fields and they appeal to different spheres of work from heavy industrial work to high-tech production. Attitudes of working-class culture are copied, for example, bold images of the sweating body in underwear-like clothing. Other symbols and materials in techno clubwear refer to extreme and dangerous situations (for example, costumes and materials of police officers or fire-fighters). Another symbolic field referred to is the world of sports, especially endurance sports like aerobics or long-distance running.

But these attitudes become transported into the context of leisure. Dancing as a mindless pleasure becomes an exciting new form of work, of working the body ("work your body" is a recurrent phrase in House tunes). The techno kids do their "work" sometimes eight hours a day, three days a week. Their form of expression disturbs the grown-ups because this kind of work fails to produce an income, only relentless pleasure. It is also an appropriate activity for expressing the hyper-narcissistic state prevalent now in Western culture. Another reference to industrial work appears in the locations of rave events: often the forgotten ruins of industrial and trade-based capitalism, the warehouse, transformed into a fun factory.

Techno, of course, exaggerates the ideal of a well-trained body by means of working it day and night into a state of hyper-fitness. In fact it pushes the body toward exhaustion. But since the natural biological resources rarely last for three days, they often receive support from a drug meant to bring the necessary energy for the dance marathon. According to McRobbie, the rave situation incorporates excessive drug abuse.

But it would repeat media prejudices to reduce techno and House to styles totally and utterly driven by the drug Ecstasy. Ecstasy is only one aspect in the set of style segments and every subculture has its special drug to match style. Nobody would describe beat or hippie style as deriving entirely from marijuana and hashish or punk from excessive beer drinking.

NATIONAL SHAPES OF AN INTERNATIONAL GLOBAL STYLE

House music as a form of dance music has been bouncing back and forth between Europe and America, perhaps because a special connection exists between African American dance styles and German musical technologies. House music has been deeply influenced by the synthetically produced music out of Germany in the seventies like the pioneer works from Kraftwerk, Can, Tangerine Dream, and Klaus Schulze. (In fact, first forms of hip hop, like electric boogie, were heavily influenced by Kraftwerk.) As Reynolds notes, the most influential piece, Kraftwerk´s instrumental "Autobahn" flattens out steady beats into the perfectly uninflected regularity of vehicular motion.

In the nineties when House music developed in Germany, U.S. DJs like Jeff Mills or old-school veterans like Frankie Knuckles celebrated their big successes in Europe; their own motherland mainly ignored them. Therefore, House and techno had to be reimported into the United States. For example, the Berlin Club Tresor plans to open a second Tresor club in Detroit.

Rave culture invites arrangements between regional and international structures. The style offers an international, quite neutral matrix understood in nearly every country and it generally receives an enthusiastic response. Therefore, this kind of dance music culture can also be interpreted as one representation of current European thought. Each country can connect to an international basic style, which makes it possible for every country to add its own special flavors (like Greek sirtaki samples and voice samples in the respective languages).

German postwar youth cultures generally embraced British and American trends, but they continually tried to add a national aspect to these imported styles. Until the punk rebellion they were unsuccessful as we have pointed out elsewhere, because they usually produced an imitation. But gradually German styles became independent, and German youth found a specific way to adapt and transform international movements. For example, experimental bands of the so-called Neue Deutsche Welle (New German Wave) like Der Plan, die Krupps, DAF (one of its former members, Robert Görl, has become a well-known techno musician) adapted New Wave and created a special national style, which often seemed harsh and doltish especially in its use of the German language. But it captured a good bit of the national atmosphere.

The geographical roots of the current techno scene in Germany clearly lie in the black community dance scenes of New York, Chicago, and Detroit. (It is, in fact, the second wave of dance music to come out of the Motor City if you think of Motown as both a dance scene and a music genre.) House music came to Germany in 1988 via Britain, when it became Acid House (heavily influenced by Spanish Balearic music and dance styles coming especially out of Ibiza). But UK Acid House was not immediately adopted by German youth culture. It appeared to be an artificial style, no infrastructure for big illegal party events had yet emerged, and what was more important, youngsters in Germany did not understand what the whole rave scene with excessive parties was all about.

But a small but fertile underground already existed, and finally in the beginning of the nineties out of different House styles, the German techno or *Tekkno* developed. It grew out of the structure of clubs and locations that already existed, especially in Berlin and Frankfurt, two centers of techno. The subculture also emerged from special constellations after the razing of the Berlin Wall. The uncertainty of the social climate encouraged the seizure of politically and commercially unmarked space. Out of the underground, the scene built up an informal network with several, sometimes quickly changing illegal locations and parties, the most famous ones being the TRESOR or the E-WERK in Berlin (which faced closure in 1995 because of government restrictions).

The German techno scene meanwhile evolved into differentiated substructures: Varieties like Hardtrance, Trance, Acid, Goa, and Tribal suggest a separatism among the musical styles whereas in Britain, these styles tend to intermingle. In the UK, German techno is called "hardcore" (which is not identical with Dutch Rotterdam Hard-core, called Gabber performed at a speed of up to 250 beats per minute). For the rave culture in Germany this display must be differentiated, because big illegal warehouse parties or gatherings in the countryside with sudden traffic jams in little villages are not typical, as they are in the UK. Large, often commercially organized events occur for the raver throughout the year, and one the indoor Mayday mega-event in Berlin, Dortmund, and Frankfurt, features all the well-known national and international DJs. For the occasion of the famous Love Parade in Berlin on the Kurfürstendamm, which mixes traditional elements of the St. Christopher's Street Day in New York and the Nottinghill Carnival in London, techno presents itself as a street style. The number of participants has exploded in the last two years from a hundred thousand to a half million. These parades are successful because even young Germans like march rhythms. Besides the Berlin Love Parade, the Union Move in Munich and the Night Move in Cologne present other occasions for the rave nation to come out of their rave closet. Normally the ravers leave their virtual rave world to integrate themselves immediately into everyday routines without affecting or disturbing them. The parades give the ravers visibility and allow them to present their style in dance performance. Because its occupation of public space is impermanent and limited to only a few hours, techno is the ideal street style.

CHANGING MODES OF FEMININITY

Dance is where girls were always found in subcultures. It was their only entitlement.

The history of dance styles is strikingly by gender specific. For girls and young women, dancing has always presented an opportunity for the experience of the body, a means for erotic self-expression and a demonstration of female ease, as McRobbie has pointed out. Up to the point when techno and

House began to dominate the dance scene—before the strident beat and the punk movement forced changes in behavior involving both sexes in the sheer enjoyment of dancing and ecstatic body movement, an inequality in the numbers of dancing woman and men had existed. Dancing has always had a different personal meaning for woman. For men, dancing had little to do with enjoyment. They saw it as a female activity and engaged themselves only in voyeuristic stares at the dancing women. If young men got up on the dance floor, it was mainly to establish contact with a dancing female.

The influence of the English Afro-Caribbean cultures in the eighties introduced boys and men into the narcissistic and autoerotic dimensions of dance. It presented a new opportunity for male self-expression, but at first only in a special form. The chance to show the special skills of the male body brought a change to male engagement in dancing. The styles originated in the black communities (rock and roll, break dancing, the acrobatic figures in the disco dancing of the seventies—Travolta´s spins in *Saturday Night Fever*, or Breakbeat, the Jungle dance style) require acrobatic skills for which male youth undergo hard training at home. Women are in general excluded from these dance cultures, if they try to enter the male circles, they lose their femininity in the eyes of the young men because this kind of dance confirms representative male images. Hip hop is a typical example for a style based totally on the rules of male competition in its break dance, graffiti, and rap expressions.

Techno and house are democratic dance movements, which render the matter of gender unimportant in the dance performance. The unequal positions between the male voyeur and the female dancer dissolve because dancing has become the motivating force for an entire youth culture, an event that gives girls a renewed confidence and prominence. The techno culture transforms the acrobatic dance pleasures that have sustained black cultures into a show of endurance and combines them with gay attitudes toward the body. Influencing the body's shape, taking care of the body, and enjoying the addictive pleasures of dance without links to sexual satisfaction become available to a wide audience. This ubiquity influences, in turn, the image of masculinity: The trope of masculinity is visually one of largely white unadorned, anti-stylish "normality." But laddishness has been replaced by friendliness. Indeed the second irony of this present social moment is that working-class boys lose their "agro" and become "new men"—through the use of Ecstasy.

Although it seems true that men do not change with various reflections of their male role, it is also clear that they do not change their basic attitudes simply because of the drug Ecstasy. If men allow all kinds of homosexual or female attitudes to enter their male world and a change to socially fixed attitudes does, in fact, occur, it is a step in the right direction. Young men have begun to recognize other possibilities—for example, training the body for a more tactile and sensuous experience of their own and other bodies—not just following traditional working-class ideals of the work-strengthened but suffering male body.

Besides the basic change in male attitudes toward dancing, girls too experience a totally new situation in the rave culture. The rave event offers a space where nearly everything is possible for a girl without fear of male sanctions. Girls can dress as freely as they like, which leads to hypersexual dress patterns in the techno and House scene. At the same time they can seal off their highly erotic dress.

The unwritten rules of the rave events protect girls. They do not countenance men trying to touch women against their will. Male voyeuristic stares mostly vanish. The rave event allows girls a maximum of freedom: They can move around freely and get into contact with young men if they like. They can talk to men without fear of sexual assault. According to McRobbie, a culture of sexual avoidance and innocence makes this possible. McRobbie's comparison is inadequate, however, because childhood is rarely synonymous with peace and harmony. Moreover, techno and House cannot be characterized by a total avoidance of direct sexuality. Eroticism is transformed into the dance style itself, and sexuality is expressed in ritual form. The dance becomes a formula for sexual intercourse, beats and rhythms imitating different states of orgasm. The dancers release their sexual tension; with ecstatic shouts their tension is diffused because it is not fixed on a potential lover or friend (it may be a form of cybersex!). Direct sexuality, usually the unpleasant aspect of dancing pleasure for girls in clubs, is suspended. The male wish for easy sexual gratification has no a chance of being realized in the rave world.

Despite all these positive implications for girls, commercialization spoils efforts at equality by reproducing parts of the old inequalities. In fact one finds few female DJs and producers (exceptions include DJ Marusha or the Dutch Miss DJAX DJ and founder of the record label DJAX UP BEATS). Girls are less involved in actively producing or playing the music; therefore they are found less often in the record shops listening to and buying new records.

COMMERCIAL HYPE OR HYPERCONSUMERIST STRATEGIES AS EVERYDAY POLITICS

There are so many dangers (drugs, sex, alcohol) and so many social and political issues . . . that Rave turns away from this heavy load and plunges headlong into a culture of avoidance and almost pure abandonment.

Ravers want desperately to escape from their burdens of responsibility, and accordingly the rave event suspends everyday rules. Ravers cannot transfer their virtual experiences into reality; these experiences function only in the virtual space of the rave event. This fabrication leads to the question of whether a dance movement like techno could have political implications. To discover a political message in a culture that tells its fans to "shut up and dance," one must look closely to notice that immersion in rave (as a parallel to virtual reality) influences patterns of love and friendship.

In Germany, there has to be a social and political impact on a youth culture, a kind of message in the music expressed in the lyrics. That music meant for amusement and entertainment must not be creative is an elemental dictum of social and cultural scientists. This attitude derives from the theoretical grounding in critical theory. Movements developing out of the structures or within the realm of the "culture industry" tend to have little power to make political statements, as introduced by Adorno. The lack of a clear message in the present instance has led to a series of theoretical attempts to interpret the phenomenon.

Does techno have, then, anything to do with politics? This argument currently rages between the administration in Berlin and the organizers of the Love Parade. The Love Parade must be announced as a political demonstration; otherwise the organizers have to pay fees for cleaning the "Ku-Damm" and for police to secure the parade. It becomes a political act because while ravers occupy public space just for fun, a party demonstrating in favor of peace expresses a kind of everyday politics. More important, ravers take control of Berlin's most important thoroughfare for their purpose. They demonstrate a party presence and themselves put an end to the discussion by demanding the "right" to party as an elementary political right. But in Germany, techno is not yet interpreted as a political movement as it is in the UK; otherwise, the Berlin administration would never allow the annual parade.

Beside the question of politics, it is a fact that techno is one of the styles (together with hip hop) fixed on products and brands. It is a consumer style reflecting the excessive consumption characteristic of western societies. There is now a complete line of products designed especially for the raver market from clothing (club wear) and food (energy drinks) to special sports (snowboarding) and raver holiday camps.

The differentiated techno style reveals an astonishing coexistence of subcultural and mainstream commercial forms. On the one hand commercialization attracts new kinds of people on familiar with the origin of the dance scene. On the other hand, the persistent underground goes back into the small clubs and returns to a personal atmosphere to develop something new. Techno remains a democratic and productive style because, like punk, it offers possibilities for many young people to produce and sell their own music. A new independent national system of producing, distributing and selling electronic dance music has developed in Germany. Small labels produce small editions of vinyl records for the direct use by the DJs in the clubs.

Techno must, then, be accepted as a form of cultural production, a form of Paul Willis's notion of "profane culture," reflecting current social attitudes. To discover a political impact in the youth culture of the nineties, traditional promotion methods especially those based on a tacit division between commercial and authentic style must be transformed. A need to just have fun and to be an excessive consumer might provoke those parents belonging to the rebellious sixties generation trying now to live reflective lifestyles. For the youth culture of the nineties, no powerful utopian parallels exist except the hope for a loving, peaceful and unifying community. International Rave culture could be regarded as an experimental laboratory where western societies could learn that forms of peaceful human relationships are still possible. But a direct transfer out of the rave system seems out of the question.

The rave zone, appearing as a virtual paradise before original sin, remains a nonreflective and self-contained zone. Love, peace, and unity as the absence of the evil, form an unreal, not transferable status of the event. It remains a zone without the "Begehren" (desire) of Lacan or "Wunsch" (wish) of Freud: a room of virtual plenty insulated from the real ambiguities outside.

References

Adorno, Th. W. (1989). Kulturindustrie (The Culture Industry). In D. & M. Horkheimer (Eds.), *Dialektik der Aufklärung* (pp. 139–188). Frankfurt, Germany: Fischer.

Chisholm, L., Büchner, P., & Krüger, H.-H. (1995). *Growing up in Europe.* Berlin and New York: de Gruyter.

McRobbie, A. (1995). *Postmodernism and popular culture.* London and New York: Routledge.

Mungham, G. (1976). *Working class youth culture.* London: Routledge and Kegan Paul.

Reynolds, S. (1995). *The sex revolts. Gender, rebellion and rock 'n' roll.* London: Serpent's Tail.

THE ELEMENTS AND ERAS OF HIP HOP CULTURE

James Peterson

In the last thirty years hip hop culture has developed from a relatively unknown and largely ignored inner city culture into a global phenomenon. The foundational elements of hip hop culture (DJ-ing, MC-ing, Breakdance, and Graffiti/Graf) are manifest in youth culture across the globe, including Japan, France, Germany, South Africa, Cuba, and the UK. Considering its humble beginnings in the South and West Bronx, the global development of hip hop is an amazing cultural feat. Yet its global popularity suggests and reflects its culturally diverse origins. Moreover, the presence of rap music and other elements of the culture in marketing and advertising signal American mainstream acceptance. In fact, it's dominance in popular culture almost hides the negative and at times malicious treatment of hip hop in the public sphere. With all of its attendant complexities and apparent contradictions, hip hop is one of the most difficult cultural phenomena to define.

In 1967, Clive Campbell, also known as the legendary DJ Kool Herc, immigrated to New York City and settled in the West Bronx. Kool Herc was born in Kingston Jamaica, the birthplace of another great musical forefather, the legend, Bob Marley. Herc, borrowed elements of yard culture in Jamaica: especially the penchant for throwing spontaneous parties outside (i.e., public spaces). For the most part, scholars and historians agree that DJ Kool Herc is one of the most notable founding figures of hip hop culture.[1] He DJ-ed some of the earliest hip hop jams, occasionally in basements, but usually outside in the streets or in the park. Kool Herc was famous for his 6 foot tall speakers, nicknamed the Herculoids. He himself stands about 6 feet 5 inches tall—literally and figuratively a giant in hip hop.

By the mid-1970s DJ Kool Herc's parties were becoming well known in New York City. In fact hip hop jams were an affordable alternative to pricey disco clubs. As early hip hop DJs began to develop the various techniques of early DJ-ing, the potential of the culture emerged in excitement amongst young B-boys and B-girls. The early hip hop DJs invented the concept of scratching, skillfully manipulating vinyl records to sonically rupture recorded music and play fragments of it back at will. Even before scratching was developed, DJs isolated and looped break beats from popular records. Break beats, that portion of a song where the music and vocals take a back seat to the beat, became the signature sound of hip hop, hence the evolution of Break Boys or B-Boys who relished the extension of the most danceable moments of popular soul and disco music. Early B-Boys would battle, and through battling the various technical aspects of break dancing were honed and developed. There were several crews of young folk who participated in the development of break dancing. One of the earliest and now most legendary breaking crews is the Rock Steady Crew. Bronx B-boys (b-boys/girls are currently known as imbibers of hip hop culture that creatively participate in two or more primary elements of the culture), Jimmy D. and Jojo established the legendary Rock Steady Crew; joined by Crazy Legs and Lenny Len in 1979).

In addition to DJs and break dancers, there were also MCs at these early hip hop jams. As a point of clarification, all MCs rap, but not all rappers are MCs. A rapper is an entertainer. An MC is an artist who is committed to perfecting the crafts of lyrical mastery and call-response audience interaction. MCs were not initially (as they are now) the front men and women of hip hop culture. Noted MC, KRS ONE once remarked that as an MC he was happy to just carry his DJs crates. These days hip hop culture, especially rap music, tends to marginalize most of the foundational elements of the culture and over emphasizes the role of the MC which stands for Master of Ceremonies in standard parlance. However, according to Rakim, an MC who is widely referred to simply as "the god," "MC means move the crowd" or "Mic Control." MCs hone their skills through freestyling and battling as well. Free style rhyming is when an MC raps without aid of previous rhymes committed to paper or memory. Much like their Jazz improvising counterparts, a free-styling MC pulls lyrical rifts and cadences from an ever-evolving repertoire in order to perform spontaneous rhymes that reflect their immediate environment or address the present opponent. Battling is when MCs engage in lyrical combat in a series of discursive turns. In fact battles between MCs have become legendary and at times notoriously violent on and off record.

The final foundational element of hip hop culture is represented by the graffiti artist. To many people, graffiti artist is an oxymoron. Graffiti is vandalism. It is against the law to spray paint names and images on public property. Somewhat unlike the other elements of hip hop culture, graffiti completely predates the development of the other three elements. Graffiti actually dates back to Old World, pre-modern times. But there are some distinct qualities to how and why graffiti has developed in hip hop culture. The earliest documented Graf moniker belongs to Greece born, Demetrius from 183 Street in the Bronx. He made himself famous by tagging Taki 183 throughout the five boroughs of NYC via subway trains. This moment is distinct for several reasons. First, considering hip hop's global prominence in the early part of the new millennium, the multi-cultural origins of hip hop certainly explain some of its universal appeal. A Greek Graf writer fit in perfectly with a diverse array of cultural constituents, including African Americans, Jamaicans, West Indians, Puerto Ricans, Asians, Dominicans, Cubans, and so forth. Second, several scholars have referred to much of the activity of early adopters of hip hop culture as a process of reclaiming public spaces.[2] Sometimes this reclamation is done through sound; consider the boom boxes of yesteryear or the current boom-box-like sound systems in cars. But sometimes this is done through the writing of names and images on/in public spaces. Third, the use of the subway, as a means to circulate the tag, Taki 183, throughout the five boroughs was a masterstroke. It underscored the urge to manipulate public property and services for the benefit of youth culture and in particular here, the processes of self identification amongst inner city youth.

In addition to the four foundational elements of hip hop culture (DJ, MC, Graf, and Dance), there are several secondary elements of the culture as well. These elements include fashion/modes of dress, entrepreneurship, and complex systems of knowledge (particularly elaborate language and other linguistic phenomenon). Fashion has always been a component of hip hop culture. After all, the DJs, B-boys, B-girls, and MCs had serious dress codes. Some of the earliest brands of choice were Adidas, Puma, Lee Jeans, Cazal (eyeglasses), and Kangol (hats). Some of the early graf artists would spray paint names and designs onto sweatshirts, jackets, sneakers, and hats. So a distinct sense of fashion was present early. As the culture grew in popularity, fashion became the outward sign of hip hop culture's entrepreneurial sensibility. Hip hop clothing brands such as Karl Kani, Cross Colours, and eventually Phat Farm, FUBU, and Rocawear all signified the fact that youth influenced by and living through hip hop culture were deeply invested in economic empowerment most readily manifest in owning one's own business.

Entrepreneurship should not be confused with aspirations to "bling." Bling Bling came into vogue during the Platinum era of hip hop (which will be discussed later), and actually reflects earlier proclivities of African American culture; what Zora Neale Hurston referred to as "the will to adorn."[3] Wearing platinum jewelry and sporting gold teeth can be viewed as a cultural strategy by young people to floss their financial means and to thereby overcome social invisibility in a materialist society. It is a means of self-identification and self-promotion that harkens back to early African American and American traditions.

The Bling Bling–Will to Adorn trajectory underscores the knowledge element of hip hop culture. Knowledge Reigns Supreme Over Nearly Everyone–KRS-ONE: a simple acronym functioning as the MC moniker of Kris Parker, formally of BDP (Boogie Down Productions)—gestures toward the value of knowledge especially for the initiates of hip hop. Outsiders or even younger hip hoppers may not have heard of KRS-ONE. They may not know who he is. They may not know that he started his recording career with the group BDP. They may not know what BDP stands for; they may not know that the Boogie Down is a nickname for the Bronx, the birthplace of hip hop. This is one example (albeit a very simple one) of thousands of linguistic cues, local references, acronyms, and code names that require constituents of hip hop culture to be "in the know." "If you don't know–you better ask somebody."

All of this creative culturally diverse energy tends to mask some of the socioeconomic factors that set the stage for hip hop's early developments. Note here, that one of the most promising scholars of hip hop culture, Imani Perry, warns against deficiency models for defining hip hop.[4] That is to say, the following discussion about the socioeconomic contexts for hip hop culture is not an attempt to account for the developments of hip hop in total. The significance of various socio-economic factors in the various developments of the culture will be readily apparent.

The outsourcing of high tech jobs has become an issue in the first decade of the new millennium, but outsourcing US jobs had been a challenge for working class and impoverished folks since the early 1970s. In the 1960s most US urban centers were economically sound based upon huge manufacturing industries. As these industries outsourced labor and developed advanced technological means to manufacture their products, unemployment increased. In New York City, this de-industrialization, was complemented by the erasure of public school support for the arts and musical training. In the Bronx, the construction of a beltway for commuters displaced thousands of residences.[5] The combination of these economic factors created a stifling environment for young people in inner cities in the mid-1970s. With residential depression and few outlets for artistic expression, young people were relegated to an economically and artistically stagnant environment. For ready reference, view the 1982 film, *Wild Style*. Not only is the film a documentary journey through the early days of hip hop culture, but it is shot in the Bronx, and unless you visited the south Bronx circa 1979, these are some of the most authentic images of the setting for the early developments of hip hop culture.

There are several other dates and historical figures of note. In 1974, Afrika Bambaataa transformed one of New York City's largest and most violent gangs into hip hop culture's first organization the ZULU nation. Even today the ZULU nation is one of the most publicly active, communally oriented organizations in hip hop. Bambaataa along with DJ Busy Bee Starski are credited with coining the term "hip hop" (in reference to those original parties/jams) in the same year. In 1975, Grand Wizard Theodore discovered the scratch, that monumental DJ-ing technique where DJs deliberately rupture a vinyl sound recording to produce the now legendary scratching sound so often associated with hip hop DJs and music producers. For more important dates, please refer to the Timepiece Timeline at the conclusion of this essay.

From these origins, hip hop's development can appropriately be broken down into several eras:

1. The Old School Era: From 1979 to 1987 hip hop culture cultivated itself in and through all of its elements usually remaining authentic to its counter cultural roots in the post-industrial challenges manifested in the urban landscape of the late-twentieth-century artists associated with this era included Grandmaster Flash and the Furious Five, The Sugarhill Gang, Lady B, Big Daddy Kane, Run DMC, Kurtis Blow, and others.

2. The Golden Age Era: From 1987-1993 Rap and rappers begin to take center stage as the culture splashes onto the mainstream platform of American popular culture. The extraordinary musical production and lyrical content of rap songs artistically eclipse most of the other primary elements of the culture (break dancing, graf art, and DJ-ing). Eventually the Recording Industry contemplates rap music as a potential billion-dollar opportunity. Mass mediated rap music and hip hop videos displace the intimate, insulated urban development of the culture. Artists associated with this era include: Run DMC, Boogie Down Productions, Eric B and Rakim, Salt N Pepa, Queen Latifah, De La Soul, A Tribe Called Quest, Public Enemy, NWA, and many others.

3. The Platinum Present: From 1994–the present hip hop culture has enjoyed the best and worst of what mass mediated popularity and cultural commodification has had to offer. The meteoric rise to popular fame of gangsta rap in the early 1990s set the stage for a marked content

shift in the lyrical discourse of rap music toward more and more violent depictions of inner city realities. Millions of magazines and records were sold, but two of hip hop's most promising artists, Biggie Smalls and Tupac Shakur, were literally gunned down in the crossfire of a media fueled battle between the so-called East and West coast constituents of hip hop culture. With the blueprint of popular success for rappers laid bare, several exceptional artists stepped into the gaping space left in the wake of Biggie and Tupac. This influx of new talent included Nas, Jay-Z, Master P, DMX, Big Pun, Snoop Doggie Dogg, Eminem, and Outkast.

The current era of hip hop is still unfolding, but since the demise of Tupac Shakur and The Notorious B.I.G., an era of battling amongst MCs and crews of MCs has taken root even as the Platinum era seems to be waning. It is no longer simply good enough to be gangsta or to be rich and "bling-ed" out. These days you need to be gangsta, rich, and prepared to at least do lyrical battle in the name of your crew or your position in hip hop culture. One needs only to study the career of Curtis Jackson (aka 50 Cent) to witness how battling has become a centerpiece in the business of hip hop culture.

By the mid 1990s, hip hop culture also emerged as an area of serious study on the university level. Courses on hip hop culture, history and aesthetics were formed on college classes across America. Due largely to student demand and interest, these courses analyzed the origins and significance of hip hop culture. Originally housed at Harvard University's W. E. B. Du Bois Institute, the hip hop archive founded in 2002 by Marcyliena Morgan is an example of this important academic and pedagogical development. Dr. Morgan has since repositioned the archive at Stanford University.

THE TIMEPIECE HIP HOP TIMELINE
COMPILED BY
JAMES PETERSON

The Old School Era (a sundial timepiece)

1967 Clive Campbell aka DJ Kool Herc (hip hop's first DJ) immigrates to the West Bronx in NYC from Jamaica.

1968 Rucker Park is a must stop for top college and pro basketball stars, eager to prove themselves. Julius Erving, Wilt Chamberlain, Kareem Abdul Jabar, establish the legacy maintained by the likes of Allen Iverson, Stephon Marbury, Ron Artest, and Elton Brand. The Rucker Tournament, the Rucker Pro League and the Entertainer's Basketball Classic are legendary touchstones for hip hop's love affair with athletics.

1968–9 James Brown records and releases *Funky Drummer* (one of the most sampled drum tracks in hip hop History) and *Say It Loud (I'm Black and I'm Proud)*.

1969   Greece born, Demetrius from 183 Street in the Bronx makes himself famous by "tagging" Taki 183 throughout the five boroughs of NYC.

1973   DJ Kool Herc DJs his first party

1974   Afrika Bambaataa leaves the Black Spades (one of the largest and most violent gangs in New York) to form hip hop's first organization, the ZULU Nation.

1974   Busy Bee Starski, DJ Hollywood, and/or Afrika Bambaataa coin the term, "hip hop."

1975   Grand Wizard Theodore discovers the scratch.

1976   The first pieces (i.e., graf-like murals) appear on New York City subway trains.

1977   Bronx B. Boys, Jimmy D., and Jojo establish the legendary Rock Steady Crew. (Joined by Crazy Legs and Lenny Len in 1979).

1979   Sugarhill Gang's *Rapper's Delight* spends twelve weeks on the Billboard Pop Chart, ushering in the era of the MC with all of its lyrical battles and authorial challenges.

1980   The Times Square Graffiti Show indicates the mainstream's brief love affair with hip hop's visual art.

1980   The High Times Crew is arrested for break dancing. The first photos of break dancing enter mainstream circulation.

1980   The first rap radio show debuts on WHBI, Mr. Magic's Rap Attack.

The Golden Age (a stopwatch timepiece)

1983   Run DMC's *Sucka MC's* signals the end of the Old School Era and the dawn of hip hop's first "pop" stars.

1984   *Roxanne Roxanne* released by UTFO spawning hundred of response "dis" records.

1984   KDAY becomes LA's and this country's first rap-formatted radio station.

1984   Rick Rubin and Russell Simmons form Def Jam in a dorm room.

1986   Run DMC's *Walk this Way* enters heavy rotation on MTV.

1988   NWA's first album, *Straight Outta Compton*, introduces Gangsta Rap to the mainstream (ICE-T, Schoolly D, and BDP have defined the genre earlier for hip hop culture).

1988   Basquiat (the first hip hop visual artist to be recognized by "high culture" art circles) dies from a heroin overdose at the age of twenty-seven.

1989   Public Enemy scores Spike Lee's film, *Do the Right Thing* (the single is titled *Fight the Power*) positioning political rap and the director at the center of urban culture.

1990   2 Live Crew is arrested for performing songs from *As Nasty as They Wanna Be*. First Amendment advocates testify on their behalf and they are released, but Explicit Lyrics Labeling is born.

1990   September—*The Fresh Prince of Bel-Air* debuts on NBC, marking the first sitcom starring a rapper.

1991   Soundscan technology becomes widespread and rap music usurps pop/rock as America's most eagerly consumed music.

1991   Rapper/actor Ice Cube, actors Cuba Gooding Jr., Lawrence Fishburne and Morris Chesnut star in the film *Boyz N the Hood*. Directed by John Singleton

1991   Lyricist Lounge in New York City starts their open mic sessions.

1991   Sway, King Tech and DJ Joe Quixx broadcast the Wake Up Show in the Bay area on KMEL.

1992   FUBU Clothing is launched

1992   Karl Kani begins production of his distinctively logoed, loose-fitting, street-chic sportswear. Within two years, aided by ads that feature artists like Snoop Doggy Dogg and Tupac Shakur, the company will earn between $30 million and $40 million.

The NOW Age (a platinum Timepiece)

1993   Hip hop's greatest producer releases his first masterpiece (*The Chronic* featuring Snoop Dogg and Tha Doggpound). Dr. Dre also produced NWA's first two albums as well as various R&B artists prior to this release.

1993   VIBE magazine is launched with Snoop Doggy Dogg on the cover. Snoop subsequently appears on the September 30th Rolling Stone cover (with Dr. Dre), even though his highly anticipated Doggy style debut hasn't come out yet.

1994   Sean Puffy Combs establishes Bad Boy Records. The Notorious B.I.G. releases *Ready to Die* (Bad Boy).

1994   February—Wu Tang Clan releases their debut album Enter the Wu Tang (36 Chambers), (Loud/RCA).

1994   Snoop Dogg releases his debut album *Doggy Style* (Death Row/Interscope).

1995   The Roots album, *Do You Want More*, brings live instruments back into hip hop popularity.

1996   September 13—Tupac Shakur dies from gunshot wounds after being shot at while driving through Las Vegas with Death Row CEO Suge Knight

1997   March—Rapper Notorious B.I.G. dies of gunshot wounds while sitting in his car after attending a Vibe magazine industry party.

1998   Dre discovers Eminem and produces Em's debut album, on Interscope Records, *The Slim Shady* LP (1999)

2000–present: Popular hip hop artists reduce lyrics to Dionysian exploits and experiences. Jay-Z and DMX supplant Biggie and Tupac as THE MCs of hip hop culture. The well-documented battle between Nas and Jay-Z coupled with the popularity of Hollywood's version of Eminem's life story (*8 Mile*) reinvigorate the dominance of MCs in hip hop and popular culture.

Notes

1 See David Toop's Rap Attack 3.
2 See Houston Baker's Black Studies Rap and the Academy and/or Tricia Rose's Black Noise.
3 Zora Neale Hurston "The Characteristics of Negro Expression."
4 See Imani Perry's Prophets of the Hood.
5 Tricia Rose Black Noise.

Resources

Books

Forman, M. (2002). *The 'hood comes first: Race, space, and place in rap and hip hop.* Middletown, CT: Wesleyan University Press.

Kitwana, B. (2002). *The hip-hop generation: Young blacks and the crisis in African-American culture.* New York: Basic Books.

Perry, I. (2004). *Prophets of the hood: Politics and poetics in hip hop.* Durham, NC: Duke University Press.

Rose, T. (1994). *Black noise: Rap music and black culture in contemporary America.* Hanover, NH: University Press of New England.

Toop, D. (2000). *Rap attack #3.* London: Serpent's Tail Press.

Web Site

www.ohhla.com (Original Hip Hop Lyrics Archive)

HIP HOP, WIGGAHS, AND WHITENESS

Melanie E. L. Bush

"Wigger" or "Wiggah" is a label considered by some as an insulting way to describe a white person who either "acts" or "wants to be" black ("wannabes") and by others, to be a white person who challenges the racial order and is a "border-crosser." The idea of "whiteness" generally refers to the characteristics, relationships, and experiences of people of European descent in a world where this identity has been depicted as superior, well-intended, and powerful. Emerging within black and Puerto Rican communities in New York City in the early 1970s, hip hop developed with artistic, musical, literary, dance, sport, engineering, social, and activist elements.

There has been significant discussion about white involvement in hip hop culture and communities. Some people believe that white youth are drawn to this movement out of their awareness of a detachment from mainstream culture and society at large. However, many people feel their involvement is evidence of yet another way that black culture, art, and history are appropriated for the benefit and wealth of whites. This essay discusses the controversy about "hip hop, 'wiggers' and 'whiteness'" as it relates to contemporary youth culture.

WHAT IS "WHITENESS"?

Formally recognized over the last two decades as a means to address a significant and missing dimension within discussions of race and ethnicity, notions of white racial identity have long been significant in the writings of scholars of color. Among the many examples include William J. Wilson, who in 1860 wrote "What Shall We Do with the White People?" analyzing presumptions of whiteness in the Declaration of Independence and during the early years of the United States nation; Frederick Douglass, who critiqued the centering of the white experience in his famous speech, "What to the Slave Is Your Fourth of July?"; and Harriet Jacobs, who in 1861 described the annual practice of "muster," a time when armed whites terrorized the enslaved population in anticipation of revolts suggesting that this institution served to unite whites across class lines. More recently Mia Bay uncovers the identification of whiteness in eighteenth and nineteenth century writings in slave narratives and by African American scholars. Disguising the idea that whites are "raced" is part of the process that allows race to have meaning.

Being white has generally been associated with ancestry from the European continent and the denial of African blood, the borders of which have shifted during different periods in history to include or exclude various groups. Many immigrants of such ancestry have enjoyed exceptional achievement upon their integration into U.S. society, however, having European heritage is often less important than whether one is identified as white in everyday interactions. Being classified or identified as "white" allows entrance to a racial club that gives status and protection based on the assumption of being nice, reasonable, and of value. Talking about "whiteness" allow us to analyze and understand that whites benefit from a variety of institutional and social arrangements that often appear (to whites) to have nothing to do with race.

Prior to the 1990s, most discussions about race were generally about the "other." Whiteness has been assumed, considered natural, normal, and made invisible, mostly to whites. For those people subordinated and oppressed by white dominant society, knowledge of the "white world" has been a matter of survival as W. E. B. Du Bois describes in his writings as "double consciousness." As one of the outgrowths of the social movements of the 1960s for equality, justice, and inclusion these assumptions about race began to be challenged. In response, particularly over the last decade, significant attention has been given to understanding race through the examination of whiteness. Initially, writers explored the impact of racialized imagery, everyday thinking, and theories about how the idea of race was created. That later developed in analysis of the educational system, cultural representation, and history. Many controversies emerged including a debate about whether whiteness should be reformed as an identity or abolished as an assumption of privilege.

Just chillin'

WHITENESS AND HIP HOP

Born of the struggles and resistance of the 1960s, the hip hop movement has developed in many different directions since that time, with much that includes very powerful analyses and critiques of racism, capitalism, and the current day context. Although often identified solely as rap, in fact hip hop is comprises many different sub-disciplines, most notably those commonly known as break dancing, b-bopping, graffiti, and m-c'ing. Many hip hoppers suggest that these cultural and artistic forms provide space to voice their perspectives and get validation in a world that seems not to care about their opinions and the future.

Young whites today often have more contact with communities of color than did previous generations, particularly in urban areas, as identity becomes increasingly complex in a highly interconnected world. Additionally, with increased media access, some believe that the rebellious and subversive quality of hip hop has become particularly appealing to white youth. Sometimes they are considered to be modern day anti-racist "race traitors," who live and experience the social deconstruction of race. Writers Charles Aaron and Salim Muwakill have suggested that they may be the last hope for

367

healing America's racial divide and pioneers in the effort; however both make clear that identity in the twenty-first century is complex. Muwakill describes these youth as boundary jumpers who are mocked by both blacks and whites. Joe Wood writes about B-boys and girls in Japan who darken their skin in an attempt to pursue African American "blackness" ("jiggers") as he discusses the complex negotiation of blackness and whiteness among Japanese youth. David Roediger says the use of "white nigger" goes back to the nineteenth century to describe either whites accepting work that was considered to be for blacks or in general breaking with cultural and racial norms.

These identities are also complex and perilous in many different ways. Mainstream appropriations of cultural symbols reshape the stories from which they emerged to make them more palatable to the dominant society. Material benefits tend to accrue to whites, for example as if Eminem created rap, white music producers were the true source of artistic creation, or that hip hop just "happened" outside the context of the communities and histories from which it emerged. As with jazz and rock 'n' roll, whites have historically been the economic beneficiaries and portrayed as the creators of black art forms that have been commercially exploited. Another consequence of the mainstreaming and money-making of hip hop is that the executives (traditionally white and male) of the music or art industries end up determining which messages and images are portrayed in mass media. Music, poetry, and art with political message about inequalities and systemic patterns do not get funded or publicized while misogynistic cultural forms get promoted.

William "Upski" Wimsatt discusses hip hop from his perspective as a white male who has oft-times been labeled a "wigger," and he connects the intellectual project of critical analysis about whiteness with the practical implications for everyday living. Known for books including *Bomb the Suburbs*, *No More Prisons* and articles such as one critiquing "wiggers," titled "We Use Words Like Mackadocious," that originally appeared in the *Source*, Wimsatt says that as a while male, he can write about hip hop and make money yet the people who taught him hip hop are either struggling to get by, in jail, or dead. He characterizes the white parts of the "hip hop nation" in several different ways. There are some, he says, who are serious about understanding hip hop culture and the history and communities from which it emerged. Others attend shows, wear hip hop style fashion, or use stereotyped "hip hop lingo." For others, the association with hip hop is solely a commercial venture and based on consumption. It is with these two last groups that the concerns about exploitation and stereotyping are particularly relevant. Wimsatt himself has shifted his energies to explicit social activism to express his views.

Jennifer McLaughlin-Calderon, aka J-Love, educator, author, and activist has written about how her racial consciousness developed within the hip hop community through social activism. She describes the delicate nature of privilege and good intentions in a "Ten Point Code of Ethics" for white hip hop heads that was published in *Redeye Magazine*, stressing the need for

deep awareness of unearned advantages, history, and respecting the originators of hip hop culture. Baba Israel, hip hop artist and educator writes
about whiteness as an enclosure that keeps people out and that maintaining awareness and actively challenging racism is a constant and continuous
effort that involves accountability to the initiators and the communities
from which it has emerged.

It is apparent that there is no consensus on what a "wigger" is and what it is
not. The label is used to refer to whites who are friends with blacks, whites
who "act black"; impersonators or originators; whites who adopt or imitate
what they believe to be "black culture"; whites who embrace elements of hair-
styles or rap; whites who are considered to act as cultural dissenters. People
who identify as "wiggers" are usually male, but not always. Similarly, "wigger" is simultaneously deemed derogatory and affectionate, racist and anti-
racist. The concept opens up the debate about the meaning of race and racial
stereotypes and as points to a common tendency among youth to question the
status quo, however issues of authenticity, credibility and white appropriation
of black creation run throughout in an analysis of hip hop, wiggahs, and whiteness.

As there are at least one hundred hip hop organizations and many individuals, often outside the mainstream radar who are writing, thinking and
acting on analyses of race and racism in today's context, this is an important area of contemporary youth culture to understand.

NOTE: Portions of this essay were published in Melanie E. L. Bush,
Breaking the Code of Good Intentions: Everyday Forms of Whiteness, Rowman
and Littlefield, Inc., Lanham, Maryland, 2004.

Resources

Books
Bay, M. (2000). *The white image in the black mind: African-American ideas about
   white people, 1830–1925.* New York: Oxford University Press.
Douglass, F. (1970). *My bondage and my freedom.* Chicago: Johnson
   Publishing Company. [Orig. published 1855.]
George, N. (1998). On white Negroes. In D. Roediger (Ed.). *Black on white:
   Black writers on what it means to be white* (pp. 225–232). New York:
   Schocken Books.
Israel, B. (2003b). White sight or white hype: White involvement in hip hop.
   Unpublished manuscript from author.
Roediger, D. R. (1998). *Black on white: Black writers on what it means to be
   white.* New York: Schocken Books.
———. (2002). *Colored white: Transcending the racial past.* Berkeley:
   University of California Press.
Wimsatt, W. U. (2001). *Bomb the suburbs.* New York: Soft Skull Press.
———. (2000). *No more prisons.* New York: Soft Skull Press.
Articles
Aaron, C. (1999, March/April). Black like them. *Utne Reader,* 92, 68.

Alexander, D. (1997, November/December). Are black people cooler than white people? *Utne Reader*, 51.

Algeo, J., & Algeo, A. (1991). Among the new words. *American Speech*, 66 (3), 316–324.

Bennett, A. (1999). Rappin' on the Tyne: White hip hop culture in Northeast England—an ethnographic study. *Sociological Review*, 47 (1), 1.

Cobley, P., & Osgerby, W. (1995). Peckham clan ain't nothin' to f*** with: Urban rap style in Britain. Unpublished paper presented at the Youth 2000 Conference. University of Teesside, Middlesborough.

DeBose, B. (2000). Black and white: 'Wiggers' and the exploitation of 'urban' culture. *Washington Informer,* 36 (19), 21.

Echeverria, S., Jr. (2003, September 4). 'Wiggers': Stealing black culture or bridging the racial divide? *Hyde Park Citizen*, Chicago, IL, p. 8.

Hill, L. (2002). Don't call me that word. *Maclea's*, 115 (8), 60.

J-Love (Jennifer Calderon). (2002, January). White like me. [Editorial.] *RedEye*, 17–18.

Muwakill, S. (1999). Aaron the wiggah. *CommonQuest*, 3 (3), 4 (1), 67.

Roediger, D. R. (1995, Winter). Guineas, wiggers, and the dramas of racialized culture. *American Literary History*, 7, 654–668.

Spiegler, M. (1996). Marketing street culture. *American Demographics*, 18 (11), 28.

Wimsatt, W. U. (1997). In defense of wiggers. *Transition. The White Issue.* 7 (1). Issue 73, 199–203.

———. (1993, May). We use words like "mackadocious." *The Source*, 64–66.

Wood, J. (1997). The yellow negro. *Transition. The White Issue.* 7 (1). Issue 73.

Web Sites

Sartwell C. (n.d.). Wiggers. Retrieved July 1, 2004 from http://www. crispinsartwell.com/longwigger.htm

Wimsatt, W. U. (1999b, October 13). Emancipation rap-clamation. *San Francisco Bay Guardian*. Retrieved June 23, 2004 from http://www.sfbg. com/AandE/34/02/lead.html

CHECK ME? . . .NO CHECK YOU!

Regina Bernard

Sex bracelets replace secret crushes; third graders make homemade thongs which replace ruffled or days of the week underwear; hair specific do-rags replace combs; sewed-in butt jeans replace bell bottoms or baggies; chasing sexual partners because of the want to become infected with HIV/AIDS, now replaces spin the bottle and tissue paper with the question "do you like me? Circle yes or no." Racial dichotomies have blurred what girls of color and white girls are into, but somehow society has managed to make these youthful ornaments racially and culturally specific.

Driving through Forest Hills, Queens, one weekday afternoon, I witnessed three young white girls sitting on the stoop of their school (which is cornered by a busy two-way traffic street). A car is waiting for the red light to change to green as it blasts Sean Paul's *Like Glue*. The music is so loud it shakes everything around me. The girls jump up from the stoop squealing at the car, "that's ma song! That's the jam right there!" They begin to get up and wind their bodies in an imitation of the West Indian waist wind. The car turns the music up, the girls proceed to take their tops off and show the driver (a black male, perhaps in his twenties) their bras, and continue squealing. What would the world of research state these girls are at risk for? In my attempt to answer this question, I can sadly state that, unfortunately, there hasn't been research done on it. However, I can check what has been tremendously written on young girls of color and their "at risk nature," and try to apply the same to this case. The "at risk" behavior seems to be the same among both groups of girls, but the reports of "at risk" results have not been the same.

How do images of people develop? What turns a trend into a stereotype that is racially and culturally specific? Socioeconomic status defines culture and, oftentimes, creates a platform to blame one specific group for its trendy cultural appeals. Lack of social access and know-how is an entrance to the development of particular racial stereotypes. The image of youth of color, particularly black and Latin images have become appealing because of its image to those whose only choice to adopt the culture, is because of its accessibility and its stray from their norm. Take body modifications for example, when Africans engage in scarification (permanent cuts and/or burns into the skin), in order to obtain community and cultural memberships, (as they have been doing for centuries), they are noted as "savage," or "uncivilized," or better still, members of the "third/sixth world." When young white men and women engage in the process of scarification, it becomes a *National Geographic* special on the trends of youth culture. While piercings and tattoos have been culturally classified, and historically adjacent to various cultures of color, once adopted by young white and affording folk, the trend setting begins and thus results in millions of copycat acts. In a time of trendy youth culture, it is fair to bear witness to white girls and girls of color who are modifying their bodies, whether with tattoos, a piercing in various places on the body, or body scarification.

Another trend that has taken flight since last year is one of risky sexual practices. Last year, an article in *Rolling Stone* magazine indicated that there are now people engaging in sexual acts with HIV-positive partners so that

371

they may contract the virus as a purposely-risky act. While countries of color watch their population slowly decline because of AIDS, the world puts forward rumors and myths that these community members engage in sexual acts with animals and are ignorant to AIDS awareness and education. However, right here in New York City, with all of the outreach and awareness that New York City organizations have undergone, there are still populations of people who have glamorized the actual contraction of the disease. While the report included men in their 30s, one can only wonder if this will trickle down to our youth for adoption as well. We are already at an alarming rate of young black women and Latinas carrying either HIV or AIDS. They outweigh the number of their white female and male counterparts. Due to its mysteriousness and lack of understanding by mainstream societies, these acts of risk, whether cultural and/or religious become attractive to those seeking to rebel against their norms.

Socioeconomically, many young blacks and Latino/as living in the barrios of New York City have limited options to them in terms of recreation. Young people of color have adopted and adapted to the cheaper versions of the "good life." Delving into a circumstance of imitation, we find ourselves addicted to name-brand shopping, fast food imbalanced diets, oversized jewelry, and privatized speech patterns that include "ghetto" as something to strive for. On any given summer night on my block you can find black and Latino adolescents and teenagers playing in empty lots (where broken bottles, garbage, rodents, stray animals, and all kinds of objects can be encountered). During hot summer days, these same young people become disillusioned by long lines for access to the public pools, libraries that close early or are not open at all, and public transportation that is minimal in the sweltering heat. As the night comes alive in these neighborhoods and enclaves of youthful energy take over, one can observe young girls who have clearly passed the threshold of puberty, affected dress codes, and rehearsed patterns to their stride. In my own youth, my apartment building stoop at night was as crowded as a nightclub on ladies' night. Bodies on top of bodies crowded the stoop, with multiple activities taking place, and much aggression. We owned our stoop; it was a place that we would never be rejected. Yet, some of the stoop members did not engage in much else. Thus, they too became "at risk."

Poverty places risk on young folk of color. As young people are also made to be ashamed of their situations and circumstances, this same level of shame contributes to them engaging in risky and oftentimes illegal behavior. "Nuclear" families living on welfare, food stamps, and WIC checks, may contribute to young folk finding ways of obtaining society's eye-candy (clothes, sneakers, jewelry, money, and other unobtainable items). Young people who live in "rough" neighborhoods or barrios are often subject to ridiculing and disrespect regarding what they are dressed in. The pressure to look a certain way is determined by what society has deemed appropriate for each socioeconomic class. For example, wearing sneakers from *outside* of the store displayed in a heap on a folding table, as opposed to the sneakers *inside* the store on a shelf and vacuum-packed in plastic makes a big difference, one, when shopping for it, and two when they actually make it to one's feet. Rendering one's self as a "have not" is not an excuse for committing crimes, large or small. However, because of the perpetuation of wealth that our society is obsessed with, it is understandable why young people exercise their powers in negative ways, thus exacerbating their oppression.

It has been researched and stated that peers ofthe young person of color who is academically successful see him or her as "acting white." The failing or the secretly achieving person of color can still manipulate his or her way through the culture of fitting in. Further, the young person of color who does achieve, and is believed to "act white," oftentimes shock teachers who do not share the same culture, race, and/or socioeconomic as them. The response, "Wow, you are *so* articulate!" The element of the surprise of the teacher is what is more insulting than the response itself. What is the response for young white boys and girls who achieve or are *so* articulate? What is the response for the young white boys and girls who use music or the adoption of another culture to resist? The response is "s/he's a teenager, and it's only a phase." When does the phase break for the young person of color?

Society is not paying close attention to all of their young. The efforts are too often targeting one particular group of young people, thus making them more open for discrimination, and tokenism. Did no one find the outfits and the behavior of the "Trenchcoat Mafia" suspicious, or at least the slightest bit curious? Did folks just believe that they were exhibiting *their* youth culture? "It's a phase, they'll grow out of it?" Before committing suicide, those boys at Columbine High School killed twelve youths and a teacher. Post-tragedy, the news filled the masses with ideas that the two boys (both white), had been suffering from teenage angst. The two boys had been reported as having suffered from being both introverted and extroverted versions of a psychopath. In New York City and Los Angeles, high schools in particular have already notified some of their teaching staff, and public safety workers about gang detection and gang safety. The gangs they look out for largely in particular are made up of young people of color. High school no longer becomes a place for learning, while morning roll call is replaced by long concert-type lines for metal detection (from head to toe), clear knapsacks that reveal even the most embarrassing of personal belongings (tampons, sanitary napkins, underwear, condoms) and massive amounts of students all attempting to attend school for the day. These youths of color enjoy during their school day "captive lunch" where hundreds upon hundreds of students share marked spaces in a small prison sized cafeteria, with gated windows nearing the ceiling, and where cliques are clearly necessary. With the visibility of metal detectors, and loud, trash-talking teenagers all filing into the same building at the same time, even the shyest of students will be aware that there is an obvious reason for metal detection, and thus feels the need to personally protect him or herself.

In order to get to the prison-like atmosphere of New York City public high schools, young black and Latino/a folk ride New York City public transportation on a daily basis. Together, their joys and pains create a deafening sound of a thousand voices, all excited about their days, and their nights ahead. The girls talk about "cute" boys and other girls who pissed them off, and boys are chatting each other down with quick tips on video games, hip hop artists, music videos, and which girl they have their eyes on. They exhibit a space of behavior that they could not endure alone. The group concept for them must exist for the strength and power in dialogue for a flowing continuity. Police officers watch them carefully. Passengers on the trains and buses watch them carefully. I carefully watch them all watching each other carefully. Young white boys and girls who ride the train "act out" in these ways, similar to black and Latino/a youth, yet no one stares. There are no cops on those trains. Out of all these young mouths, the words "Nigga" escapes, with affection, with venom, and with awesome cluelessness.

Academics, researchers, teachers, and people with the power to label, have decided that these same black and Latino/a youth are a population "at risk" and live in the "inner city." Being born and raised in Hell's Kitchen, New York City, I am still awaiting to see an "inner city" neighborhood. What attracts young minds the most? Risk! It doesn't matter if you are an "inner-city" resident, as young people, we want to *know* exactly what is so *risky* about piercing/tattooing our bodies, drinking beer or forty ounces of malt liquor, smoking marijuana, and engaging in random and barely-familiar sex. How is it that both sets of youth (of color and white) are engaging in this risky behavior, but it is the group of color who remains at risk? The answer cannot simply be based on neighborhood can it? Let's look at the similarities in the following example, and disparity in the analysis. Drinking a beer in a paper bag in broad daylight on the number seven train is okay, but drinking a forty-ounce of malt liquor on a street corner is problematic, and classified as characteristic of the "ghetto." Is it possible, that youth of color can help break their own stereotype? Is it possible that young people of color can have a plan B if engaging in at risk behavior or never leaving the inner-city gives them yet another set of assumptions about their already-made futures? Do young white teenagers not get pregnant? Do young Asian teenagers not have premature sex? Do neither of these groups smoke pot nor drink beer? Do neither of these groups hang out on corners of their barrios? Before answering these questions, let's ask "then what?" after each. Now apply the same questions and "then what?" to the youth of color.

The "at risk" label for white youth is perhaps based on who they interact with. Even this is problematic. Why is a white person who lives with low-socioeconomic black neighbors considered "white trash?" If their socioeconomic status renders them as "trash," what are the folk of color who can't seem to move out of those neighborhoods deemed as? Perhaps, the "at risk" for young white women consists of deadly-diets, anorexia and bulimia,

Mickey Mouse Club stars turned hypersexualized, and which sorority to pledge to. For young white men, the "at risk" could possibly be, which Ivy League will they apply to, where will they go during the summer, and how much they adopt black culture. The concept of at risk is racially reinforced through multiple lenses of the media. Youth, white-, and female-oriented magazines advertise sexual advice, tanning and makeup tips, and offer prom-central specific issues. The one and only one advertisement geared towards the young woman of color, is the advertisement for a "Drug Free America." The advertisement offers a picture of a young black woman who appears to be dejected and depressed, but rather, she adds, "I am my own anti-drug." Not only has she been tokenized, she also is a walking poster woman for the "at risk" black young woman who considers using drugs, as though for most of us, using drugs is a readily available and likely option.

On the homepage of Planned Parenthood Federation of America, Inc.'s Web site, there are about nine small pictures of couples, and families, six of which are people of color. The organization is supported by a famous white male actor (depicted on the Web site). The message is clear. The targets are individuals and families of color, the "voice of reason" is a famous white actor. However, white, black, and Latino/a young girls alike, are claiming that like "Destiny's Child" no one is "ready for their jelly" as well. Both white and girls of color are gaining advice from Christina Milian's *Dip it Low*, with a trendy beat, and soulful singing, she assures listeners that if you: "Dip it low/Pick it up slow/Roll it all around poke it out, like ya back broke/Pop, pop, pop that thang/I'ma show you how to make your man say ooh." Why then is the planning of parenthood a necessity only for young people of color? Aren't both white and girls of color receiving musical messages that engage their minds to sex? Someone has either deliberately or mistakenly forgotten that these kinds of targets are a result of the larger social issue on several levels. Based on Planned Parenthood the known fact that girls of color become teenage mothers more than white girls is a direct correlation between girls of color and how early they begin having sex. However, what are the remedies and opportunities of social access that girls of color are afforded? We cannot hide our single-parented child behind large family homes, white picket fences, or secret ladies clubs. The entire apartment building sees the sixteen-year-old and her pregnant belly, and watches as her mother hangs her head in shame. One can only ask whether or not white girls become teenage mothers, and in cases where the child is not put at some type of risk after birth, what are their options as well?

It is clear. We are not taking the time to understand our young folk, whether of color or white. Neither are we taking them very seriously as a group rather than as a racially divided source of study. Society has helped to create, stereotypes, and stigmas for young people of color, thus leaving them to their own devices, and society's judgments. White students can freely learn, and freely arm themselves with shotguns instead of college applications, because no one is listening, and no one is looking, because no one suspects them of anything. Black and Latino/a students are knowingly and unknowingly playing into a stereotype that holds them responsible for sociological studies and many of society's ills.

While much despair exists among our youth, there are many youth of color that are working towards taking the responsibility to disseminate stereotypes that do not belong to them. While still remaining latch-key kids, heads of households during the day, and sometimes during the evening, youths of color are empowering themselves despite their predisposed maps of plans. For example, my undergraduate students at Baruch College in New York City have learned to negotiate their learning space with me. I have replaced their traditional final exam, which I ruled as a "punishment" to learning, with a hands-on approach to now using what they have learned in my course, and their life experiences to better those who come after them.

We have begun the process of creating various packets and products that lead the youth of color to various aspects of their liberation. These packets are based on an ongoing assignment in which my students are to document their observations of stereotypes that surround black/Latino/a youth. From these observations, students have found ways to concentrate their liberation packets in connection to the stereotypes they have observed. Part of the larger idea within these liberation products, are ways to remedy or refusals of participation in supporting the stereotype. When I teach my students, I teach from what they bring, not from what I have solely designed as necessary knowledge. We engage in each other's histories, so that we are not appropriating anyone else's culture, but rather, we are working together to find ways in checking ourselves, so erroneously no else has to.

Resources
Web Sites
Alvarez, S. (2000). *Body Piercing.* Retrieved September 18, 2005 from http://www.terra.com/specials/bodyart/roots_bp.htm
Cullen, D. (2004, April 20). The Depressive and the Psychopath. *Slate Magazine MSN.* Retrieved September 18, 2005 from http://slate.msn.com/id/2099203/#ContinueArticle
Planned Parenthood Federation of America. Retrieved September 18, 2005 from http://www.plannedparenthood.org/
Sex Bracelets: Your Complete Guide to Sex Bracelets. (2004). Retrieved September 18, 2005 from http://www.sex-bracelets.com
Films
Girlhood. (2004). Fox Lorber.
Thirteen. (2002). 20th Century Fox.
Music
Destiny's Child. (2001). "Bootylicious." *Survivor.*
Christina Milian. (2004). "Dip it Low." *It's About Time.*
Sean Paul. (2003). "Like Glue." *Dutty Rock.*
Tupac. (1998). "Changes." *Greatest Hits.*

Self Reflection

Shakeisha Morris

You just bought your new Rolls Royce
When I just had to make a choice
Between groceries and rent
And I just spent my last twenty-
five cents on a bag of chips
Now I gotta go borrow some money
Yeah that's what you got and I'm not
Mad at you but you got dough and I don't
See why I can't go out and get a decent job
My last resort is now to rob
A playa like you
Maybe I'm just a fool
for wanting what you got
but maybe if I stop
Hatin' on you and just drop
Everything that I'm doing and plan for a better tomorrow
Cause who do I think I'm fooling?
I'm livin' in a world of sorrow
Pain and poverty in this society
But how I'm livin'
Is what I'm choosin'
I'm waiting for a brighter day to come
But for now I'm on my way to church
Cause I need to be saved some.

Fashion, Brands, and Logos

Birgit Richard

VARIETY WITHOUT SUBSTANCE? TENDENCIES IN YOUTH FASHION

It is becoming increasingly difficult for the adult or post-adolescent observer to find adolescent styles, in a rapidly changing world of fashion, that are uniformly designed. Since the end of the 1980s, we therefore talk about an inflation of styles. In youth cultures, all stylistic means are released by punk, analogous to dada in the fine arts. It creates a *tabula rasa* for the future utilization of stylistic elements and crosses all borders that hitherto existed in the field of youth cultures. The climax of this utilization is reached in the post-Punk-era, when the discovery of this style makes the accessories available in department stores with only a minimum of delay. A loss of substance on the level of content leads to a loss of parts of the identity-shaping power of quite a number of the new styles. However, only rapid change provides the chance of dissociation from the adult world. The inter-locking of styles makes it more difficult to assign particular categories and, therefore, to merchandise individual styles. Youth cultures have since been permanently running from market mechanisms getting a grip on the style increasingly fast and becoming ever more subtle, and from the transforma-tion of their stylistic elements into an "adult" form, serving the purpose of preserving the imaginary image of a youthful appearance.

The disappearance of stylistic extremes has to be similarly taken note of. They enable the observer to detect and assign punk extremely fast. The process of dissociation of adolescents today can be observed in small sty-listic, but no less meaningful deviations. With some delay, analogous to the fine arts, the inefficiency of avant-garde strategies of shock and prov-ocation, later inherited by the haute couture in the 1990s, is shown. The exhibits of the exhibition "Avantgarderobe" allow us to follow the devel-opment of these spectacular, almost purposeless forms having ended up in the haute couture, for example. *Comme des Garçons*, during the course of the century.

For contemporary youth cultures a policy of differences, of small differ-ences, is decisive. We should oppose researchers studying youth cultures and journalists who diagnose an arbitrary aestheticism and eclecticism in the incoming postmodern era, and proclaim the result that clothes no longer convey a meaning. This approach shows the hysteria of adults, sup-ported by the media, who, in contrast to the adolescents, can no longer find an organizing pattern in the confusion of styles.

Punk is the youth culture that initiates the development of today's variety of styles. From this point on, there is no longer any predominating youth culture like there was in the 1950s, 1960s, and even in the 1970s, but a simultaneous pluralism of styles. Punk turns the counterpart of youth cultures to the collage, the bricolage, by the combination of set pieces of the most important postwar youth cultures with profane items of ordinary life, appearing here as segments of styles of a new quality, into a new extreme manifestation. The chronological order of youth cultures is muddled up.

Older styles like punk, Goth, skinheads, or heavy metal have today become fixed classic youth and adolescent cultures, which have a permanent place in the spectrum of styles. Variants on styles in these systems have developed: "Gothic punks" or "Grufties" (the German term), skater-punks, and surf-punks or wavers. In addition, the number of designations for stylistic variants of core areas of youth cultures has increased out of proportion: at the beginning of the 1990s we find, among others, rave from Manchester, a new psychedelic movement; the crusties as a form of music of the new age Travellers, and the grunge. At the end of the 1980s there are the New Beat, Electronic Body Music, and in the mid-1980s, hip hop and the U.S. house scene. In the 1990s we detect an increase of popular movements of dance music in particular: acid house, house, techno, ambient, hardtrance, breakbeats, gabber techno, drum+bass, triphop, bigbeat, ragga, downtempo, illbient, to call to mind just a few. Among these musical-organizing terms, no longer do all of them have counterparts in an independent image of style and fashion elements that can be directly assigned.

STYLE-LOOPS: TIME-LOOPS IN FASHION

The 1980s and 1990s are characterized by an appearance of styles of revival. There is now the opportunity to live an historical style of youth culture as an aesthetic quotation. Punk reanimates the styles of the 1950s, teds or rockabillies. At the end of the 1980s, the 1960s (sixties, neo-hippies) are reanimated and at the beginning of the 1990s there is a revival of styles of the 1970s and neo-punk. The contemporary revival of the 1980s, which can be observed at the end of the 1990s, creates a revival-loop: punk already is a combination of revival-elements of the 1950s and contemporary attributes of fashion, so that now a dual time-loop is created.

Three forms of recollection can be found among contemporary youth cultures: retro, old school, and revival. We have to differentiate between a transformation of stylistic elements and a reanimation of a historical atmosphere that does not take the contents of the historical style into consideration and does not reactivate it either.

Retro is the imitation of elements or complete sets of clothing of centuries past, a nostalgic looking back on times past. Revival already etymologically comprises the dimension of updating. Style and stylistic features are not supposed to be preserved, but are open for change. A vivid revival takes place when contemporary tailoring patterns are combined with original fabrics, or vice versa.

In contrast to the modeling of the past mentioned above, the so-called old-school-phenomenon, first appearing with hip hop as well as techno, shows a completely new form of self-referential recollection: reverting to the original forms gone now becomes an internal process of the style and demonstrates the possibility of an autopoiesis of systems of youth cultures. This preservation of old elements of the style and their incalculable revitalization outstrips and eludes economic exploitation and selectively creates an autonomous economic cycle between scene-boutique and flea market.

CONSUMER-GUERILLA AND "ADBUSTING"

The history of the youth cultures in the postwar period starts with the development of youth-specific commercial structures. "Teenager" is the target-group of new consumer goods, tailor-made for their hedonistic needs. Basically, any youth culture is since determined by a certain kind of participation in consumer society, as is demonstrated by Hebdige in his analyses, which are supported by Willis's concept of the profane or common culture.

Youth cultures predominantly are consumer communities, which create important stylistic elements by making a fetish of particular goods. The profane goods do not primarily get their meaning from their representationalism, but from a selection during the act of consumption and the subsequent symbolic transformation of the raw material commercially available, which muddles up the ordinary regular order of goods and the business cycle. Adolescents, by their deliberate misuse, create new stylistic elements in music and fashion. These first have to be recognized as being essential. Then it is taken up as an existing trend by the cultural industry, which processes it for a mass consumption as expansive as possible. At this moment, a scene draws the line between authenticity and commercial plagiarism.

The material products of youth cultures implement structures of communication of a new quality into the landscape of consumption. For example, the respective scene-shops are no anonymous temples of consumption, but have the whole cosmos of the style on offer. Where you buy your records, there often is a DJ, putting records on. In comparison with the huge superstores for consumer electronics, the record-shops of the scene rather resemble a corner-shop and serve the purpose of listening to music, exchanging information and, of course, selling goods.

The youth cultures of the 1990s and beyond necessitate a new definition of the relationship between authenticity and commercialism. However, it is not sufficient to say goodbye to the term "subculture" that stands for criticism of consumption, as it is done by Baacke/Ferchhoff or Türck. Genesis and commercial spreading of youth and subculture are no longer linked in a hierarchical, multistage cycle of development, being taken over, manipulation and end of the style. The coexistence of subversion and commercialism is predominantly caused by the rapidly fast-spreading and the instantaneous development of variants of styles. Techno culture and hip hop scenes represent examples of a new structuring: for the first time in the history of youth cultures, they demonstrate simultaneity between the avant-garde underground and the broad mainstream parts.

Furthermore, a large part of the youth cultures in the 1990s no longer evades commercial pressure, but uses brands and signets as stylistic elements for working on and with symbolism. The adolescents of the 1990s apply the new strategy of a "consumer-guerilla," a free playing around with various brands. The overemphasis on consumption, hyperconsumption, is a different form of dealing with society. Three different forms of handling consumer goods can be detected in contemporary youth cultures:

1. Hyperconsumption by adolescents is a mirror-image of a society with a fixation about consumption. If we assume that adolescent styles always reflect certain dark sides of a society, they are the reflection, carried to extremes, of a parental generation lusting after consumption and, for example, voluntarily submitting to social constraints forcing them to buy a new luxury car every two years. It is a symbol for an overindividualization triggered by the market-economy, a power of the segments of the market.
2. Hyperconsumption serves the purpose of a defiant strategy of dissociation from those parts of the parental generation that try to live more consciously and closer to nature and to waste no resources. With unquestioned excessive consumption adolescents are able to disconcert even liberal and understanding parents.
3. Hyperconsumption becomes a targeted subversive act at a moment, when the scene and the designers of the scene playfully appropriate signets of others and are sued by companies like Shell or Telekom. Owing to the opportunities offered by modern lay-out programs, this redesign is unproblematic. This so-called "adbusting" points to the fact, that the cultural industry has secured the rights to putatively public symbols and emblems. Strategies like "adbusting" are directed against the generation that tries to cast in concrete its ideals of a protest movement. They oppose a culture of discourse verbally orientated.

The descriptions above referred to the fact that the traditional confrontation of youth cultures with the cultural industry is a thing of the past. However, this does not mean that they live in unison with contemporary social formations. The openly shown opposition to a world of consumption no longer can be found among a large part of youth cultures, since it is pointless to try to escape from commercial demands on these scenes and from trend scouts of industry. None of the existing youth cultures is still a protest culture critical of consumption, like they were found in the 1960s and are still taken as a benchmark. Since styles always react to a particular time, other ways of handling consumer goods have developed. A targeted consideration with the means of an immanent analysis of the aesthetics of contemporary youth fashions will also reveal an (unconscious) social content.

Talking about the disappearance of independent youth cultures consciously overlooks the temporary autonomous zones, which have developed, for example, by the reappearance of vinyl-records in the techno, house, and hip hop scenes, the foundation of small record labels and self-operated record shops, the production of collections of clothes for the scene, and the use of data-standards for music such as MP3s. Aesthetics, music and dance-style continually selectively create niches for adolescent strategies of dissociation. Regardless of the negative moulding of the symbolic raw materials for the development of the styles by the consumer industry in the 1990s, characterized by the immediate adoption of ideas of the scene, it should not be forgotten that it becomes increasingly important that the market-segments should be defined from the perspective of the consumer. Especially in regard to clothing, a sense for the needs and demands of a scene is essential. The "Adidas old school" trend, which suddenly reanimated old synthetic track suits of the 1970s and was passed on to the ravers, after the track suits had been retrieved from wardrobes of the parents and from flea markets by the hip hop scene, could not have been predicted by any marketing strategist.

A forgotten element of ordinary culture is discovered by the adolescents, gets a symbolic meaning, and becomes an important stylistic element. The stylistic segment therefore develops within the youth culture itself. Only then can manufacturers of sports-items pursue a follow-up by, for example, offering the old sports-shoe design from the 1970s as a re-edition.

HYSTERICAL PRODUCTION

Youth cultures face a harsher economic practice of fashion consumption, production, and marketing, with an ever-decreasing half-life of representationalism. The short periods of production permit an immediate reaction to detectable trends. Especially in the field of clubwear and streetwear, the seasonal four-stage process and a long period of preliminary planning can be done away with. Aided by computers, even small businesses are able to produce in-production-cycles of 6–8 weeks.

The digitalization and individualization of fashion leads to a metastatic variety of colors, symbols, shapes, and unusual high-tech fabrics, which requires an ever-increasing competence of selection by the consumer. The confusion of the complete range of fashion on offer turns the brand into a point of reference. Even with items of the scenes of youth cultures, the surplus is so great that the scenes themselves lose track. To create a cult-brand of clothing and to be able to preserve it becomes increasingly difficult. This also applies to items of clothing which, two decades ago, were represented with one model per brand and were almost never subject to a change in fashion: gym-shoes. Besides a wide varietal range of forms of "sneakers," the market is determined by permanently changing collections and regionally differing models.

The permanent change and the loss of orientation among the variety of product-variants is counteracted by classic products, such as the Levis 501 among jeans. However, these also lose their function as points of reference, when adolescent consumers prefer new forms of multi-functional work-pants. The so-called chino or cargo pants have outstripped the classic pair of jeans. Levis reacts with new models like the creased Levis Sta Prest.

The permanent making of a fetish into representationalism, and the continuous transfer of objects into cult-objects leads to the pulping of the cult and to the privatisation of the symbols. A devaluation takes place, from the cult of the profane to the cult of the mass-fetish, easily replaceable.

In the field of clubwear and streetwear, even a half-life of brands of half a year or a year is rather short. Therefore, fashion/clothing is increasingly detached from contexts of a particular stylistic set. The devaluation makes stylistic elements nomadic. In a short time they wander from youth culture to youth culture, after having been brought on the market. Nevertheless, the starting-point of stylistic elements determined by brands can always be detected, since the brand represents a network of meanings that has to suit the style, or otherwise it calls for a different design.

ARCHAEOLOGY OF THE NOMADIC: TRANSITIVENESS

Youth cultures have developed a special system of dealing with the transitiveness of their stylistic elements by feeding them back into the business cycle. This protects youth fashion from final decay and reduces the business cycle of fashion to a bearable and clear term. It also attempts to circumvent the commercial standard-terms of the business cycle for elements of fashion. Youth fashions both accelerate and slow down the business cycle for fashion. The half-life of fashion vanishes with the interconnection with digital media. It decreases corresponding to the half-life of computer systems and software solutions. The reproducibility and creation of variants by pressing a button contradicts a potential perpetuity of a product. It is replaced sooner, has a shorter life span, but there is a certain probability that it will re-enter the system.

An adult strategy to deal with the transitiveness of the individual is to let the exterior, the clothing, grow older instead of the individual itself. At the surface, clothes appear increasingly older, the human body increasingly younger. Pre-aged or pre-used clothes have the function of providing relief and offer a projection surface for the processes of ageing and dying. The stage-managed used character suggests being alive by hinting at an individual history and infinity, qualities missing in items of clothes. In a magic ritual, the liberation of the body from the process of ageing takes place in the symbolic act of getting dressed, transferring transitivenss to a simulated process of ageing on the exterior. In the end, the exterior is more alive, more active, and more intelligent than those who wear it. The individual gets choked, so to speak, by its young exterior, feigning age.

Fashion photography represents another facet of this tendency with "Heroin Death" and "Handicapped Chic." It demonstrates that it is better to have an artificial exterior take over the role of director, as, for example, in the photographs of Ines von Lamsweerde, by offering insights into the depth of the corporeal which has not been technologically arranged and digitally processed. It opens up the exterior of pretension, tears the smooth surfaces, and reveals embarrassing, "puny," anorexic bodies, which no one really wants to see the way they are shown. There is only one solution to overcome the pure horror of the misshapen body: a suitable brand of clothes.

Disabilities and physical deficiencies bear witness to the generally damaged corporeal, additionally ennobled by clothes. The frailness of the body becomes visible by contrasting it with the perpetuity of the brand. Labelling the brand on bodies, for example, Versace on Kristen McMenamy's body, relies on the transcendence of the brand's name. For the insecure, adolescent bodies it is an opportunity to follow this putatively safe way by labeling brands on their bodies. In general, the fixation about a robust brand in youth cultures has other motivations as well. Here, print-campaigns for youth-specific products stress the perpetuity and infinity of particular brands and fabrics. The product and the brand survive the individual (Eastpak or Doc Martens advertising), which long since has become a victim of circumstances. The durability of the brand is stage-managed to emphasize the inferiority and frailness of the human body against the background of the fabrics produced by humans. These print-campaigns are tailor-made for adolescents, since they have not yet become a victim of the panic-stricken fear of ageing and death. They trust their own body in combination with a product offering security beyond death. The extreme durability of the items represents the chance to live an extreme life-style in using them; carried to its extremes with the motto "live fast, die young." The durability of the material also qualifies the object as a solid stylistic element.

The fashion of youth cultures is per se directed towards a perpetuity of its stylistic elements, since these serve the consolidation of the style. The discarded stylistic elements then circulate in the basic equipment storage room of the cosmos of youth cultures and await their rediscovery.

ARCHAEOLOGY OF THE NOMADIC: ARCHIVING

Even though it seems absurd, the efforts to preserve ephemeral fashion, especially by styles of youth culture that exert a great influence on the media, design, fashion, and the arts of society as a whole, are no futile or pointless endeavour. A small, exemplary part of the cultural history of ordinary life is thus recorded. Theoretics of art and design theory/education do not give a lot of attention to this, although it puts at their disposal essential explanatory patterns for the genesis of contemporary forms. A collection serves the recon-structing, archaeological examination of alien cultures within one's own and tries to comprehend and appreciate cultural practices of youth cultures. The alien area within one's own culture is not assimilated, but its fashion and aesthetics are perceived as meaningful phenomena, bearing witness to the creativity of adolescents in handling consumer goods.

The collection of fashion puts the part of ordinary culture, which plays an important role for children and adolescents, at the observer's disposal. On the basis of having concrete material ready, an immanent analysis of the design of fashion and products can be pursued and social references can be filtered out. The results gained are then disseminated via the medium techno-kit, the archive, and later via a virtual counterpart on the Internet.

The interaction between the social systems aesthetics of ordinary life, arts, and design should be observed to increase our ability to find out whether there is an aesthetic expansion of forms of communication in youth cultures, and how these might penetrate other systems and get trans-formed there. The interaction between systems of fashion demonstrates that unconditional excitement about or the fervent hope for youth cultures changing society in a major way are as unsuitable as the prejudice that these are herds shepherded and steered by the cultural industry.

The collection of objects of various youth cultures is a conflicting process, as it shows that a closed stylistic image is a construct. Styles of youth cultures are processes with meaningful selective accumulations of objects, and a phase of relatively closed autopoetic reproduction of the stylistic elements of communication. This is the starting-point of the material Jugendkultur-Archiv in Frankfurt, which was launched by myself. It collects youth fash-ions (punk, Gothic punk, hip hop, disco, techno, house, drum+bass, ambient, trip hop, acid, hardtrance, gabber, bigbeat . . .), and objects such as maga-zines and flyers, and attempts to preserve a segment of the world of products of adolescents, especially of what, in the 1990s, is called clubwear and streetwear. With the help of the artificial intervention of an archive, which freezes the ephemeral, we can demonstrate that all elements of the cosmos of youth cultures are of a nomadic nature and continually at the disposal of the internal communication. They can always be re-infused into the cycle of sty-listic elements by medial processes like zapping, switching, and surfing, the nonlinear combination of images and objects. Thereby, the special usage of media by youth cultures and their public relations activities are taken into consideration as well.

The archiving of these objects has to follow the "flow" of things, which means, it has to be continuously in motion. Thus, the ideal extension of an archive dealing with youth fashions is its virtual counterpart on the Internet. The material, "having at hand" basis, however, remains essential for the anal-ysis of design-forms of youth cultures. The virtual "Jugendkulturarchiv" also picks out the role of the media in geographical transfer-processes of styles, for example between the United States and Europe. Today's styles in Europe are a manifestation of a western affluent culture and its handling of consumer goods. The fact, that style re-interprets stigmas developing in a context of poverty and repression into symbols of a positive identity and, therefore, after the geographical transfer, conveys connotations like autonomy, is neglected by the standardized complaint about the loss of substance and the faith in brands of contemporary youth cultures. The expectation in regard to stylistic principles of youth cultures thus reads: the contemporary youth cultures shall realize a particular attitude supposed to be authentic. For earlier generations, authenticity only comes along with poverty and ghetto or physical or verbal rebellion. This paradoxical demand overlooks that style is not created by deprivation itself, but by a detachment from the relevant living conditions taking the form of parody, like the "playing the dozens" strategy of the black communities.

BRAND-LABEL-LOGO

The visual manifestation of the brand in the so-called logo determines the design of the whole item of clothing, which, as a paraphrase of the brand, becomes an icon and therefore a carrier of information contained in images. The representation of the self increasingly focuses on labeled and iconized surfaces. The transfer of graffiti-strokes from "driving walls" on subway-trains onto clothes is an outstanding example. The strokes do not show any legible writings, but a pure picture. The imprint, as a means of surface-design, renders the cut as a form of shaping, depth unimportant. Veiling and unveiling of the body is a kind of self-wrapping. Just as on the surfaces of products, character-branding takes place (e.g., comic strip heroes on food-packaging).

The neutral standard-forms of items of clothing, the so-called basics (T-shirts, sweat-shirts), can be used as carriers or a matrix for picture or written information. Their smooth surfaces show no disturbing elements like buttons.

The visual variations of the brand and the labels on the inside and outside of clothes become the dominating feature of design, determined by graphical design in the mid-1990s, and alongside the back and front of clothes, the sleeves get imprints as well. Clothes get painted and labeled and become an "all over painting," analogous to tattoos which also cover the whole body.

As late as the 1970s, it is rare to find an item of clothing characterized by a visible trademark, imprints, or embroidering. A preliminary stage to branding is do-it-yourself letters to iron on. Only in the 1980s do we see the T-shirt-print. In youth cultures, it first appears in the form of fan or tour T-shirts. These show the admired stars and are exclusively available at concerts. Labelling, characters, cartoon characters, faces of rock stars, or their logos become important set pieces of design.

The surface makes the self-assignment of the individual fairly easy, since it can be expressed rather explicitly by strokes or images. However, it requires an increasing competence of differentiation in the observer. In the contemporary youth cultures, the deciphering and assignment of the visual emblems alone lead to expertise and the status of an insider. The design of the surface has to be divided into the brand and its visualization, the brandmark or logo, and the label. The latter today requires its own line of design, label design, since the inside of clothes and the signs attached become surfaces for articulation as well. While the labels placed in the inside of clothes are supposed to serve the security aspect and shall avoid plagiarism and faking and lead to extremely complex systems comparable to bank notes (e.g. Diesel jeans are numbered), the outer label is a surface for communication additionally attached. Therefore, this form of labeling simultaneously serves the purposes of security and recognition. Especially in the 1990s, we observe a logo-overkill, when all possible places in and on the clothes, and all separate parts like buttons, zippers, and capes bear a trademark.

A logo is partially a self-referential phenomenon, entirely serving a corporate identity. It condenses the meaning of the brand and the company producing it, and owes its existence to its visual stimulus. The function of the logo is representation, not discussion. However, only at first glance does the logo function as an unambiguous significant-significant-chain. Here, it is essential that the visual variation of the brand lets the brand's distinctive features remain visible; the design should not change the brand in a way that might make it unrecognizable. Behind any logo in youth cultures we find a secondary complex reference-system, which requires an examination of the style to be able to assign it correctly. There rarely are "mono" logos; companies either alter their brands/trademarks or there are various basic visual designs in the first place, which get varied (an example is the brand Stüssy, which uses two different strokes, or Homeboy). The creation of variants on styles of youth cultures does also lead to a creation of variants on brands in so-called "sub-labels" to be able to reach the greatest number of styles with one brand, but also to offer each individual style its own visual manifestation. However, sub-labels and small segments of the market are much sooner forgotten than monolithically constructed brands.

The processes of youth cultures question the visual permanence of brand trademarks. Variants are not allowed by the classic trademarks for legal reasons. The corporate identity needs the inalterability of the trademark, for instance an alteration of the star of Mercedes is unthinkable. Logos are general symbols of social acceleration. The contraction and combination of language and image results in icons, emoticons, strokes, and initials or pictograms in immediately perceptible visual condensations. The shifting and visual processing of logos and trademarks in youth cultures refers to the occupation of language and images by the cultural industry, both in the public and the private sphere. Youth cultures, by the means of alteration of designs and illegal appropriation, achieve a partial re-occupation of occupied spheres of language and images.

CONCLUSION

In the United States of America, logo-culture and brand plagiarism convey another message than in Europe, where youth cultures counteract the "hippie-jabbering" of their parental generation by a soundless logo-culture. This represents a culture of denial and disobedience, withdrawing from the spoken language. The heated talk about a youth culture in denial of protest shows that the objective of dissociation from the adult world was attained.

Playing around with brands and logos is meaningful, too. The youth cultures neither stick to internal borders between the styles, nor to genres of fashion like sport and work wear, and thus circumvent the purity of brands and ideologically motivated brand-policies. The extremely condensed design of trademarks is not only an economic end in itself, but represents a complete lack of references. As everywhere, the brand of course indicates the manufacturer.

On a secondary level it is then assigned to a particular life-style, thereby becoming meaningful. Here the shifting by youth cultures sets in from milieu such as sailing (Helly Hansen) or surfing (Stüssy) to the hip hop and house scenes. Cult-brands like Stüssy create an ideology of brands which relies on a cut down of resources, for example using only selected dealers who are licensed, a myth of development linked to a famous athlete, and a limited clientele. An expropriation that contradicts the brand's philosophy is frowned upon: Stüssy's brand-policy exclusively targets the hip hop community and people associated with surfing, despite advertisements in techno and house magazines. Another case of "misuse" is the expropriation of collections by Tommy Hilfiger, who with his racist orientation would rather prohibit the black community from wearing his clothes. Both cases make the brand, which the scene's eyes are set on, even more attractive and thus paradoxically boost sales again, so that this could also be considered part of the marketing strategy.

RETRO

Heike Jenß

Retro is regarded as one of the most important stylistic features of postmodern fashion. As a cultural phenomenon retro-looks are not only limited to dress, but they appear in all other design forms such as cars or furniture, as well as in music, film, and even in food. Up to this point, numerous writings have been dedicated to the implications of retro. However, most interpretations remain on a level that generalizes the *meaning* of retro as either a sign of a specifically postmodern "anything goes" attitude, or as a symptom of a nostalgic yearning for the past. Even if there are approaches that situate retro in the context of a changing perception of history that is no longer linear but more mosaic-like—in accordance to the continuous representation of histories in film and new media—nostalgia theory has repeatedly gained in actuality: Fashion magazines have been applauding the designer collections for fall/winter 2003 that embrace the fashions of the 1960s or the more recent 1980s—decades which are retrospectively seen through rose-colored glasses as better and more innocent times that people are yearning for in order to recover from the trauma caused by 9/11.

Is it really the fear of future insecurities that particularly younger people engage while playing with fashion time? What is so appealing about retro—and what impact does retro actually have in the context of body and dress practices? By drawing on the history of retro in fashion and youth cultural appropriation, this essay will be outlining some of the meanings that have been ascribed to the use and consumption of historic styles. Thus it will show that what is celebrated in the fashion press as brand-new retro, linked with an actual retro-mood in society, has been a constant in fashion and youth cultural style practices for some time, following less of a "yearning for yesterday" than a longing for the unique and different. Before turning to histories and meanings, however, I will first focus on the term "retro" itself and how it relates to the connection of dress and time.

RETRO IN DRESS

Considering the many articles dealing with retro that can be found in magazines, fashion books, or theoretical publications, it can be said that there are actually very heterogeneous understandings of what "retro" is. This is because retro is used as an all-encompassing catch-word, applied to a phenomenon which is actually very differentiated in itself: Depending on the complete style and analogues to its various appearances, ranging from real old, fake old, respectively "authentic reproduction," historic style mix, concentration on historic key-elements, or the transformation of old forms via new materials,—what is called "retro" can have multiple facets and effects. Birgit Richard defines retro as an unchanged, nostalgic recourse to historic elements, an opposite to revival, which etymologically indicates a dimension of change. O'Hara Callan's dictionary of fashion lists retro as a word "used to describe clothing from a previous era, usually at least twenty years earlier. […] These clothes though revisionist in attitude, are remade to work with current looks . . ." Having come into more frequent use during the 1990s and perceived as an established fashionable term now that is also applied to new retro editions, the term can now no longer be restricted to the meaning of either "original" or "copy."

The word "retro" is of Latin origin and means "back" or "backwards." Used or understood as short form for retrospective or "retro-look," it hints to the impact it has in dress: A retro-look is produced by engaging in and "looking back" at fashion history, using old forms as models. At the same time the "retro-look" in dress itself visualizes and presents a look to—or from—the past. When worn and completed as an appearance, it can signify the body as "anachronistic," generating memories or subtle associations with images from the past, playing on the potential of dress as a cultural signal of time and a component of cultural memory.

Dress and fashion are in many ways directly linked with our category and conception of time. As a time-sign, a garment can indicate when it was made and worn, and the duration and passing of time, hence its decay and fashionable temporality. For Christopher Breward fashion is a cultural clock ticking with the rhythm of the industrialized order of production, distribution, promotion, consumption, and eventually transience, which it aims to erase in each new season. Dress becomes obsolete by going out of fashion, therefore it has to distance itself from its most recent past, working against the immediately remindable time, and pushing away the boredom of the old with the new looks. Categorized and put in the order of a chronological structure, material survivals and images of fashion history then become "dated" and regimented by our conception of time. Already the recognition of a few single elements of dress seems to be enough to conceive an object's entire context, subsuming the most diverse fashions of an era or decade under a sequential time-unit. Recognizing and perceiving past dress forms in the everyday practice of fashion as "very fifties" or "so eighties-like," corresponds to the chronological measurement and order of dress according to "decade-labels," which have become a feature of dress just like fabric and color.

However, this feature can only be perceived as a materialized retrospective and allusion to the past if it is recognized as such by the present time. This means that particularly young people who have not biographically experienced the decades appropriated through contemporary retro-looks, such as the 1960s or 1970s, need to be familiar with these time-signs. As a side-effect, media such as film, photography, and Internet images, play a key role in the education and mediation of a fashion-historic consciousness and knowledge. To speak of Walter Benjamin, in the age of technical reproduction the reproduced is detached from tradition and the passing of time and can always become actualized. Thus, dressed bodies become eternally available via pictorial representations, and can inspire retro-appearances as well as enable their decoding. This is one reason why retro is regarded as a particular postmodern phenomenon that is closely allied with the development of information technology and images.

RETRO IN RETROSPECTIVE

When we look back at the history of dress, we find that "retro" is, however, not a new or particular postmodern phenomenon. As one study shows, the revival or use of historic dress styles can be dated back at least to the 16th century, even though in the early days they were mainly restricted to courtly festivities and masquerades. In fashionable dress, however, the most prominent of earlier revivals is certainly the idealization of antiquity around 1800, expressed in the *mode a la greque* that was stimulated through the archaeological finds of Pompeii and Herculaneum in 1738. Based on an increasing interest and a wider accessibility of history and historical artifacts as inspirational sources during the course of the following century, attempts towards a replay of historic forms culminated in a real obsession with the past.

These recourses to fashion history were also linked with the political. What Eric Hobsbawn calls the "invention of tradition" as evident in the use of civil uniforms based on 18th century aristocratic dress, used at European courts, was not only restricted to the Old World. Cynthia Cooper has shown in her study of fancy dress balls held by Canada's Governors' General, that the engagement in historic dress modes was also highly popular among the Victorians in the New World. For a big historical fancy dress ball held in Ottawa in 1896, guests dressed up in costumes representing the 800 years of Canadian history. The effect of this ball was a thrilling historical mosaic showing all the figures of Canada's past from the Norsemen onwards, enthusiastically performed by the cream of Ottawa's society. During a period of political crisis and polarization in French and English Canadian relations, these historical balls served as an historic-cultural education and fostered care for this nation's roots.

But beyond events such as masquerades or courtly rituals, 19th century fashion was infiltrated with historical references. The middle-ages and the renaissance, en vogue in literature, theater, and decorative arts were highly influencing. It was also in this context that particularly younger people and artists associated with Romanticism, started to incorporate former dress modes in their wardrobes. Sir Walter Scott was well-known for his enthusiasm for historic dress and presented, together with Lord Byron, an important role model for European youth from 1815 to 1840. In France it was nineteen-year-old Theophile Gautier who rejected the "grayish" conformism of bourgeois dress, cultivating a more "picturesque" archaic aesthetic in dress. The dress of the young Romantics was historically based. The young Romantics' style-mix, as described in Gautier's book *Les Jeunes France*, published in 1833, resemble very much the style practices usually associated with contemporary style sampling. However, rooted in the context of 19th century Romanticism, these historic references in appearance were also linked with the concept of originality, individualism, and anticonformism, which became a key idea associated with the use of anachronistic dress that can be traced to the context of contemporary retro-practices, too.

Compared to these early examples of "retro," the appropriation of dress history today nonetheless has a different quality. Changes in the production, distribution, and consumption of dress have made clothing available on a far broader level, leading to an ever more increasing amount of surplus goods that may enter into a second circle of consumption. Even though there are many examples of revisiting the more distant past in contemporary fashion design, and haute couture particularly, as Vivienne Westwood or John Galliano show, we witness in youth culture an interest in the fashion of the more recent past that is actually more accessible through this discarded clothing.

Therefore, not only is the visual databank of fashion and youth cultural styles made up through photographs and movies that stimulate retro-styles, the engagement with dress history might develop also on a concrete material or "touch level": through the wardrobes of parents, secondhand shops, jumble sales, and last but not least through newly produced retro-garments. So compared to earlier examples of using historical dress, which were still very much confined to the upper social classes or elitist circles such as artists, retro-styles are now components of a lot of young people's everyday clothing practice, though particularly among the middle-classes.

Many fashion brands aimed at young consumers, such as Diesel, Levis, or H & M include retro-lines in their collections. And companies such as Adidas or Puma react precisely to the demand for the real thing among the young and hip, by relaunching a collection of their own "originals," charged with (branded) history. However, the ongoing attraction of retro-looks among young people and their interlinked practices of self-fashioning and consumption cannot simply be explained in terms of market strategies or techniques imposed from above in a trickle-down process. Rather on the contrary, as will be shown, retro-looks must be seen in the broader context of the secondhand market as an alternative to the established market of first-circle consumption. Hence the next sections will outline an overview of retro-styles among youth subcultures and their culmination and as retro-scenes and youth cultural constants.

YOUTH RUMMAGING THROUGH HISTORY

With the Neo-Edwardians or Teddy Boys, examples of historic references among youth cultures can be traced back to the very beginnings of postwar youth culture. The retro-style of the Neo-Edwardians, was a mix of styles. Modeled on "Teddy," Edward VII, in the context of post-war culture the style was reminiscent of British elite culture. At the same time the style was also highly subversive, presenting a bricolage of classes. The look consisted of the characterizing long "drape" overcoat with velvet collar and cuffs, combined with waistcoat, drainpipe trousers, and crepe-soled shoes. The clothes had been made-to-measure, though in the beginning, cast-offs had also been used and skillfully adapted to the look. Apparently women did not participate in this style; this might be due to the restricted opportunities for girls to participate in youth street culture at that time. However, a prominent example for revivalism in female fashion is certainly Dior's hourglass-shaped "New Look," launched in 1947, that determined fashion throughout the 1950s.

However, in America the young beats were already using old clothes as a way to avoid the world of mass produced, ready-made clothing. Young women were buying fur coats, satin dresses, and silk-blouses that survived from the 1930s and 1940s. In the context of the mid-1950s they subverted not only categories of taste but also gender conceptions.

The mods, which were to become a mass phenomenon by 1964, dismissed in the beginning any obvious historic references. They wanted to be and look "modern." Although here too, it can be observed that the idea of modernity was linked with references to the past, namely the 1920s. The bob reappeared in the numerous variances designed by Vidal Sassoon. And in fact, the entire body shape produced by the mini, as the most prominent fashion invention of the 1960s, combined with flat shoes and a slim bodyline focusing on the legs, can be seen as a tribute to the 1920s. That era presented an early model for women's emancipation and for the idealization of youth, which were to become a leitmotif during the 1960s. However, the apparently supermodern fashions based on pop-art or influenced by the high-tech materials and geometric shapes of the space-age were also eventually a revival, influenced by futurism in art, utopian literature, and early science-fiction cartoons. The futuristic retro-looks in fashion were followed again by the incorporation of elements from the 19th century, now the flamboyant Regency style associated with the "Peacock Revolution." Colorful shirts with frills in the front and on the cuffs, Paisley patterns, short coats with high collars, as well as long hair, hinted already to the style of the psychedelics and hippies, who formed into a counterculture by 1966.

Although the secondhand market is not at all an invention of the postwar period, but has in fact a long tradition, the development of retro, as it is popular among young people today, must be linked with changes in the evaluation and consumption of used dress that evolved during the decade of the 1960s. The hippies' use of thrift shops and finally their professionalization as subcultural entrepreneurs certainly had the most important impact on the establishment of the secondhand market as an alternative source for fashion. The charity shops which were a new source of income for welfare organizations provided another particularly interesting and cheap source to create new styles by using outmoded fashions. Boutiques, aimed at the young consumer and incorporating historic pieces of clothing, like old military uniforms, were soon to follow. Acquiring original items on flea markets and jumble sales began to turn into an established pastime and eventually attracted also the middle classes as customers.

Among the young the wearing of old clothes was intended as an anti-establishment comment, a reaction to the new throw-away attitude that came along with the explosion of mass-produced clothing in the 1960s. However, the parental generation who had experienced need during the war was disgusted by this reuse of old garments. This was due to the fact that they had been worn by "other people," showing traces of wear such as sweat or holes. Perceived as "trash" and "rags" that others no longer want, secondhand clothing had the touch of poverty. However, instead of marking an alliance with the genuinely poor, who really depended on handed-down garments, the hippies' "dressing down" has been interpreted as an "act of unintended class condescension." Thus anachronistic dress was again linked with the rather elitist idea of originality and individuality that was also part of the aforementioned Romantics' use of historical dress styles.

The entrepreneurial structures in the context of the alternative second-hand fashion market developed even further within the context of punk culture during the 1970s and 1980s. The do-it-yourself aesthetic of the punk style relied heavily on the incorporation of discarded items of dress. Impulses for style bricolage were provided by material culture as well as by the exploding world of imagery. Youth could not only refer back to "history" through media, but it could self-referentially refer back to specific youth subcultural styles, hence referring to its own history.

Paul Weller, who was back then singer in the punk influenced band "The Jam" became interested in the former style of the mods by 1974, ten years after the mods' heyday. Inspired through a photograph of a group of mods, he began to focus on the clothes, music, films, and literature of the time. Appropriating clothing from mod culture, such as straight trousers and jackets, was for a fifteen-year-old youngster a way to distinguish himself from the dominant fashion taste of the 1970s. For those who had worn the clothes at the same age when they were in fashion, and regarded them ten years later simply as passé, this might have been an affront. Apparently, historic distance is a key to the functioning of retro-looks. According to James Laver's cycle of fashion and taste, a fashion is perceived as hideous after a distance of ten years, after twenty years it is ridiculous, after thirty years it is amusing. However, it is debatable if his scheme, constructed in 1945, still has the same validity in a time where people seem to have become more used to anachronistic appearances, when fashion images from the most diverse periods circulate synchronically on Web sites and TV channels as well as in contemporary retro-appearances, blurring strict differentiations into past, present and future. If then, in consequence, past fashions are no longer perceived as bygone but as options of present time, how can people then be nostalgic for it?

RETRO AS PROTECTION WEAR?

Nostalgia was originally a medical diagnosis for homesickness, introduced in 1678 by humanist Johannes Hofer, who observed a heavily melancholic mood and depression among sailors who have been a long time away from home. Today the term is less understood as a yearning for a certain place than for a certain bygone time. Following nostalgia theory, the recourse to historic fashions can be seen as a sign of a particular relation to history and tradition, which is marked by a regressive attitude towards contemporary conditions in society, such as the progress of modernity and high technology, and the acceleration of time; going back to the "good old days." Considering again the comments on the fall/winter collections in 2003, this theory has apparently not lost in actuality, linking retro-styles aroused through terrorism and war. But again, is it as simple as that—is it a declining faith in the future that makes young people "look retro"?

Protagonists of postmodern theory have suggested that the reference to history is in fact more random or superficial. Frederic Jameson sees in retro, or more precisely in retro-movies, a "cannibalistic plundering of the past" that can only result in a pastiche or simulacrum, thus reminding one of Jean Baudrillard's characterization of fashion as the endless recycling of the dead. In the 1990s Ted Polhemus has transferred this discourse in postmodern theory to his survey on post-war youth cultures. He regards anything after punk as either "straight retroisms," like the diverse retro-groups who copy historic subcultural styles (i.e. "retro-mods") or postmodern remixes of several elements from past styles that come up with "new results," like Techno, using sampling as a creative production technique. Due to media, the progress of linear subcultural history has been interrupted and exploded into the simultaneity of the formerly non-simultaneous. According to Polhemus, subcultural history presents today a supermarket of style from which young people can choose and consume subcultural styles, disconnected from their former cultural contexts, like tins on a supermarket shelf. Meaning, however, is in this way no longer created, but just reproduced, or rather simulated on a surface level. Like Jameson's complaint about retro, this interpretation gives youth a certain randomness in the process of style-creation and self-performance, as well as a superficiality and ignorance towards "original" historic meanings and contexts. Polhemus seems to idealize a moment in the history of youth cultures, when "real" subcultural styles were originally created and not simply appropriated and turned "retro" by the young ones. As shown here, retro has been incorporated into youth culture right from the beginning of the postwar period, culminating in the style of the punks which was made up from a mixture of elements taken from numerous former youth cultural styles as well as from the more conventional history of dress.

For Polhemus, punk had the ultimate shock-effect that makes it impossible for the following generation to compete with or top. However, maybe it is precisely the brazen appropriation of "their" youth-style among a new youth-generation that bears a thorn in the former generation's eye. As the contemporary slogan for Adidas' retro-trainers indicates, one that identifies the new old "Record" as a model "from a time when you had thin soles and thick hair," retro-styles produce to some degree also a generational gap. This might be particularly valid in the context of youth-scenes that aim at historic accuracy in their "authentic reproduction" of historic styles. By wearing nearly exclusively original 1960s garments or by getting them done, modeled on original items completed with an original-like make-up, hair, and even body posture, retro-styles such as in the contemporary sixties-scene even outdo the original. In their minutely detailed reproduction of the former style and strive towards "authenticity," the young retro-stylists show an anachronistic appearance that would—at least in such a consequential way—rarely be worn by the people who wore the style "originally" back in the 1960s.

Youth cultural styles have certainly become selectable, ensembles that can be consumed dislocated from their former cultural context, due to an image associated with the respective time that has a contemporary appeal. The 1960s, which may appear to them "different," and exotic rather than bygone, have been consciously selected as a style out of the multi-optional world of fashion and imagery. The appropriation of 1960s originals enables the appropriation of some bits from that decade, which is appreciated because of its style, music, as well as the retrospectively constructed positive and dynamic image of the time. Via retro-dress they can get in touch with the period. However, at the same time original garments are utilized to mark off knowledge in terms of cultural capital and social distinction. The engagement into "everything sixties," the hunt for originals on jumble sales, as well as in virtual auction houses like eBay, the development of the associated fashion and music knowledge, provides the sixties-stylists with a way to distinguish from others as well as to get reintegrated into a network of like-minded people with whom they can enthusiastically engage in their "theme."

However, even if these retro-practices aim at the construction of an imaginary past, fabricated through body, dress, private space in sixties-design and sixties-events, their interpretation in terms of nostalgia as a "declining confidence in the present" and regressive attitude (i.e. towards modern technology) would be too superficial. Rather they must be seen as a consequence of the process of modernization influenced by modern technology such as mass-production and the image producing media, which made a phenomenon like retro possible on an even broader scale. Eventually sixties-stylists use the Internet themselves to communicate with enthusiasts worldwide, find fashion icons from the 1960s, or buy rare records and items of dress, thus allying their fable of the old with modern high technology.

CONCLUSION

As Gregson et al. have demonstrated in their study among students in Britain, there can be far more modes in the appropriation of retro-dress, and in the context of using clothing from one single era. Young people may use retro-dress without even knowing that they do, or in order to caricature a former style that they can exaggerate. The idea of using retro-dress in a carnivalesque mode, as an occasional party-style, goes back even to the roots of fashion revivals in courtly masquerade. Furthermore, there are also the sophisticated modes of "appropriately appreciating" retro-dress, by combining old dress with new clothes to mark off an individual style that can be correspondingly decoded by a "knowing audience."

As Valerie Steele rightly acknowledges, meanings of retro have constantly fluctuated. Just as the retro versions of former fashions never have the same appearance or meaning as in the cultural context when they were "originally" worn. Following Gabriele Mentges, fashion must be understood as a complex cultural practice, in which the forms and meanings are not a given or predicated, instead they are always newly negotiated by the historic actors. But due to the fact that dress practices are elaborated strategies for the definition and localization of self, youth styles can in reality not as simply be picked and mixed like soup-cans, as Polhemus's *Supermarket of Style* suggests. Retro-practices must be situated in the context of the development of an alternative fashion market, or more generally within the context of the ongoing fragmentation of fashion and youth culture that are interlinked with processes of individualization. Dress practices have become more and more elaborated, assisting and constituting in the formation and presentation of a "unique self."

Secondhand dress, even if formerly mass produced as well, that has become "unique" due to historical distance, is obviously very suitable for dressing the knowledgable individual self. But retro-items are, beyond that, also an instrument to step at least partly outside of the rhythm of fashion production. Focusing on one period of dress only, or mainly on secondhand consumption, can provide a certain immunity against contemporary mass-clothing produced under the dark circumstances of a globalized production scheme. For youth in the industrialized affluent West, who generate identity through consumption practices, retro-dress is a means to perform knowledge and "authenticity." At the same time retro-styles provide a tool to get in touch with a historic reference system that may be invaded to construct or to subvert linkages with (youth cultural) histories, leading eventually to their further continuation.

Resources
Chenoune, F. (1993). *A history of men's fashion.* New York: Flammarion.

Ginsburg, M. (1980). Rags to riches: The second-hand clothes trade 1700–1978. *Costume*, (14), 121–135.

McRobbie, A. (1994). Second-hand dresses and the role of the ragmarket. In A. McRobbie (Ed.). *Postmodernism and popular culture* (pp. 135–153). London and New York: Routledge.

O'Neill, A. (2000). John Stephen: A Carnaby Street presentation of masculinity 1957–1975. *Fashion Theory*, 4, 487–506.

FASHION AND TECHNO STYLE

Birgit Richard

The particularities of fashion as commodity style will be worked out on the basis of the creative principles of the techno style, which characterize the visual field as well as the field of music. Essential techniques like transformation and modulation are less a break with the foregoing, or a juxtaposition of the disparate, but rather a creation of variants—with small but therefore very significant differences. For the production of variants, Photoshop or Roland TB 303 filters present typical instruments for modulation. In the context of dress, modulation and transformation are mainly applied to brand logos, which are printed on "basics." The brand logo is looped analogously to music and forms an invariant core. Size, color, and fabric make up the differentiations from the original or from the brand logo expropriated via adbusting.

Another principle is artificiality: Sleeping and waking sequences are structured in a new order that ignores the natural rhythm or separation of life into day and night. The parole of excessive dance runs counter to the bourgeois week schedule, allocating the weekend the function of rest and recovery. As the music is computer generated, it is artificial, too. The pitching of natural voices generate childlike tones, reminding one of Mickey Mouse (as in gabber). Further hints of the synthetic as well as the technical can be found in the artificial childhood of the girlie-look, in dyed hair, wrong lashes, shrill neon colors, and materials such as extravagant high-tech polymers in clothes. There are actually parallels to the color ecstasy back in the first decade of the twentieth century, when fashion, stimulated by the futurists, preferred colors with an artificial expression, such as violet, orange, purple, and jade-green.

In the techno and house scene nature always appears in plastic versions, like sunflowers or artificial lawns. The emphasis lies on special, man-made, and chemically produced materials—heavy duty stuff—which is extremely durable, non-inflammable, and resistant to water, acid, or oil.

Further principles are self-containment and stylistic hermetic in the culmination of events, the rave or club night. The spaces of the techno and house scene are like isolated laboratories, in which the various combinations of party people are tested to create the right "chemistry" for the night. This hermetic is also based on specific criteria of exclusion, differentiated according to dress style. Like all other subcultures, techno, too, claims equality within the style. But the postulation of equality functions only on a style intern level. In the moment of an event social differences, such as class and gender, are in fact deactivated. However, in advance of this, there are strict and steady selection principles regulating the entry. The door politics of the club scene generate a different social order. Via the establishment of internal style hierarchies the scene is subdivided into a manipulative dancing crowd (comparable to the users of computers) and into a privileged producing elite: Analogous to computer programmers these are DJs and producers. In the market these internal style hierarchies are expressed by certain groups of commodities: The CD-compilation is targeted at users, whereas vinyl pressings or the White Label are produced for the practicing DJ. Hobby mixer, and Technics reproductions are aimed at the hobby-DJ, and the original Technics SL 1200 Mk 2 is used by the professional. These kinds of hierarchies are less expressed in fashion than in institutions like VIP lounges and VIP cards and face control or door politics.

In addition to the social subdivisions in the scene, the individual tends to shield the body from external influences with special accessories and materials: Skintight and partly impermeable surfaces like neoprene, latex, PVC, and leather, or objects like lollipops, dummies, or gas masks shut the body orifices and conserve the body like a mummy, delimiting it against a body-hostile surrounding. Keeping the body fit for the event, by saving its energy and temperature, similar to a diving or space suit, is an apparently quite paradoxical practice, because it forces and intensifies the process of "radiation" and ecstasy caused by drugs and heat. For dancing excesses workwear is rather dysfunctional, due to the solid quality of the durable and protective materials, people literally wear themselves out in them. This is similar to the flared worker's pants; they not only indicate a loss of functionality in workwear, they also present a direct hindrance for work and thus a safety risk.

The reduction of sight through dark shades and protective glasses used for welding, the limitation of olfactory nerve and breathing via gas- or dust-masks, and the restriction of movement and dancing through bulky plateau shoes change the perception. This "material" limitation of perception runs counter to an "immaterial" mind-expansion achieved through chemical aids, like substances for inhaling (Vick's Vaporub) and designer drugs.

This kind of dress generates associations, which lead far beyond the basic material level. Simultaneously, they are an imaginary protection against invisible "immaterial" dangers like radiation (laser or x-ray) and chemical substances (acids), but also a conscious exposure to risks: An expression for the effect of drugs is "Verstrahltsein," a German world indicating radioactive contamination (one of the music styles is called "acid" not only because of the tones of the 303 machine).

Literal superficiality is the next structural principle, from which reflection and layer, the two further principles, can be derived. An entire item of clothing, even arm holes and lining, is designed on a surface structure via imprints, applications, and layout. Here design reaches no longer into a deep structure. Specialized high-tech materials turn the bodies into reflecting and communicative surfaces—somehow positioned between billboard and screen, and moving between the color walls of light installations.

Layers are also produced by mix and remix techniques in the endless tracks of sound carpets that produce overlappings and interweavings. Also the organizational structure of the style is set up as a layer. Labels (record as well as clubwear companies) with many sub-labels also represent a layered, nonhierarchical structure. Layers in dress are produced by the connection and overlapping of particular time-specific elements, for example when the historic item from the secondhand market is combined with futuristic high-tech materials. Layers are also formed when numerous garments, like T-shirts, are worn on top of the other. Tied around the waist, like an apron over trousers, the prints are still kept visible. Clothing layers are turned upside down when bras and skinny undershirts turn into visible party-dress.

Similar to the design of flyers, layers are superficial, remaining two-dimensional. Emblems in the form of logos and brand signs are the only point of dress, which develops certain three-dimensional effects, for example in the case of blinking labels or op-art structures.

Reflecting labels and neon colors correspond to the structural principle of radiation and visibility. The individual appears like a light-object. Shiny materials reflect the light and transform the body into a projecting surface, which sends simulated and even real light signals. Non-verbal forms of communication, like gesture in dance, send and receive signals, too. In techno an exchange of information and energy becomes highly visible through reflections: Dress is electrified by punctual blinking and turns the body into a temporal vision of light. This kind of metamorphosis is a sign for the voluntary transformation into an immaterial appearance, flying across spaces. Fluorescent objects such as a necklace or stick held in the hand and laser-pointers reinforce this impression.

Material presence is alternately interrupted and accentuated. Communication with others is kept at a distance and at the same time wanted. Due to their own transitoriness as a vision of light, flashing and reflecting materials are no paradoxical remedies against the fleetness of the body within the virtual space of the rave—but instead, they display the ambiguity of bodily presence in virtual spaces.

SYMBOLIC REPRESENTATION

By the expropriation of objects and structures, the fashion of the techno and house scene produces a very disparate field of references, which refers to diverse areas of function in society.

The central area of reference, connected to all others, is the area of work. Its adaptation in workwear also integrates the forms of protective wear. They are durable and robust products, easily purchased on the mass market

Makeup and tattoos change identity

(Doc Martens, Carhartt, Dickies), and they are relatively cheap in the United States. When youth cultures discover these commodities for their styles, they often become expensive prestige objects. There are two contrary spheres of production visible, representing the past and future of work: One is the clean and sterile high-tech production of processors and microchips, a work in weightless virtual worlds, with accessories like white gloves; and the other is the parallel sphere of traditional field of craft, or rather, machine supported bodily work, with heavy, bulky protective wear, gas- and dusk-masks, and protective glasses.

Workwear represents the step from concrete to immaterial work. The reflector jackets of street cleaners, canalization workers, road workers and autobahn service or the boots of construction workers (like Caterpillar Walking Machines) promise the event of "real" physical (though low paid and low valued) work. Apart from its warning colors and reflecting applications, the jacket of the street cleaner is especially interesting because it indicates the discrepancy between the dying industrial and high-tech work for a limited number of "elected" people, and low service "Mcjobs" for the others. But workwear can also be found among other youth cultures. In the 1980s new wavers wore roofer's shoes, the hippies and the ecological movement used overalls and undershirts, and the punks utilized worker's boots with toe-caps made by Doc Martens. Also the flares of the 1970s, the so-called Manchester trousers, originated in the area of workwear.

Beyond the references to industrial work, the symbolism of techno clothing is also taken from extreme situations like emergency, accident, catastrophes, or dangerous substances—representing another specific work field. Concrete borrowings come from the field of public security, police, fire workers, first-aid doctors, national security, and drug police. British and American elements are especially used, because of the more shrill colors. Catastrophes and permanent emergency are "normality" during an event, as the siren, the rave signal and terms like mayday show. Thus techno is a preparation for survival in extreme situations. The collections of Daniel Poole offer survival packs and jackets, enabling a person to wear everything directly on the body—in a sense of an urban support system.

Workwear gets a rather utopian character when it refers to the future work in space. Visual ciphers from old science fiction novels and movies, and recently also from the Japanese manga comics, present here the main means of stylization. As "utopian dress" futuristic elements form a new direction in the fashion of the 1960s, alongside miniskirts and hot-pants: In 1966 Courreges launched silver space clothes, Pierre Cardin created transparent boots, and Paco Rabanne made dresses of plastic rhombus connected with metal hooks. The movie *Barbarella*, produced in 1968, can be seen as a model for the space look now popular in the techno scene. It features Jane Fonda in an artificial—and at the same time seductive—dress with transparent plastic holes. Television series give another, highly important creative input to youth culture–style creations. The techno and house scene favors uniform-like shirts, as if they have jumped out of the spaceship Enterprise or Orion.

Further visual formulas referring to future and extraterrestrial life are all the emblems showing motifs such as stars and planets, rockets, spaceships, cockpits, or the stylized head of a Roswell alien. Furthermore, the literary figure of the cyber punk turns into a direct model for fashion. This is mainly because of his outlaw image and striving for autonomy, uncoupled from the hegemony of economic power. The punk parole "no future" is altered into "our future"—and the only option to maintain in a technologically dominated society is the appropriation of technology for own purposes.

Another area of reference is sports. Sports turn into work, into an endlessly perpetuating marathon. Sportswear is either directly appropriated respectively reanimated, like the blue Adidas jackets from the 1970s, or adopted in single striking elements, like stripes on sleeves. The collections of Fila, Helly Hansen, and Tommy Hilfiger are highly popular because of the signaling character of primary colors and the pure shape of the brand logos. As outdoor garments they are made of simple, catchy forms and high-tech materials. Further areas of reference to sports are motorcross (the trousers and jackets worn by Sven Väth in the middle of the 1990s) sailing (jackets and T-shirts), snowboarding (shoes and glasses), football (strips as loveparade T-shirts), skiing (old jackets from the 1970s,) and skating (shoes and trousers).

It is remarkable that the garments for outdoor activities are utilized. The use of this clothing is not really appropriate for warm indoor spaces and can therefore be seen as indicative for shifting outdoors into indoors. The exterior enters into the interior when world and public space are (via the Internet) connected with indoor spaces such as cafes or clubs.

Fun-Guerrilla and Profanation: Military Elements in Youth Cultures

Military combat gear also loses its function indoors. Uniform elements became very important style components in all postwar youth cultures. McRobbie dates the beginning of the utilization of military clothing back to the hippies of the 1960s. Actually, the youth cultural usage of uniform pieces goes back to the 1950s. The uniform is an extreme form of conventional clothing. Its original function is to impress or frighten the enemy during direct conflict. For this reason uniforms are kept in loud and flashy colors until World War I. Afterwards the aspect of concealment and camouflage is of primary importance. Military pieces of dress are chosen by youth cultures, similar to workwear, because of financial or practical reasons. Functionality and durability of materials play an important role. However, the camouflage aspect is here of less significance, instead the net of connotations, into which a military garment is woven, as well as its immediate aesthetic effect is highly important.

Military stands for a particularly strict order in society. With the use or appropriation of military accessories youth cultures express their opposition to society. The military dress is deprived of their "frightening dignity" by direct alterations like inscriptions, tears, or the combination with rather contrasting garments, like underwear. Hippies marked their military parkas with peace signs, symbols opposing militarism and the governmental authority. Inscriptions and badges desecrate uniform elements. Another strategy is to render them useless of their original function, for example by changing the colors of camouflage suits. Violet, red, or orange patterns no longer serve to conceal and camouflage, instead they draw the attention to the wearer. In this they also refer to the military strategy of dazzling the opponent side. The intention of dazzle paintings (a protection paint for ships used in World War I) was not to make the ships invisible, but to irritate and confuse the enemy's perception.

It is remarkable, though not surprising, that youth cultures only rarely use the complete uniforms of a higher rank or a complete combat gear. This would be directly associated with military megalomania and obedience. Significantly, precisely for this reason, these garments are chosen by right wing youth cultures, like Nazi-skinheads. They are willed to demonstrate aggression, a nationalistic attitude, patriarchal power, group membership, and a return to "old values."

Another exception is Public Enemy's combat style and the aggression among the visual language of many gangsta rappers, who work consciously with military elements to underline their readiness to fight for the Nation of Islam and the Fivepercenters.

Among gay cultures, in the context of sadomasochistic plays, uniform pieces serve the connotation of subordination and unlimited power. They are used to exaggerate and overdo the heterosexual image of manliness.

All the other youth cultures usually play with only single military elements. Neither do they understand them in a literal sense nor do they take them seriously. A brief overview of the forms of direct appropriations of military dress shows this: Accessories like sunglasses are originally a military item. Today they function as a certificate of coolness and are either worn on the nose or on the top of the head decorating the hair (since the 1970s). Sunglasses were developed for pilots in the 1920s as a protection against the harsh light during high altitude flying, which caused headaches and sickness. The forerunner of the legendary Ray Ban with green wad and Lomb glasses, made in 1937, was developed for the U.S. Marines.

In the manner of Marlon Brando in *The Wild One*, the young "rowdies" of the 1950s wore World War II pilot jackets, Perfecto Bronx model, produced by Schott, New York. In the 1960s, the British mods preferred oversize parkas with U.S. Airforce emblems. Their opponents, the rockers, in contrast wore Wehrmacht helmets and emblems. The peace-loving hippies returned to army parkas in the 1970s. The punk style consists of a whole range of military garments: army trousers, often dyed, with many pockets, army boots and Doc Martens worker boots, camouflage prints, cartridge belts, and long, dark green coats formerly worn by the Gestapo. The aspect of functionality, the price, and durability—appropriate to the life in the streets—plays a very important part in the punk streetstyle. Additionally, another meaningful function of military elements among the punks is the reinforcement of a distanced but nonetheless threatening habitus. The new wavers of the 1980s differentiate the style of the punks further by wearing short, black or gray wool jackets with the Swiss cross on the buttons, which were originally worn by the Swiss mountain infantry.

Calf-high Doc Martens with 18 holes and bomber-jackets are a reference to aggression and male combat-readiness among the male skinheads. Female punks wear ankle-high Doc Martens and army trousers as a practical demonstration of a different and autonomous female role. Female punks are also the first to introduce a combination of raw military footwear worn with a skirt or dress. Even if this is today fully absorbed by fashion, in the late 1970s and early 1980s women in high and bulky boots were still scorned because of their "unwomanliness." In the 1990s military accessories are a direct expression of girls' aggressiveness and combat-readiness, as displayed by the cartoon character Tankgirl or by the Riot Grrrls.

Like in many other youth cultures, techno and house involve military discourses, reinterpreting them as aesthetic phenomena. Around 1994 and 1995 camouflage patterns, visible in many youth cultures (punk, skinhead, hip hop, rastafari) in diverse patterns and color combinations, are also particularly significant in techno. The camouflage aspect is subverted by producing the pattern in a wide range of flashy colors, and by applying it to all sorts of garments, including shoes and skirts. In the middle of the 1990s, winter or snow camouflage was very popular. Outside of snow-capped surroundings, this pattern is extremely salient. Therefore, camouflage is not used to hide oneself, but to arouse attention. Visibility is the motto on events. The use of other colors can cause the contrary effect, namely getting invisible in the crowd on the dance floor.

So in techno and house the aggressive touch of camouflage gets annulled. The operational area is the party-battlefield. These actions are all an expression of the fun-guerrilla. They conquer urban space following the Beastie Boys' motto "You gotta fight for your right to party!"

However, to be able to realize the progress of time within the dark space of the party, there is a renaissance of digital watches with fluorescent faces, like Casio's G-shock. They are a reference to the clock-faces of pilot watches with self-reflecting radium. Further military elements are neon colors, which have a function similar to signal rockets: they show a person's positioning in the space of the event and send a sign of presence. Fixing something with the laser-pointer corresponds to the targeting with infrared and laser weapons: they no longer fix objects through the reticule, but focus and mark them via a red laser spot. This is an additional, technical way of communication in the party context, an immaterial, nearly telepresent method to tap on somebody's shoulder. The stomping rhythm is reminiscent of marching, samples imitate the noise of battle and rifle fire, and the rave signal resembles a military alarm signal. The special light effects, the reduction of the color spectrum, and the concentration on white light, either produced by stroboscope-flashes resembling dazzle-rockets or big searchlight-projectors, constructing a carpet of light, are similar to the anti-aircraft rays of Albert Speer's light-dome, though minimized and turned down about ninety degrees.

To the eyes of outsiders, techno exposes the dancers to extreme conditions, which are, however, not perceived as exceptional by the members of the style. This is the serious side of the training toward new worlds of perceptions. The other side is the fun side: pasteboard tanks (Berlin Ensemble

1997 and Rake ten: Camel The Move 1994, record label DJAX Up beats loveparade 1997) and military vehicles are popular motives for lorries on parades like Street Parade in Zurich and Love Parade in Berlin—who are not incidentally called parades and refer in themselves to something military. However, together with camouflage and water-filled pump guns (supersoakers), they represent a rather obsolete military area. Blinking dress elements and laser pointers hint of the future direction of military transformation: The visible forms of weapons are turned into toys—the weapons of the future will no longer be visible.

The Infantile and the Androgynous

The reference area of childhood shows a willful, stylistic step outside of the adult world. The rejection of aging and the cultivation of a shrill and child-like taste form the basis of a prejudice-free get together and a feeling of safety in the big substitute family of the event. As a fashionable element, the recourse to child-like elements is nothing new. Oscar Wilde wore a suit that was perceived as infantile, the so-called Lord Fauntleroy suit, which consisted of short trousers and a velvet jacket. Even today adults tend to dress for leisure activities or holiday like little children. They wear shapeless garments that can be easily put on, like jogging-pants with elastic waistbands or shoes with Velcro fastenings. This "temporary childwear" is made of the traditional materials of children's clothing, such as cotton and jersey, in baby colors and cute patterns.

As in the techno and house scene decades later, the women of the 1960s also looked like children. Make-up and haircuts produced a big head with big baby eyes. The childlike body was constructed through simple clothing shapes, like mini-dresses and baby-doll, slip-dresses and geometric forms. This impression is further increased by the beauty ideal of the time: a thin body with slim legs and skinny torso. Elements of children's wear can also be seen among men, who wore jackets without lapels, anoraks, cords, turtlenecks, and bright colors. For Alison Lurie, these infantile elements in fashion are a sign of an economically secure time. By the time of the recession at the end of the 1970s, infantilism was for a while out of fashion.[1]

All of the described elements are now revived in the club and event scene, labeled as girlie, cutie, and babe. Heidi-plaits, hair-slides, the miniaturization of accessories like backpack and rucksack, toys (water pistols), and sweets as necklaces are significant components of this style. The infantile look is complex; the entire children's world is ready for disposition. Even drugs like ecstasy pills get a child-like face, displaying smileys, Fred Flintstone, dinosaurs, or dolphins.

The girlie image in the context of the techno and house scene is not a construction of an individualistic, antifeminist social climate. Instead of a regressive step, it is the creation of a safety space for girls and young women. The indicated accusation applies only to the media images of girlies, which have to be seen in close connection with commercial interests. Girls and women symbolize with the original girlie concept, with an infantile, pre-sexual outfit, an innocent and at the same time autonomous engagement with their body. They signal that sexual attraction is not the aim of this partial body exposure. By categorizing themselves as child-like, they display the wish to be left alone. To men this presentation signals a taboo zone. And many men also wear necklaces with wooden pearls, known from childhood, and engage as fun guerrillas in children's pleasures, armed with plastic pump guns and colored water pistols. The recourse to infantile elements allows men to get rid of the macho postures of being sexually impressive and instead experience a rather free or playful relation the other sex.

However, there are also different body concepts and practices integrated into the house and techno scene, adopted, for example, from the gay or fetish cultures. Incorporating androgynous elements, particularly male body images, tend to blur gender boundaries visually. Fashion blurs the crusted structures of gender constructions, even when the androgynous forms serve only an aesthetic differentiation. Men who wear make-up or skirts are often still stuck in these experimental poses. Only very few of them are real cross-dressers, transvestites, or drags. Gay posing becomes fashion, alongside a coquettish play with bisexuality à la Madonna or Dennis Rodman. However, it is decisive for the laboratory of the techno event and house club that the visual experiments toward a re-coding of the male body is eventually possible.

Because of a wider and more differentiated range of styles, men are usually the trendsetters of the scene, like in hip hop. In techno and house many men also tend to cross the borderlines of gender and style. In contrast, with the exception of the girlie-look, women's wear in techno develops no autonomous line, but is often a "gendered" copy of men's wear (like Adidas mini-dresses and Puma trainers with high heels). So a crossing of gender-boundaries by girls can only be seen in transformed sportswear and in bulky shoes; however, also significant is the adaptation of a gay dance style. But nonetheless, there is no connection to female androgyny, as it could be seen in the 1920s among the garconne, the seductress who flattened her breasts with bandages to get a boyish appearance.

Men are on their way to becoming fashion victims, and in their narcissistic poses they touch on the style strategies of the gay scene, as described in movies like *Paris Is Burning* or in "vogueing." The changes in male body images and experiences is mainly initiated by the cultural practices of gay, black minorities in the United States, transferred to Europe by the early acid house scene and the house clubs of the 1990s. In the techno and house culture they are regarded as opinion leaders. Because of a mixture of street credibility, black coolness, and gay dancing ecstasy, they stand for an authentic party culture.

Urban blacks are the dandies of today, the true heirs of Beau Brummel; their "boss vines" show a concern for fit and detail rare elsewhere, and a talent for daring combination of color and fabric that a professional designer might envy.[2]

The plushy and kitsch-like interior of many house clubs, with gold, brocade and a preference for cheesy devotional articles is mainly stimulated through the creative means of travesty, the artificial and ecstatic exaggeration of femininity. Alongside the unveiling of the fragile construction of visual gender norms, the cross-dressing strategies of this scene refer to media-technological techniques, like gender switching or bending, popular on the Internet.[3]

Retro, Revival, Old School

Beyond the techniques of cross-dressing, techno and house work with the symbolism of super-high-tech, orientated toward the future but juxtaposed with three retrograde forms: retro, old school, and revival.

Retro here means the imitation of elements or complete dress ensembles of past decades, as a nostalgic retrospect to the past. Barbara Burman-Baines differentiates classical, rural, historical, and exotic revivals. She signifies revival as a form of retrospection, which is characterized not by change but by the search for lost values like simplicity, the natural, and classical severity.[4] With respect to the youth cultures' engagement in historical elements, the term "retro" is more suitable to comprehend the unchanged, nostalgic recourse. Revival already etymologically incorporates the dimension of change within a revival. It is not intended to preserve styles and stylistic features; instead they are open to change and alterations. An actualization happens also via the release and reintroduction of original forms, materials, and glossy fabrics like satin, lurex, or PVC, which were highly popular among the disco scene of the 1970s and are now incorporated into the new context of club culture.

Disco revival is an attempt toward the establishment of an anti-fashion. The resistance to fashion regularly produces new fashions. An apparently overcome aesthetic faux pas that some part of the generation of the 1970s felt helplessly exposed to, it returns in all of its disproportionality, dysfunctionality, and contrariness in tight and oversize forms. Flares, go-go dancers, and rounded or extremely long collars find their way into the house club culture. The recognizable shrill, high-tech fabrics are juxtaposed by the proletarian, square, and "bad taste" of the 1970s. The bulky and misshapen forms, such as over-dimensional flares, plateau shoes, and poly-fibers, make an especially traumatic reappearance. The janitor look—consisting of training jackets, undershirts, proper polyacryl jumpers in beige or brown and a haircut with proper parting—is, if at all, only very lately recognized as subversion. In the over fulfillment of a rather conforming and proper style, the look seems to correspond to an accused escapism. However, with reference to the ecstatic style of the British mods, this uptight style is clearly differentiated from the success-orientated and expensive conformity of the yuppies back in the 1980s, because here they use the overtly unspectacular, not the labeled, but the proletarian common article.

The mentioned revival elements are a sign for the simultaneity of the different time levels—past, present, and future—which are now synthesized in one style. A completely different form of self-referentiality or retrospection, in distinction to the aforementioned modulations of the past, is presented by the so-called old school phenomenon, which appeared for the first time in the techno and hip hop scenes. This is a style-internal revival, produced by the recourse to the archetypes of the own style during its time of origin and demonstrates the autopoiesis of youth cultural systems.

SIMULTANEITY OF THE CONTRARY

One characteristic feature of the contemporary house and techno culture is an (unconsciously generated) dialectical relation of contrasts, quite in the sense of Adorno. The sixes XXS and XXL exist parallel, however, not without causing a special tension. Tight and small dresses in children's sizes appear alongside extremely wide and baggy clothing, as is common in hip hop. Oversized XXL is produced by the amount of fabric, not by applications or linings. Particularly eye-catching is the reoccupation of the object, with a strong emphasis on the material and its qualities for a differentiation of products, and the use of particular durable and raw special materials.

Another contrast is the "naturality" of the naked male torso and the partly bare female body or the natural fabrics and ethnic symbolism (introduced via musical directions such as goa) in opposite to the entirely synthetic dancing context. The direct manipulation and inscriptions into the surface of the body, via tattoo and piercing, produce a contrast between the "restored" primitive body and the technological music, lighting, and spatial surrounding.

Nudity and exposure do not display a "natural" body, but a body whose surface has been designed by workouts and Wonderbras, illustrating the potential constructiveness of body images. The upheaval toward a maximum robotization and the forcing of alienation can also be traced in phenomena such as hybrid plateau-trainers. For a better visibility the actors in Greek tragedies wore stage shoes with high soles, the so called cothurne. And the Venetian courtesans of the fifteenth century are not even able to walk in their high plateau shoes (zoccoli) without assistance. Depending on somebody for support, they confirm Veblens's thesis of the women as valuable property. The actual form of the plateau shoe, the Monsterlette, produced by Buffalo Boots, is a hybrid between a calf-high plateau boot, sneaker, and the snow- or moon-boot of the 1970s. Although they are extremely high, these shoes do not have a fetish character. Because they do not show the fragility of high heels, they do not assign the wearer the image of a dangerous seductress. In contrast, the Monsterlette connects the wearer securely with the ground, signaling autonomy instead of a helpless female need for protection. Though in the case of techno and house, bulky footwear indicates "take off" as well as being down to earth. Like the astronaut returning from space or virtual reality, men and women experience via their footwear—after an event back on earth—the everyday reality. Their footwear and balloon-like clothing, resembling Oskar Schlemmer's Triadic Ballet, turns them into mutants incapable of moving. This is closely linked to another aspect of simultaneous contrasts: traveling between absolute freedom of corporeality, floating to the music ("fly"), and the conscious hindrance of corporal freedom by heavy boots and insulating garments.

MICRO-SOCIETY OF THE FUTURE

Music, as a connecting element, temporarily produces a higher state of consciousness, a take off from the finite, corporal worlds. This corresponds with the utopias of the new technologies, aiming at the body's preparation towards a life in space.[5]

Motifs such as astronauts, cyborgs, and aliens open up a huge spectrum of new corporal worlds, ranging from the discovery of new living forms to the desire of being extraterrestrial or of leaving the human system and turning into a technoid machine. The symbolical robotization of the human body leads to an identification with alien and nonhuman forms. In that sense, glaring hair colors, common among the scene, do not serve any ideas of provocation (as among punk), but as an extension of the too-small color range of natural hair. Thus they can be understood as a hint or attempt toward a new specie. The insect-glasses of the late 1990s produced by Global Eye Wear or Funk (although oversized "frog" glasses have been around since 1967) conceal the face and construct an image of an extraterrestrial being. They can also be compared to head-mounted displays. "Additional eye-lights," small lamps positioned right beside the eyes (as used in Orbital performances), are a further instrument for the creation of an extraterrestrial look.

The techno and house scene generate a closed symbolic system. As an autopoietical system it can be transferred to many places all over the world. The style coexists with work, both are no longer incompatible, as in the case of punk. As parallel worlds they are even partly structured identically. They serve the training of a new form of living, a simultaneous existence in many parallel natural and virtual worlds. The important segments of society, such as work, leisure, sports, combat, war, executive, emergency, technology, are in the scope of a nonstationary micro-society shifted, respectively represented in distortion. Furthermore, the scene synthesizes a combination of primitive and "civilized" living forms, thus societies from various epochs.

However, as any other form of society, the techno and house scene has a hierarchy and is a distortion mirror of the characteristics and structures of the adult world. In the deconstructional manner of the architects Eisenmann or Liebeskind, the values of society are decentralized exaggerated or consciously filled with senseless voids.

Via symbols and emblems, the scene refers abstractly to the future and the world of technology. Flashing applications on clothing, small lights, shining lollipops, laser pointers, and numerous other reflecting and radiating objects are low-complex technologies. Thereby the scene constructs unconsciously an image of new technology with infantile means. They test the images of tomorrow in a childish-naive and playful manner, stepping into the future in a rather child-like nature. As described above, with the help of toys, dress, and accessories, future as well as war and evil are symbolized in a child's view.

During the event, the techno and house scene simulates on a pre-technological level the existence in a material-corporal world, which is determined by immaterial impulses and stimuli. As analyzed, the shift between material and immaterial happens abstract-symbolically via medial clothing, similar to concrete techniques like wearable computing. Above that, the scene tests a further characteristic of the future, which is an important criterion of wearables, too: They wear/carry anything directly with their body, chain purses, small backpacks, or Daniel Poole survival packs.

Notes

1   See Lurie (1981), pp. 81–83.
2   See Lurie (1981), p. 98.
3   See Stone (1996), p. 65.
4   See Baines (1991), p. 10.
5   See Extropy Institute, Max More, http://www.primenet.com/maxmore

Resources

Books

Baines, B. B. (1991). *Fashion revivals from the Elisabethan age to the present day.* London: Drama Book Specialists.

Lurie, A. (1981). *The language of clothes.* New York: Random House.

Stone, A. R. (1996). *The war of desire and technology at the close of the mechanical age.* Cambridge, MA: The MIT Press.

Web Sites

Digital Life Consortium. Retrieved September 18, 2005 from http://dl.media.mit.edu/

Frog Design Mind. Retrieved September 18, 2005 from http://www.frogdesign.com

IBM Journal. Retrieved September 18, 2005 from http://www.almaden.ibm.com/journal/sj/mit/sectione/zimmerman.txt

WEARABLES

Birgit Richard

We wear clothes, put on jewelry, sit on chairs, and walk on carpets that all share the same profound failing: they are blind, deaf, and very dumb. Cuff links don't in fact, link with anything else. Fabrics look pretty, but should have brain, too. Glasses help sight, but they don't see. Hardware and software should merge into "underware." Your shoes should be retrieving the day's personalized news from the carpet before you even have time to take off your coat.

Since the beginning of the 1990s, we have seen research, especially American, on "wearable computing"—in short "wearables"—examining how mobile media-technology can be worn directly on the body and become connected. The integration of technical instruments (wearables) into the clothing layers produces an external—at the moment still visible—technological layer or envelope. This is going to have a basic influence on the human's bodily senses and perception, producing even a new skin ego. In her book *What Do Cyborgs Eat? Logic in an Information Society*, Margaret Morse regards oral incorporation as the dominant modus of subject construction within the new technologies. One of these forms consists of an embracing of the other, for example through a layer of muscles, trained in workout, which covers the skin itself, or through covering the body with a technological second skin such as "wearables."

Wearable computing turns technology into dress and thus into fashion. In contrast to the expensive and unique items like datasuits or suits for special applications, such as art installations (see Stahl Stenslie cyberex-suit or the suit for the installation of Ars Electronica 1997), wearables are intended to be affordable in a certain time by all people. Thereby the datasuit, formerly not wearable without special technical units, uncouples and turns into an ordinary everyday object. No longer fixed to a technical naval-string it will then be governed by a remote control principle. This leads to a mobilization of telepresence, as the users no longer sit in a control center, but are mobile themselves, operating and influencing from a distance.

The universalized smart clothing has then been detached from the original military function of the future, where wearable computer systems and networks play an important part. Military concepts such as "21CLW," the twenty-first century land warrior, are dependent on the development of wearables. But there are also medical applications of wearables: Blind people will be able to see again via artificial eyes, already tested on animals. They consist of glasses with implanted cameras that forward recorded visual information to a wearable computer, which again sends impulses to the optic center in the brain, causing a visual impression.

In contrast to this, the new medial garments are not a sign of disability, not an artificial limb in the classical sense. They are initiated to expand human capabilities, though at the moment they are still causing bodily hindrances. Everyday surroundings are not suitable for the movements of robots or men such as Steve Mann, who observes the external world via a camera. The desire, that a simultaneous look at the head-mounted display and the external environment will not reduce the freedom of movement ("without running into people"), is not yet achievable (actually, on Ars Electronica 1997 Steve Mann needed some assistance to find the sanitary facilities). However, Steve Mann is the first who stepped outside of the laboratory and shifted science fiction visions into reality. He is called a cyborg, and people find his media-supported presence weird and scary. His perception of an augmented reality converts two different layers, in the connection of virtual and "real" reality, on one screen. The "private eye," in the form of glasses, displays also additional information to the observed surrounding, mediated, for example, in texts.

For quite a long time now, these visions have been realized in movies: The cyborg (Arnold Schwarzenegger) in *Terminator 2* is already equipped with this augmented reality. By targeting an object, his retina projects additional information about locality, weapon system, and individuals. In *True Lies* the secret agent wears sunglasses that expand his perception; they function as a screen for a micro-camera. In addition to movies, the ideas of wearable technologies are particularly developed in literary cyberpunk stories, such as Bruce Sterling's *Artificial Kid*.

In the case of Sterling's *Artificial Kid*, technology keeps a distance from the body. It circles around him and is not integrated as instrumental means into the clothing. William Gibson's character Molly in *Neuromancer* introduces another aspect of medial clothing, which is the combination of dress and weapon: Numerous double-edged scalpels are fired out of a container positioned behind the protagonist's nails.

Wearables are a highly popular topic in movies: In the James Bond movies it is the task of Mr. Q to integrate secret weapons invisibly into garments and elsewhere so that they are quickly at hand. Dress is turned into deadly danger, which is able to look through a camera. Steady connections and hybrid mutations from body into weapon via digital techniques like morphing are realized in newer science fiction movies such as *Spawn* or *Stargate*. Through the medial technology in dress, the entire surroundings can be organized by remote control, as shown in *Stargate*.

The utopias and experiments of literature are only rarely consequential and turn technology via data into immaterial accessories, as practiced by Agentur Bilwet's figure of the datadandy. Actually the datadandy has not developed yet. At the moment "fashionable" technology does not manifest itself in an abstract form. It enters directly into fashion, embodied in materials, production techniques, or futuristic symbolism. Media turns into intelligent clothing, "smart clothing," occupying the gaps and holes that body and dress offer. Especially body decorations regarded as primitive pave the way for high technology. Opening the body through tears and piercing, they are a preparation for the future invasion of technology. Thus, in the future, a receiver in a piercing of the bellybutton would be a good place to implant technology.

The integration of technology into the body happens in two stages: Starting with mobile objects, media-technological extensions such as Walkman and Watchman, leading via pager (advertisement and textual messages can slip via pager directly onto the body, see Quix by Bravo), cellular phones, watches (like Swatch the Beep), and PDAs, which are both sender and receiver, to wearable processors with Internet facilities, namely online-wear.

Miniaturization up to nano-units, as well as the reduction of weight, are actually the technical preconditions for wearable media-packages. Concepts like "fluid machines," a cooperation of AT&T and NEC, the projects by Frogdesign, Carnegie Mellon University in Pittsburgh and IBM Almaden Research Center in San Jose (Thomas G. Zimmermann) to name only a few, show that the elements are in fact already small enough and that there are also materials available, but it is their connection that causes problems.

Like multimedia applications, wearables are set up to incorporate all possible functions of consumer electronics, including CD players, fax machines, and pagers. Christian Nürnberger observed on the Funkausstellung in Berlin 1997 that people can get car radios with an integrated mobile phone, organizers with digital cameras, and pocket computers with fax and Internet access. In his view the trend goes in the direction of a vibrator with integrated PC, telephone, face-solarium, fax, cosmetic mirror, camera, soap-dispenser, and Internet.

Actually, this requires the development of a universal language, like html or java for the World Wide Web, which offers also an option for personal design (in the sense of an electronic hand-me-down fashion, a pendant to basic clothing). The requirements for the data transfer have to be identical for all people. Therefore, through the simplification of individual bodynets, which will then emerge, a non-visible software uniform can be developed. The original creators and inventors of wearables in the scientific laboratories still prefer the LINUX system. An absorption of the Microsoft or IBM systems, which is just driven by economical interests, has at this stage not taken place.

In the MIT media laboratory wearables belong to the department "Things that think." Dress conceals media, making them always available for the user. The development of wearables is realized on three levels: The lowest level engages in the hardware design of the objects. This is the only level of material design, which allows fashionable variations. The next step is the connection of the wearables and their integration into bigger networks.

The last and highest level is the design of the entire information architecture, the integration into the entire system, and the retrieval of knowledge.

The "mobilization" of the objects (naturally, their development originates in military purposes) is followed by civil applications. Their aim is the integration of technology: Implanting receivers in the ear, equipping collars with senders, or fitting mobile phones into jewelry. Actual examples for already existing wearable computer systems are UPS, mobile ticket machines, worn by the conductors of German Bundesbahn. In this way already existing "stupid" clothes can become "smart objects." Due to their specific positioning on the body, they have a task within the personal computernet: Shoes, "smart sneakers" (designed by Thad Starner of MIT and produced by Nike), are used as energy generators or as receivers. Glasses can house screens. Caps, worn on the top of the head and thus the highest point, function as stations for sending and receiving data. Smart underwear controls the physical condition and regulates body temperature. Integrated affective sensors measure blood pressure and pulse.

For military purposes smart clothes are equipped with special functions. The twenty-first-century land warrior has particular equipment analogous to its specifications. The medial soldier wears a helmet with a display (one-eyed optic), showing data to the unit and information about the enemy. He is woven into a net in which his position can be immediately traced via a laser range finder and a global positioning system. Integrated into this system are also various tools for the extension of perception and weapons.

Wearable computing turns media into dress and dress into media. Through this direct technical extension, the body becomes a sending and receiving surface. Media degrade the body to carrier material. The harmless term "clothing" averts from the significant invasion of technology. The theoretical-ideological condition for the technological body conquest and occupation is the proclamation of its inferiority—due to the "flesh factor" (title of Ars Electronica 1997)—for example on the side of "Radical Humanities" in the context of media- and hacker-culture, as well as in publications such as Mondo 2000 or WIRED.

Andrew Ross unveils the technological ideology, which stands behind the growing "smartness" of the entire object world: Humans become "outsmarted," because "smartness" is transferred to the lifeless object world. This automated intelligence illustrates: *"human-made object world becomes an alternative home of intelligence."* In contrast to human smartness, which always overshoots the mark, the smart intelligence of objects is cost saving, systematic, user-friendly, and can be subordinated under programmed structures. The economic complex strives after the production of this submissive, unscrupulous, non-neurotic, anatomically correct form of intelligence. The thesis "machines get smarter, people get dumber" creates the impression that the human being is at the limit of its mind capacity and in an urgent need of intelligent products. The "promethic shame" (Anders) is reinforced because superior technology is directly applied to the body.

The goal of concepts such as "ubiquitous computing" (Mark Weiser, MIT) is the "augmented reality": a world, enriched with intelligent clothing, furniture, and spaces. The medializing of objects is followed by the integration of humans into the networks of electrified garments. The internal network of the body via smart dress, which will be worn by all people in ten years time, is an intermediary state, as long as technology is not able to enter directly into bio-substance, to implant microchips (in twenty years), respectively cultivate genetically nano- and processor technologies in our bodies (in thirty years according to the prognosis of Neil Gershenfeld, MIT). As a flexible communication-junction the human being can move objects, far and near, by remote control via the personal body-network (PAN, Personal Area Network). Through the BodyNet an individual is connected to a network, like a mobile phone in stand-by mode, and can be localized in the net as a dialogical junction, visible in its data movements. This enables the construction of movement profiles, which can be reinterpreted in concrete spatial movements (see the Swisscom scandal at the end of 1997). Smart dress, especially underwear, similar to the "smart toilette" of the "Tronhaus," is also able to compile a personal health profile. In the case of aberration or irregularities the data will be immediately sent to the doctor.

Furthermore, through techniques like "tagging" the industry can analyze customer's purchasing habits and register electronically the course of articles. In stores tags have already had control functions for a long time, for example, electronic devices to prevent shoplifting. New models are able, via implanted chips, to trace the way from the shop to the customer, thereby weaving an invisible net of garments. Sending out invisible signals, the producers are able to localize the positioning of their articles. Future applications are imaginable, as tagging, respectively registered and actively sending garments that would increase the success in the search for criminals or terrorists. The news that a personalized pair of Levi's can be made responsible for the capture of a criminal—due to individual size and traces of use—could become the norm.

Dress influences its wearer. Even comfortable casual clothing is never entirely neutral or unobtrusive. Therefore, wearables will significantly change our habitus and the way and manner of moving around in the world. The technicians and producers have the illusion that there will a wearable computer "that's always with you, is comfortable and easy to keep and use, and it is as unobtrusive as clothing."

Instruments for espionage, such as micro-cameras or bugs, function as models for design because they are invisible and unobtrusive. Wearables will be controllable by voice or twiddler, a mixture of a mouse and a one-handed keyboard, allowing a "hands-free" operation. However, as a technical extension they cause unfamiliar sounds and movements directly on the body. Facing the vision of a rotating mirror of the "private eye," it is still doubtful that wearable media are unobtrusive. Another problem that stands against their unobtrusive integration is the supply of energy. Accumulators are actually the heaviest elements and last for approximately eight hours. They will restructure the rhythm of the day into three accu-phases.

Wearables are yet not real components of clothing, but invaders and technoid alien elements, such as the additional munitions hooked to the belt of a soldier. For everyday use of computer wear, manufacturing is particularly focused on the durability of the small computer boxes as well as shock resistance. Design and comfort are still of secondary importance.

DRESSED IN COMPUTERS

Are wearables used like conventional dress? When are they worn? Except for sports, sex, showering, and sleeping, they can be worn at all times, their developers answer. They only disturb in activities in which people wear less clothing, as well as in the context of wetness or excretion.

In the future, a day will start with putting on one's intelligence. So when one awakes in the morning, being in a dumb (and very human) state, the smart, thinking uniform is already waiting. The German term *"reizwäsche"* gets a new dimension of meaning, as computer wear always has to be equipped with electronic impulses. The energy supply is the basic element, forming a kind of immaterial underwear. Its components also have to be exchanged on a regular basis, so that the common male-chauvinist question in everyday married life will be "Darling, can you lay out a fresh accu for me?"

The human being of the future has to care for his body and his health on two levels: material and immaterial. Both of them have to be protected against viruses and violent infringements. The now "independent" dress requires regular update, repair, and safety care. It needs the "mending" of security gaps and burst seams or the replacement of buttons. The electronic clothing of the normal user is, similar to the Internet, a partly open system and therefore not safe against viruses and invasion. Other persons could get hold of the data of the bodynet and through this data quasi-enter into the bodies of others. If the exchange of data is possible via a handshake and all information on a person is immediately present, then this is always a revelation of personal data, as it is impossible to prepare the data according to the opposite person.

But security problems are no topic in the development of software. Instead scientists promise that when one wears intelligent clothing, one will never again forget something or somebody. In an immaterial sphere, navigational systems, thesaurus, dictionary, calling cards, or telephone numbers, as well as personally gained knowledge are parallel and continuously running. Quick searching machines guarantee immediate access to all needed information. Software-accessories for media clothing are programs for face recognition, which compare and classify the face of the opposite with portraits saved in the personal or public database.

So the problem of information overload sticks directly to the body. On the one hand all the personally relevant information has to be fed into the system—if one does not want to wear standard softw(e)ar. On the other hand, according to the degree of personal control, the human being is clad or locked into an invisible aura of information, losing the privilege to forget something intentionally. A computer does not forget—only completely in the case of systemic catastrophes, so there is no selective oblivion. Intelligent clothing keeps everything in mind, what has been implanted, remembering even what the human being would prefer to forget. Therefore it transports the unconsciousness in digital form.

WORK IN MOTION: THE MOBILE OFFICE

The decisive criterion of wearables is that one can move in them. This means not necessarily mobility, but the main interest lies in the option to move away from the workplace, without losing track of work. American scientists regard it as disturbing to work in a fixed environment. For the "radical humanists," the breaking away from fixed spatial-material structures is a very significant aspect. The elite of information society prefers a residence in wilderness, a life in nature, though with complete media-technological facilities. Behind this lies the hope to lead a free and self-determined life at the edge of civilization, (New Edge) and to get rid of the traditional restrictions of work. However, they overlook that only very few privileged people can afford such a "self-determined" life.

Moving away from the fixed workspace suggests total independence and freedom, the release from a fairly bad treatment of the body caused by the standardized workplaces. However, the freedom of movement is an illusion, because media clothing, programmed and standardized through hardware and software, mobilizes the entire office and glues it to the body. Thus, working people mutate into an office on legs. Work is always present, bodily perceivable. Its corporal nearness is a liability to work overtime—it is impossible to escape from work. Just like in connected tele-work, the employer can control minutely how long and on which task somebody works. The illusion of personal freedom and a free timing of the work is made possible by a subtle control, exercised by a telepresent employer. This can be understood as a subversion of the punk maxim "if you move, you don't feel the chains," which is the principle of bondage trousers, a voluntary fastening, drastically demonstrating with each step the restriction of one's own freedom of movements. The mobility of wearables is similar to that of electronic cuffs, which are used in the U.S. for prisoners placed under house arrest or for young delinquents in Britain. In this way control organs are always informed about the positioning of the prisoners.

SELF-SUFFICIENCY OF ELECTRIFIED OBJECTS

Smart clothing makes dress independent and emancipated. Objects communicate with each other and feed each other with information. In Thomas G. Zimmermann's vision of modern family life, the human being is even entirely excluded: The shoes in the closet exchange news on the daily activities of their user. Humans do not have to talk about the things of daily life; it is carried out by objects. Things even have an autonomous perception, their own senses. It might happen that only the glasses see, but not the person who wears them. The human is the sender of impulses; his task is to collect the communicative data for the machines. Dress, however, leaves its passive state behind. Through electrification it becomes "active wear," in a literal sense.

Wearables generate electric fields with changing impulses on the body. They are not immediately perceivable, but it is imaginable to reinforce them, as it is practiced in art (Stahl Stenslie, Stelarc, Huge Harry). Wearables are a sign of a Lilliput syndrome: Like Gulliver, human beings are surrounded by tiny material particles, which contain artificial organs like agents (see MIT, gesture and narrative language group) or artificial life forms, which can communicate with each other even without any action on the human's part. Electronic parasites inhabit the host "human," who feeds them with energy. This settlement of intelligent nano-populations and immaterial agents form the human's second skin, a quasi-home. The technology of wearables reverses the relation of human being and surrounding, as the human formerly occupied it all as his hostage.

Furthermore, as the example of Steve Mann shows, dress is no longer a private matter. It becomes a surface in public space, it expropriates and publishes human perception. As an interface it transfers individual views. Wearables present an exceptional state, turning humans into permanent spies of humans—against their will. The look is split in the moment when it can switch between display and external world. This diffusion of the senses turns the individual into a "divisum," which is yet not in the state of coordinating all the different motorial actions with different perceptive impulses, as the combination of car and mobile phone shows. Thus electronic dress, which can theoretically stress the senses and transfer them at the same time to other localities, reinforces sensual diffusion.

DIGITAL FASHIONS

To return to the relation of fashion and technology, a slight variation of Manfred Schneider's three stage model of information media will now be applied to the development of wearables. The model transfers the principle of "trickle down" from fashion to technology. In the first instance a technological instrument is a prototype, which is used only by an avant-garde group of users (military, industry, science). When it is put on the market, it is rare, expensive, and exclusive. However, at that stage it is already user-friendly : Its use does not demand a technical expert. The instrument is first appropriated by the economic and political elite, becoming a public as well as private means of distinction. "The powerbook as decoration is the pride of many salon-digitalist, who mocks with actuality, hype, and fashion . . . When he is plugged off the net, his personality evaporates."

With the new instrument of technology they can clearly express the principle of conspicuous consumption. Then in the third stage mass-consumers start to identify with the product. Mass production is paralleled by a further technical simplification and cost reduction. However, during this stage the gadgets do not lose their distinctive features entirely, as Schneider argues. Distinctions just get more subtle. In a phase of universal dissemination one can easily disqualify oneself by the use of wrong variants: a bulky, turquoise mobile phone is not really a status symbol.

Wearables are currently in the test period for their inventors. They are purely functionally defined and show no intentional aesthetic implications. What Morse states regarding smart food, namely that it is not tasty and only a medicine for body tuning, applies to smart clothing, too. Everything "smart" has, per se, no aesthetic design. Therefore wearables, as future components of everyday wear, will provoke new questions regarding individual style and self-performance. Is there a society of immaterial decorated data-dandies and unfashionable computer-nerds emerging, whose insignificant flesh—namely the body-facade—tells nothing about the inner beauty of the collected immaterial data? The fashionable attributes of the new programmer elite are of a technological naturek their clothing plays a subordinated part and can be put into the traditional dress segment of "casuals" (remember Bill Gates as a young programmer).

"Perfume and pink stockings are just replaced by valuable intels, delicate data-gloves, data-glasses decorated with ruby and fine sensors on his eyebrows and the wings of his nose."

The person who can telephone by the means of a pin and earring will be regarded as avant-garde. As in the area of mobile phones the "almost" invisibleness will become an important status symbol. Only the members of the old economic elite will impress each other with the latest Armani design. The new sort of clothing and accessories will be made-to-measure, purchasable in the computer store. Thereby, to become a fashionable medium, wearables have to pass the stage of standardization and become mass-confection. Without standards, dress cannot fulfill its communicative promise. There is no sense in being the only one wearing a certain system, because there can happen no exchange with others. So for the present, there will be no haute couture of wearables—data-suits without compatibility are useless.

Visually marking signs for new systems will emerge to suit people's wish for distinction. However, even insiders are not able to recognize the latest processor or the newest gadget in dress. A perfect media-dress will stand out by the exclusivity of a personal filter, sorting out digital junk immediately. But they, too, are not visible. Socio-economic development will contradict the scientist's original idea of invisible wearables. Like in youth cultures, the design of labels and logos will play an important part in the demonstrative display of differences in the immaterial. T-shirts saying "Intel Inside" already exist, but for the future prints listing the data capacity of the worn processors are thinkable, too. Maybe the electronically enriched clothing will also show small embroideries, similar to labels, which give information about the worn system. And wearables will also produce fashionable and unfashionable systems. There will be secondhand ware and retro-aesthetics, featuring old-school processors. However, they will never be a serious functional competition to actual models. Because technology never falls behind its possible systems and its own velocity, they will remind to past systems only as aesthetic surface.

Resources
Web Sites
Digital Life Consortium. Retrieved September 18, 2005 from http://dl.media. mit.edu/

Mentges, G. Piercing. Frog Design Mind. Retrieved September 18, 2005 from http://www.frogdesign.com

PIERCING

Gabriele Mentges

"Piercing is like a drug. Once you have begun, you must continue." This is the comment one of my students made. Being herself pierced, she was engaged in a project on body modifications that I carried out at the Institute of Cultural History of Textiles at Dortmund University.

Body ornaments like piercing and tattoo have been around in non-Western cultures as well as in certain subcultural contexts for quite a while now. In Western industrial cultures, however—on a broader scale—they turned up in mainstream *fashion* and in the numerous youth culture styles only within the last decade. They imply a profound transformation in the use of jewelry and corporal ornamentation: decorative body ornaments are moving increasingly toward the surface of the skin, or rather, onto certain bare parts of the body.

Piercings are actually only one variant of body modifications. There are other, apparently more extreme practices that go even further—and thus deeper into the skin: like branding, scarification, cutting, and implants. However, in the following I will focus on piercings, as they turned out to be among the most popular forms of body modification in current practice.

As material objects, piercings can have a great variety of forms, such as rings or rod-shapes. To avoid infections they should be made of metals like gold, niobium, or high-grade steel, as it is used in surgery. The piercing is often set on the so-called thresholds or openings of the body, like the ear, the mouth, or the genitals. The tongue, eyebrows, nose, ear, and—depending on the way you dress—the navel are the body parts where the piercing can be seen by the public. Where and how the piercing is going to be set always depends on the part of the body. The genital piercing in particular demands a special fitting. The piercing apparatus has to be adapted to the individual size of the penis, for example.

Piercings and all the other cited corporeal artifacts differ remarkably from sartorial accessories: They are no longer simply an adjunct to the body, but become themselves a part of the body, as discussed by Featherstone. To put it more precisely: they move beneath the surface and penetrate the skin as the ultimate frontier of the body. Therefore, the skin must be seen less as a corporal-biological frontier but rather, as a culturally established boundary.

It seems that a new relationship between the body and its representation is emerging, one that is closely linked with the question of gender.

Before I will turn to these issues, however, first some notes on the empirical basis of this entry: The following remarks and reflections are based on interviews and ethnographic investigations that my students have carried out with young people living in the industrial area of the Ruhr-Valley. This area has the highest population density in Germany, as well as the highest concentration of industries. Since the decline of the coal industry, it is also marked by social contrasts and economical problems. It is an urban region made up by a net of nearby cities, and is also connected by the dynamic of a great number of clubs and youth-cultural scenes. The people interviewed were between 13 to 35 years old (time period 1999–2000, 2002), and came from all sorts of social backgrounds, ranging from students and social workers to traders and craftsmen. The group can be broadly divided into "pierced," "non-pierced," and people working as piercers or as manufacturers of piercing jewelry. In addition to these first-hand informants, the students also asked a school-class of young boys and girls about their views on and experiences with piercing.

The print media and related sources, such as television, provided another source of material. The media discussion of piercing stimulates not only the discussion in the public, but contributes also to the lust of sensation concerning piercing practices. Beyond thathealth experts have also been interviewed about piercing and body modification.

This entry will be structured with respect to these different groups and perspectives. I will first focus on the side of the actors, meaning the people that are pierced and those who work in piercing studios, and then will focus on the other side, on the perception of piercing by those people who are "non-pierced," including our own perspective, those of health institutions and the media.

To use the terms of Goffmann's theory as a metaphor, our study was framed by several perspectives: One focused on the actors on the stage, the other on the spectators in front or behind the stage. This is also the side where the social-

More teens than ever before are getting "tats"

medical discourses on the effects of piercing is located, held by medics and the legal part of society. The metaphor of the "stage" implies that it is possible to change sides, and also that there is something like a "spectacle" going on. Neither the sides nor the perspectives are definitely fixed, nor the participation or involvement in each. The process of negotiating piercing—and by this body modification—is in Western society, in full swing.

So toward an exploration of the cultural boundaries between the different groups and their body practices, I want to consider all aspects of the discussion, reading the rejection of piercing as a practice too.

VIEWS ON THE BODY

It is not surprising that the body was the center of all interest and all arguments collected in favor of, as well as against piercing: I will first briefly summarize some of the "activist's" arguments.

For one young woman, her pierced navel aroused a sensation of pregnancy. It also intensified her corporal feeling and her sexual sensations. Another young women with a pierced tongue noted that she liked to have something in her mouth to play around with. She also said that the piercing has reinforced her sense of taste and intensified the feeling of kissing. Others, with genital piercings, said they liked to intensify their bodily sensation simply by moving around. During love-games and sexual contacts, they could attain a very particular pleasure. That is nearly always the case with intimate piercings. A twenty-three-year-old dental technician said that her pierced vagina stimulates her sexual excitement. She added, "This kind of bodily experience is like a threshold between pain and pleasure."

Pierced body parts draw erotic attention from the others or give an erotic feeling to oneself. One young student reported that each morning, when he looks at himself in the mirror, he finds himself reassured and in a better personal condition and feeling toward himself. "There are also many couples who use piercing to refresh their sex life," remarked a young woman, working as a piercer. She added, "Piercing forces you to confront yourself with your own body. That can be fun, but sometimes it can also be quite annoying. With your piercing you can experience the most strange things, there can be very unpleasant situations, you have to go through.

Piercing embraces the entire body, its senses, and its feelings. But it seems to depend less on the gaze of others, which is usually associated with the appearance and has so much importance in dress and fashion. So my first assumption was that piercings might stand for a different kind of representation, of a rather unusual imagination of the body. This sort of corporeal ornamentation intensifies the own bodily feeling and experience; however, it doesn't necessarily need the gaze of others. Already the fact that it is hidden from the public eye, its secrecy and intimacy, can provide a special delight, which adds to the concrete corporeal feeling.

The piercers, on the other hand, claim the role of a healer who has a greater experience in setting piercings than a medic. In fact, many people prefer piercers, with studios similar to tattoo-shops, instead of doctors because they think they are more competent in finding the right places on their body.

Piercers, both men and women, seemed to enjoy talking about their profession. They were even looking for publicity. They proved to be very eager and conscious, at least verbally, to heal the wounds they have inflicted on their clients. Looking after their clients seems to have as much importance as the procedure of piercing itself. Considering their fragile and contested status in society, the necessity to be so eager with the concerns of their patients seems to be quite obvious. Piercing is actually not regarded as a profession. Yet all the piercers are extremely engaged in their profession and convinced of a deeper sense of piercing. Most of them don't consider piercing simply as a job, but as the realization and expression of their way of life. Perhaps piercings and tattoos can be understood as body-codes, which communicate a certain kind of consensus between otherwise very diverse sorts of people.

Turning to the other perspective, now, it became evident that non-pierced people fear the sight of the—as they called it—mutilated body. Mutilation was treated as an equivalent to non-beauty. An elderly lady, for example, associated tattoos and piercings with pirates and criminals. Many people are also simply afraid of the disadvantages they might be confronted with at their work place. Indeed, some employers refuse piercings at all and also in many official institutions, like the army, piercings are not accepted. The main arguments or reasons for the rejection of piercing refer to aspects of hygiene and medicine. People were afraid of hurting themselves and worried about the wounds, which could get infected and cause problems when one gets older.

A great number of the non-pierced people, among them the younger ones, however, accept a certain kind, or, more precisely, a certain degree of piercing. They favor nose piercing, perhaps navel piercing, but reject intimate piercing completely. Aspects of hygiene, disease, and aging were the main reasons for their refusal. There were also older people who favored piercing, although the great majority who seem in favor of piercing belong to the younger generation.

In reconsidering the arguments, the crucial question that separates the groups is whether you are authorized to do damage to your own body or, to put in a positive way, if you are allowed to practice body modifications. This question determines even the pure aesthetic argument.

This problem leads directly into the center of the medical-hygienic discourse, but touches first on a legal interest. In actual German law, piercing can be labeled a bodily harm, and hence constitute a criminal offence. For this reason professional piercers generally ask teenagers to certify the agreement of their parents. This is the reason why, in the eyes of the law and in traditional medicine, piercing is considered an illegal, or, at least, a very doubtful practice. A warning from the federal secretary of health, for example, recalls the risks of infections caused by piercing, such as the transfer of AIDS and jaundice. Official representatives often try to criminalize piercing or at least they pathologize it. Print media tends to horrify the new techniques as well, when implying that each stitch runs a risk.

Nonetheless, health insurance plans are forced to accept piercing as a reality and correspondingly they "inform" people by warning about the risks and recommending health doctors instead of piercing studios.

THE INTACT BODY

The official argumentation proves to be rather ambiguous. The verdict of law only concerns piercers, but—strangely enough—not the "competitive" profession of the jewelers. They are allowed to practice piercing and, considering the common fashion of the earring, they have been authorized to do that for quite a long time now. A director of a health center, who was interviewed about this problem, avoided approaching that topic at all.

The condemnation of piercing practices, on the side of health institutions and by law, can be seen as a form of social and cultural exclusion of a non-desired competition. Medical discourse once again defends its hegemony. Yet it also reflects the manner, in which this discourse is culturally situated. In her article on piercing Karmen MacKendrick discusses the crucial points of the public discussion on piercing. I agree with her in so far as she refuses the medical or pathological reading of piercing as cultural practise. She is also right in rejecting the argument that piercing continues the misogynist practises of western beauty culture. Instead she centers her main argument on technology or, precisely, on the context of modern technology.

Strategies of conforming to the actual cultural body discourse and strategies of subversion are both engaged, adds MacKendrick, based on Foucault's theory. Media-theorist Birgit Richard argues even more pointedly when she interprets the new body modifications as an experimental preparation toward the future employment of high-tech in and on our bodies.

But beyond medicine and law, there are also the religious traditions that are challenged. Christian tradition maintains the rule that the body must be kept free from injury. However, on the other hand, as Scarry points out, representations of Christ involve bodily images.

PAIN AND MEDICAL DISCOURSE

In the medical history of Western culture the ambiguous position and treatment of the body is well reflected. Since the Renaissance the human body has been submitted to the experiments of surgery and hence to the opening of the body for dissection. The interest in having a look into the inside of the body finds its continuation in the actual Visual Human Project, a three-dimensional digital model of the body. Contemporary artists like Stellarc and Orlan today test and challenge new body experiments with their art.

Surgery and, above all, plastic surgery is specialized in the transformation of the body and its single parts. Pieces of the body can be removed, replaced, and modified. Following its official definition, plastic surgery aims at the correction of deformed bodily parts. In reality, however, this practice goes a few steps further, ranging from silicon breasts to lip implants, transformed noses, accentuated cheekbones, anti-wrinkle skin-lifting, and so on. In her essay on female artificial bodies, art historian Katharina Sykora depicts the different ways of approaching the body during the last three hundred years. Back in the eighteenth century, the category of nature entered the center of the bourgeois conception of the body. Even though the promotion of "natural" behavior does not exclude body modifications by corsets and other dress instruments. Despite this ideological norm, women, and sometimes even men, were regularly breaking these norms by wearing corsets or other means to form and shape their bodies.

Today, it is, above all, the female body where plastic surgery finds its most interesting and exciting territory. Interestingly Sykora compares plastic surgery in its intention of beautification to the tailor of the nineteenth century. Like the tailor, she points out; the surgeon works with needle, stitches, and scissors to execute his operations. The piercers and tattooers seem to work in the very same way. Their studios resemble very much a surgery cabinet: you see instruments such as needles, scissors, couches, gynecological chairs, a lavatory, sterilization, gloves, sheets, and other medical instruments. One is surprised by the cleanliness of the white walls and the medical atmosphere of the entire surrounding.

But in contrast to the medical surgery, these interiors are completed by large mirrors, posters, and photographs of modified body parts that hint to the special character of this work place. Apparently it is the special mixture of this environment that increases the excitement and interest of people who decide to get a piercing done from a studio. In many ways the experience of those who are pierced resembles people's usual suffering from "normal" medical treatment, of which the scariest one is certainly the treatment of the dentist.

A young women, who is a social worker by profession, mentioned that she did not feel any pain but an exciting rush of adrenaline during the piercing procedure. When she left the piercing studio with her new tongue piercing, she was "high." In the beginning she perceived the piercing as an alien element, but after a few days she thought that something was missing from her body when she had to remove it for cleaning. Another young woman, age twenty-three, who also has her tongue pierced, reported that she was afraid of the pain, but the piercer calmed her down by being very kind and helpful. The piercing procedure itself didn't cause a lot of harm; yet she was suffering afterwards. However, even if she could not eat but only drink for a few days, she said that "in view of what you are getting in return, it is worth the pain" (club manager). Another young women mentioned that it was a special kick for her to master her own fear (employee of hotel business).

Turning to the side of research, this experience of pain has provoked a set of interesting interpretations. Michel Maffesoli argues, for example, that traditional patterns of sociability are nowadays reproduced in forms of neotribalism. Piercing is also defined in terms of an anti-fashion strategy to escape consumer society. Others like Le Breton highlights piercing as a new form of 'rite de passage'. Indeed similarities with traditional societies cannot be neglected: Cultural anthropologist Pierre Clastre, for example, has reported how Native Americans marked their rite of passage from childhood to adulthood with rituals of tattooing and scarifications. The body was used as a register or documentary for cultural and social memory: a corporeal means against oblivion.

All researchers agree that piercing and tattoo must be considered as part of the new great body project, which is dedicated to the construction of a coherent self-identity. Indeed, sociologist Jean-Yves Pidoux adds that piercing expresses the wish to transform the body into an icon, inscribed with indestructible signs.

The recapturing of autonomy-niches is characteristic of modern youth-cultures, who strive after the distinction from mainstream consumption practices and common social values. However as research on tattoos, at least in the United States, has shown they are not limited to youth cultures only, but spread among members of the middle classes from young to old (fifty-five years). During the 1980s, for example, tattooing among women was conceived as one way of liberating the female boy and reinforcing female self-validity. However, the similarity to medical practice refers to a further dimension that is quite a more subversive character. We are dealing with a transfer of medical forms of experience into an aesthetic-cultural practice. This indicates, above all, a regain of the autonomy of one's own body against the power of traditional medicine.

SKIN AND CULTURAL BOUNDARIES

Véronique Zbinden regards pain in this context as a stimulation of lust and sexual energy. She speaks of a regained control over pain. Not only is this dimension included in body modifications, moreover, they hint at a complex set of cultural relations and patterns, which can be read according to their multiple potential meanings.

Elaine Scarry has repeatedly stressed the difficulty of formulating pain in speech. Piercing does not only articulate the body, it also situates pain within a cultural surrounding, thus "naming" it. This is already another critique against the hegemonic medical practice, which separates pain from the individual, thus creating and fixing it as an abstraction. What is new and original about this articulation of pain in Western societies is the manner and way it is produced, that is via the insertion or penetration of objects into the body. However, if we take Elaine Scarry's definition of objects for granted, saying that it is body enlargement, what happens when these objects are actually incorporated by the body?

Since the eighteenth century the skin has been considered the ultimate frontier of the body, dividing between inside and outside as well as between the individual and his environment. The skin has to be viewed both as an organic and cultural boundary. In her profound study on skin, Claudia Benthien has examined the various cultural perceptions of the human skin. Skin serves as a metaphor for the housing, vicariously for the human body. However, this meaning has been applied to skin only in the eighteenth century and was paralleled with a new understanding of the body: The skin was now viewed as a wrapping or concealment of the inner corporeal container, awakening an interest in penetrating into its inside content.

In the nineteenth century, medical theory treated skin as a potential carrier of infectious bacteria, thus claiming corporal and social distance to the skin as well as to the individual person. The cultural perception of skin now turned increasingly into a distant-perception.

Referring to the cultural imagery of the body, Benthien notes the outstanding significance of the skin: Skin, like no other part of the body, serves both as the representation of the corporeal unity, and for what is concealed. With the examination of the cultural meaning of skin, the concept of boundary is called into question, the boundary between inside and outside, the self and the other.

Feeling—the sense closely connected to the skin—is not only a psychological process, it is in fact rooted in the concrete haptic feeling. Didier Anzieu showed this convincingly: For him, skin is an organic, as well as an imaginative reality. It is a protection of our individuality, as well as the immediate instrument and side of exchange with the other. Therefore, modern psychology seeks the problem of psychological disorientation in the interface between the perception of the boundary and the own *image du corps*. Viewing the spectacle of all the performing tattooed and pierced bodies in events like the Berlin love-parade, the "festival of performing bodies" as one newspaper called it, the nudity of bodies is eye-catching, though gender-specific.

Apparently, as far as conveyed in the media images, we witness here a new kind of search for nearness between humans—at least human bodies—suggesting a boundlessness. Are we really dealing here with a new hitherto unknown body-experience and design, loosening the old, firm, and skin-limited body? What does this mean to the relation of identity, body, and gender?

At first sight, as far as the culture of piercing is concerned, we find a certain promotion of an androgynous body politic. However, returning to the immense and huge love parade, we can observe highly gender specific features: the male body is eroticized in a very different manner than the female body. The latter is still completely exhibited—whereas among men, the erotic gaze focuses on the breast, and therefore only on the upper part of the male body. At least, I dare to maintain that traditional gender differentiations become less outspoken, they are more implicit than before and they are using other forms of articulation.

CONSTRUCTION OF THE SELF AND GENDERING

In Western societies piercing refers to surgery. It does not only defy actual health prescriptions for the skin but also the traditional conception of the body in the whole. This means, on the one hand, to decontextualize techniques and technology and, on the other, to push the consequences of technology to an outermost limit, that is the incorporation of technology into the own body. And this implies a further connection between body and material culture, as the body is opened to the material and human environment. The skin no longer fixes an ultimate frontier between the self and the other. Is a new concept of identity coming up, in which the definition of self is no longer attached to the body?

In his short but very concise essay on jewelry, George Simmel centers the interest in jewels in the classical conception of person and identity. Wearing jewelry means to him an extension of the human body, which enables a person to radiate power by the means of the particular quality of brilliant and reflecting precious stones. For Simmel the culturally given ability of distinction and dissociation represents a necessity for individual and social autonomy.

Media scientists favor the argument that a new concept of the body as techno-flesh is emerging. They take for granted that the human body can serve as an appropriate field for future experiments with genetic and bio-technology, as well as information technology. However, they apply the same paradigm of group and individual membership. Of course, it is a provocation of the traditional uniqueness of the body in so far as the skin is proclaimed dress. When Kate Ince discusses Orlan's performance art she notes that, if the skin is no longer the frontier between dress and the body, the status of dress as well as of skin is changing. And citing Orlan, she concludes, "The body is but a costume."

CONCLUSIONS

Being part of the experiences of youth cultures, piercing has the status of a ritual inside the consumer culture that opens a large field of action. Thus it refers to new forms of socialization that develop outside the traditional frame of family, school, and other institutions in order to shape new cultural values and behavior. But body modification also seems to challenge a highly and thoroughly technological society with all its paradoxes, its contradictions, its hypocrisy, and its cultural normalizations; sciences are not excluded from this challenge. Therefore, the remarkable pleasure that is demonstrated by the pierced as well as by professional piercer in their talk about their own feelings and experiences calls the method of interview itself into question. At the very least, we must not only revise our scientific tools concerning youth cultures, but we have to ask if they have turned scientific research into a stage, and the scientist into an actor too.

GOTH

Birgit Richard

The subculture of the goths (in Germany called "grufties") started in Britain in the early 1980s and derives from the gloomy, resigned side of punk and new wave, in the field of music called "dark wave" or "doom." It is noticeable that there are many coexisting terms for this style. The goths take the Gothic novels of the romantic period as a point of reference, which can be deduced from the English expression "Gothic punk." They also like to call themselves "the blacks." The German term gruftie derives from the motif Gruft" (tomb). It is not a proud dissociation from the normal citizen, but a kind of stigma. This self-labeling is not completely unproblematic, so in the 1990s the not totally serious Gothcode 1.1. (resembling a program with updates) was supposed to make it easier to get in touch with other "blacks" on the Internet. A person can decipher from codes what category another gothic assigns himself or herself. There is, for example, the "Jammergoth." Life is a permanent existential crisis—you simultaneously weigh up what is more unsettling, the expanding conflict in Bosnia or the transitoriness of things. Or there is the "shy goth: please, don't look at me. . . . I hope they are not talking to me." Other manifestations are the muntergoth, grantelgruftie, sarkigoth, and der-goth-der-nur-noch-dahinvegetiert (German terms expressing different kinds of character and philosophies of life).

THE MELANCHOLIC CONDITION OF THE "BLACKS"

The large acceptance of the Internet indicates that gothics are not a "street style." The public sphere is not of essential importance for the presentation of the style. Meetings are held in private or at isolated places like cemeteries, where the scene is not disturbed. You enter the black scene, when a certain philosophy of life shall be expressed: loneliness, isolation, lacking affection and communication, problems at school, identity problems, and disappointment in first love affairs. Helsper gives another reason: the basic alienation from and indifference to children in the family. In addition, the style opposes highly controlled structures like they can still often be found in small towns and villages. Far away from parents and schools, which no longer offer any security or support, the style becomes a place for reproducing socialization. The individual gets a forum and a symbolic-cultural opportunity to express herself or himself to deal with problems and doubts about the meaning of life in an imaginary way. Introverted sadness and melancholy, which are based on disappointments subjectively experienced and collectively shared by all members and trigger a mental processing of a resigned and pessimistic philosophy of life, are characteristic. A network of the lonely is formed, who also realize their strong desire for contact at particular meeting points, such as "black discos," where, however, you rather get the impression of a cultivated isolation.

The Internet, too, as a new medium of communication through international links, selectively does away with the individual isolation. The existing "black nets," which were launched on festivals and by fanzines, are expanded. The web offers the opportunity to communicate directly and exchange information with like-minded people (e.g., information on concerts and records, gothic clubs and scene-boutiques, films, comics, books, poems, and online games), which is independent of physical proximity. The decisive structural feature for gothics is the link to other gothic-sites (e.g., Death Homepage [1995], The Darkening of the Light, The Dark Side [all September 1996]), which guarantees that a permanent linking-up with other "blacks" all over the world can be sustained.

The Net is also a carrier of the style's values, such as the important internal taboos of the style. One of these is the "gool," the gravedigger, digging up mortal remains in cemeteries to use them to decorate rooms or person. This figure, very popular in the relevant media and attracting attention by rituals at the grave and necrophilic activities, which is perceived to be the epitome of the gothic style, is rejected by a large part of the scene. Digging up mortal remains, for gothics, represents a proximity to death that is no longer tolerable, because the direct intrusion into the sphere of the dead lacks the due respect. These extreme gothics, who only leave their flats at night and no longer go to discos, have done away with the constituent, existentially important social contacts of the style, which enable them to process their basic mentality of proximity to death.

A myth of a forbidden zone of the black culture is formed. The persona "gool," inaccessible for strangers to the cult, is, despite the vehement verbal rejection, a fascinating feature of the scene. It represents the existence of real death, while the rest of the scene stylizes death. The rejection of these practices sets limits to the fascination with death specific to this group. The second fascinating feature thus mentally processed is suicide. The notion of suicide is familiar. However, it is not accepted as a solution to their own existential problems, but as an admitted failure due to their own emotions of loss, death, and sadness. Therefore, the goths are no subculture of death, driving members to commit suicide, as is reported in the media and asserted by politicians, but rather the opposite: an attempt to pursue a critical and joint analysis of their own loneliness and proximity to death. In the awareness that they live here and now and have to deal with their problems, they develop a different relationship to death, having overcome the overwhelming fear of death shown by other human beings.

Another important part of the style is the preoccupation with religion. Supported by the process of the "bricolage of religion," the gothics deal with elements of Christianity, religions of other ethnic groups, and occult traditions. The latter are attractive for goths because they are linked to another era or to another stage of the development of civilizations. Symbolism rejected as irrational by other parts of society enables them to express dissatisfaction with the institutionalized church and the completely rationalized modern civilization.

The reflecting examination of religious and occult traditions does not lead to an occult gothic religion. The opposite is true: It would be contradictory if the Gothics voluntarily entered a restricting, closed system, after having stylistically broken out of a rustic-religious one-track environment. The "main article of faith" is not the belief in Satan or God, as reported by the media—Gothics can rather be considered to be atheists—but a belief in death as a higher power no mortal is able to elude. The "bricolage of religion" creates a kind of private religion of death, which reminds its followers of their mortality, but has no comforting function of providing relief.

COMPONENTS OF BLACK STYLE

Among its prominent representatives the Gothic style runs through the whole environment of life: their room, clothes, hairdo, music, dance, places, spheres, media (fanzines—magazines/Internet). The World Wide Web enables gothics to transfer music and pictures of bands they admire, such as Sisters of Mercy, Cure, Alien Sex Fiend, Ann Clarke, Skinny Puppy, Fields of Nephilim, Christian Death, and Current 93, from generation to generation.

As with all subcultures, the epicenter is the music. From all areas of Independent Music examples with sad or dark lyrics or musical structures, which correspond to their melancholic sense of life are filtered out. Sound collages of ordinary noises, quotations from religious contexts (Gregorian chants or instruments like church organs), harpsichord sounds and self-manufactured instruments made of bones are put alongside punk and electronic body music.

The preoccupation with lyrics dealing with unrequited love, death, and religion serves the purpose of an outlet to overcome depressions endangering their existence. A band such as Joy Division is supposed to be very authentic because the depressive basic mentality of vocalist Ian Curtis, who committed suicide because of an unhappy love affair, can be found in their lyrics and music. The absolutely passive anti-dance of the gothics is a meditative concentration of energy on the inner sphere of the individual, a retreat into an inner exile. The autistic form of dancing, reminiscent of movements of Frankenstein's monster, is also described as North-South-Course by those who mock the style. It consists of a monotonous, staggering walk up and down an imaginary line, without ever heeding the music's rhythm. The body movements have nothing to do with physical activity, a release of energy, or aggressions, quite unlike the pogo of the punks or the self-experience of the body by hippies.

VAMPIRES, MONKS, AND WITCHES: BLACK OUTFITS

The rooms of the "blacks" are designed in a special manner with small altars on which accessories such as grave-ribbons, crucifixes, grave-lamps, candles, and skulls are arranged. Pen-cases formed like coffins are supposed to symbolize death as useable items in ordinary life to be aware of the individual's own mortality. Caves draped in black with tombstone-walls are fairly extreme examples within the scene and are partly smiled upon, partly admired. However, in contrast to media reports, we do not find coffins used as beds or corpses, for that matter. The room shall reconstruct the dark atmosphere of the cemetery, its proximity to death, or serve as a cave that shelters from a threatening outside world. The accessories also bear witness to an element of fun in dealing with things that are unsettling for other people.

Very unusual and standing out from the contemporary, versatile fashion-range is the "blacks'" very homogenously designed way of clothing, reminiscent of figures from centuries past. This style of clothing does not correspond to the "confrontation dress" of punk, which is supposed to be provocative. To be sure, it is nevertheless shocking, but any confrontation is unintentional.

The dissociation of the goths is successful: the color black, which dominates the style, is primarily associated with old age, death, loss, and mourning. At a time when punk made it possible to wear all sorts of colors—for example, neon colors—for clothes, a color loaded with meaning is deliberately chosen as a dissociation from a carefree life, characterized by superficiality and consumption.

The goths combine the various cultural meanings of the color they are familiar with. For them, black is the expression of a sense of emptiness, a meaninglessness, and a symbol for despair and resignation. Beyond, it is an expression of mourning for mankind, which is quite possibly doomed, a premise the gothics cannot do anything about. Besides, the color points to the self-chosen ascetic isolation of monks. For the goths, the central meaning of the color black is the symbolization of inevitable death. The "blacks," as they typically call themselves, alongside the necrophile component of the color, also promote the traditional symbolization of the evil and the negative, which are turned into positive ideals.

The goths put the color black—under normal circumstances intended for the temporary phase of mourning, therefore having a special position in the spectrum of colors—into the context of ordinary situations. It is detached from any particular purposes as regards time, place, or situation and, as a decisive feature of the style, is applied to all situations in life. The color black is contrasted by silver metal studs and ornaments on accessories and clothes, floral motifs like the rose or symbols of death like the skull. We find the pointed, tightly tailored buckled shoe, recalling the pointed shoes of the outgoing middle ages, embroidered with death's-head or bat buckles.

The gothic style is accumulative; belts, bracelets, earrings, buckles never appear in a simple manner. The clothes are unordinary and the opposite of what we might consider comfortable clothes for everyday life. Furthermore, they demonstrate a detached attitude toward the body. Items of clothing such as wide capes, wraps, scarves, Dracula-capes, monks' habits and cassocks, and Turkish pants on men do not permit drawing conclusions on the veiled body. The body's sexually distinctive marks, otherwise so important in society, have no central place in the style's philosophy, since the erotic is passionately referred to death.

The goths have nothing to do with the actively aggressive principle of torn clothes and the aesthetics of ugliness and poverty, on which punk is based. A poetical stage-production creates female, "beautiful" angels of death, corresponding to romantic ideals of the nineteenth century. Thus the preferred materials are soft, traditional, and natural fabrics like lace, velvet, or silk, less frequently leather, patent–leather, or rubber, representing a tough sexuality.

The four basic patterns of hairdo are an essential hallmark of the goths. The most prominent hairdo is the "plate" (also called flat anti-tank mine or plate skull). Gothics talk about "making (themselves) the plate." The covering hair is plastered with incredible amounts of hairspray and formed into a plate-like, flat thing. Another hairdo derives from the shaved head of the punks, leaving only a ridge between brow and neck, although in most cases hair here is worn longer and backcombed. We also find the waver-hairdo, with upstanding covering hair and very short or shaved-off hair on the sides and above the neck. These manifestations are mostly worn by male goths.

Women prefer black, long, uncombed-looking hair, which is extremely backcombed and supposed to be reminiscent of the tangled hair of witches. In contrast to the fanzines, on the Internet we can find practical advice on how to comb hair in a "gothic style," dye it black, or "paint to death," and put on make-up, black eye shadow, lipstick, and nail varnish to counteract a chalky white face. This "dead" way of putting on make-up, "painting to death" or "walking around dead" as the gothics of both sexes call it, creates the symbolic comprehensive picture of the dead in living bodies or of vampires (i.e., unworldly figures) and anticipates the fate of the future dead and shall express solidarity with the dead.

The everyday clothes and make-up of the gothics with their materials, colors, and tailoring patterns represent a permanent celebration of death and mourning.

BLACK ART: ANKH, BAT, AND RUIN

Motifs and symbols of jewelry essentially derive from three closely linked areas: death and physical mortality, Christianity and religions of other cultural backgrounds, and the magic.

Since goths are fascinated by everything that has to do with death, consequentially their favorite motifs in jewelry are death's heads, skeletons, and bones. The latter, when worn on clothes as real items, become a materialized memento mori, a personal relic.

The religious symbolism used comprises only a few accessories, such as crucifixes, stars of David, ankh (an Egyptian symbol), or the pentagram. The most provocative symbol is the cross turned upside down, a historico-cultural symbol of Satanism, which in turn reverses rituals of Christianity. Here, it serves as a distinguishing feature from the normal Christian symbol and is simultaneously provocation and diffuse criticism of religion and the institutionalized church. Also when following traditional religious symbolism, the cross has different levels of meaning: it represents a deinstitutionalized Christian faith, a kind of protective pendant against evil, or is simply an embellishment. Alongside skeletons and death's heads, it refers to anguish and transitoriness.

The embellishment with religious accessories from other cultural backgrounds and eras is directed against the primacy of a restrictive Christian doctrine. With this act of secularization, the gothics conquer the last bastion of fixed symbols for the process of Bricolage. This not only consists of a radical re-codification of Christian symbols, but, through the combination with other symbols, also an opening-up of new dimensions of meaning.

In the border area between life and death we find the phenomenon of the walking dead, the undead, who are returning (for example, the pale, bloodsucking vampire). The gothics stylize themselves as beings who populate the world between life and death. A preferred motif in jewelry, thus deriving, is the bat, an "ugly, dangerous, bloodsucking" beast of the night. This irrational prejudice is accounted for by the bat's association with the powers of evil. While the punks actually carry around their symbolic animal, the rat, which is also discriminated against, the gothics have selected an imaginary zoo of animals which, because of their color or nocturnal life, according to Christian definition since the Middle ages, are supposed to have been symbolic animals of evil. The zoo includes spiders in particular—since so many people are disgusted by spiders, the spider's web is a frequently appearing ornament on clothes—plus flies, ravens or crows, amphibians, lizards or salamanders, newts, owls, snakes, and beetles. The symbolic animals have the important function of taking over the drifting souls of dead humans. Thus the gothics use originally religious symbols of death and of evil in which, nevertheless, folksy superstition has been kept intact.

The imaginary worlds of the gothics also comprise atmospherically charged pictures of dark palaces, castles, dungeons, and nocturnal scenarios, veiled by fog and the light of a full moon. For the imaginative dealing with these unordinary worlds of images, the Web offers ideal conditions. As a technological medium, it permits the construction of virtual-imaginary worlds detached from tough reality. Here, the imaginary figures of the past described above can flourish.

Concerning real spheres, the gothics predominantly use "gothic-like," dark places such as cemeteries and ruins. The motif "industrial ruin," for punks a symbol of acceptance and use of the urban sphere, is of no interest to gothics. Only an old, crumbling church with a cemetery in a lonely landscape represents an undefinable value, long gone elsewhere, that was able to survive on the fringes of a consumer society. The aura of decay and isolation creates a strong sense of belonging together for the time of the original construction of the building. The ruin is the skeleton of a building and symbolizes the process of ageing of humans and objects.

The places the "blacks" prefer are characterized by silence, isolation, gloominess, and death. It is especially the cemetery, a place detached from most people's ordinary life, thereby acquiring its aura of the forbidden and mysterious, that is turned into their normal venue by goths. They benefit from the reluctance of normal citizens to encounter death and mortality. In the twentieth century, most people do not like to go to cemeteries, a place where proximity to death is the greatest. For gothics, this is the decisive reason to stay there. Their everyday sojourn and their mourning, independent of an individual's fate—at their graves, they linger over the history of the dead unknown to them—revives the traditional public function of a cemetery.

PROVOCATIVE DANCES MACABRES

Gothics are a retrospective youth culture. The whole style is a complex, historically orientated form of coming to terms with melancholy and depression, mentally combining individual and collective death (the fate of mankind, apocalypse, last days, and destruction of the environment). The gothics have extreme and direct ways of dealing with death, unsettling for the rest of society. This is owing to the partial release and the removal of taboos of notions and images of death. They construct niches in various media, where the seemingly archaic, atavistic symbols and images can be circulated (e.g., picture galleries on the Web). The myths of the scene are repeated here. The desire for an ever-present encyclopedia, a genealogy of the images of the style can be realized here in an adequate fashion. The most important function of the gothic homepages on the Internet is therefore, besides the online communication, the collection and exchange of images and symbols of death. Repetition and the creation of variants on a basic repertory of images (e.g., gothic image database, gothic/images/index) turn the Net into the virtual archive of the style. It is the keeper of the stories (e.g., about the gool, ghoul, the gravedigger) and the immaterial image-representations of the out-of-the-ordinary symbolism of the style mentioned above, so that they are constantly at the disposal of the internal autopoesis of the style.

The goths protect themselves against the latent fascination with these pictures and concepts of death by carefully drawing a line when it comes to the realization of necrophilic fantasies. The determined examination of decay and dissolution of physical substance takes place on the imaginary level of ciphers and symbols. While the development of a style in youth cultures normally constitutes an imaginary resolution of real contradictions in the process of reproduction, the gothic style is all about the symbolic stylization of loss, death, and mourning experienced in reality. The aesthetic anticipation of the individual's own death and the realization of the process of mourning through their stylization of a walking dead between life and death suspend the necessity of the individual's own death in its suicidal variant.

Through the symbolic articulation of death, dying, and mourning in their style, which develops via communication within the scene, they do away with deficits in society. The scene considers itself to be a subcultural elite, the only ones working against the social suppression of death, which finds its manifestation in speechlessness. Since the beginning of the nineteenth century, a large part of society no longer digests the finiteness of the human existence, because the fear of death and the fear of the return of the dead has become overwhelming, much to the profitable advantage of a number of film genres (e.g., vampire or horror films). Goths stage-manage a subcultural dance macabre by stripping off the term's historical meaning and taking it literally. They are the real reminder of death, a living and naturalistic memento mori, aesthetically and verbally anticipating the future, age-defined metamorphosis.

The goths are one of the most conspicuous subcultures because they work against the suppression of death and ageing with their deathly pale faces in a time when sun-studio tanned complexions are the epitome of health. They become the terror of a deathless producing-and-consuming culture, which marginalizes the process of dying and bodily decay to be able to proclaim the ideal of perpetual youth. Putting death at the center of their style and their lives becomes a provocation by a subcultural group of adolescents who cannot be forgiven by society. Youth has to look fresh and "tasty"; it is not supposed to walk around "dead." In a society with an ever-increasing average life expectancy, dealing with death is suitable only when a certain age has been reached.

The goths, on the basis of traditions of various epochs, cultural backgrounds, and media, test the development of their own rituals to come to terms with death. They represent unordinary places and stylistic elements, excluded from the rationally defined modern age because of their embodiment of death or evil.

To make the socially special and detached character of death a matter of ordinary life is a criticism of the increasing social rejection of death in a modern age, that is, of a completely rationalized ordinary life in which the extraordinary, the "extremely alien" (Sturm) character of death is only permitted at certain times and places. Thus, the goths are a subculture that, on the aesthetic level, does not shirk the responsibility of the modern individual to create rituals for dealing with the finiteness of life.

SKATEBOARDING: BETWEEN MAINSTREAM AND PUNK ROCK

Curry Malott

After more than five decades of transformation, skateboarding has emerged with at least two competing foci: skateboarding as mainstreamed, corporate, money-making *sport*; and skateboarding as punk rock, *do-it-yourself* (DIY) performance art (not a sport) and *outlaw way of life*. To best understand the social phenomena known by its practitioners simply as "skating," one must comprehend these two opposing manifestations of skateboarding. What follows is therefore a discussion of the tension between mainstream skating and skatepunks (or sk8punx). As a skatepunk myself, who first became a part of the culture more than twenty years ago, I put more emphasis in the following paragraphs on sk8punx because I believe, while not immune to the hegemonies of the dominant society such as greed, apathy, white supremacy, homophobia, and sexism, it has served the purposes of emancipation more than those of social control compared to what I refer to as the skateclones of capital.

THE NEVERENDING STRUGGLE

As the mainstream, white, straight, middle-class, politically conservative skating scene of the 1970s waned in popularity, those dominating the business side of the industry, predominantly non-skaters, began to pull their capital investments out of skateboarding because it was becoming less and less profitable. Skateboarding was therefore on its way out as a middle-class cure for boredom in a meaningless, commodified world, and thus as an agent of social control. However, burying skateboarding as a dyeing fad was too late because it was taking on a life of its own outside the market mechanisms of capital.

That is, before skateboarding could die of natural causes, a handful of professional skaters who were into punk rock during the late 1970s, such as Duane Peters, became punk rock skaters, sk8punx, transforming their lives into an underground culture more concerned with an alternative, "who cares?" life style than mainstream acceptance (i.e., the punk rock revolution of 1977 embodied in the music of The Clash, Sex Pistols, Sham 69, Stiff Little Fingers, Ramones, etc.). Combined with punk rock, skateboarding was therefore taking on an outlaw persona appealing to the generation of the late 1970s and 1980s who had seen not only the potentialities of the social movements of the 1960s sold out to and destroyed by a capitalist-dominated state, but also saw their futures downsized and outsourced as previously industrialized regions of the United States became de-industrialized, therefore weakening the collective bargaining power of the working and middle classes (thank you Ronald Reagan, a.k.a. Ronnie Baby (the Nazi) coined by Mike Muir of Southern California's punk/metal band Suicidal Tendencies).

Perceiving (however intuitive) the system of dominant society as only concerned with the interests of the increasingly wealthy white male ruling-class elite and viewing (however misguided) the progressive and revolutionary social movements as too rigid in their demands they placed on themselves and others for appropriate behavior, many punk rockers emerged giving the finger to both the left and the right proclaiming, to paraphrase the Sex Pistols, that we might not know exactly *what* we want, but we know *how* we are going to get it. For predominantly white and Latino sk8punks coming to the fore on the Western coast of the First Nations' land now known as the United States of America, this call was interpreted as DIY, manifesting itself in many sk8punk owned and operated skate companies and punk rock record labels.

However, while there was a nihilistic tendency among some U.S. skatepunks, there has always been a strong sense of social justice running through the genre connected to the social movements of the 1960s and 1970s fighting for self-determination and freedom from coercive power. This progressive tendency among skatepunks was represented in bands such as the Dead Kennedys and Minor Threat, challenging the more reactionary elements within the culture. Representing the socially just tendencies in the scene during the 1980s was the Dead Kennedys song "Nazi Punks F*** Off" recorded in 1980 and resulting in many violent confrontations between DK lead singer, Jello Biafra, and Nazi skinheads. This song, embodying both the f*** you attitude of punk rock and the social justice of the 1960s and 1970s social movements, is still played today by bands such as New York City's Sheer Terror. The ground on which this fight was often fought was therefore at punk rock concerts and skateboarding contests.

Although the skateboarding industry has consistently been for-profit, the 1980s was marked by a surge in skater owned and operated businesses, some more concerned with providing quality gear and supporting the culture, and some more interested in becoming rich through mainstream acceptance, a source of tension among skaters. That is, the board you rode and the logos you sported said a lot about *how* punk rock you saw yourself. The *most punk* were those who covered up the graphics on their boards with their own art/logos—those who *really* did not give a f*** about anything commercial.

Whereas some skater-owned companies were barely surviving, such as Skullskates, who personified the most offensive and rebellious aspects of the skate-pirate, f***-you culture, others were making a lot of money, such as Powell-Peralta. Contributing to Powell's capitalist success was their dream team line-up of pro riders including Tony Hawk, Rodney Mullen, Steve Caballero, Lance Mountain, Tommy Guerrero, and Mike McGill, and the brightly colored graphics on their boards and t-shirts, which were influenced by southern California's Chicano art, coupled with an aggressive marketing campaign that included skateboard videos and advertisements adorning the pages of *Thrasher* magazine, the lifeblood of the culture. Through this campaign the Powell-Peralta skate team was painted as a group of fun-loving, non-offensive, safe jokesters. As a result, they sold millions of boards to young middle-class white kids largely due to the assumption that they did not offend their conservative parents. In other words, it has been argued that Powell's marketing campaign was not only designed to appeal to youngsters, but perhaps more importantly, to parents, who were the ones actually buying these products for their children.

However, despite the relatively mainstream success of Powell-Peralta, during the 1980s skateboarding was associated with rebellious youth, and in many towns and cities across the United States skaters were deemed as outlaws experiencing police brutality and harassment, regardless of what graphics they brandished on their boards and t-shirts. Although the image of skaters as social outcasts has persisted to some degree into the twenty-first century, skating has witnessed a level of mainstream acceptance never before experienced. One need only turn on their television and wait a few minutes for a Mountain Dew commercial to witness x-treme skaters "doing the dew," or tune into ESPN for the X-Games where the likes of Tony Hawk, the world's wealthiest skateboarder, can be seen demonstrating his aerial maneuvers devoid of any counter hegemonic content. Better yet, one can consume professional skater Bam Margera's show on MTV where he and his friends play pranks on family and friends in much the same style as the old Powell-Peralta skateboard videos.

For some, such as Steve Caballero, the commercialization of skateboarding and skateboarders represents the needed distance from the outlaw image of skating necessary for legitimizing their sport, which translates into more money for more skaters, and thus economic stability in a mainstream middle-class context. For veteran professional skateboarder Rodney Mullen the popularization of skateboarding has put him in a position to offshore the manufacturing of Consolidated Skateboard Distributor to China threatening the livelihood of many small skater-owned-and-operated companies.

For others, the mainstream success of skateboarding has meant that their culture is under attack and in danger of being sold out, watered-down, sucked dry of profitability, and discarded for the next trend. One need only follow the debates raging within *Thrasher* to get a sense of how heated this issue is between skateboarders. As a result, many life-long sk8punx are on a heightened state of terrorist alert, code red, if you will. On their side is the fact that sk8punx survived the 1990s, a lull in skateboardings' popularity, and thus a time when little money was being spent on skateboarding.

There is little doubt that many small skater-run companies will not be able to compete with skateboards made with super-exploited Chinese labor made available by international trade agreements such as the General Agreement on Trade and Tariffs (GATT). However, if the globalization of skateboard manufacturing is *successful*, and many sk8punx are no longer able to support themselves as they have been, they will not go away. In other words, our industry can be overrun, but our spirit cannot be broken. In short, this fight is far from over.

Many skater-owned and operated companies, such as Punk Rock Skateboards, are creating advertisements that stress their independence from cheap, non-skater labor while Consolidated is creating ads that argue it is not a crime to make money. The globalization of skateboard manufacturing has also resulted in sk8punx upping the radical ante. Black Label, for example, a skater owned and operated company started by long-time pro skater John Lucero, has Duane Peters as one of its pro riders, which is highly unorthodox given the fact that he is well into his forties and most pro skaters are in their twenties. Lucero has three different Duane Peters pro-models out and a video, *Who Cares: The Duane Peters Story.*

In the world of skateboarding Duane Peters is known as the most punk rock skater of all times. He has invented more tricks than he can remember, has been homeless, in and out of prison and county jails throughout his twenties in an effort to get off of heroin, was an alcoholic, and is known as the master of disaster. According to many respected old-time skaters such as Tony Alva, Duane's passion and attitude are as strong today as they were in 1981 when he was one of the best skaters the world over. Duane is not only a professional skater, but he is also the lead singer of the punk rock bands, the U.S. Bombs and Die Hunns. The U.S. Bombs has been deemed one of the best punk rock bands ever, a daunting feat given the hundreds upon hundreds of punk bands that have come and gone in the past thirty plus years.

Themes tackled in Duane's lyrics range from getting off drugs and skateboarding to governmental and corporate economic and racist attacks against the working class. Found on Die Hunns' official Web page are links to various sites dedicated to civil liberties and other issues related to social justice, such as critiquing the prison industrial complex, the Patriot Act, and George W. Bush. Duane and Hunns bass player Corey Parks urge readers to take time out to read these pages to "find out what's going on all around us." Summing up their position, they argue "as punk rockers we've all got [to] stick together."

Peters represents the hardcore, aggressive, antiauthority attitude typical of the sk8punk counterculture. Like the contradictory "who cares?" philosophy of punk rock Peters uses both homophobic language while simultaneously supporting homosexuality. For example, captured in an interview response to snowboarding, Peters argues that "[t]here's so many queers in Huntington that just turn me off." Supporting homosexuality, Duane explains to the crowd at a U.S. Bombs show how he believes that he figured out why they had come to the show: "to f***, man and woman, or man and man, or woman and woman, it's the 1990s, it's a PC world, so whatever you want, but we are here to f***." In another interview reminiscing on the early punk days Peters argues that "we had a homosexual friend that we were really proud of."

Duane Peters used to skate for Beer City skateboards and recorded a split seven-inch on Beer City's label Beer City Records with the U.S. Bombs. The Bombs also recorded on Alive and then Hell Cat records. Peters now records on his own Disaster records. Having Duane Peters as a pro rider on Black Label commands a certain amount of respect from skatepunks of multiple generations, securing a strong following unhindered by the commodification of skateboarding as mainstream skate-clones for capital.

Sk8punx on the street, however, exist on the margins and resist from outside the boundaries of the industry and the imperatives of capitalist expansionism more generally. Thus, in their daily lives, many skatepunx refuse to participate in dominant society by not seeking legitimate employment and living on the streets. However, the isolation can be counterproductive because being isolated distances them from spaces where they can form alliances with other groups to create broader coalitions for social change. Others work jobs to survive but disrupt the social order by not conforming to accepted modes of dress, patterns of speech, and forms of dialect, and use public and private spaces such as steps and handrails as skating spots and canvases for graffiti art. By simply being a punker and skating, both individually and collectively, sk8punx resist dominant society. Still, other punks are on the streets because they have no other place to go. They symbolize the United States' abandoning of children and the country's overall poor populations.

In a sense, the lifestyle characteristic of sk8punx as well as that of dominant society, including skateclones for capital, could be conceptualized in terms of a continuum where sk8punx are at one extreme and dominant society is at the other extreme. Sk8punx tend to be relatively extreme because, by definition, countercultures are measured against the norms of dominant society; the further away on the continuum countercultures exist the more marginalized they are. The pressure of living on the margin sometimes takes its toll. It is because sk8punx have a tendency to be extreme, and because the pressures to conform work so well that there is a high turnover rate.

This high turnover rate also makes punk susceptible to co-optation because it suggests that it is not a cohesive movement and therefore easily infiltrated. For example, at times the most influential punk is predominantly ideologically aligned with Leftist politics while at other times geared more toward postmodernist defeatism, or even at times Right-wing conservatism. The punk style has been co-opted and rearticulated as something different and foreign to the punk scene; that is, the Gen-X, slacker styles for sale at the mall. In addition, as argued above, the conservative, positive image of skate-boarding has recently become widespread in the mass media as evidenced by the X Games, commercials against kids smoking shown before movies at popular theatres and on TV, and through white, male middle-class, straight, skating legends. Such messages cleanse skateboarding of any of its counter hegemonic roots. Like punk rock in general, when skaters are portrayed as counter hegemonic, they are portrayed as slackers or Gen-Xers devoid of any real meaning or purpose.

However, although these messages might have a negative impact on the public's perception of who sk8punx are and what they are about, they do not have the power to destroy the spaces created by sk8punk countercul-tural formations. For example, in a number of interviews in *Thrasher*, Mark Hubbard, skater and world-class skate park on-sight builder and designer and owner/operator of Grind Line skate park construction, has noted how those interested in exploiting the profitability of skateboarding are in no position to meet the needs of skaters because they do not have the intimate, continuously changing nature of skateboarding, and thus could never replace the Skate Nation (skaters united worldwide beyond nation states). The future is not written, and thus the struggle between sk8punx and skateclones of capital is yet undetermined. Two things, however, are cer-tain: capital, until it is defeated, will continue to expand beyond its bound-aries and intensify within the areas it already exists, and sk8punkx will not go out without a fight. Long live the Sk8 Nation!

Resource

Malott, C., & Pena, M. (2004). *Punk rocker's revolution*. New York: Peter Lang Publishing.

AIR & STYLE SNOWBOARDING CONTEST

Klaus Neumann-Braun and Axel Schmidt

This entry deals with the communicative processing of the Air & Style Snowboarding Event. The music industry and others operating in the youth culture scene continue to organize an increasing number of such events. These normally take place in unusual venues and aim at providing a "complete experience," targeting all the senses, and affording their "lifestyle clientele" an otherwise difficult-to-create feeling of togetherness. Events such as the Love Parade, the Street Parade, or the Wave Gothic Meeting (still) seem to recognize no limits in their number or size. For those attending such events they occupy a particular role in the flow of everyday life, standing out from it and casting a shadow over it, both before and afterwards, when it becomes the stuff of narration. For those taking part, such an event is not simply a one-off experience limited to a particular time and space, it is also a symbolic entity, which during the course of time takes on diverse forms, influenced by expectation, memory and fantasy. In communication with others these diverse feelings find structure, expression and modification. I will therefore, in the following, consider a snowboarding event from two combined perspectives: (1) the perception of the visitor, and (2) the communicative activity involved.

THE EVENT: THE AIR & STYLE CONTEST IN INNSBRUCK

The Air & Style Snowboard Contest has been held in the Berg Isel Stadium in Innsbruck, Austria, for seven years. Formerly more of a local event, it now forms one of the core components of the international snowboarding scene. Here the world's best snowboarders have the chance to demonstrate their skills on the purpose-built ramp beneath the giant ski jump of the mountain stadium. In its first year the event received 2,000 visitors, nowadays the figure is closer to 40,000, the majority of those attending aged between thirteen and twenty-five. The event is organized by *Monster Backside Magazine*, a snowboard periodical, and is supported by noteworthy advertisers, such as G-Shock (Casio), who are the main sponsors, as well as MTV, Audi, Warsteiner, Reef, and Quicksilver, the last two being two of the scene's leading fashion labels. The highlight of the tournament is the Contest, a competition between the snowboarders to do the highest, longest, most stylish jump. Concerts, parties, and fire and light spectacles, as well as merchandising stands and numerous smaller contests form the backdrop to the competition's proceedings. The bands and DJs are those familiar to and popular with members of the snowboarding public. This has meant in recent times those from the Hip Hop and Grunge/Crossover fields. Before and during the contests in 1998 the groups Therapy and Cypress Hill played, both bands being in the middle of European tours. After the day's events MTV, in collaboration with the Ministry of Sound and the firm Nintendo, organized a post-contest party, which took place on several floors of a renowned Innsbruck concert hall.

BEFORE THE EVENT: THE BUILDUP OF EXPECTATION

In the group of fifteen- to seventeen-year-old male youths observed by us, specific preparation for the forthcoming event was seen to take place. This consisted of all manner of reflection upon it and of making the forthcoming event comprehensible. The announcements and flyers of the organizers contained much of symbolic significance for the young and provided a lot of scope for fantasy and imagination, the spectacular being a recurrent motif. With which specific communicative practices did the observed group structure their expectations and ideas about the imminent event?

First, *imaginative reflection* should be mentioned. From six to four weeks before the event the youths began seeking to exceed each other in their conception as to what would take place. This consisted of wish projection and the romanticization of individual aspects: the youths imagined that the sexiest, most attractive women would be attending, that the parties taking place there would be the coolest, and the musical acts were almost deified. Furthermore, even the journey there afforded a certain magical quality. In conversation with work colleagues, the separation of the event from the sphere of normal, everyday activity was repeatedly emphasized. Both processes led to the formation of sayings (one cue-word being "Innsbruck") and ritualized running gags, which both served the function of bonding those traveling together.

Secondly, *practical reflection* also took place; the youth became frantically busy. Planning and preparation were discussed extensively to the point of excess. This was revealed particularly in the meaningless and unnecessary questions put to the team observing the group, as well as in complicated, continually re-negotiated arrangements with each other.

Thirdly, *reflection through boasting* was noted to take place. Boasting to those unable to travel to the event fulfilled the function of transforming the destination into something special. Alongside the function of reflection however, the activity also played a role in supporting group building. Those traveling to the event saw themselves as a privileged group compared to those remaining at home.

These various processes allowed those involved to take individual episodes from an anticipated future experience, to represent them orally and to charge them with diffuse attributes and expectations. The short reference "Innsbruck" functioned as a manifestation of the future event and became in the time leading up to it a key word, representing for the group all of their specific themes and everything they had considered particular about it and remote from everyday life.

DURING THE EVENT: PROBLEMS AND DISILLUSIONMENT

For the group we observed, the day of the "mega event" ran as follows: As no tickets had yet been purchased, the group, despite arriving late the previous night, had to get up extremely early on the morning of the event to avoid the risk of being unable to get tickets after the long journey. The situation in front of the stadium was chaotic, none of the organizers being able to give information as to where and when tickets would be available. The youth wandered to and fro in front of the stadium entrance in order to be sure that the decisive moment would not be missed. Although the temperature was between –15 and –20° C and not all of the group were wearing appropriate winter clothing, they waited for the next two and a half hours there. By 12 o'clock all had tickets for the contest as well as for the after-show party, which led again to feverish excitement. There were four hours to go until the event began and as they were all frozen, the group decided to head back to the pension where they lay on their beds, talked, and watched television. Not until 5 pm did they manage to pull themselves together again which led to slight tension amongst them. The return to the stadium proved to be more troublesome than had previously been the case in the morning as many of the approaching streets were now completely closed, and all parking spaces occupied. Participation in the event was accordingly delayed once again and the whole group began to moan and complain about the inconvenience. On arrival the crater-shaped Berg Isel Stadium was already packed and the band Therapy was already playing. All seats were already taken. The group of youth we observed positioned themselves near the stadium exit by the highest row of seats, where they stayed for the remainder of the event. From this position, however, both the stage and the jump could only be seen with difficulty. The amplification system was insufficient to cover the whole stadium and the concert's atmosphere did not reach the position where our group was standing. Despite the thronging crowds and the resulting proximity of the visitors to one another, there was no contact with any other visitors, nor with the much spoken-about female snowboarders, as they had previously longed for.

After a short time the group began to be troubled by the cold, which had been underestimated by all of them. The youth slowly became restless as another four or five hours lay ahead of them. The excitement generated by the appearance of Cypress Hill and the contest itself, disappeared quickly. The group seemed to be longing for the end of the event shortly after its beginning. The countless jumps, which did not differ spectacularly from one another, were followed by the youth only sporadically. During the supposedly exciting finale of the contest, the group was already discussing how they could leave the stadium before the crowds. Immediately following the announcement of the victor, the group left. Excitedly the youth went then to the after-contest party, which according to their expectations would be *the* event of the year. There was a great deal of congestion in front of the entrance to the four vast factory halls and a little patience was needed during the preliminary security checks. The jostling of the masses continued in the various rooms of the event and the group was unsure where they should seat themselves and wandered through the extremely hot, loud hall until they found a small podium with tables and chairs at the end of one of the halls. As in the stadium the group, having found a place, remained very static for the rest of the evening and did not join in with events there. The music being too loud however to converse, the activity of the group consisted for the rest of the evening of observing what was happening and smoking. None of the youths attempted to make contact with another of the visitors. *The* party of the year proved to be a flop, the wished-for "ultimate kick" eluding the youth.

447

AFTER THE EVENT: PROCESSING OF DISCREPANT EXPERIENCES

When the group's previous expectations are compared with the actual course of events during the evening a clear discrepancy between expectations and reality can be established. Above all, the fantasies the group had about the event, with all their socio-symbolic associations, proved to be excessive, and the group was unable to find this imagined excess in reality. The questions now arises as to how this disillusionment fits into the everyday life of the youth, and how is it processed? Generally speaking, the youth tried to absorb and defuse such discrepant experience within the group. This took place through *communicative processes aimed at reducing the discord between expectation and reality*:

First an intensive search for the causes of the perceived failure took place, which led to the *dramatization of external reasons*; the supposedly peculiar behavior of other visitors in an unfamiliar place, combined with an "uncool" party took the blame for everything—according to the motto, "the people there were strange."

Second, *renormalization* took place: Along with a search for reasons, the youths started to adjust to the new situation. They tried to minimize the disillusionment ("we didn't miss anything, the party was s*** anyway"). They also endeavored to find positive aspects in the new situation ("wicked, let's go to McDonald's again"). Both functioned as strategies, which allowed the redefinition of the experienced disillusionment in order to avoid those aspects that would have damaged the image of the group.

Third, a *collection of the highlights suitable for inclusion in later stories* about the day took place. The youths began to sort out the positive and presentable aspects of the event. Individual aspects and single elements of the event were selected (e.g., the performance of Cypress Hill) and were dramatized and condensed.

This all happened while the groups was leaving the disappointing party. In the following we will consider what of the event was taken home to the group's everyday clique.

MEMORIES OF THE EVENT: LEGENDS AND TROPHIES

First, it can be said that the actual experiences of the event were *retrospectively ordered according to their presentability to the group's everyday clique*. The discrepancies associated with the event were completely revised, now becoming dramatic stories. On the journey home the youths began to review the event and concentrated on those aspects which had already been discussed before the event, and which appeared to be acceptable for narration. For instance, the boring after-show contest party was changed by the youths to an extreme bodily experience; the party was so extreme that it hurt the eyes and lungs, and brought on claustrophobia, a typical comment being "we could have died there." Whether these extreme descriptions were meant positively or negatively was left open. Most important was the enjoyment of the extraordinary and delight in the extremes. The general *pattern of the event's processing*, in other words, that which remains in memory of such an event, can be summarized as follows:

The interactive production of "legends," consisted of stylizing individual aspects of the event and taking them to extremes as well as the construction of absurd scenarios. This procedure took its starting point from real situations, which were then subsequently transformed.

In contrast to that, the *recollection and presentation of trophies* refers to the subsequent recurrence of significant youth culture names and labels, such as Air & Style, or Cypress Hill. In contrast to the aforementioned legend-forming, such symbolically important labels need no special format, providing presentable stories as they are. The simple statement of fact ("I saw Cypress Hill live") is enough to conjure up appropriate images in the recipient. In this way it is easier to separate what was expected from the actual experience. After the event it is apparently unimportant for the youth whether or not cult band Cypress Hill were good or how they played, or whether or not the Air & Style Contest was cold and stressful. Important is simply the fact that one was there, and that one is able to present this being there as a trophy to those who stayed at home.

CONCLUSION: "INNSBRUCK WAS AMAZING"

The above has sought until now to demonstrate how youth-cultural events are appropriated by the young. An attempt has also been made to reconstruct the event from the perspective of an actual participating group of youths. The representation corresponds closely to the empirical material, including field notes and recordings of conversations with the youths. The analytical preparation of the data presented here allows for a variety of follow-ups and interpretations. To conclude, however, I shall concentrate on a combination of two points, namely the connection between a symbolic, global youth culture scene as a large virtual society, and the concrete local peer group.

INSIDE YOUTH-CULTURAL CONTEXTS: EVENTS AS A "CORE DEVOID OF MEANING"

To the first point: in the 1970s and 1980s youth culture formed itself according to extra-symbolic bricolage processes, which meant that objects and symbols of the official culture were taken, decontextualized, and transformed. In the 1990s the jungle of youth culture appeared for many to become impenetrable, and with this came a lack in understanding of the diverse scenes' many reference points. The consumer goods market, the media, and advertising all play a decisive role in this diversification process: youth cultures arise from the marketing process, which constructs target-groups according to music, clothing and consumer preferences. This allows advertising to target its consumers effectively. This is supposed to guarantee success for certain brands which then lend a certain attractiveness to the associated event or media packet, such as snowboard, hip hop, or cross-over. These brands represent youth-cultural trophies, which are used by the participating youths to lend meaning to an event in its preconstruction and reconstruction. In this manner a "core devoid of meaning," as I will call it, is formed. Along with the actual experience, which is often lacking in spectacle, disillusioning, or simply frustrating, stands the before and after, which are surprisingly resistant to disappointment and ambiguity, and avoid too much detail. In the before and after, the event is established as a schematized substrate. Processes of communicative reflection play an essential role in the modification and stabilization of the event's interpretation as contrasted to its actual course. Participants reassure each other that they were there, but little more is actually expressed.

GLOBAL EVENTS AS OCCASIONS FOR LOCAL PEER GROUP ACTIVITY

Up to now, however, what we have considered has made clear that the various offerings of the youth culture scene should not be considered as individual isolated units, but as a symbolic framework which is further developed and supplemented according to the group's or individual's developmental needs. In our case the sex of the participants and the constitution of the group stood particularly in the foreground. On the one hand this finding demonstrates that youth culture and its commercial manifestations emerge first of all through their communicative processing by a group of participants. Issues relevant to everyday life are actualized in a new and extraordinary framework. On the other hand, however, such peer-group specific interaction concerning youth culture allows us an insight into the everyday life of a youth clique: the fact that the observed group behaved in *this* particular manner reveals something to us of each individual's values, leading to the aforementioned result, namely "Innsbruck was wild," despite the disillusionment and disappointment. This leads us to further conclusions regarding the specific forms of identity management within the group as regards their interaction with youth cultural events. Beyond all conceptions of youth culture as an internationalized community, and eclectic biography-building sensory experience, the observations show one thing: youth spend their everyday life principally in a peer group formed locally and have to slot the various offerings of youth culture into their everyday existence, using the usual coping strategies in the process. The observed youth displayed distance to the public event and this functioned with regard to their lives' context as a protective mechanism, which combined two motifs: the glamour of saying "I've been somewhere to be envied," which functioned as a trophy, had to be combined with the problem of being in a strange, unfamiliar situation. The youth discussed overcame this problem by traveling through these strange surroundings as a *local peer group*. In light of this, the question is raised as to how much of a global culture children and youths are actually capable of accepting or are ready to recognize?

PAINTBALL: FROM MARKING TREES TO SPORT

Shirley R. Steinberg

The third most popular participation sport in the early twenty-first century is only twenty years old. Next to inline skating and skateboarding, paintball places third, with snowboarding and skiing coming in fourth and fifth. A game most identified with males, females are beginning to enjoy the fast, strategic sport as well. Disagreements about how paintball evolved are reduced to two scenarios. Those in New Hampshire claim that the sport was developed by rangers marking trees for cutting. By shooting a patch of paint on the trees, the lumberjacks could quickly identify their marks. The other popular claim comes from the American West, where ranchers would shoot paint on to cattle in order to identify them.

The New Hampshire version is gaining in popularity, and certainly, New Hampshire places prominently in popularity among paintballers. Scores of groups and single players head for the woods in New England in search of the perfect paintball venue. Woods and varied terrain lend themselves to enjoyable and varied games. Not only is paintball fun, strategic, and challenging, it is also used by different corporations and groups to develop skills among employees.

Essential to paintball is equipment. Everyone wears a mask; this is required on every field or paintball course. One cannot enter a playing field without first putting on the mask. The paintball gun is essential, as are the paintballs. Most games last about twenty minutes, and if organized in teams, the team that is still standing or that captures the goal wins.

Players can be outfitted for paintball for about $200. However, as a paintballer becomes more involved in the sport, a mask or a belt pack could cost that much. A state-of-the-art gun can run well over $1,000. A fast gun can shoot out fourteen balls per second. This is much faster than the original pump-action guns from twenty years ago. Paintball facilities allow rental of equipment, or one's personal equipment can be used. Parks sell paintballs, and sometimes one is allowed to bring one's own paint. The ball is made of a gelatin capsule; in fact, drug companies manufacture the casing of paintballs.

The ball is filled with a water-based food dye. When balls are loaded into the gun, they are shot out by compressed air or CO_2. It is important to choose good paint. Cheap paintballs are purchased from large chain stores, and can be too hard and not break easily on contact.

Paintball facilities differ in themes and in difficulty. Some paintball fields are set up for speedball. Speedball is played on a field with large inflatable shapes that the players hide behind and shoot. It is, as its name implies, very fast, and one tends to win by barraging the opponent with hails of balls. Some paintball parks have thematic fields. One such excellent park is OSG Paintball (Outdoor Strategic Games) in Center Barnstead, New Hampshire.[1] Boasting seven fields, players can chose from a medieval-themed castle, an air field, a village, forest courses, a western town, and an urban town. Players can play capture the flag, capture the castle, or eliminate the other team.

Groups can rent paintball facilities for many different reasons. Ranging from birthday and bachelor parties to corporate training, paintball attracts many different people. Youth (usually twelve and over) play paintball as they emulate their activities from video games. Companies use paintball to teach cooperation and communication skills. Successful paintball requires that the players work as a team. The best teams have learned how to talk to one another, giving instructions and information in spotting the opposition. The more a team plays together, the more the members are able to assist one another in evading and attacking the opposition.

Naturally there are risks to paintball. It must be played in a seriously controlled environment. Strong nets should surround the field, and no one should enter a playing area without a good mask. Not only the face, but the ears should be covered by a good mask. Cheap mass-market masks are dangerous and can split. Guns must have barrel plugs when players leave the field, and weapons should never be discharged outside of the controlled area. A paintball can go as fast as 300 feet per second—well over 100 miles per hour. Think of a major league baseball being pitched. The average fastball is about 95 mph, and one knows the harm a baseball can cause if a player is hit. Paintballs, while soft and only filled with paint, are dangerous bullets that can harm or kill if shot at a close range or too fast. A responsible paintball park will regulate the speed of the guns, and Doppler radar is used to measure the balls as they leave the gun. Any speed over 300 feet per second is too fast, and guns must be adjusted to be lower than that speed. It is important to monitor the shots throughout the day, as when a day gets hotter, the velocity of the balls increase, and without measurement, the guns could shoot much, much faster. Parents and caregivers should not allow kids to play paintball in the back yard or park without supervision. Accidents happen at an alarming rate when there is no regulation, and blindness, serious injury, and even death is possible.

A good paintball park will have referees on each field, someone who is a responsible employee and who oversees the rules and safety of the game and players. Games should not run much longer than twenty minutes, as the momentum of the game can be lost, and it is easier and more pleasurable to start a new game. When a player is hit, they usually raise their gun and proclaim that they are out. They immediately leave the playing area and wait for the next game.

Paintballers roleplaying in military gear

An unexpected offshoot from paintball in New Hampshire has been the growth of the trees in the woods. Because of the way paintball is played, the weeds and weed trees are destroyed by the players underfoot, yet the larger trees, the hardwood trees, are able to flourish and grow without competition from the weeds taking the nourishment.

Paint guns can cost well over $1000.00

Note

1 Many thanks to Dave and Gordon of OSG Paintball in Center Barnstead, New Hampshire.

Resources

http://www.draxxus.com/history/paintballs. asp? flash=1. Retrieved August 1, 2005.

www.osgpaintball.com. Retrieved August 1, 2005.

A New Hampshire original: Paintball

Public Pedagogy as Spectacle: The Case of Professional Wrestling

Peter Pericles Trifonas

Recent cultural figures from Walt Disney to Homer Simpson have analyzed, commented on, put into practice, resisted, and exemplified the dimensions of popular culture as a public pedagogy. Popular culture filters the interests and obsessions of an audience yearning for an ethics of fun into easily digestible forms of entertainment not always morally sanguine. This is easy to see if we take a look at the spectacle of professional wrestling.

Let us put aside for the time being the intellectual and ethical questions of why anyone would want to watch professional wrestling in the first place. You might object: "Yeah, I know it's fake. So what? I like to watch professional wrestling anyway!" Its remarkable popularity worldwide as a form of entertainment is indisputable. But there are also those who dismiss professional wrestling as the cultural epitome of bad taste and totally devoid of educational possibilities, as an event that exploits the strongest of human emotions—love and hatred—for profit, not for the edification of the spectator. It is easy to reject professional wrestling on aesthetic, pedagogical, or moral grounds. Shapely female courtesans with ample lung capacity buttress their weighty cleavage with the tiniest of sticking plasters while groping the slippery thighs of an equally stunning opponent for a firm hold during a corn oil match to the death. Long-haired body builders in spandex tights strike venal poses for the frenetic females (and males!) in the audience as they recount with surgical precision the anatomical details of last night's slaughter of a fellow wrestler as he was "taken apart, piece by piece." Tales of betrayal, adultery, greed, jealousy, and even theft abound.

Yet, as a form of public pedagogy, there is more to the spectacle of professional wrestling than meets the eye. Understanding its appeal is like trying to explain why stopping your vehicle to gawk at the morbid aftermath of a car accident is construed as a natural human response. We thrive on spectacles, especially bad ones. Sometimes we don't know why. Spectacles that display the struggle between luck and destiny makes us feel alive, as we witness the tragedy of someone else we neither know nor will likely ever see again. So we stop to look at the traffic accident in order to unconsciously reaffirm our sense of safety and well being—we are alive while somebody else is suffering. In professional wrestling, the sense of survival is conveyed through the spectacle we know is fake. There is no point in watching a match we know is fixed other than to release our anxiety in a scapegoat, the bad person who suffers for our sins.

The excess of the spectacle naturalizes the idiosyncratic nature of the cultural values we find represented in the world of professional wrestling. The big sweaty men in tights we love to hate, yet might secretly admire, are more than their muscle-bound, greased, and hairy selves. They are cultural icons of meaning—moral archetypes, muscularly overdeveloped signs—that we engage and interpret as we would competing ideas and values. Arbitrary notions of 'what is good' and 'what is bad' are symbolized through the dress, speech, and actions of characters who are combatants in the ring. For this reason, professional wrestling cannot be classified as a sport, that is, a true competition among equals. Like a play, professional wrestling is scripted. The outcome is determined in advance of actual matches. Sport depends on competition fuelled by the technical mastery of participants. Its entertainment value derives from the fact that the contest is always up for grabs, the destiny of the players nebulous. Sport is drama. Anything can happen. Uncertainty fuels the drama and sustains the desire to watch until the outcome is apparent. Some would say that sport is honest. But unlike wrestling, sport is lifeless.

That is not to say that in sport the participants and spectators are without emotion, don't take sides, cause riots, or take up arms against each other in the name of loyal allegiances to individual players and teams. But contests of skill are not allegories of sport itself, as a game of abilities with fixed rules depends upon the outcome and not on the spectacle itself. Reactions determined by the conventions of sports do not directly relate to the great struggles experienced in life. Rather, they relate to the performance of sport played as a game. It is an artificial contest—not real life. No moral judgment is required of the player to participate in the game of football or of the spectator to watch it. One cannot go outside the rules of competition to interpret the meaning of the action on the field. For example, it would be absurd to say, "Averri scored a goal to punish research scientists supporting the opposing team because he doesn't believe in using live animals to test cosmetics." Social morality isn't on display through every action the players perform for the sake of sporting competition. It would be as absurd and meaningless to say that the spectators began to bludgeon each other with fists because they disagreed about the validity of Averri's ethical stances regardless of the goal. Life does not intervene in the playing of sports. Every time a fan makes an aesthetic or ethical judgment about a sport or its players it is in relation to the rules of the game and its code of morality construed by the dictates of skilful performance. Otherwise the basis for the opinion would be ridiculous.

The enjoyment of professional wrestling, however, flourishes and increases primarily through witnessing the raw spectacle of life's great stories acted out in the ring as a play of moralities. Not to mention the ethical diatribes, free psychoanalysis, pop philosophy and generous smatterings of sexual counseling that constitute the narrative thread of each and every match and entangle the stories of the wrestlers with our own lives. Wrestling consumes life. Nothing more, nothing less. It swallows life whole and spits it back at the audience as an ersatz form of experience. It is an allegory of human existence that begs a response. Spectator emotion is driven by moral judgments that go outside the rules of the "contest" itself. The outcome becomes secondary because the power of wrestling lies in the ability of the wrestlers to stage the event, the struggle, which is a real product of conflicts in human affairs outside the ring. Who wins does not really matter. What is of concern to an audience is the extent to which judgments about professional wrestlers and wrestling matches can be made by drawing on a knowledge of life experience itself. Spectators use aesthetic and moral principles that they have learned in their everyday lives to form allegiances and antipathies. They learn how to reflect on life from the spectacle of wrestling as it relates to the reality their experience, which is why it is easy to condemn professional wrestling as a public pedagogy—its teachings run the gamut of ethical and unethical predicaments and challenges of everyday life. But life intervenes. Wrestling makes plain the struggle of good and bad and universalizes it for the viewer by establishing moral archetypes to which the spectator responds regardless of whether they want to or not. The spectacle is predicated on the play of ethical and social norms of behavior that we experience in our everyday lives and take for granted. We cannot but respond.

In the squared circle, the stylistic and rhetorical flourishes of the wrestlers as performers, not simply athletes, support moral values. The spectator is forced to take sides according to the moral codes and cultural values of a society. For example, "good" characters are referred to as "technically accomplished athletes." They are well-spoken defenders of dominant but arbitrary ideologies and cultural institutions like "the family," "the American way," "civil rights," "justice," and "democracy." Professional wrestling in the United States during World War II depicted clean-cut "good old boys" of unimpeachable character taking on monocled Nazi caricatures with bad German accents. The nationalistic spirit of the times made it possible to exploit the situation of real violence that was being experienced on the battlefield for the purpose of entertainment and patriotic moralizing. American wrestling heroes exacting symbolic revenge on the representative of an enemy nation was indeed a cathartic experience. The good guy always won! Consequently, there was hope that evil would not triumph in the real world.

"Bad" characters use dirty tricks to subvert what the "good" characters stand for, in order to bring about a New World Order—which incidentally was also the name of a wrestling cohort of evildoers and misfits. This group of characters walks on the dark side of the fine edge between good and evil. They punctuate their talk with profanity, a distinctly pejorative masculine bravado replete with homophobic and misogynistic references. That is, if they speak at all. Sometimes menacing grimaces, guttural growls, the pumping of fists and the gnashing of teeth are enough to make a point. These less than savory characters might include a Satanic high priest, a porn star, or even a raving lunatic who, having escaped from an unidentified asylum, wears a mask to conceal his identity. Whether it be raising the dead, seducing a wrestler's companion, or talking to a sock puppet, their actions are exaggerations of real life intended to make visible the inner state of their troubled souls. Nothing is left to the imagination. We see and hear everything except the depth of their capacity for evil.

Moral standards that guide the interpretation of human behavior that generalizes the experience of viewing are tied to the wrestling spectacle. The pedagogical value of wrestling as an educational spectacle is in how it tries to bring about a consensus of how we perceive reality, encounter the human condition and act in respect to the difference of others as a community. There is always a "good" character and a "bad" character. Morally upright figures never fight each other. Never! Even though we know the world of wrestling is a stage-managed sport, its excessive spectacles of human experience—its exhibitions of pain, suffering, betrayal, guilt, treachery, cruelty, desire, and elation—allow the viewer a purer or less ambivalent identification with the actors. Some of the wrestlers' symbolic names also facilitate stock responses: for example, the Rock, Stone Cold, the Undertaker, The Phenom, Mankind, The Patriot, Sergeant Slaughter, Kane (the man whose face no one has ever seen!), Vader. The whole point is to have raw-nerved, unadulterated emotion take over the intellectual response. It is an exposed and untempered sentiment but not without an ideological bent that is colored by a moral sense of taste. The audience quickly has to take sides for the spectacle of wrestling to be effective. They are separated into communities of the good versus the bad. In wrestling matches, as in mythology, imaginary sagas of life and death struggles pitting good against evil are played out before an audience ready to identify within such a play of morality the primordial ethical situations of the human condition. Wrestling exploits the mythological archetypes that preoccupy a consciousness of taste and judgment. A darkly masked figure, a face of evil, squares off against a crowd favorite who displays and defends all that is good in a culture.

The mythical spectacle of wrestling relies on viewers' unconscious desire to work out the psychic and ethical tensions within the ideology of culture. It feeds on the audience's sense of right and wrong. One side or the other is supported on the basis of taste standards and aesthetic and moral judgments. But ultimately, the ethical, social, and political boundaries of society and culture frame the way we perceive the mythic struggles among the wrestlers in the ring. Spectators are publicly judged—praised or mocked—according to a display of sympathies and choices of taste. Any rejection or show of support reveals a sense of taste that is morally categorized as good or bad. Let us not forget the system of fashion made up of saleable commodities that accompanies professional wrestling—T-shirts, belts, flags, hats, pins, pens, belt buckles, stickers, water-bottles, coffee mugs, bikinis, and so on—as it brands the sport and markets it for public consumption. By having such items we provide others with a quick and easy way to interpret the meaning of the life-world we inhabit with a view to explaining our present through the archetypes of the past. In other words, your fan gear and paraphernalia represent the "world order" you support and consider yourself to be a part of, the ideological orientations you embrace and the narratives you spin, with respect to the schematic of life and living provided by the professional wrestling scene.

This symbolic element of the spectacle as it defines "good" and "bad" demands the viewer's attention and simplifies aesthetic and moral responses, which accounts for the tremendous popularity of wrestling. It plays on bias and prejudice, likes and desires. It reduces the excesses of meaning that are present in everyday life. There is no need for interpretation, because differences are made audibly and visibly obvious. The spectacle of wrestling as a public form of informal pedagogy therefore becomes ideological, a mythical rendering of experience. It is "what-goes-without-saying." What is good is good and what is bad is bad. There is no in-between. Professional wrestling suspends the need for a critical questioning of cultural representations and the stories we tell ourselves about reality. It reinforces in a most crude way the aesthetic and ethical stereotypes of as either good or bad. Simply through the wrestlers bringing to life and making graphic the moral consequences of human beliefs and choices. The mythic spectacle naturalizes the distortion of reality that wrestling performs in order to arouse the sentiments of an audience and create fan allegiances. It allows us to gloss over the unsavory elements of violence and verbal abuse that form the seedy underbelly of each match by forcing us to search for a higher meaning that can be taken on as a ready-made truth about existence. The reward of finding the goodness of truth in such an unlikely place would redeem us of desire to watch and the guilt we feel at enjoying watching the sordid spectacle of professional wrestling. Morality becomes the emotional and psychological aftereffect of an uneasy viewing, the moral dimension made clear by the fact that the 'the bad guys' wear black masks.

Resources
Pericles, P. T. (2001). *Umberto Eco and football.* Cambridge: Icon Books.
———. (2001). *Barthes and the Empire of Signs.* Cambridge: Icon Books.

If You're From DR Don't Be Ashamed

Jessenia Diaz

If you were in DR, the land from which I came
Dimelo Mi Pana is something you would say
Y si tu vas you'll stay for more than a day
Because *mi terra* is what's up, it's not a game
So represent like Ralphy 'n Ed who play *la musica*
Like the *bachatas' n tipicos que a Soli le gustan*
Talking bout Soli, Nery 'n Wally are the same
So like them if you're from DR don't be ashamed
Our land may be little but we got it all
Del campo al monumento standing tall
Our flag, the colors red, *blanco* y blue
And writing this poem won't really do
To describe DR we need a book
Cause like I said my land is off the hook
I'm talking bout everything all in one spot
The people, the beaches the temperatures hot
The *platanos* we eat, the times we share
I can't wait *pa irme* just to be there
The breezes, the sun and all the vain
Oh how I wish I could take a plane
Because being here is not the same
DR is special in so many ways
So si tu eres Dominican don't be ashamed

Editors' note: DR refers to the Dominican Republic

Politics and Youth Activism

The Heaven? The Hell? The In-Between?

Nicole Daniel

The life of the worries of the world of the living.
The people of the city of the small town.
From the murderers to the supposedly saints.
Why are they here?
Hold up! Wait. What am I saying? Why the hell am I here?
We criticize the people that we see
We snub our noses at them but still
We can't see what we do and
Even if it is something wrong we say
Oh it's me it's ok its no big deal.
But still we watch the world with scorn.
Why do we always have to say:
What is wrong with the world?
We need to stop talking about what is wrong, Like why we at war?
Why is Bush still here? Why is there so much poverty?
Come on people we need to stand up!
Come on make a movement don't just sit still
You say that they try to keep you down.
Well aren't you tired of just saying it and not doing anything? Well my people
rise up!
We can make a difference
The African American, Hispanic, and the Asians.
So if you are tired of sitting down
get up and fight for your right.
Your right to be free and say
Who you would like to help lead you to your destiny of greatness?

YOUTH MOBILIZATION: STRENGTH IN NUMBERS

Faith Bynoe

Community organizing by youth, a long-held tradition in the United States, has been an impetus for many movements, especially the Civil Rights Movement, which peaked from 1953 to 1968, and the Black Power and Brown Power movements from 1964 to 1975. The work in the Civil Rights and Black and Brown Power movements is exemplified by groups like the Student Nonviolent Christian Coalition (SNCC), the Southern Christian Leadership Counsel (SCLC), the Black Panther Party, the Young Lords, and the Brown Berets.

These organizations had a broad power base and impacted many lives. Fueled by the belief that equal rights were afforded to all citizens of the country regardless of race or ethnicity, the youth in these organizations were highly effective in recruiting their peers and mobilizing their communities. Youth garnered support from their communities and participated in the enforcement of issues such as dismantling Jim Crow laws and securing voting rights for the disenfranchised, equal funding for education, reallocation of funding (local and state) to support personal and civic safety, beautification of neighborhoods, and installation of traffic lights, as well as providing free meals for poor children. For many groups, founding an organization in one city was just the beginning. Organizations like SNCC, the Brown Berets, and the Black Panther Party rose to national prominence as they reached out and recruited young people in other cities and started local chapters regionally and nationally. As young people worked and participated in the Civil Rights, Black Power, and Brown Power movements, they were provided with the confirmation that regardless of ethnicity, race, or locale, residents in cities around the country could identify with a common set of concerns and issues. The lifespan of many of these organizations was short, but their values and many of their tactical strategies, as well as some of their inconsistencies, would provide valuable lessons learned.

YOUTH ORGANIZATIONS OF THE CIVIL RIGHTS MOVEMENT

By 1960, Civil Rights organizations like SNCC and SCLC provided a vehicle for students, of all races and ethnicities, to participate in the protests and civil disobedience within the South. As youth were recruited to these organizations they engaged and mobilized people, including other youth and adults. By working with organizations like SNCC and SCLC, young people from around the country participated in protests such as the Freedom Rides of 1961, and marches such as the ones in Montgomery, Alabama, in 1963 and 1964. Local laws changed as buses, shops, and other public places were desegregated. Not only were these youth groups highly effective within their respective communities, but they were influential nationally. The Civil Rights Movement garnered national attention by the media, and influenced state and federal laws with the passage of the Civil Rights Act of 1964 and the Voting Rights Act of 1965.

Mobilizing young people from around the country proved to be a shrewd strategic plan. It broadened the power base of youth organizations in the Civil Rights Movement in multiple ways. The number of participants in organizations increased, and as young people traveled back to their respective communities, these members became recruiters. They gave firsthand accounts of the injustices that occurred and were able to engage their peers. Concurrently, organizations in the South were able to engage and broaden their local power base. College students and adolescents from the South were integral participants to many of the protests. Young people walked out of their high schools and colleges to participate in marches and sit-ins in local restaurants and libraries. The stream of nonviolent youth protesters never deteriorated. Youth from the South and from around the country viewed their participation in the Civil Rights Movement as a personal and collective responsibility to their communities. As the Civil Rights Movement drew to a close, the personal and collective responsibility that young people prescribed to led to the establishment of new movements and new leadership.

THE BLACK AND BROWN POWER MOVEMENTS

As the Civil Rights Movement was ending, the inception of other organizations ushered in new movements created to fill the needs of specific populations. Some of these groups included the Black Panther Party (1966), the Young Lords (1968), the Brown Berets (1967), the American Indians Movement (1968), the Red Guard (1969), I Wor Kuen (1969), the Young Patriot

Organization (1968), and the Third World Women's Alliance (1970). Representing blacks, Latinos, American Indians, Asians, poor whites, and women, each organization engaged and empowered their particular constituencies by increasing awareness of their civil rights and promoting collective unity. These organizations understood that as poor people entitled to their civic rights they were underrepresented and invisible to the dominant middle- and upper-class whites that held power.

The founding of the Black Panther Party in 1966 confirmed the transition from the Civil Rights Movement to the Black and Brown Power movements. (The Brown Power movement encompasses the work of Latinos, Asians, and the later stages of the Chicano Rights movement.) The Black and Brown Power movements grew out of a need for self-empowerment and acceptance of diverse perspectives and cultures by minority groups (black, Asian, and Latino). As these movements established the importance of self-empowerment and promoted the acknowledgement and celebration of cultural diversity as a norm, these groups no longer preached a single philosophy of nonviolence but promoted a stance of self-defense of their communities.

As each organization empowered their respective ethnic peoples, it was not to isolate themselves or become separatists, but to acknowledge the strengths and diversities of these groups as they gained equal footing with their middle- and upper-class white counterparts. Promoting self-empowerment proved to be a shrewd tactical strategy that led to multiple accomplishments. Youth around the country organized walkouts and sit-ins to illuminate the poor education system. They took over hospitals and churches to demonstrate the need for better direct services for the homeless, substance abusers, and poor. They supported unions by providing food for striking workers, and by joining picket lines. They blocked major roadways with piles of garbage to demonstrate city government's neglect of poor neighborhoods. Youth organizations also practiced cooperative capitalism by pooling their money and opening businesses.

All of these actions resulted in high schools and colleges broadening their curriculum to reflect the history of many races and ethnicities, the opening of cultural centers, and increases in tutorial programs and bilingual education, as well as the hiring of multiracial teachers, administration, and staff. Hospitals that were to be permanently closed were reopened to provide better health care services; churches became responsive to their community and congregation by providing direct services. The organizations of the Black and Brown Power movements also provided direct services to the community. These services included free meals for poor children, clothing drives, political education classes, child care, nutrition classes, senior drop-in centers, testing for sickle cell anemia, voter registration drives, and the creation of profitable cooperative businesses such as pool halls and youth centers. As groups of community residents increased their awareness of ethnicity and identity, they felt empowered to talk about and act on the issues that were plaguing their communities. This illustrated the need for all community residents to have a voice in decision making. Community members became active in direct service programs, and became civically engaged in their neighborhoods.

YOUNG WOMEN LEADERSHIP OF THE CIVIL RIGHTS, BLACK POWER, AND BROWN POWER MOVEMENTS

Women were prominent leaders throughout the Civil Rights and Black and Brown Power movements. During the Civil Rights Movement Ella Baker galvanized her male and female colleagues to create SNCC. By 1964 SNCC was a four-year-old organization. To continue its development two white female SNCC members, Casey Hayden and Mary King, wrote a then-anonymous document titled "Position Paper." This written document was the first of its kind to publicly discuss the issue of women's roles within movements. By distributing this document, men and women across race and ethnicity began to acknowledge sexism as an issue. "Position Paper" and subsequent dialogues provided a spark to the women's movement. Other organizations used "Position Paper" as a catalyst to debate and problem solve. In 1968, Frances Beal established the Black Women's Liberation Committee (BWLC) a division within SNCC that addressed issues specific to young women. By 1970, BWLC evolved into the influential Third World Women's Alliance, a multiracial organization.

Although black, Asian, and Latina women participated in the women's movement, many women of color aligned themselves to organizations around racial lines first and gender second. Many women of color believed that some of their needs as an ethnic minority were not addressed in the women's movement. As women participated in the Black and Brown Power movements they demonstrated impressive leadership skills by devising and implementing activities and programs throughout their various organizations. Black, Latina, and Chicana women like Cathleen Kleaver, Elaine Brown, Assata Shakur, Maria Varela, Elizabeth Sutherland Martinez, Gloria Cruz, and Denise Oliver held active and prominent leadership roles in the Black Panther Party, SNCC, and the Young Lords.

Young women were instrumental in the development of their organizations. Angela Davis was the Minister of Communications in the Black Panther Party, Elaine Brown was Black Panther Party Chief, and Denise Oliver was a founding member of the Young Lords. Oliver and other Latinas within the Young Lords influenced their male counterparts to revise their thirteen-point plan to reflect equity across gender. With young women as leaders and members in these organizations a broader perspective and the needs of women in the community were recognized. Young women organized marches and actions against education systems, as well as free breakfast and lunch programs for poor children. They also advocated for reproductive rights that included prenatal and postnatal care for poor women, affordable day care, an end to sterilization abuse, and legalization of contraception and abortion. By identifying issues important to women and creating programs and activities, thousands of youth and young adults felt their needs were included and became more engaged in the movement.

TARGETING ORGANIZATIONS' WEAKNESSES: J. EDGAR HOOVER AND COINTELPRO

By 1969 many of the organizations of the Black and Brown Power movement had been established for no more than three years; the mean age of the organizations was two years. SNCC, the oldest organization (nine years old), was almost defunct. Young in their development and attempting to find the balance of managing internal dynamics, meeting the needs of their constituents, and fending off the pressures of the government, members identified problems of trust across inter and intraracial coalitions, classism, and sexism. Very effective in their communities but perceived as radicals by many conservative whites, these organizations became targeted by the federal government.

Deemed dangerous by FBI director J. Edgar Hoover, these organizations were placed on watch lists, and files were opened on the organization and many of their members. Hoover created a division within the FBI called COINTELPRO, a federally funded program that enabled Hoover to identify organizations as "enemies of the state." Contingent on this label Hoover sent FBI agents to infiltrate the organizations' operations with the explicit orders to dismantle and eradicate their power bases. This work was done with blatant disregard to civil rights and often broke laws by framing, and subsequently incarcerating, members of organizations, and turning young organizers into informants. The main objective of COINTELPRO was to expose and exacerbate the internal problems of these organizations by creating a chaotic frenzy that would result in the implosion of the organization because of internal strife. By systematically destroying organizations, the Black and Brown Power movements would be discredited and rendered defunct.

As organizations began to problem solve, and to model healthy developmental skills, they were stymied by mounting pressures from FBI's informants. Distracted by a pervasive enemy, the organizations' focus was diverted from strengthening these partnerships and the coalitions were never nurtured to their fullest potential and began to fade.

LESSONS LEARNED: BUILDING COALITIONS AND ALLIANCES

Although racial lines divided groups like the Panthers, Berets, and the Young Lords, leaders and party members learned from their Civil Rights predecessors and understood the importance of broadening their power base. Members of the Black and Brown Power movements understood that the issues people of color were dealing with were not specific to a particular ethnic group but overlapped because of the racial and economic inequities of the poor and working class. The Black Panther Party understood the importance of building alliances with other groups that held similar vision and missions and would frequently collaborate with different groups and organizations around the country like the Red Guard, the America Indian Movement, and Los Siete de la Raza.

Coalition building was a wise strategy and well received by many of the organizations' respected leaders. The first attempt to formalize a partnership was the inception of the Rainbow Coalition. Created on June 7, 1969, the Rainbow Coalition consisted of the Black Panther Party, the Young Lords, and the Young Patriot Organization. Each organization's constituency represented blacks, Latinos, and poor whites, respectively. The Coalition understood that although each organization had a specific target audience, each had intersecting points of interest and concern. By acknowledging each group's racial differences, the Coalition acknowledged the need of each organization to work within their respective ethnic group to deal with cultural issues. The Coalition could embrace the similarities of the diverse races and create a larger power base as they confronted legal, economic, and political issues that affected their communities.

The leaders of the Black and Brown Power movements, having learned from the Civil Rights organizations, recognized to be effective in creating systemic change it was imperative to build coalitions across class and race. The Black and Brown Power movements engaged the poor and working-class by partnering with auto and farm workers, through outreach and mobilization of unemployed youth, and by reaching out to working class GIs who came home from the Vietnam War.

By building coalitions that engaged people across class and race accomplishments that were specific to one neighborhood had an effect on a larger community. In the Bay area, New York, Chicago, and Los Angeles, the Black Panthers, Young Lords, Brown Berets, and Red Guard provided free breakfast to poor children. By 1975 the federal government provided free breakfast to poor children in schools and summer camps around the country.

CONCLUSION

The Civil Rights, Black Power, and Brown Power movements engaged youth of all races, ethnicities, and classes. Their age ranged from fourteen to mid-twenties; they were both men and women; they attended high school and college; they were unemployed, gang members, or GIs. Youth were diverse in their culture and each movement provided a space for an awakening of their racial and ethnic identities. But these movements also provided a space for youth to become engaged and active participants in making their history.

Although short-lived, the organizations in the Civil Rights, Black Power, and Brown Power movements had powerful and long-lasting effects. Organizations had a direct effect on the communities they lived in and they influenced the creation of state and federal policies that were beneficial to the poor, they influenced revisions of state education systems, and they participated in electing people of color to government. They also influenced the next generation of youth organizations, including Californians for Justice, North Carolina Lamda Youth Network, the Prison Moratorium Project, the Malcolm X Grassroots Movement, 21 Century Youth Leadership Movement, and Youth in Action. These groups continue to organize in their communities and influence local and national policy changes around issues like education, health care services, juvenile justice, immigration, and gay and lesbian rights.

Current youth organizations have learned from their predecessors. To support the developmental needs of youth organizations, intermediary organizations like School of Unity and Liberation (SOUL), the Movement Strategy Center, Active Element Foundation, and the Local Initiative Training and Education Network (LISN) provides technical assistance nationally. Technical assistance includes strategic planning, and the development of organizing, grant writing, research, and media skills. Youth organizations may be specific to a region; but with the assistance of intermediaries they are broadening their power base, building coalitions and creating systemic change.

Resources

Books

Anderson-Bricker, K. (1999). "Triple jeopardy": Black women and the growth of feminist consciousness in SNCC, 1964–1975. In B. Collier-Thomas & V. P. Franklin (Eds.), *Still lifting, still climbing: Contemporary African-American women's activism* (pp. 49–69). New York: New York University Press.

Melendez, M. (2003). *We took the streets*. New York: St. Martin's Press.

Munoz, C. (1989). *Youth, identity, power: The Chicano movement*. London: Verso.

Navarro, A. (1995). *Mexican American youth organization: Avant-garde of the Chicano movement in Texas.* Austin: University of Texas Press.

Roth, B. (1999). The mobilizing of the vanguard center: Black feminist emergence in the 1960's and 1970. In B. Collier-Thomas & V. P. Franklin (Eds.), *Still lifting, still climbing: Contemporary African-American women's activism* (pp. 70–90). New York: New York University Press.

Web Sites

Asian American Movement E-zine: Progressive radical and revolutionary Asian American perspectives. Retrieved September 10, 2005 from http://www.aamovement.net/index.html

Fight back! Luche y Resiste! (2003). The Brown Berets: Young Chicano revolutionaries. California heritage collection: The Barcraft Library.

Retrieved September 10, 2005 from http://sunsite.berkeley.edu/ CalHeritage/panthers/coalition.htm and http://www.fightbacknews. org/2003winter/brownberets.htm
Latino education network service: de los barrios las Americas. (n.d.). Retrieved September 10, 2005 from http://palante.org

KIDS AGAINST CAPITAL

Pepi Leistyna

In this day and age of neo-liberal globalization, it is of particular importance to address how class structures and struggles dramatically affect the diversity of youth around the globe as they bare the brunt of a long legacy of, and increasing subjugation to, the economic, political, and cultural logic of capital. Of the 6.3 billion people that currently live on this planet, almost half of them are under the age of twenty-five. Half the world's 1 billion poor are children. Victims of the residue of a brutal history of colonial rule, and now the imperial grasp and draconian mandates of deregulation and structural adjustment, 11 million of these kids under the age of five die annually because of malnutrition, dirty water, disease, and poor housing. Hundreds of millions of youth around the world are not getting a formal education and millions are trapped in sweatshops or caught up in military conflicts where they are often forced into fighting someone else's economic wars.

The United States is the biggest proponent of the neo-liberal ideology of privatization and deregulation, and its role in a global economy and in "helping" developing countries. But what kind of example does the United States really set?

A COGENT CASE OF NEOLIBERAL FAILURE

Although talking about social class in the United States is taboo, class divisions and conflicts are rampant. In this postindustrial society—a society dependent on service industries, knowledge production, and information technology rather than manufacturing to generate capital—the average wage is 29 percent less than it was during the days of heavy industry. The average income in the United States is shrinking, and workers are earning less, adjusting for inflation, than they did a quarter century ago. Median household income is $43,318, which is down $1,604 from 1999. Income has dipped for the poorest 20 percent of the population across the country. Meanwhile, the ratio of average CEO pay in the United States to the average blue-collar worker pay in the same corporation is 470 to 1.

The gap between the rich and the poor in the United States is the largest it's ever been since the government started collecting information in 1947. In fact, the United States has the most unequal distribution of wealth and income in the industrialized world, with 35.9 million people living below the poverty level. Bear in mind the federal poverty thresholds: for one person under 65, the poverty level is $9,214; for two people under 65 with one

Students work overtime on independent projects

child, it is $12,207. Twenty-nine percent of families in the United States make less than what is currently estimated to meet basic needs. The number of people living in extreme poverty—less than half the amount of the poverty line—is 15.3 million.

Children are hit the hardest by economic oppression that accompanies the logic of these late stages of capitalism. By 2003, as the poverty rate rose for the third consecutive year in the United States, 12.9 million children were poor. That year, 1.3 million people were added to the poverty pile, with kids representing over half of this increase—733,000. The homeless population in the United States is 3.9 million (a number projected to increase 5 percent each year), and 1.3 million (or 39 percent) of the American homeless are children. The nation ranks seventeenth of all industrialized countries in efforts to eradicate poverty among the young, and twenty-third in infant mortality.

The percentage of people without heath insurance in the United States has also risen for three consecutive years: 1.4 million people were added to the list of uninsured in 2003, 43.6 million Americans currently lack health insurance, and 9.2 million of them are children. These statistics are especially disconcerting and revealing given that the top health care executives at the top ten managed health care companies make on average $11.7 million per year.

The richest 1 percent of Americans controls about 40 percent of the nation's wealth; the top 5 percent has more than 60 percent. As far as political influence is concerned, some 80 percent of all political contributions now come from less than 1 percent of the population. It should thus come as no surprise that most of the public policy debate remains in the confines of the Wall Street agenda; especially given that the nation's wealthiest 10 percent own almost 90 percent of all stocks and mutual funds. While almost one in two Americans don't own stocks, and those outside the wealthiest 10 percent own very few, the ubiquitous numbers from the stock exchange falsely imply that the market will help those in need and the country as a whole.

Unemployment in the United States has vacillated between 5.6 and 6 percent since 2001. It is important to note that this figure does not include part-time workers, long-term unemployed who have stopped looking for work, people temporarily serving in the military, the homeless, or the millions of people who are currently incarcerated. Approximately 3 million jobs have been lost during this period. These job losses are not merely lay-offs caused by hard economic times; nor are they a direct result of 9/11 as many politicians would like the public to believe. With capital flight and global outsourcing, both blue collar and white collar jobs have been and continue to be exported by U.S. corporations to nations that pay below a living wage and that ensure that workers have no protection under labor unions and laws that regulate corporate interests and power. By cheap labor, we're usually talking between 13.5 and 36 cents an hour in countries often run by totalitarian regimes. We're also talking about a total disregard for child-labor laws and environmental protections.

As the Federal Reserve has noted, these outsourced jobs won't be returning to the United States even if there is a major upswing in the nation's economy. The current administration, which embraces outsourcing as good productive practice, boasts creating new jobs for Americans, but it neglects to inform the public that these are overwhelmingly part-time, adjunct, minimum-wage positions that provide no pension, union protection, adequate child care, or health care benefits. Part-time, temp, or subcontracted jobs currently make up 30 percent of the workforce, and this number is rapidly increasing.

As the federal minimum wage is currently $5.15 an hour, a figure that has been stagnant for seven years (while the Congress during that same period of time gave itself annual raises totaling an increase of some $16,700), full-time minimum-wage workers in the United States make about $10,712 a year—recall that the poverty line for an individual is $9,214. This makes it impossible to afford adequate housing throughout the country. It's no wonder that one out of every five homeless people is employed. It is important to note that contrary to popular myth, the majority of minimum-wage workers are not teenagers: 71.4 percent are over the age of twenty.

Although the average worker in this country now has to labor for more hours each year to make ends meet than in the last three decades, the current administration is adamantly opposed to raising the minimum wage and has been working diligently to revise the 1938 Fair Labor Standards

Act that would take away the forty-hour workweek, and it wants to limit overtime pay that more than 8 million people rely on to financially stay afloat.

In need of government protections and tax relief, workers in the United States don't get the royal treatment that corporations do. Sixty percent of U.S. companies pay no income tax. By the year 2000, the corporate share of taxes had fallen to 17 percent. Corporations find creative ways to keep from paying the 35 percent tax on profits that they are legally compelled to cover. From 1999 to 2002, U.S. transnational corporations augmented their profits in no- or low-tax international zones by 68 percent. In 2002, U.S. companies made $149 billion in eighteen tax-haven countries. Kept legal by the Congress, which has effectively disarmed the Internal Revenue Service, the existing tax code encourages outsourcing of labor by permitting deferral of taxes on profits earned outside the United States, and gives companies a dollar-for-dollar credit on taxes paid in foreign countries; these practices translate into a subsidy for offshore investment. In 2003, the average pay increase for CEOs who outsourced the majority of their service jobs was 46 percent, compared to just a 9 percent increase for those who kept most jobs here in the States. It is estimated that 14 million jobs are at serious risk of being sent outside the country.

It's now 2005 and the nation has accrued over 7 trillion dollars in debt and the president, through frantic spending, has accumulated a $445 billion budget deficit—the highest in the nation's history. Meanwhile, backed by a Republican-majority Congress, the president has created tax cuts of $1.7 trillion that favor the rich. This conscious effort to wipe out any money to sustain the public sector makes the privatization of healthcare, Medicare and Medicaid, social security, and schools the only available option. The not-so-hidden agenda of the Bush administration's "ownership society" is to shift the tax burden onto wages and salaries as the real meaty cuts go for taxes on savings and investments, dividends, and capital gains on stocks, bonds, and real estate—in other words, to the elite people that already own the country. Meanwhile, in the guise of "compassionate conservatism," neo-liberals continue to blame the poor for their limited access to quality education, job training, child care, and a living wage.

The government's aforementioned tax cuts to the rich don't include the $400-plus billion that is annually funneled through the Pentagon's military industrial complex. Here the government socializes risk and investment while the public pays for the research and product development, but privatizes the profits. The military also provides a security force for corporate interests as is clearly evident in the current operations in oil-rich Iraq—so much for laissez-faire and the natural flow of the market.

In the end, the working class not only pays for endless wars with their tax dollars and by sustaining program cuts that fund these adventures in capitalism, but with the lives of their children as well as they are offered limited opportunities in schools and the workplace and consequently turn to the armed forces where they make up the majority of combat soldiers— even though many of them are not old enough to legally drink or vote. For their service, government in the past three years has cut funds for veteran's health care, closed seven veteran hospitals, tried to cut Federal Impact Aid offered since 1950 to school districts that provide educational services to military children that live off base, proposed doubling costs for prescription drugs for veterans, and the Pentagon had even planned to cut pay for troops serving in Iraq and Afghanistan.

SCHOOLS AS THE BATTLEGROUND FOR CLASS WARFARE

Corporate-guided education feeds into this neo-liberal disaster as it functions to reproduce the "normalcy" of capitalist social relations and generate a semiliterate and semiskilled workforce.

Since President Bush signed into law the Elementary and Secondary Education Act of 2001, better known as No Child Left Behind (NCLB), high-stakes testing has been officially embraced and positioned to be the panacea of academic underachievement in public schools in the United States. The act engenders a hitherto unheard of, and unconstitutional, transfer of power to federal and state governments, granting them the rights to largely determine the goals and outcomes of these educational institutions.

Embracing what is in fact an old neo-liberal approach dressed up as innovative reform, and disregarding the blatant contradiction with their "downsize the government" platform, proponents of this market-driven educational model make use of words and phrases like "equity," "efficiency," and "the enhancement of global competitiveness" to continue to sell their agenda to the public. However, this same political machinery— this synergy between government and the corporate sector—shrouds, in the name of excellence and "choice," neoliberal efforts to privatize public schools by forcing their failure and collapse and subsequently channeling public funds to private firms that relish the idea that mandatory education means mandatory consumers.

In this "no corporation left behind" agenda, where 6 million children have thus far been left in the wake, and where the White House has under funded its efforts by over $6 billion, devoted advocates of current education legislation effectively disguise the motivations of a profit-driven testing industry led by publishing power houses like McGraw-Hill, which is the largest producer of standardized tests in the country. No Child Left Behind leaves little to no room for success in public schools, but plenty of room for profits—$7 billion in materials alone.

This corporate model of public education is not concerned with infusing civic responsibility in preparation for public life. Educational institutions are currently not designed to engage students in studying labor history or reading the world critically, creatively, and independently; nor are they intended to nurture politically active citizens. On the contrary, schools function to leave many students, predominantly working class, racially subordinated, and poor kids, at the bottom of the academic hierarchy and consequently with limited occupational choices, if any. For those "throwaway" masses, constant exposure to discrimination, gross inequities in schools funded primarily through property taxes, limited, exclusionary, and distorted curricula, and ill-prepared teachers, work to virtually ensure the self-fulfilling prophesy of youth failure, deviance, and resistance. The government's response is more standardization, zero-tolerance policies and practices, and the militarization of these public spaces with the addition of armed guards, security systems, and random raids. There is no consideration for the realities of discrimination, unemployment, poverty, the alienating and commodified junk culture, or the destructive logic of the market that deeply affects young people's lives.

IS THE DUMP BIG ENOUGH FOR ALL THESE KIDS?

In order to bankroll their corporate exploits, the leaders of this market-driven society are slashing funding for education, health care, and other public needs and services. In doing so, millions of young people are confronted with a bleak future and left to fend for themselves in the nation's streets. In an effort to explain away and consequently do away with these "disposable" youth, the State is working overtime to publicly criminalize and manage them with repressive and punitive social policies.

As part of this effort, prisons are being used within the feudalism of today's capitalist social relations to lock up what's seen as superfluous populations that the powers that be have no immediate use for. The prison population in the United States has skyrocketed over 200 percent since 1980. There are now over 2 million people in jail in the United States, and although it has only 5 percent of the world's population, it has 25 percent of its prisoners. The United States surpassed Russia in the year 2000 and now has the world's highest incarceration rate. It is 5 to 17 times higher than all other Western nations. By the close of the millennium, 6.3 million people were on probation, in jail or prison, or on parole in this country.

Over 70 percent of prisoners in the United States are from non-European racial and ethnic backgrounds. African American males make up the largest number of those entering prisons each year. Racially subordinated women are also being incarcerated in epidemic proportions. One can only imagine the psychological and academic effects on children when their parents are locked up. And yet, this insatiable appetite for incarceration comes from the same bunch that preaches "family values" and the need for parents to play a bigger role in children's lives. Patriarchy and white supremacy function in coordination with the logic of capital to keep women poor, and the racially subordinated and working poor locked down in prisons and disenfranchised from voting in many states.

CLASS CONSCIOUSNESS

Economic growth over the past fifteen years has not helped the economically oppressed, and the nation is in dire need of effective policy responses that change the current mode of production rather than rely on the myths of the "free" market. Within this antagonistic economic climate, mass upheavals and uprisings are possible, but the elite classes work diligently to suppress political and cultural dissent and the dissemination of substantive information to the public. For example, in 1998 there were 24,000 documented acts of corporate lawbreaking, yet the media barely gave it a notice. As such, it shouldn't be surprising that so many people were suddenly shocked by the recently discovered abuses and atrocities of corporate giants of the likes of Enron, Tyco, and Worldcom. Because profit-driven journalism only allows for spectacle and infotainment, as it is controlled by corporate elite who wish to protect their own interests and not offend their advertisers, there was no early investigation into such malfeasance.

At the same time, within corporate-dominated media, the business press that addresses the financial concerns of so few saturates the society and readily demonizes organized labor in the public eye. While workers in unions earn 30 percent more than non-union people doing the same job, and get far more guaranteed benefits such as a pension and healthcare, the assault on organized labor has been devastating. By 2002, only 13.2 percent of wage and salary workers in the United States were union members—a number that has been getting smaller every year since the "Reagan Revolution." Regardless of the federal law (Section 7 of the National Labor Relations Act) that gives workers the right to organize, the harsh reality is that those who try to exercise their rights often face serious repercussions. Up to 20,000 people a year are fired or punished for trying to unionize. Low-wage earners in particular face an atmosphere of intimidation and as a result many, desperate for work, steer clear of union activity.

While the myth of a liberal media bias persists, Hollywood, and the corporate media giants—Viacom, News Corporation, AOL Time Warner, General Electric, and Walt Disney have rarely produced positive representations of the working class or poor. When poverty manages to make its way into the media it is usually played out in a rags to riches narrative that feeds into the myths of meritocracy, rugged individualism, the American dream, and the "pull yourself up by your bootstraps" ethos. In the end, these types of representation work to justify class relations and structures and the outsourcing of jobs by blaming the victim for having a poor work ethic, being financially irresponsible, having bad family values, having little interest in education and advancement, or, in some genetic twist, for not having the necessary smarts. Corporate media's pedagogical forces have worked to shape public consciousness about youth and the working class and poor and they have worked to shape and justify socially-sanctioned practices and policies that go against the best interests of labor and those in need.

CLASS ACTION

And this is the great "success" model that neo-liberals are boasting and selling globally, or more accurately, forcing down the throats of the world. In order to combat this aforementioned long list of abuses of power, it is crucial to formulate more inclusive and effective political subjects and democratizing networks that are able to analyze political moments and consequently develop critical responses to oppression that have both local and global dimensions. Rather than forcing young people to ingest commodified culture as the only legitimate road to happiness and success, they should be encouraged to explore and envision different ways of organizing social relations that can work to restore the centrality of politics over the tyranny of market forces. Any hope to change the current class structure locally and globally includes an analysis of the material conditions of society, of ownership and political regulation, and encourages theorizing about how culture shapes our sense of political agency and mediates the relations between everyday class struggles and structures of power.

The youth of the world can certainly be looked to as a democratizing force capable of dismantling the structured inequalities of class-based societies. It is for this very reason that conservatives and capitalists fear them so and vigilantly work to contain and control them. Those of us who believe in the virtues of participatory democratic movements and social policies and institutions developed to help ensure the public's well being, and who understand the glaring contradiction between capitalism and democracy, need to work to physically, emotionally, intellectually, and spiritually unleash youth so that they can forge anti-imperialist, multi-interest coalitions that can present a real challenge to neo-liberalism in the global fight of kids against capital.

GUERRILLA JOURNALISM

Drew Traulsen

For nearly a century, young people whose ideas, interests, and opinions have been deemed irrelevant by the mainstream media and publishing outlets have been producing their own independent, noncommercial, non-professional, small-circulation publications called "fanzines." In doing so, young people have moved control of the presses out of the hands of large media outlets and into the hands of ordinary people and fostered a significant, independent underground community.

The term "fanzine" is a combination of two words, "fan" and "magazine" (also called "zines"). They are noncommercial, nonprofessional, small-circulation publications that are often produced, published, and distributed by a single individual. The fact that they are privately funded, have irregular publication schedules, and are individually distributed, sets them apart from mainstream magazines. Fanzine topics vary and include almost anything imaginable. They are generated and sold by independent individuals who operate without the editorial and publishing controls placed on the major media outlets and are usually produced for fun and the sheer will to be heard rather than for profit.

Fanzines have existed in the United States for close to a century and are important for a number of reasons. First is the fact that they have established and fostered a significant subculture with a tradition of correspondence between enthusiasts of all types. These underground networks have used their peripheral status and new technological inventions to print and promote interests and opinions considered insignificant by major media outlets. Most important, fanzines have hijacked control of the presses away from the major media outlets and produced an important primary source for gauging the pulse of youth culture. Lastly, coupled with a "do-it-yourself" (DIY) work ethic and a penchant for rebellion, the fanzine tradition seems to bear not only historical and cultural significance but a boundless future as well.

The earliest fanzine on record is Hugo Gernsback's 1926 venture titled *Amazing Stories*. Gernsback, an avid science fiction fan and storywriter, wanted to collect and publish stories written by like-minded individuals. In a move that would both galvanize the science fiction community and begin a wave of other fanzine publications, *Amazing Stories* started printing the full addresses of each contributor. Readers were encouraged to submit suggestions or discuss the published works. In this way, *Amazing Stories* served as much more than a science fiction publication; it also established a sense of community among fanzine creators and readers that survives to this day.

One of the many discussion groups formed out of *Amazing Stories*' practice of printing full addresses of its contributors was *The Science Correspondence Club* (SCC). In 1930, the SCC published its own science fiction fanzine titled The Comet. The Comet was significant for two main reasons. First, it set the standard for science fiction and fantasy based fanzines, not too mention the soon to explode comic book industry, for the next three decades (one of which, *Science Fiction*, was published by Jerome Siegel and Joe Shuster, who would later become famous as the creators of the *Superman* comic). Secondly, and more importantly, *The Comet* utilized the new invention of the mimeograph-duplicating machine to cheaply print each issue. Use of new technology, a dominating force in the revolutionizing of mainstream journalism, would repeatedly influence the fanzine community over the ensuing decades.

As the prosperity of the Roaring Twenties gave way to the high unemployment, homelessness, and starvation of the Great Depression, a new form of fanzine evolved. Out of the left-wing folk music movement and led by such notable individuals as Pete Seeger, Woody Guthrie, Lee Hays, and Alan Lomax, sprang *People's Songs Incorporated. People's Songs* was run not only by musicians, but also by average young people interested in the power of music and its ability to foment change. The belief that protest music could inspire and motivate people was based on longstanding American social traditions such as the abolitionist, labor, populist, and socialist movements. Through songs and live performances, musicians cried out for labor equality, civil rights, civil liberties, and peace. In an attempt to raise awareness of social issues, *People's Songs Inc.* began publishing the *People's Songs Bulletin* in 1945.

The *People's Songs Bulletin* was much more than a collection of sheet music and lyrics; it also established booking/management services, a song archive and recording opportunities for folk musicians. Much like the science fiction fanzines of the preceding decade, *People's Songs Bulletin* encouraged song submissions and published letters from readers and labor unions covering a wide range of social topics. In their submissions disclaimer the editors noted that, "People's Songs is interested in folk songs, work songs, and the best in song tradition, but not to the exclusion of new songs. It works not as a folklore society, but as an organization serving the cultural needs of the people." In this way, the *People's Songs Bulletin* maintained two traditions that have dominated fanzine culture: First, it provided a publication outlet to those who had none and second, it fostered a sense of community by inspiring readers to submit and communicate with one another. Although the *People's Songs Bulletin* was a short-lived venture, its replacement, *Sing Out!*, first published in 1950, continues many of the same traditions to this day.

As World War II gave way to the Cold War, a new generation of marginalized young people would take up the fanzine tradition. The Beats, such as William Burroughs, Babs Gonzales, Allen Ginsberg, and Jack Kerouac, began espousing ideas of individuality, mysticism and a relaxing of social and sexual inhibitions. Some of these individuals, as well as fans of their work, began issuing small audience, small circulation zines called "chapbooks." Chapbooks were collections of literary work such as poetry, short stories and artwork either shunned or deemed culturally irrelevant by mainstream publishers. By seizing the opportunity to publish their own work, the Beats were, in essence, carrying the fanzine tradition forward. Such endeavors, and their creators, would inspire a whole new generation of literary, music and radical fanzines as the homogeneity of the 1950s gave way to the turbulent decade that followed.

The 1960s and its political and social upheavals spawned a revolution in the publication of alternative media. Although not referred to as fanzines, these publications became commonly known as the "underground press." The youth of America during this period sought an alternative because the mainstream press was not concerned with issues important to young people. Underground publications responded, "by editorializing on civil rights, social welfare, colonialism, flower children, international peace movements and the inhumanity of war." With time, these topics would expand into "fan" related subjects such as literature, art, music, and drug use. The most recognized papers of this movement formed the Underground Press Syndicate (UPS) in 1967. Publications of the UPS included the *Los Angeles Free Press*, New York's *East Village Other*, the *Berkeley Barb*, San Francisco's *Oracle*, Detroit's *Fifth Estate*, Chicago's *Seed*, and Austin's *Rag*. At its height, the UPS included more than a hundred other alternative publications.

The underground press would have an immense affect on the future of fanzine publication. The first of two significant aspects of the underground press was individual control over all aspects of the publication process. Whether conceiving story ideas, researching, interviewing, editorializing, taking pictures, doing graphic design/paste-up artwork or delivering and selling the final product, many alternative journalists were exposed to every aspect of the process. The second important aspect of the underground press was this DIY work ethic coupled with inexpensive offset printing, justifying typewriters, and the camera-ready copy processes, which coalesced to give voice to the dissenter and led to a proliferation of alternative media. As the 1960s wore on, some underground publications began to focus on the confrontational social and political aspects of the burgeoning rock-n-roll music scene.

By the late 1960s the underground press had expanded to include not only social and political commentary, but literary experimentation and critiques and analyses of the rebelliousness of sex, drugs, and rock-n-roll music. Counterculture musicians such as Bob Dylan, The Fugs, The MC5, Joan Baez, Country Joe MacDonald & the Fish, Buffalo Springfield, Creedence Clearwater Revival and Crosby, Stills, Nash & Young were all vocal critics of American policies both at home and abroad. In response, more than five hundred underground fanzines began monitoring, recording and publishing the activities and opinions of rock musicians and counterculture figures (the most well-known during this period was Rolling Stone). This expanded focus led to a wider readership as young people not initially attracted to the underground press were drawn in by the focus on rock-n-roll music. The effect of such a shift ultimately increased the number of zines being produced and created a tight-knit network of counterculture individuals. This network would later inspire a whole new wave of fanzines in the coming decade.

Despite rock-n-roll's evolution into a strong counter-cultural force, the mainstream media tended to ignore it. On the other hand, large record companies, realizing the huge marketing potential of the underground press, began pouring large amounts of money into advertising. As a result of this corporate co-opting of the counterculture's views, media and music, by the middle 1970s rock-n-roll had degenerated into overproduced, corporate, arena rock that many believed had lost its rebellious edge. To many young people this was unacceptable. The stage was set for nothing short of a new youth rebellion, counterculture, music, and fanzine revolution.

The emergence of punk rock music in the mid 1970s most significantly impacted the history of fanzines. Punk rock attacked the overindulgent lifestyles of rock musicians and the overproduced nature of their music. This new form of music was characterized by edgy, anarchic, and nihilistic anthems that railed against the status quo. Punk rock became the new counterculture as young people opposed the corporate stranglehold on rock music, fashion, and the press, while championing unopposed individuality. Music historians argue over the origins of the punk rock phenomena, but most agree it began in the United States with the Ramones in 1973 and in England with a band called the Sex Pistols in 1976. Like history repeating itself, a whole new wave of fanzines was born to cover this new youth movement.

Two zines that covered the early punk rock scene and would ultimately shape the future of the fanzine tradition were New York's *Punk* and England's *Sniffin' Glue*. *Punk* used slick printing and an almost comic book design, while Sniffin' Glue utilized sloppy hand lettering, typewritten text, and poorly produced photographs. Fanzines that reported the punk rock scene, like their counterculture predecessors, focused on issues and music that the mainstream found unimportant or irrelevant. While their styles were widely different, both *Punk* and *Sniffin' Glue* set the bar for a wave of fanzine production, the likes of which had never been seen before. By the early 1980s large circulation fanzines such as Los Angeles' *Flipside* and San Francisco's *Maximum Rock 'n' Roll*, not to mention hundreds of smaller publications, catered to the punk rock underground.

No other inventions would have greater effects on the production of fanzines than the Xerox machine and the personal computer. The proliferation of the Xerox machine in the early 1980s provided anyone with an interest in anything the opportunity to publish his or her own fanzine. The advent of the personal computer and its desktop publishing and printing capabilities would allow for completely self-contained fanzine publication. By the late 1980s the combination of punk rock's underground spirit, the DIY work ethic and new technology led to an explosion in fanzine publication. This explosion was so vast that a fanzine titled *The Factsheet Five* (F5) was established that attempted to review and catalog all other zine publications.

Founded by Mike Gunderloy in 1982, each issue of F5 described fanzines and listed both their prices and contact addresses. Much like the discussion groups that had formed out of the science fiction, folk music, Beat era and UPS, *F5* allowed a whole new generation of fanzine enthusiasts an opportunity to correspond with one another. The *F5* was so popular that, by 1985, its size had increased from a two page Xeroxed pamphlet to a bimonthly with close to 150 pages and a circulation of more than 10,000.

Presently there are an estimated 20,000 fanzines being produced in the United States alone. Examples of current fanzine topics include the following:

music, extreme sports, classic television shows and movies, religions and cultures, serial killers, racism, sex and sexual deviance, bird watching, pro- and anti-drug and alcohol, literature, bowling, politics, amusement park deaths, personal diaries, roller coasters, travel diaries, physical abuse—and the list expands on a daily basis.

Although fanzines are still far from the cultural mainstream, they may not be relegated to the periphery much longer. Some of the larger circulation zines have begun accepting corporate advertising to offset publication costs. Much like corporate interests had realized the potential of marketing to the counterculture in the 1960s, it seems they are again realizing the economic potential of the underground youth market. This has created an interesting problem within the fanzine community. Fanzine publishers have to negotiate the difficult line between anti-corporate, socially critical ethics and the desire to reach more of an audience. Although there are numerous zines that have resisted corporate influence, there are also those who have increasingly felt the strain and given in.

Fanzine production, like the world of traditional journalism, has been impacted greatly by new inventions. The recent proliferation of personal computers and use of the Internet to get information has prompted many mainstream publications to venture into cyberspace. Fanzines are no exception. Unfortunately, e-zines are difficult to locate because many online publishers refer to them as their "personal Web page" rather than by name or topic. Attempts to catalogue e-zines, much like the F5 had done in print form, has been an arduous task that some have begun but most have abandoned.

The use of the Internet for publication of fanzines has also sparked a heated debate within the fanzine community. Proponents see the Internet as a way of reaching millions of potential readers while avoiding huge printing costs. Conversely, opponents argue that it isolates those individuals who have no access to computers. Opponents also argue that e-zines are unable to provide the reader with the DIY aesthetic of the printed fanzine, thus giving the reader only a small part of the true fanzine experience. They also believe that the e-zine is an easily co-opted medium where the possibility of corporate collusion is not easily discerned. Regardless of the debate though, the clash between the old-school purists and the e-zine proponents seems far from resolution. It seems the choice will ultimately reside with the consumer.

Resources
Books

Duncombe, S. (1997). *Notes from the underground*. New York: Verso.

Emery, M., Emery, E., & Roberts, N. (2000). *The press and America: An interpretive history of the mass media*. Boston: Allyn and Bacon.

Glessing, R. (1970). *The underground press in America*. Bloomington: University of Indiana Press.

Gunderloy, M. (1988). *How to publish a fanzine*. Washington, DC: Loompanics Unlimited.

Lieberman, R. (1979). *My song is my weapon*. Urbana: University of Illinois Press.

Streitmatter, R. (2001). *Voices of revolution*. New York: Columbia University Press.

Wertham, F. (1973). *The world of fanzines: A special form of communication*. Carbondale: Southern Illinois University Press.

Articles

Chezzi, D. (2000). The counterculture zine. *MacLean's*, 113 (47).

Gross, D. (1994). Zine but not heard. *Time*, 144 (10).

Web Sites

Friedman, S. (n.d.). A brief history of zines. Retrieved November 14, 2003 from http://www.essentialmedia.com/shop/seth.html

Romensko, J. (1993). Fanzines explained. Retrieved November 14, 2003 from http://www.obscurestore.com/zinesajr.html

Stoneman, P. (2001). Fanzines: Their production, culture and future. Retrieved November 14, 2003 from http://www.lundwood.u-net.com/fandissy/fdtitle.html

YOUTH PEACE-BUILDERS IN COMMUNITY ORGANIZATIONS

Leonisa Ardizzone

Community organizations offer a supportive outlet for youth interested in working for peace. Youth often seek organizations outside of school that will allow them to work for social change. This interest stems from the present condition of youth today, namely that they encounter many obstacles—including poverty, violence, and marginalization—that often result in feelings of despair, or harmful behaviors. This condition has led to the scapegoating of youth in society. Popular media and politicians like to blame societal ills on youth, deliberately marginalizing them and actively removing them from political and social movements. Many youth have chosen to confront media-propagated stereotypes by becoming involved positively in their own communities. For example, youth in New York City have created or joined pro-social organizations that allow them to work for change. Inner-city youth begin their path to peace-building for a few reasons: a desire to learn more; an interest in counteracting negative views of youth; and witnessing injustice in their communities. The community groups they work with address the three core values of peace education: Planetary Stewardship, Humane Relationship, Global Citizenship—values that encompass an ethic of care for the environment, an interest in intercultural understanding and the ability to see oneself as part of a much greater whole. Through these organizations youth are able to explore: global issues and the role of youth in the movement for peace and justice, local concerns such as tenant rights and police harassment, environmental stewardship, and war and militarism.

Motivation to become involved in these pro-social organizations occurs for a number of reasons. Naturally, some reasons fall into the mundane category—as a way to enhance their transcripts and/or college applications or a way to meet girls and make new friends. Others join groups because of an interest in learning especially about topics they do not feel are covered in school, which can be quite extensive. For example, youth want to learn about foreign policy and international issues, what role they can have in their community and what issues need to be addressed locally, and how local ideas connect to global concerns. Still others are motivated by a sense of social responsibility—a desire to help people and share information. Many youth are motivated to join these particular youth organizations because of their interest in finding and using their voice. As youth often feel silenced by society, voice is a powerful motivator. They feel very strongly about changing the public's perception of teenagers; they do not like being seen as screw-ups with nothing to offer society. Community organizations provide youth with the opportunity to examine these misconceptions and develop methods to counteract this bad press.

The most powerful motivator for youth peace-builders is a critical experience(s) such as witnessing injustice or personally feeling oppressed, thus wanting to change the societal situation that caused it. Examples of these experiences include seeing friends get arrested because of their race, being harassed by police because of their skin color, being forced to follow curfews based on the neighborhood they live in, working with death-row inmates, and being disrespected by boys. The commonality among these experiences is their relationship to structural violence. Structural violence (also known as indirect violence)—or the violence that is embedded in social structures causing oppression, alienation and marginalization (showing up as poverty, hopelessness, unequal education, sexism, racism, etc.)—can serve as a powerful motivating force for change. Many youth peace-builders articulate feelings of dehumanization (a form of structural violence) namely that they are treated differently because of their age (i.e., being followed in stores or harassed by police in the streets). For many of them, their race and ethnicity adds to this "burden" of age, and they find that the dehumanizing treatment they receive by adults and authority figures is a motivating factor for them to work for social change.

Structural violence as motivation has been present in youth and political movements for many years. Certainly, in the past, disillusionment with authority sparked student involvement (i.e., Vietnam War protests, Civil Rights Movement). However, it now more often than not leads to depression and apathy coupled with an eroding ethic of social responsibility. Researchers explain that young people experiencing traumatic events lose interest in the world and often will alter their behavior to hide fear. Nevertheless, many youth not only demonstrate an understanding of structural violence but also an interest in working to change oppressive structures. Hopelessness and apathy are not the answers for them.

Simply, experiences that serve as motivation can best be explained by something "clicking." These critical experiences allow youth to see the world differently, an experience occurs that raises their consciousness, compelling them to take action for the greater good. Inner-city youth witness and experience structural violence on a regular basis but they may not always "get it." They may not see racism or failing schools, or they might just see it as their lot in life, or believe that they personally will overcome it. However, hopefully many do "get it" and when they do get it, ideally they will respond. Whereas the most common response observed (by researchers and popular media) is that of direct violence (physical violence, such as fighting, abuse, gun violence), many other youth represent an alternative view: the choice to become a peace-builder and an agent for social change evidence of which exists in the history of activism. Through the informal education settings of their respective youth organizations, these committed youth not only become aware of the structural and direct violence that surrounds them but they are also given the opportunity to take action. Therefore, the path of structural violence leading to direct violence is altered and the route from structural violence to social action is established.

Once youth are motivated to take action and find a community organization to serve as an outlet for their peace-building, the real transformation occurs. Membership in these organizations furthers their interest in "seeing the big picture" and understanding the contradictions. Youth take action for social change and find that their community organization better supports their learning and personal growth than their schooling. Many urban youth feel that formal education in public schools is often inequitable, and irrelevant. Youth consider themselves under-represented in the curriculum, unengaged by the pedagogy, and disregarded by teachers. Often teachers do not listen to them or allow them to have a say in course content. However, their non-formal education experiences through community organizations are quite different. Involved youth see their engagement with these groups as a way to learn more and many agree that their organization teaches them a lot, more so than formal school. They feel they learn about the complexity of society and how to "deal" in difficult situations. They also tend to learn a lot more about global issues and international topics.

The organizations offer youth the chance to become empowered through choice and voice. Youth like: having a choice of what they can learn about and pursue; having the opportunity to share their opinions with others; designing learning experiences—either workshops or outreach education; being agents of change, and changing peoples' perceptions of youth. These are examples of how these non-formal organizations provide youth with learning opportunities they do not feel they receive in school. The nature of these organizations is the key to their success in providing youth with these aforementioned feelings of empowerment. These organizations seek to develop youth, but also to help them become thoughtful citizens, and provide them with an outlet to confront issues of structural and direct violence. Because they are not bound by the structures of formal education, they can offer learners more flexibility and freedom to question, find answers, and act. These characteristics make these youth organizations different from others—such as athletic, religio-cultural, or vocational—in that they don't just serve as a means to help youth stay out of trouble, but they offer youth a chance to be part of the solution.

For inner-city youth, who live in poverty and feel marginalized or dehumanized, this means that they have the opportunity through youth programs to question the structural violence inherent in their situation. This questioning begins the process of raising their critical consciousness and potentially those of their friends, family, and community members. In doing this, they no longer accept the status quo and they begin to work for social change. More importantly, they are active in the development of these youth organizations. Many youth organizations that address peace-building are founded by youth, organized, administrated, and facilitated by youth. They are in charge of their own social movement. Therefore, if society is interested in supporting youth who are motivated to become peace-builders, support should exist for the creation of opportunities that facilitate consciousness-raising providing youth the space, both physical and intellectual, to do so. Community organizations not only offer a social setting but also opportunities to direct their own learning, practice social responsibility, use their voices, and further their critical experiences. Involvement in youth organizations is a critical experience for many, fostering social responsibility and a commitment to peace, justice, and social change.

Resources

Books

Canada, G. (1995). *Fist stick knife gun: A personal history of violence in America*. Boston: Beacon Press.

Clark, T. (1975). *The oppression of youth*. New York: Harper Colophon.

Fine, M. (1991). *Framing dropouts: Notes on the politics of an urban public high school*. Albany: State University of New York Press.

Freire, P. (1973). *Education for critical consciousness*. New York: Continuum.

Galtung, J. (1976). *Peace and social structure: Essays in peace research, volume two*. Copenhagen: Christian Eljers.

———. (1978). *Peace and social structure: Essays in peace research, volume three*. Copenhagen: Christian Eljers.

Garbarino, J., Kostelny, K., & Dubrow, N. (1991). *No place to be a child: Growing up in a war zone*. Lexington, MA: Lexington Books.

Kelley, E. C. (1962). *In defense of youth*. Englewood Cliffs, NJ: Prentice Hall.

Males, M. A. (1996). *The scapegoat generation: America's war on adolescents*. Monroe, ME: Common Courage Press.

Ogbu, J. (1974). *The next generation: An ethnography of education in an urban neighborhood*. New York: Academic Press.

Reardon, B. A. (1988). *Comprehensive peace education: Educating for global responsibility*. New York: Teachers College Press.

Article

Ardizzone, L. (2003). Generating peace: a study of non-formal youth organizations. *Peace & Change*, 28 (3), 420–445.

YOUTH IN THE BLACK PANTHER PARTY

J. Vern Cromartie

Founded in 1966 in Oakland, California, by Huey P. Newton and Bobby Seale, the Black Panther Party quickly became a source of identification for many youth. Two years after Newton and Seale established the organization, the Black Panther Party had some five thousand members and forty chapters and branches in various states, including California, Washington, Oregon, Colorado, Texas, Louisiana, Tennessee, North Carolina, Maryland, Illinois, New Jersey, and New York. Kathleen Cleaver, former communications secretary of the Black Panther Party, has reported that most members of the Black Panther Party were teenagers or joined as teenagers and most members were females. Seale, former chairman of the Black Panther Party, has written in his autobiography, *A Lonely Rage*, that by 1968 over 60 percent of the members were females.

Youth who joined the Black Panther Party were expected to participate in all aspects of the organization, including its community service projects and leadership structure. During its sixteen years of existence from 1966 to

THE NEXT LEGA-C

Joshua (Lega-C) Rodriguez

By any means necessary, I was taught to achieve.
Heard the dream by Doctor King and was taught to believe,
Seen the force of Malcolm X and I changed in my ways.
Quotin' many lines of Pac, prayin' for better days.
All this oppression faced got me pressure faced in the face
Hopin' soon we'd be accepted not neglected by race.
How many must it take to perish into the earth
Before equality and justice is provided at birth?
What's even worse, we all are facing similar fates
And nobody cares enough to even right the mistakes.
Well I'm awake and care,
So I'ma take it to there,
Even if the only thing that stands behind me is air.
Conceived a mortar,
Meant to lose my life
For the plan of the unity of nations and the binding of man.
Most people ran but I accepted faith in my heart
That I'd die at 29 to take a place in the start, inside a nation,
Where there's one man helping his brother,
Unity around the world due to helping each other
And by my mother I swear
To right this life that I live
Just to make a better planet for the future of kids
And what it is I realized that nothing is for free
Rosa Parks made the start to make them finally see
And as for me I'm just a liberator to be,
And a strong declaration is what's makin' me.
They say we are free but never will that finally be
Spend my life to make it happen even tough I want see
But what I will see is freedom in the next pregnancy
Passin' on the torch from heaven
To the next Lega-C.

1982, the Black Panther Party established more than sixteen community service projects. Those projects, as Charles E. Jones has pointed out, became known within the organization as survival programs and included the Intercommunal News Service (*Black Panther*); Free Breakfast for Children; Petition Campaign—Referendum for Decentralized Police Departments; Liberation School/Intercommunal Youth Institute; People's Free Medical Research Clinic; Free Clothing Program; Free Busing to Prisons Program; Seniors Against Fearful Environment (SAFE); Sickle Cell Anemia Research Foundation; Free Housing Cooperative Program; Free Shoe Program; Free Pest Control Program; Free Plumbing and Maintenance Program; Free Food Program; Child Development Center; and the Free Ambulance Program.

Consequently, many youth became involved with the Black Panther Party as actual members, community workers, or supporters because of their attraction to the projects and/or ideology of nationalism and intercommunalism. Among the youth who got involved as members were Bobby Hutton, Joan "Tarika" Lewis, Regina Jennings, and Mumia Abu-Jamal.

Bobby Hutton, also known as "Li'l Bobby," joined the Black Panther Party at the age of fifteen in 1966. Hutton became the first person to join the organization after Newton and Seale. During the first few months of the Black Panther Party, Hutton helped Newton and Seale to sell copies of *The Red Book* by Mao Tse-Tung's at the University of California, Berkeley, take part in armed patrols of Oakland police, and disseminate the first issues of *The Black Panther*, the official organ of the organization. He also helped to recruit other teenagers to the organization.

Hutton participated in several colossal events of the Black Panther Party, including the Sacramento armed demonstration and the April 6, 1968, shoot-out in Oakland, which led to his death and earned his recognition as "the first to fall" among the original six members of the Black Panther Party. Hutton is buried on a hill in Oakland's Mountain View Cemetery.

Joan "Tarika" Lewis, also known as Matilaba, joined the Black Panther Party in 1967 at the age of sixteen. She has received recognition as the first female to join the Black Panther Party. After becoming involved in the Oakland office, Lewis participated in political education classes and was trained in weaponry.

During her first year of service, Lewis was appointed to a section leader position and ran drills for a Black Panther cadre. In addition, she became an assistant to Emory Douglass, the minister of culture. Before leaving the organization in January 1969 as a result of a purge, Lewis published some of her illustrations under the name Matilaba in the organization's newspaper. After her departure from the organization, Lewis proceeded to become a graphic artist and well-respected jazz violinist. She has performed in jazz combos with the legendary John Handy. During the production of Mario Van Peebles' film *Panther*, Lewis served as an on-the-set consultant and even acted in a small role.

Regina Jennings joined the Black Panther Party during the summer of 1968 when she was sixteen years old. She took a plane from Philadelphia,

Pennsylvania to Oakland to join the organization. Jennings has related that she initially joined with a serious drug problem. She has credited the organization with helping her to overcome that problem.

According to Jennings, she participated in political education classes and the community service projects. Among other things, Jennings recalled that she fed children breakfast, passed out bags of groceries to the poor, sold Black Panther newspapers, and organized dances for teenagers. Jennings served in the Black Panther Party from 1968 to 1974. Eventually, Jennings returned to school and earned a Ph.D. degree in African American studies from Temple University in 1993 and went into academia as a professor.

Mumia Abu-Jamal became an official member of the Black Panther Party during the spring of 1969 at the age of fifteen. In May 1969, Abu-Jamal became a founding member and Lieutenant of Information of the Philadelphia chapter. While in the organization from 1969 to 1971, Abu-Jamal served stints with the organization in New York and Oakland in addition to Philadelphia. Abu-Jamal has said that he spent a lot of his time in the Black Panther Party writing, reading, editing, shoveling sand for sandbags, selling Black Panther newspapers, and working security.

Following his departure from the organization, Abu-Jamal was active as a community activist, broadcast journalist, and taxi cab driver. In December 1981, Abu-Jamal was charged with killing police officer Daniel Faulkner. After being tried before Albert Sabo in Philadelphia, Abu-Jamal was convicted and sentenced to death. While on death row and appealing his case, Abu-Jamal managed to write several books and earn a M.A. degree in humanities from California State University, Dominguez Hills.

With the aim of recruiting youth like Hutton, Lewis, Jennings, and Jamal to its ranks, the Black Panther Party established a Junior Panther Program in Oakland during 1967. In this program, young children, ranging from age eight to fourteen, were taught black history and revolutionary principles so that they would develop a commitment to self-determination for the black population. Both Junior Panthers and young Party members were recruited in working-class communities. In fact, the leadership of the Black Panther Party consciously sought out the lumpen proletariat to join the ranks of the organization.

Nevertheless, young Party members were also recruited at college campuses. Although the Black Panther Party eventually faced decline and destruction due to internal and external social forces, the organization represented an effort by youth to formulate a theory and practice of fundamental social transformation.

Resources

Books
Abu-Jamal, M. (2004). *We want freedom: A life in the Black Panther Party.* Cambridge, MA: South End Press.
Brown, E. (1992). *A taste of power: A black woman's story.* New York: Pantheon Books.

Cleaver, K. (2004). Introduction. In M. Abu-Jamal. *We want freedom: A life in the Black Panther Party.* Cambridge, MA: South End Press.

Cleaver, K., & Katsiaficas, G. (Eds.). (2001). *Liberation, imagination, and the Black Panther Party: A new look at the Panthers and their legacy.* New York: Routledge.

Erikson, E. H., & Newton, H. P. (1973). *In search of common ground: Conversations with Erik H. Erikson and Huey P. Newton.* New York: Norton.

Hilliard, D., & Cole, L. (1993). *This side of glory: The autobiography of David Hilliard and the story of the Black Panther Party.* Boston: Little Brown and Company.

Jones, C. E. (Ed.). (1998). *The Black Panther Party reconsidered.* Baltimore: Black Classic Press.

Newton, H. P. (1973). *Revolutionary suicide.* New York: Harcourt Brace Jovanovich.

———. (1972). *To die for the people: The writings of Huey P. Newton.* New York: Random House.

Seale, B. (1978). *A lonely rage: The autobiography of Bobby Seale.* New York: Times Books.

———. (1970). *Seize the time: The story of the Black Panther Party and Huey P. Newton.* New York: Vintage Books.

Van Peebles, M., Taylor, U. Y., & Lewis, J. T. (1995). *Panther: A pictorial history of the Black Panthers and the story behind the film.* New York: Newmarket Press.

Article

Jennings, R. (1991, February). A Panther remembers. *Essence, 2,* 21.

A BORIKUA GUERRERO YOUTH ORGANIZING

Joseph Carroll-Miranda

How can I begin this essay without being too egotistical, while being true and just to all of my crew who have been with me for over ten years? As a tight crew, we organized on issues regarding the environment, Puerto Rico's self-determination, social justice, anti-militarism, homophobia, xeno-phobia, the decriminalization of drugs, university reform, neo-liberalism, and national-international student governments. How we chose to work and organize, within Puerto Rico, marked a new generation of organizing spawned by us: Borikua Youth. How and why we organized the way we did will be the main focus of this essay, hence the title. The following will be my voice that is always connected to a we that represents my crew. I am not speaking for the crew but rather representing the crew. This is the story of a Borikua Guerrero.

I can't begin by saying that I was always a youth organizer. What I have to seriously recognize is that this all started with a general discontent with what I was being taught in high school. Like King Tone from the Almighty Latin King Queen Nation (ALKQN) says in the documentary *Black and Gold*, "Why was I never taught the true history of Puerto Rico" or the truth of where I am from? I was pissed at the fact that I was never told of the nationalist revolutions of the 1930s, 1940s, and 1950s. I was never told that in the late 1940s most of the people wanted independence for our motherland. I was never told how the United States invaded Puerto Rico and took military control that is alive and kicking to this day. I was never told that in 1934 and 1937 there were two massacres by the U.S. military against peaceful manifestations of those who were proud of being Puerto Rican. I was always told by my history teacher that Pedro Albizu Campos was crazy. I was never told that most revolutions failed because of snitching. All of this and much of the dumbed-down curriculum of our schools forced me to organize within my first group in high school. We created the MEC Movimiento Estudiantil de Concientizacion (Student Movement of Concientization). As such we wanted to learn and expose the true history of ourselves and our colonial rule. Naturally, we gravitated to historically neglected nationalistic roots. At this time I have to give props to all those within the punk/skinhead crew that while kicking it and drinking in the streets we talked about what we never were taught in schools.

When I finished high school I went to the University of Puerto Rico. This university was famous for its revolutionary student movement, of which I wanted to be a part. Within the first weeks of class, a student organization received all of the students with a welcoming activity. This activity used spoken word, music, and speeches as to why we should be organized as students. Notions of democracy, student government, and music seduced me into FUPI (Federacion Universitaria Pro Independencia/University Federation Pro Independence). Without knowing it, I was enrolling in a student group that was responsible for kicking the ROTC off of the main campus during the Vietnam War. This organization spearheaded multiple strikes, protests, and actions that helped consolidate the student government in Puerto Rico.

Our organizing was unique. Art and music was the way we busted out knowledge. Murals, sculptures, music festivals, and spoken word were the way we did things. Everything else eventually fell in place. We organized many music festivals that helped us organize pickets, marches, manifestations, and strikes. If it were not for the music and the art, we would be considered as a bunch of bores that are too self-righteous to get down with *la gente*. Bomba, Plena, rumba, rock, and hip hop were some of the music that was always present in our activities. This was not always like this.

We learned over time that revolutions can be and must be fun if we want to add rather then subtract people in the movement. We worked hard in establishing what we knew as Temporary Autonomous Zones (TAZ). As such we owned the place for a specific time and space. Sometimes it was hours and other times it was days and even years. We never asked for permission, we just notified and did things regardless. This is how we did over twenty murals in five years all over the university, the city, and country. We had/have the attitude that we were the revolution. It was a way of life.

Through the arts and music we raised awareness on issues such as the so called 500 years of the discovery of America and Puerto Rico. One of the murals we did was one ridiculing the notion of discovery in a cartoon of some Tainos laughing their asses off at the fact that "dice que se llama Colon y viene a descubrirnos" ["He says he is Columbus and he came here to discover us."] The mural also said, "Somos Boricuas Milenarios, Pa'l Carajo el V centenario" ["We are Milenary boricuas, screw the V centenary."] This was an extremely popular mural that we ended up making t-shirts out of because a lot of people loved it.

Every year we did welcoming activities that were tighter and tighter. There were more musicians, artists, and organizations that wanted to be a part of this. Our organization grew in ways people were intimidated by our crew. As an integral part of our organizing, we kicked it in bars recruiting people while having fun. Most of our activities were planned in the streets while hanging out. This made us unpredictable, nomadic, and decentralized. Our organizing skills were so good that we had a coherent national student movement engaging in issues of a Latin American university reform.

We were part of the OCLAE: Organizacion Cantinenetal y Caribena Latino Americana de Estudiantes (Caribbean and Continental Latin American Student Organization). In fact in the mid-1990s, we changed the bylaws and *principios* of this organization with the help of the delegations from Peru, Bolivia, Argentina, and Paraguay. As a student movement we needed to incorporate issues such as eradicating homophobia, xenophobia, discrimination against anyone with mental, sensorial, or physical impairment, and the decriminalization and demilitarization of drugs. Such acts gave us a great deal of heat and beef.

About a year or two after this fact most of the so-called left in the island were upset that we were talking about these issues. Under the threat of a serious throw down, it came to such a drama that we chose to quit FUPI and created a new more open minded organization called KAL: Kolectivo Laternativa Libertaria (Libertarian Alternative Kolective). As such, KAL embraced an openly decentralized mode of organizing that used performance and art as one of the main avenues of getting the word spread out. Within the first few months we organized so heavily that we helped mobilize more than 8,000 students from the University to el Capitolio (Puerto Rico's Capitol Hill).

In order to do this we did numerous rallies, murals, and music festivals. It was the bomb and as such we had a great deal of respect from everybody. During this time we wanted to do more aggressive tactics in terms of the environment and we embraced notions of ECODEFENSE. We started engaging in civil disobedience. We paralyzed numerous construction projects that intended to cut down trees. We were extremely successful in some of the cases, in the others we just raised awareness and made the six o'clock news on numerous occasions.

In time many of the mobilizations were a collective initiative against a government policy of taking over 40 million dollars from the university budget. This initiative was paralyzed due to aggressive student organizing. The conditions within the University were so ripe that a movement against neo-liberal policies emerged. This was called El Frente Estudiantil en Contral el Neo-Liberalismo, better know as el Frente (Student Front against Neo-Liberalism). We were a serious force to be reckoned with. On two occasions the Governor of Puerto Rico Pedro Rosello and Secretary of State Norma Burgos had to be escorted out of the university for they were terrified that university students were about to lynch them for their neo-liberal attacks and policies.

On the occasion with Norma Burgos, the fact was that when the government functionary left the Riot Police entered the University, a clear violation of University Autonomy. Last time this happened was the heated strikes of the early 1980s where political and physical repression were extremely harsh to the point of gun battles. We made such a presence that even the head of police showed up on the scene where many students booed, mooned, fingered, and were kicked out of the university. The show of force proved to the country that we meant business and were a threat to the *status quo*. They had choppers with snipers, and riot police that were kicked out by the whole university community. This meant that students, faculty, staff and university police all got in a human line and pushed the riot police off of campus. This was a historical event without precedent. For the first time in the university history the university police re-vindicated themselves and protected those whom they had historically beaten with batons. Such event led to the culmination of a peak activity called Nunca Mas (never again) where we established a university policy where the policy of nonconfrontation was the way to solve all internal disputes. To this day this is modus operandi.

The Frente Estudiantil was very well organized after several university activities, rallies, festivals, and campaigns. We reached a peak when the government wanted to sell the publicly owned telephone company. The phone workers organized a strike against this neo-liberal initiative. As students we were with the workers in solidarity in the strike activities. We built a solid coalition of students and workers. We helped each other and we were living in the streets for weeks. The strike was so effective that the government needed to use the riot police to break the strike. With sheer violence and terror both workers and students fell victim to police brutality. The violence culminated after we ridiculed the riot police's chief into an extremely vulnerable position where it appeared that he was being beaten. This was not the case and the press made it a point, nonetheless they went to another strike site and beat at least three workers unconscious, with blood gushing out of their heads, leaving them comatose. One of our close friends, who was a student and a telephone company worker, had his head cracked open and took his blood and threw it at the riot police's faces. This made major headlines and made the whole labor movement and people of Puerto Rico extremely upset. The whole country was paralyzed for two days; the dock workers, electricity workers, and water services workers paralyzed the international airport with such elegance that although riot police were deployed they were not used because these workers were bigger and stronger and were ready for war. Many of these workers had two-by-fours with a tiny flag or an iron rod with little signs. They were all defiantly yelling moving their hands in an inviting way "*Vente vente*!!" ("Come on, bring it on!"). The whole country was in euphoria as we took control of the whole country. People were bringing food, money, and resources in ways that it appeared we were truly a collective society that would make any socialism weep. Due to this strike and experience we learned a great deal of tactics, strategies and the undeniable notion that under the right conditions people rise up and demand respect and dignity from oppressive situations in a spontaneous manner.

Through our Borikua organizing style we learned the importance of organized civil disobedience. As we engaged with solidarity activities with the EZLN and denouncing the Massacre in Acteal we were trained in civil disobedience and with the anonymous crucial support of affinity groups. This catapulted most of us into a very active part of the civil disobedience campaign to stop the U.S. bombing of Vieques. Many of us who worked together in the university composed the youth component of the civil disobedience in Vieques and in the United States.

In time, many of us went to the United States and continued our student careers. In New York and Washington, DC, in Spain, France, and New Mexico, we all gave our own twist of organizing wherever we were. For instance, the New York crew organized around Vieques that led to activities such as shutting down the entrance of the United Nations with celebrities such as Ruben Blades and Rosie Perez, interrupted a New York Yankees game, and decorated the Statue of Liberty's forehead with banners and flags, raising the issue of U.S. militarism and the bombing of Vieques, Puerto Rico. After more than 1,000 civil disobedient arrests, festivals, rallies, organizing, and support groups, and over four years of defiant struggle, the U.S. Navy stopped the bombing of Vieques in May 2003. This is a major historical victory for those with a serious demilitarization agenda.

As for myself, I ended up in the land of enchantment, better known as New Mexico. I have always kept in touch with my crew and we have kept working on numerous projects together. While in New Mexico I have worked with the Movimiento Estudiantil de Concientizacion (MECHA), Cop Watch, Migra Watch, Vieques solidarity organizing/activities and planning in establishing a chapter of Indymedia. My experiences with the Borikua organizing has catapulted me into positions where we try to establish a culture of resistance here in the borderland.

To my surprise when I came here for the first time in 1998, there was not a section of political organizers in campus. Previously and currently in Puerto Rico you can go to a specific place and hook up with like-minded people. This is kind of similar to Peoples Park in UC Berkeley. So I met an old school skatepunk and we started with a simple literature table that transmuted itself into a free speech movement. The administration at that time deemed a literature table threatening on campus. We were told that we could not do this, and hence we started our struggle. The struggle we engaged in had a serious Borikua taste to it. We engaged in speak outs, rallies, music festivals, drum circles, and cardboard murals among other situationalist tactics. This was never done in New Mexico State University's history. After almost two years of struggle, the whole university is now a free speech zone.

Looking at the anti-globalization movement in Seattle, DC, Prague, and Cancun, we embrace each other's history of activism Borikua style, for we see them being done all over the world. When we first started doing this in the early 1990s we though we were all alone. Now in 2004 most grassroots organizations have basic things such as decentralized power and collective consensus decision making—nomadic, unpredictable, and extremely creative—utilizing music and art as a central way of organizing and having an attitude that we are not here to ask but to do. Most of these groups have very democratic internal dynamics where the minority is not squashed. We build upon differences and multiple positionalities so as to do different things at different times and spaces without imposing one specific action or tactic to the whole group. This flexibility and shape-shifting ability makes it extremely difficult to disrupt these groups through repression and COINTELPRO styles of infiltration. The youth is organizing in such different ways that traditional actions such as pickets and marches are challenged. Hacktivism, Indymedia Activism, and CopWatch are doing things in different ways.

Underground hip hop and punk and hard core scenes are engaging in their own revolutionary movements that are giving us seductive forms of activism that includes youth rather than repels it. This is what I think the Borikua style organizing and other anti-globalization styles of organizing have to offer youth and society in general. We can do things in our own way, with our own flavor and style. This is what makes revolutionary struggle worthwhile. Youth oriented activism should be about celebrating and defending life. Therefore music, poetry, arts, and youthful expression have to be at the core. What we do bring into the struggle is something that we all must decide ourselves, as long as we are working for a world where many worlds can fit, then we are definitely working for better days and walking in the right direction. This is what revolutionary movements should be all about. Umbuntu Agalamosa Ashe To! (We are all connected in a revolution built upon wisdom and spirituality so let it be so!)

Resources
Books
BBB. (2004). *Pie any means necessary.* Oakland, CA: AK Press.
Critical Art Ensemble. (1995). *On electronic civil disobedience and other unpopular ideas.* Brooklyn, NY: Autonomedia.
Hakim, B. (1994). *Temporary autonomaus zone ontological anarchy, poetic terrorism.* Brooklyn, NY: Autonomedia.
Jornad, T. (2002). *Activism!: Direct action, hacktivism and the future of society.* London: Reaktion Books.
Lash, K. (1999). *Culture Jam: How to reverse America's suicidal consumer binge.* New York: Harper Collins Books.
McDonald, D. (1995). *The root is man.* Brooklyn, NY: Autonomeida.
Sued, G. (2001). *Vieques: Cronicas desde la desobediencia.* San Juan, PR: La Grieta.
Torres, A., & Velazquez, J. E. (1998). *The Puerto Rican movement: Voices from the diaspora.* Philadelphia: Temple University Press.
Welton, N., & Wolf, L. (2001). *Global uprising: Confronting the tyrannies of the 21st century. Stories from a new generation of activists.* Canada: New Society Publishers.
Video
Big Noise Films. (1999). *Black and gold.*
Big Noise Films. (2001). *This is what democracy looks like.*

SLAM! GENRE FOR SOCIAL ACTIVISM

Stacey Miller

SLAM is a hybrid of spoken word and performed poetry, sometimes with music, that gives individuals an opportunity to voice their opinions and feelings on any topic; conveys urgency, action, and excitement; can be a competitive art of performance poetry; is rooted in resistance and rebellion, often capricious; and can offer an emotional outlet to our youth and provide an opportunity to explore personal convictions and truths, and at the same time, recognize human commonalties. It breaks out of dominant structures of binary poetry and calls for the writer to not only craft for the self but for others. It can expand the genre of poetry and bring the teaching of poetry into a whole new frame for social action, and is a way for students to make meaning of the world around them as they unpack complex issues and "meaning make."

This entry is written to expand the landscape of SLAM as a genre for social action. It is written to those who strive to validate any student's experience, who seek to inspire in students an extension of former ways of thinking and creating, who seek to extend former ways of examining the self, and who strive to create a soulful and humanistic connection to poetry and its elements.

SLAMMIN' BACK INTO HISTORY

The roots of SLAM poetry are historically situated in traditional poetry, the poetry of the Beats, and in hip hop music. SLAM taps into the rhyme scheme and versification of traditional poetry but also creates its own hybrid of convention and form that is based in modern poetry. SLAM reaches back into the poetry of the Beats and revives an unconventional use of rhyme scheme, syntax, and use of grammar.

The maturation of SLAM poetry most definitively evolves out of its relationship to contemporary hip hop music. Just as some musicians have crossed over into the acting world, poetry has passed through the music world and morphed into a new genre of poetry called SLAM. Essentially hip hop, which arrived at the tail end of disco in the late 1970s, broke the musical and rhythmic beats in disco music and birthed the notion of hip hop as a subgenre of music. Music rapper, TL Rock sang a song titled "It's Yours," and when Def Jam broke down the beats of the song, he almost single-handedly helped disco morph into hip hop and initiated the birth of the movement. In the late 1980s, hip hop stopped acting as party music and became a way to catalyze a new form of sharing sociopolitical issues in the music world. Hip hop became a dominant force in the music world, defined by social issues and political sensibilities and laid the foundation for what was to later become SLAM poetry (some critics argue that SLAM predates hip hop). SLAM's reification arrived when poet Marc Smith started a poetry reading which placed an emphasis on performance and laid the groundwork for the brand of poetry that would eventually be exhibited in SLAM. Smith approached Dave Jemilo, the owner of the Green Mill (a Chicago jazz club and former haunt of Al Capone), with a plan to host a weekly poetry competition on Sunday nights. Jemilo welcomed him, and the Uptown Poetry SLAM was born. Smith drew on baseball and bridge terminology for the name, and instituted the basic features of the competition, including judges chosen from the audience and cash prizes for the winner. Poets "tried out" their SLAMS and refined their practice at these events. SLAM poets were essentially birthed by and validated by the judges at the competitions. As an outgrowth of these SLAM competitions, poets studied each others' techniques and use of language and matured in the crafting of SLAM.

SLAM poetry evolved out of hip hop and has crossed into the poetic genre, taking on a whole new direction and has gained even more momentum over the past

Teens unite in political action

ten years. SLAM is therefore, a crossover genre from the music world into the world of poetry. SLAM, as a discourse for identity, is understood as spoken word, performed poetry, a hybrid sometimes with music and gives individuals an opportunity to voice their opinions and feelings. SLAM is rooted in resistance and rebellion; it can offer an outlet to our youth, an opportunity to explore personal convictions and truths, and at the same time, recognize human commonalities. SLAM has no boundaries of topics or themes; it provides an opportunity for individuals to voice their opinions and angst on any topic such as: homophobia, politics, spirituality, memories, race, class, gender, rape, abuse, and love. SLAM conveys urgency, action, and excitement and can be a competitive art of performance poetry. It puts a dual emphasis on writing and performance and encourages poets to focus on what they're saying and how they're saying it. SLAMS are often performed at a poetry slam, an event in which poets perform their work and are judged by members of the audience. The performance aspect of SLAM is tantalizing. Poets might use their bodies and hands to convey their feelings and tones, they may move around on the stage, or their clothing may reflect their attitude toward the topics in their SLAMS.

SLAMMIN' INTO THEORY: SLAM AS IDENTITY, DISCOURSE, AND ARTIFACT

I am located in the margin. I make a definite distinction between the marginality which is imposed by oppressive structures and that marginality one chooses as a site of resistance-as location of radical openness and possibility.

bell hooks, 1990

Prejudice perpetuates divisive hierarchies in our country and in our schools. In particular, youth who are targeted or perceived as "different" are disenfranchised from the educational system and can be victimized by these hierarchies. Students can be marginalized within the schooling experience when the discourses they bring from home are mismatched against those of the schools. We cannot talk about discourses without speaking about identity because students' identities are formed by these school systems and the prejudices within. Gee defines discourses as "a socially accepted association among ways of using language, of thinking, and of acting that can be used to identify oneself as a member of a socially meaningful group or 'social network'" and which grant us access to a particular group which has a particular identity. However, when schools ignore home discourse as a viable source of scaffolding and bridge into institutional schooling, it reinforces this marginalization and the mismatch between home and school discourse becomes painfully teleological. Gee suggests that our core identities are formed by and within those discourses and each individual is on a trajectory through "discourse space," a space that opens up the possibility for acceptance into a social or affinity group.

Identities, according to Michel Foucault, are constructed by the effects of power, and that the constitution of self is vulnerable as a result of power. The education system, which plays a role in constructing its students' identities, is founded on principles and discourses based in hegemony. These epistemologies shape why we believe what we believe and who we believe and why. Hegemony, therefore, unapologetically distances students both covertly and overtly from graduating with a healthy perspective of their own power in the world by ignoring or invalidating their experience and/or home discourse.

Though school districts attempt to address prejudice, most educational systems fall prey to institutionalized prejudice. Institutionalized prejudice is the reproduction of white privilege as it is reinforced by government, universities, school systems, and the corporations that have absolute fiscal and social policy control over what goes on in schools. On this, hooks concurs that for the most part, institutions have perpetuated the notion of prejudice through the reproduction of white privilege. Sadly enough, some students' emotional and psychological well-being suffers because of a lack of validation for their actual or perceived differences.

Academic research often constructs youth as rebellious with raging hormones and lacks in its focus on how youth are constructed and construct themselves in resistance to dominant culture. Research also lacks in examining how youth "reinvent literacies for unique contexts and how they use literacy as a tool to navigate complex technologies and social worlds." To the contrary, Freire and Macedo suggest that the students' rebelliousness be used as a platform to look at how you invent, sustain, and morph new literacies and how it empowers them within dominant culture. Because disenfranchised students already feel marginalized, this resistance often takes place from the margins.

Existing in and surviving from the margin forces individuals to be creative in their ways of surviving. Since youth culture is highly creative and often exists on the margins, it has appropriated concepts from dominant culture and then created a hybrid to ensure its survival. Bakhtin suggests that language creativity comes from the hybrid between genres. Youth culture involves itself in a vast array of constantly shifting and invention of identity artifacts and art forms. An identity artifact is a functional instrument that shapes the identity of a group or individual and which also reflects the expression of a group or individual. Appropriated by youth culture, SLAM poetry is an outgrowth of resistance to dominant culture, and is an art form that has taken its place in the margins of the schooling process. SLAM is best understood as hybrid genre of poetry that is rooted in resistance and rebellion and is an expression of a combination of sociopolitical feelings. It is likely that youth culture will continue to appropriate concepts from dominant culture and form hybrid artifacts as dominant culture attempts to codify and reify SLAM poetry and other hybrids. Marginal culture must continually reinvent itself if it hopes to survive from the margins. SLAM is likely to appropriate from new and old artifacts and continually live and survive as a hybrid of creativity and resistance.

CRAFTING SLAM AS A NEW POETIC GENRE

SLAM, as a viable subgenre of poetry, offers our youth a renewed sense of power by allowing them to take control of their own language and discourse, which is an iconoclastic act in the eyes of some. In a country where students are seduced away from self-knowledge and self-awareness, SLAM poetry acts as a contraceptive against the struggles often present in our day-to-day lives. SLAM poetry as an identity, discourse and artifact can validate lives as it offers students a new identity, a way to recycle language, reframe the struggle of the marginalized into social activism, validate primary discourse and help students make meaning of their own lives. SLAM, taught as a discourse in academia, can affirm or contest identities that schools attempt to construct. The sense of empowerment that SLAM poetry can offer can help students make meaning and unpack the world around them as they voice their opinions on complex issues. The making of meaning may instill a way of how to "meaning make" or a way to help them make sense of the world around them. The liberation that comes from SLAM may open new possibilities for challenging dominant culture.

Since genres are frames for social action, SLAM can be situated as both a genre and as an agent of social action and transformation. SLAM, framed within a genre for social action, is an agent of transformation, and a tool that is used by a student to act upon the world in order to transform it. SLAM, as an artifact of resistance culture personifies a necessary survival strategy within compulsory schooling and as an identity and discourse that reflects a way in which students may express themselves in opposition to dominant culture. To fully define what SLAM is sends it toward codification and possibly reification, thus losing its potency. It is more essential to make meaning of it and attempt to understand its power from the margin, rather than attempt to define what it actually is.

What demarks SLAM as its own genre is detailed below.

THE ELEMENTS OF SLAM

The elements of SLAM are an extension of traditional forms of poetry, accepted upon versification and grammatical rules. SLAM can adopt a combination of poetic forms but it may also invent a new hybrid or form. The crafting of SLAM, though seeming to be carefree and simplistic, is on the contrary, extremely difficult to craft; a well-crafted SLAM is highly articulate, highly provocative, sophisticated in detail, sophisticated in performance knowledge (i.e., how to create a rise in the audience), sophisticated in convention (meter, rhyme, stanza), sophisticated in syntactical strategies (juxtaposition) and sophisticated in use of figurative language (allusion, alliteration, assonance consonance, paradox). Further, the crafter often conveys the entrapment of individuals by norms and promotes a call to transgress and understand the hegemonic patriarchy that keeps individuals from meeting her or his potential. The purpose is twofold: to generally create a reaction in the audience, and to convey aroused feelings in the soul—offering some form of spiritual purging and enlightenment for the self and for the audience. SLAM can ultimately expand the genre of poetry and bring the teaching of poetry into a whole new frame for social action.

Type of Poem

SLAM is a dramatic or didactic poem whose form is open, is made up of elements of a ballad, and is a dramatic monologue (the flow is unconventional, commas are displaced, capitals don't appear where they should, and the structure is rhythmical).

Form of Poem

Commonly, a SLAM's form is open (unconventional) and may use or dismiss rules of grammar.

Versification

SLAMS are highly subjective and its stanzas are based on where the rhyme breaks, where an idea or word morphs into a new subject or thought, where a new subject or voice is heard, or simply where the crafter feels it necessary to pause in thought. SLAM meter is based on how the crafter rhymes words/syllables and where the beat needs to be broken or shifted. Most fundamental and alluring about SLAM is its uniqueness in rhyme. Most SLAMS do rhyme, or words tend to morph into new words, or ideas morph into new concepts. A key in crafting SLAM is to select generative words—words that generate discussions on sociopolitical issues, that convey the most meaning with maximum impact and affect. Its rhyme scheme is non-traditional, such that it does not have conventional rhyme and meter but contains vertical or horizontal rhymes that may be internal, and whereby the beats that break or shift may morph into new words and ideas. Words may be repeated, deleted, or morphed for effect; themes are often revisited from stanza to stanza and figurative language and syntactical strategies are used to affect the pace.

Performance

SLAM is written to be performed. The crafter understands how to use pace and bring the SLAM to climax, then use denouement and anagnorisis, and create a resolution or resting point to have maximum effect on the audience and leave them wanting more.

SLAMMIN' INTO THA' FUTURE

SLAM can save lives and liberate silent voices of the marginalized. The power inherent in SLAM is that it gives students a voice and if academia wants to stifle that voice, it may co-opt SLAM for other purposes. So how do we make meaning of this phenomenon without co-opting it and how do we preserve it as an authentic discourse from the margins? A danger that SLAM poetry may face is its consumption by the poetic genre to be codified and reified into a discourse that loses its power and authenticity as it bumps up against other discourses in academia. How then can SLAM maintain its power and language and be included in the poetic genre? Can SLAM remain authentic in the margin of poetry? Is there a place for marginal discourse that is still viable at academic and institutional levels? To teach SLAM in school as a discourse, is to instill a sense of identity, to arm pupils with an artifact, a canon to contest prejudices that others try to pass on, and also trajects them toward a discourse that celebrates life and diversity. SLAM, if taught as a genre, although grounded in resistance and rebellion, can act as a way of helping students understand a genre study, while also empowering them to create powerful and meaningful poems and artifacts. SLAM, as a genre, builds upon traditional forms of poetic genres but also encourages a call to social action and can teach students how to weave in and out of dominant discourse. Our youth, with an affirmed authentic self can seek to transform the world through a subjective self that does not ascribe to the construction that the school system seeks to impose upon them. Consequently, the world/

environment becomes vulnerable to a new subjectivity as it transacts with authentic selves, free of institutional constructions.

Resources
Books
Alan, E. Z. (2003). *Stolen snapshots: I am not a poet*. New York: Alliterative Authors.
Apple, M. (2002). *Official knowledge*. New York: Routledge.
Bakhtin, M. (1986). *Speech genres and other essays*. Austin: University of Texas Press.
Eleveld, M. (Ed.). (2003). *The spoken word revolution: Slam, hip hop and the poetry of a new generation*. Naperville, IL: Sourcebooks.
Freire, P., & Macedo, D. (1987). *Literacy: Reading the word and the world*. Westport, CT: Bergin & Garvey.
Foucault, M. (1988). *The final Foucault*. In J. Bernauer & D. Rasmussen (Eds.), Cambridge, MA: MIT Press.
———. (1980). *Power-knowledge: Selected interviews and other writings, 1972–1977*. C. Gordon (Ed. & Trans.). New York: Pantheon Books.
hooks, b. (1994). *Teaching to transgress*. New York: Routledge.
———. (1990). *Yearnings: Race, gender and cultural politics*. Boston: South End Press.
Riesman, D. (1954). *Individualism reconsidered*. New York: Free Press.
Williams, S. (2001). "The life of Saul Williams." Taos Poetry Circus, World Poetry Bout, Taos.

Articles
Gee, J. (2001). Identity as an analytic lens for research in education. *Review of Research in Education*, 25, 91–125.
———. (1989). Literacy, discourse, and linguistics: Introduction. *Journal of Education*, 171, 5–25.
———. (1992). Socio-cultural approaches to literacy. *Annual Review of Applied Linguistics*, 12, 31–48.
Leander, K. (2002). Locating Latanya: The situated production of identity artifacts in classroom interaction. *Research in the Teaching of English*, 37, 198–250.
Moje, E. (2002). Reframing adolescent literacy research for new times: Studying youth as a resource. *Reading Research and Instruction*, 41, 211–227.

Web Sites
Background on Slam Poetry. Slam-nation: Background of Slam poetry. Data Wranglers. Retrieved September 15, 2005 from http:\\www.slamnation.com/info/backgrnd.htm
Heintz, K. (1994). Incomplete history of slam. Slam Poetry in Chicago. Retrieved September 15, 2005 from http:\\www.epoets.net/library/slam/converge.html

PSI. (2001). Poetry Slam Inc. Retrieved September 15, 2005 from www. poetryslam.com/faq.htm

WPBA. (2000). WPBA. World Poetry Bout Association-Poetry Circus. Retrieved September 15, 2005 from http:\\www.poetrycircus.org

FEMINISTS' DAUGHTERS

Ainhoa Flecha

Many people often complain about the fact that youth are not interested in social movements. They say, for instance, that young women are not interested in feminism. Nevertheless, what I argue is that young women feel enthusiastic about feminism, but we often reject our mother's feminism. We don't feel identified with a rigid version of feminism that was previously built and now just gives us the opportunity to either accept it as such or reject it. In order to get young women engaged by feminism we need to present it to them as something dynamic to which they can contribute by raising new issues. Young women do feel that feminist concerns, such as birth control, education, equal salaries, and so on, are important. Several women's groups are developing a new feminism, based on equality of differences. A feminism that seeks the participation of all women, especially of those women who have remained invisible, those who have been traditionally excluded from the feminist theory. Through an egalitarian dialogue among all women, we can develop a new movement which can represent us better and with which young women would feel identified.

Along the history of the feminist movement, there have been different trends, which have usually been called waves. The first wave of feminism, also called feminism of equality, started in the nineteenth century and extended its influence through the seventies. During the first decades of the feminist movement, the aims were the emancipation of women and obtaining equal rights for women. They demanded that women had the right tovote, could do the same jobs as men did, could have the same educational and other opportunities. Other relevant demands had to do with birth control or the right to divorce. In short, they were fighting for legal, economic, and reproductive equality. They wanted to have the same opportunities that men had and to have the right to decide by themselves. As a result of this movement, important changes were accomplished. Our society had no other option than beginning to consider some of the feminist demands. Many countries in the world started to recognize legal equality for women,

What I want to do...What I do

George Sanchez

I want to accomplish great things
I want to be successful in many fields
But what I want is different from what I do
And what I do isn't what I should.

I have set a lot of goals
I have tried to change
I have tried it all
But most of it never works.

I have tried poetry, and even sports
I wanted to do a lot.
And have failed many times
But I am still going on.

What I want to do is great
What I do is a disaster
What I want to do... What I do
What I don't do is give up.

and the right to vote was given to them. In the personal sphere, in many places divorce was legalized and the means for birth control extended. Moreover, women entered the field of education, up to a point that today, on average, they to do better than men at all educational levels. These changes also allowed women to improve their situation in the labor market.

The first wave feminism, however, was soon criticized because it confused equality with homogenization. On the one hand, wanting to be as men made them reject femininity and all its values. All behaviors traditionally attributed to women were considered submission. Instead of rethinking the world from a feminine point of view, they assumed traditionally masculine roles and behaviors. In this sense, for instance competitiveness was exalted while motherhood was rejected. On the other hand, they did not consider the differences that existed among women. They omitted that oppression is not the same for a higher-class white woman than for a black poor woman, and that the opportunities that feminism was accomplishing did not benefit both of them in the same way. A few white, higher-class and highly educated women set themselves up as representatives of all women, deciding for themselves what all women wanted. As a consequence of this, feminism progressively moved away from the majority of women. Most women refused feminism because it did not represent their needs and did not defend their interests.

These critics came especially from women from different ethnic identities, such as bell hooks and Gloria Anzaldúa, who did not identify with that version of feminism. As a result of the voices of many women who claimed that they were not represented by mainstream feminism, a second wave started to emerge in the seventies. Second wave feminism emphasized the idea of difference. It emerged as a reaction against the homogenization of the first wave, and it rejected masculine values emphasizing women's values. They believed women were different to men and thus the aim did not have to be adopting masculine behaviors. They also claimed the existence of differences among women. They noted differences such as ethnic background, cultural experience, sexual identity, and so on. They highlighted the idea that not all women suffered the same kind of oppression and that the achievements that the feminist movement was obtaining—higher education, better salaries, reproductive rights, and so on—were benefiting upper-class white women, but not all women.

However, the problem came when the emphasis on difference diluted the aim of equality. This lead to a fragmentation of the movement originated by the idea that due to difference we cannot understand each other, neither can we work together—that is, we cannot reach agreements of what we want as women. As a consequence of this fragmentation, the feminist movement lost influence and plunged into a crisis that would last until our days. Postmodern thought also influenced this crisis, since they radicalized difference from the feminist theory—as we can see in the works of scholars like Kristeva or Irigaray—and took distance from the social movement.

Today, a new feminism based on equality of differences is emerging. Dialogic feminism strives for equality. It starts from the idea that all women, without having to renounce their different identities, can take part in an egalitarian dialogue through which they establish what they want as women and agree upon joint actions to make that happen. There are groups of Romaní women, Arab women, black women, and working-class women, with no academic skills that are clamoring for a more inclusive feminism in which they can take part. They do not want a small group of privileged women to tell them how they have to live their lives in order to become liberated women. They want their own voices to be heard and included in the feminist theory. We use the concept "other women" to refer to the non-academic women who have been traditionally excluded from the feminist movement. Feminist theory was led by women who had attended college and occupied privileged positions in society. They were listened to in academia, but they never listened to other women with no academic background who worked in other contexts (i.e., in factories, supermarkets, domestic cleaning, etc.). In the feminist discourse we would be able to listen to a woman graduate, probably a professor at some university, but never to an illiterate mother of five children. Both first wave and second wave leaders left an image of feminism as a privileged women, man-hating movement. This is what young women have received and that's the kind of feminism they don't identify with.

Let's look at some examples. Drom Kotar Mestipen is a Romaní Association of Women with the aim to fight against the multiple discriminations that affect Romaní women. They promote an open dialogue among women of different ages, academic levels, and ethnic backgrounds. As a result of this dialogue they obtain very rich reflections that help to identify the main barriers faced by Romaní women and to develop strategies that can contribute to overcome them. One of the most important issues on which they focus is education. They believe education is essential to gain opportunities in our society and that's why one of their main goals is to improve the educational level of gypsy women.

The Federation of Cultural and Educational Associations of Adult People (FACEPA) is another good example that we can find in Spain. This federation promotes a Women's Group, made up by different non-academic women who meet once a month to discuss issues that affect them, as women. Through these dialogues they get to understand each other and develop strategies to accomplish a main goal: the transformation of gender relations in a way that benefits all women. In a conference on Women and Social Transformation, Judith Butler dialogued with these women, with Romaní and low literate women, and stated that they had given back to us the meaning of the feminist struggle, why it is so urgent and necessary. The feminism of the twenty-first century is a dialogic feminism that includes the voices of all women who are still in the margins, invisible.

Multiple associations of "other women" are contributing to this dialogic feminism. That is a feminism through which all women can share experiences and agree common goals but in which they are not forced to give up part of their culture. Traditional feminism makes them choose between feminism and their identity. And they do not want to do that. Feminism consists in achieving further freedom for women, giving women the opportunity to choose how they want to live their lives. We can take the French "Veil Act" as an example. We, Westerners, decide that the *hijab* (veil) is an expression of oppression against Muslim women. And therefore we decide that it is better for them not to wear it and we ban it. But have we listened to them? Do we know better than them what is best for them? When FACEPA Women's Group discussed the issue of the *hijab*, there were Muslim women among the participants. They stated that they were wearing the *hijab* because they wanted to and that nobody was forcing them to do so. They demanded their right to wear the *hijab*, and they did not want to be seen as submissive women for the simple reason of wearing it. The group discussed the issue and agreed that what is really important is to let everybody choose, and that any woman should have the right to choose whether she wants to wear the *hijab* or not. Feminism needs to seek freedom, and not allowing a woman to wear the veil is the same as forcing her to wear it.

These feminist movements have another issue in common: they all have young participants. Although traditional feminism is complaining about the fact that young women are not interested in feminism, we can see young women encouraged in these women's groups. When interviewing these young women they state that they reject the traditional version of feminism, which in the name of difference forgot about equality. They share the goals of feminism and they join dialogic feminism. They demand a feminism that gets to include all voices, including their own. When young women reject feminism it is because we receive the image of feminism as something static, already built up by our mothers and that we have to rather accept it or not. Instead, dialogic feminism provides opportunities to build up a new movement oriented to the struggle for social change, a feminism in which working class and academic women fight together to the transformation of gender relations.

If we want that young women get involved into feminism, we need to make it an encouraging movement. Dialogic feminism gives us the framework through which we can develop a democratic and enthusiastic movement capable to encourage young women.

Resources

Beck-Gernsheim, E., Butler, J., & Puigvert, L. (2003). *Women and social transformation*. New York: Peter Lang.

De Botton, L., Puigvert, L., & Sanchez, M. (2005). *The inclusion of the other women. Breaking the silence through dialogic learning*. Dordrecht: Springer.

THIRD WAVE FEMINISM

Rhonda Hammer

"Third wave feminism" is a term that has been used by a number of women, as well as popular media, to describe contemporary versions of feminism that evolved in the early 1980s and continue to the present. Some have associated this term with young feminists who were influenced by the legacies of feminism's second wave, which began in the mid-1960s. Yet the term is highly contested and has been employed to describe a number of diverse feminist and anti-feminist theories and practices. Like the term "feminism" in general, there is no definitive description or agreed-upon consensus of what constitutes a feminist third wave. In fact, many feminists argue that because feminism is always changing and in progress, and because there is no clearly identifiable boundary between the second and third waves, identifying a third wave of feminism is fallacious. Others assert that historical, social, political, economic, technological, and generational differences between the feminist second wave and the so-called third wave are distinct and demand an exclusive label. Within this loose category of feminism's third wave are a multiplicity of movements, philosophies, and practices. However, to even talk about a feminist third wave necessitates an understanding of what characterizes those periods or movements that have been identified as first and second wave feminism. And it is also essential to recognize that young women, girls, or radical youth cultural dissidents have always been central to feminism's ongoing local and global developments before, within, and between these hypothetical waves.

The "wave" analogy is an interesting one, and has provoked many debates. At one level, there are feminists who argue that it is an appropriate metaphor, which manages to capture the similarities, differences, continuities, discontinuities, and evolutions of feminism as a transformational series of movements, epistemologies, and activisms. For some, it becomes a useful way to classify historical periods of feminist struggles; others, however, contend that to reduce the multiple dimensions of feminism to two (or three) waves tends to oversimplify the complexities of feminism's ever-changing nature and progress, as well as to distract from the realities that feminism is hardly restricted to Euro-American relations and contexts.

Indeed, one of the problems associated with the conceptions of feminism as a series of two or three waves is that the first two waves are often associated with the domination of ideas and experiences of privileged white, middle-class, Eurocentric feminists—a charge that has also been lodged against some of those who identify themselves as third wave. Although white, privileged, liberal-reformist women played a large role in the advancement of Western feminism, there was also a diversity of marginalized women—a wide variety of cultural and political persuasions and beliefs—who were leaders and activists in both of the so-called waves (as well as in what many are calling the "third wave"). However, the first and second waves were distinctive, and a brief exploration of these historical periods and their differences provides a necessary overview of the complex dimensions involved in the development of contemporary Western feminism.

The feminist "first wave" is generally identified with the mobilization of strong feminist movements in the mid-nineteenth and early twentieth centuries in Europe and North America that were concerned with a number of egalitarian and radical issues which included equal rights for women, educational and legal reform, abolition of slavery, and "suffrage" (the right to vote). Although the first wave is often characterized as the struggle for women's suffrage, a plethora of feminist, humanitarian, and radical politics were advanced during this period—especially those that were identified as falling under the rubric of "the tyranny of men." It is within this context that many young women, in particular, began to question the institution of marriage, in which women and children were literally the property of men.

Many contemporary feminists forget that it was as early as 1792 that Mary Wollstonecraft (1759–1797), in her influential enlightenment treatise *The Vindication of the Rights of Women,* argued that women, like men, were rational beings. She contended that it was, in large part, due to lack of, or misguided, education of girls that women appeared to be irrational and subordinate.

Anticipating central concerns of first, second, and so-called third wave feminism, Wollstonecraft also argued that social constructions of feminine beauty and fashion were serious impediments to women's sense of autonomy, freedom, and equal rights. Some feminists contend that dimensions of the feminist first wave were highly influenced by Wollstonecraft's writings and that criticism of male-oriented portrayals of beauty and fashion were part of this movement's struggles. Emphasis on thinness, mediated by debilitating fashions that celebrated tight waists, long skirts, and high heels impeded women's ability to perform everyday tasks and proved detrimental to women's health. It was not uncommon for upper- and middle-class women to pass out from the binding constraints of this type of clothing, reinforcing the stereotype of privileged women's inherent weakness and inferiority. In 1851, U.S. feminists introduced a far more liberating style of dress, known as the "bloomer" or "bloomer dress" (named for editor Amelia Bloomer, who had advocated its adoption in her journal *Lily*). However, few women actually adopted the fashion, described as loose trousers under mid-calf dresses, due to the public scorn, ridicule, and harassment directed at those who wore it.

Radical cultural reforms in the arenas of women's art, dance, literature, journalism, and music were also a large part of the feminist first wave. Although much of the European first wave feminism finds its rudiments in the libertarian and enlightenment principles and practices of the French Revolution, the anti-slavery movement, especially in the United States, is identified as one of the most important influences on the development of the feminist first wave. It was the anti-slavery movement, many contend, that inspired numerous white women and women of color to politically organize against their own oppression.

In fact, the first U.S. women's rights convention, in Seneca Falls, New York, in 1848—which demanded an end to all discrimination based on sex—was initiated in response to the prohibition of women's participation in the 1840 World's Anti-Slavery convention in London (an organization that supported equal rights for black men, but not for women). Many of the most powerful and influential first wave feminists were black women, some of whom were ex-slaves like Sojourner Truth (1797–1883) and Harriet Tubman (1843–1913), who were also involved in abolitionist movements and the Underground Railroad (a covert escape route to the North and Canada from the Southern slave states).

It is hardly surprising then that numbers of first wave feminists not only demanded the right to vote, but also fought for massive reforms in the arenas of property rights, labor, education, divorce laws, child custody, prison conditions, and sexual liberation, to name a few. Numerous first-wavers also addressed the mostly legal, inhumane practices of rape and the abuse of women and children, especially by husbands and fathers.

The end of the first wave is often associated with the periods in the early twentieth century during and after World War I (1914–1918), when most women, in the Western world, were granted the right to vote. Moreover, many experts argue that the rise in income for the growing middle classes in the 1920s, which primarily allowed for white middle-class women to enjoy new lifestyles, also contributed to the dissipation of the feminist first wave. However, it cannot be forgotten that the courageous feminists of the first wave had succeeded in initiating many reforms. Yet it was believed, by far too many, that once women were afforded these rights of citizenship they would no longer be treated as a subspecies of human beings.

Hence, although feminist, human rights, and social justice struggles continued throughout the early 1920s to the mid-1960s, it is not until the 1960s that what is called the "second wave" of feminism rolls in. One of the most contested debates concerning the feminist second wave involves the false characterization of the second wave as a predominantly white, middle-class, liberal movement. Although numerous second wavers followed in the footsteps of some of their first wave "grandmothers" and continued to press for reformist/liberal agendas, many more advocated far more radical ideas, actions, and programs. Indeed, the multifarious dimensions of feminism are reflected in the highly diverse philosophies, practices and politics embraced by what has been identified as the feminist second wave.

A large majority of second wave feminists were young women and girls who were part of the massive baby boom generation (1946–1964) born during the period of economic prosperity that followed World War II. Many were the first in their families to have university educations and were highly influenced by or involved in civil rights struggles and radical youth cultural movements. Others were disenchanted with social conventions following the war that had forced women back into traditional roles, especially those that idealized women as full-time wives and mothers. At the same time, there were limited opportunities for employment outside of the home, except for those in the usual feminized low-waged arenas.

Consequently, many women's dissatisfaction with their societal and economic positions, as well as with a host of sexually discriminatory attitudes and policies provoked what many refer to as a new feminist wave of awareness and protest. Moreover, unlike the first wave, the politics of the family, reproduction, and sexual liberation of women became central concerns of second wave feminism. The second wave is loosely described as beginning in the 1960s and cresting in the 1970s although there is much debate as to whether it ended or continues to go on. Moreover, the diversity of the second wave makes it particularly difficult to describe as any kind of unified movement.

Contrary to popular myth, many argue that the second wave of feminism was most influenced by women who advocated far more revolutionary politics than those of liberal, mainstream feminists, and who became involved in what were called "women's liberation" groups that were often defined as radical or socialist. To put it very simply, radical feminists identified patriarchy as the major determinant of women's oppression, whereas socialist feminists perceived capitalism and male domination as the central ingredient of women's subordination. Whereas most liberal feminism advocated progressive reforms of the system, these feminists supported forms of systemic change.

Radical and socialist politics also infused women's liberation groups that were especially concerned with celebrating difference. This included lesbian and women of color feminists, to name a few. Much of this movement was lead by young women in their twenties who had been veterans of sixties activism and become disillusioned with the sexism that pervaded so many of the counterculture youth politics andr New Left liberation forums and organizations. Indeed, in the United States, many of these political movements, including feminism, were influenced by the black, Chicano, and American Indian liberation movements, and it is hardly surprising that black women and women of color were leading figures in the evolution and development of second wave feminist theory and practice. In fact, some of these women employed the term "third wave feminism," in the early 1980s, to describe their unique form of anti-racist feminism that was written from the perspective of the marginalized.

Hence, initially the term "third wave feminism" characterized a feminism mediated by the terrains of race and multicultural alliances, rather than age. Often it "talked back to" and challenged dominant and exclusionary forms of white feminism, while incorporating dimensions of "consciousness raising" in powerful narrative and autobiographical style. This "coming to voice," many explained, was a unique mode of "everyday theorizing" that made apparent the importance of a central feminist idea: that "the personal is political." It is this kind of resistant feminism, which exploded in the 1980s, that examined not only the intersections between race, class, culture, and sexuality but also the celebration—and coalition politics—of difference. Within this context, the relevance of what has been called "the politics of hybridity" was of central concern.

Indeed, the "new hybridity" is a term used to express the "multiple identities" of many contemporary girls and women, especially in the United States. This concept has been central to describing a new generation of critical resistant feminists—primarily women of color—with multiple ethnicities, cultures, and class experiences whom, in the early 1990s, began to describe their work as third wave feminism. Many of these younger feminists had grown up during or after the 1960s and 1970s era of social movements and consequently most had the advantages of either formal or informal feminist education. Translating from the theories and writings of their resistant feminist predecessors, their own particular personal, sociopolitical, and economic contexts are taken into account and mediate their feminist perspectives.

Further, more radical notions of gender and sexuality have become a significant dimension of this kind of resistant feminism. The incorporation and advancement of "queer theory" (which argues that sexual identities are not fixed, and questions the social construction of heterosexuality as the norm) has also become an important part of much of these kinds of critical feminist thought. However, some of these resistant feminists have distanced themselves from the label "third wave feminism" or do not use it to describe their work, due to what many identify as a conservative appropriation of this term, as well as an emphasis, by some who call themselves third wavers, on age rather than issues.

The 1980s saw the emergence of a backlash against feminism that, many argue, continues today. It corresponds with the dominance of new right, conservative family values and politics that gained prominence during the Reagan/Thatcher/Bush Sr. (and Jr.) administrations. The media, especially, promoted the myth that there was no longer a need for feminism, as women had already achieved equal rights. Moreover, many conservative women, some who were blatantly antifeminist, as well as a number of self-serving women who attained celebrity status, adopted the term "third wave feminist," (which was often used interchangeably with "postfeminist") to promote their own political interests. This popularized so-called third wave or postfeminism often one-dimensionalized and demonized feminism, and feminists associated with the second wave.

The false stereotype of feminists as anti-male, humorless, unattractive, and out of touch with young women's needs and values was actively promoted. An imaginary picture of an ultra-leftist, evil feminist cult, which brainwashed young women through women's studies programs, was invented and aggressively promulgated. Feminists involved in violence against women movements were especially attacked and accused of exaggerating these realities and promoting what was called "victim feminism." Popularized media marketed feminism became a euphemism for what many feminists describe as "lifestyle" or "sex and shopping" fake feminism that advocates ultra-capitalist and consumerist values, self-centered materialism, and Western ideals.

The media, advertising, and beauty industries, which were especially threatened by feminist critiques, contributed to the establishment of a pseudo-post or third wave feminism—directed at young women—that was predicated on greed, power, anti-intellectualism, and freedom to consume designer fashions and beauty products. Indeed, within this context any woman can be a feminist, regardless of her politics, and some young women who assumed this postfeminist or third wave guise achieved celebrity status, supporting this kind of consumer, "power" feminism. This kind of popularized feminism, in actuality, embraces highly traditional values and ideals about youth, Eurocentric notions of beauty, hedonistic pleasure, and "pursuit of men," which are central beliefs of dominant sexist and racist ideologies.

Meanwhile, conservative women's groups and right-wing movements effected detrimental shifts in government polices directed at assisting battered women and children, reproductive freedom, and abortion rights as well as social welfare programs (which continue to escalate well into the new millennium). Moreover, even within the bastions of power, women continue to be dramatically underrepresented and underpaid, and the domination of white men continues, although the myth about western women's empowerment persists.

However, this continuing backlash against feminism helped inspire the development of another form of third wave feminism in the 1990s. Many of these third wave feminists tended to define themselves as a new and separate generation, largely defined by age, that is both influenced and at odds with dimensions of second wave feminism. Some identify third wave feminism as comprising women born between 1963 and 1974, while others define this new wave as that of a multiplicity of feminist activities of girls and women between the ages of fifteen and thirty.

Much of this third wave scholarship also employs autobiographical formats, some of which criticizes primarily mainstream, middle-class, second wave feminists who are their mothers, or of their mother's generation. Many of these second wave feminists, they argue, are ignoring or paying little heed to the needs and different experiences and politics of young women and are resistant to sharing power with—or passing the feminist torch to—their proverbial daughters. Although these kinds of writings have provoked much fascinating debate as well as recognition of the kinds of power relations that permeate many forms of feminism, some of this work has been criticized as being more akin to personal testimony that is devoid of any political or theoretical basis.

Third wave feminism in the United States are often associated with a nonprofit national organization called the Third Wave Foundation that was founded in 1992 and backed by the MS Foundation for Women. This philanthropic organization's mandate is committed to combating inequalities young women face as a result of age, gender, race, sexual orientation, economic, or educational status. The organization, like many other third wave feminist groups, encourages young women to aspire to leadership roles and social activism and to "reclaim" feminisms. Indeed, many third wave feminists attack dimensions of mass mediated popular lifestyle feminisms and the backlash against women and feminisms through unique forms of cultural resistance. In fact, there has been a powerful and exciting employment of new technologies, subversive art and music, as well as guerrilla action that have framed a number of contemporary feminist endeavors. Young women have been at the forefront of these kinds of activities, although only some have described their work as third wave.

Many identify cyberspace politics, the Internet, Web sites, the development of feminists "zines" and resistant, alternative forms of art and music, which began in the 1990s, as being the new feminist frontiers. Some credit the Riot Grrrls, a counter-cultural white middle-class group of punk rock women, "unofficially" formed in Washington, DC, in 1991—who published a controversial feminist zine—as inspiring the development of much of contemporary feminist pop counter-culture. Indeed, some new feminist studies are concerned with the exploration of what is called "girl culture" at both local and global levels, to further understand and empower girls and women of all ages.

Although the notion of feminist waves is useful, it is also contentious and the idea of a feminist third wave is especially complex and problematic. However, what an exploration of the so-called third wave reveals is that girls and young women often moved to the forefront of feminism theory and practice, and that feminism—which is a plurality of visions, ideas, and lived experiences—is especially relevant to, and alive within contemporary youth.

Resources

Dicker, R., & Peipmeier, A. (Eds.). (2003). *Catching a wave: Reclaiming feminism for the 21st century.* Boston: Northeastern University Press.

Hernandez, D., & Rehman, B. (Eds.). (2002). *Colonize this! Young women of color on today's feminism.* New York: Seal Press.

Heywood, L., & Drake, J. (Eds.). (1997). *Third wave agenda: Being feminist, doing feminism.* Minneapolis: University of Minnesota Press.

hooks, b. (2000). *Feminism is for everybody: Passionate politics.* Boston: South End Press.

CONTEMPORARY PUNK ROCK AND ACTIVISM

Leonisa Ardizzone

Punk rock has long been the voice of counterculture, and current punk artists are using their voices as political activists. Punk (or hard rock) lyrics created by youth and for youth, express concern—or anger—over pressing political issues. The music provides youth with both an opportunity and an outlet for consciousness-raising. As youth are being denied political and social authority, they often search for outlets to become more vocal, political, and present. Alternate forms of expression—including music, art, video, and the Internet—have provided a medium for the global youth movement to flourish. Although many adults may dismiss youth culture and the music it creates, youth know full well the power this outlet has. It becomes a way to unite and work together for social change.

Since the concept of "adolescence" began, young people have been marginalized. As early as the beginning of the twentieth century, a youth subculture was created mainly due to the societal view that youth possess a potential for delinquency. The idea of youth subculture originally started as an inner-city phenomenon related to street gangs, but found its way to representing all youth regardless of social class. The youth subculture offers youth different norms and customs, including styles of dress, and language fads different from adults. Though lost on many adults and not traditionally categorized as art, the expressions, symbols, signs, and art of young people have cultural significance. Young people invest meaning in their social practices and life spaces, their personal style, clothing choice, use of music and television, friendship groups, music-making, and dance. These pursuits are not trivial or inconsequential—they are actually quite crucial to both individual and group identities and cultural survival. These forms of symbolic creativity are a necessary part of everyday life for young people and should be seen as integral to the human condition.

The term "grounded aesthetic," coined by youth researcher Paul Willis, refers to a creative element where meaning is attributed to symbols and practices that provides motivation to recognize alternate futures and to understand oneself as a powerful, creative force that can bring those ideas to fruition. Punk rock is an example of a grounded aesthetic. Youth use the lens of punk rock to interpret media and derive meaning for themselves. Consumption is also a part of this aesthetic as it helps shape identity and cultural forms and leads to cultural empowerment. For example, the music youth purchase, or download, or share, contributes to youth empowerment—if

517

they are taking part in political punk or hip hop they are either making a statement or embarking on a process of self-education.

Youth culture is most obviously observed through television, video/film, computer/Internet, magazines, and music. For example, young people are very knowledgeable about music—it is a site of their common culture. Lyrics call up imagery and symbolism that express the feelings of young people—often allowing them to define themselves through popular music. Furthermore, music often serves as a form of informal education both socially and politically. In the past, folk music as performed by Joan Baez and Bob Dylan represented the voices of dissenting youth. More recently, rap, hip hop, and alternative rock artists such as Chuck D of Public Enemy and Rage Against the Machine have become the voice for disenfranchised youth. The popularity of these artists, as evidenced by their album and merchandise sales and concert attendance, illustrates that music is a significant outlet for disenfranchised youth. Youth consumption of subversive art forms, including stories, art, poetry, and film-making, indicates the importance of the arts in general as an outlet for marginalized populations.

Cultural theorists (e.g., Bhabha and hooks) argue that there is tremendous power in the margins or in-between spaces since it is at these locations where collective experiences, community interest, and cultural value are negotiated. By expressing themselves by whatever means, those on the margins, including young people, can offer others life lessons on how the larger society thinks and lives. The artistic and aesthetic expressions of the disenfranchised enable marginalized spaces to become locations for counter-hegemonic cultural practice. Being on the margin speaks to the need for the oppressed to move out from oppressive boundaries, by shaping and determining responses to existing cultural norms. Furthermore, it allows youth to imagine and envision alternate aesthetic acts such as punk rock. Therefore, the margin, the location of the oppressed, is a site of possibility and a location for resistance.

Repeatedly, marginalized populations struggling to find a voice for resistance have found a viable alternative through punk rock and other more mainstream popular media. Giving youth the opportunity to express themselves through their culture, whether in song, film, poetry, or art, gives validity to these marginal voices and the notion that knowing does not need to be clearly defined or expressed. Activism in these contexts can take many forms utilizing a variety of media. For example, young people use their music, dress, photography and video, street arts such as graffiti, and the Internet, as a way of expressing their voices and creating a global youth movement. Not only do these modes of expression unite them, but they also educate them—many get their understanding of world politics from lyrics, videos and Web sites. These media serve as a call to action—youth often report a personal transformation related to song lyrics they heard or a Web site they visited that allowed them to see the world differently.

Punk rock serves as a powerful outlet for those on the margin. Many groups today made up of young rockers and rappers write political music—a la Bob Dylan—with an edge. Bands like Rage Against the Machine, Propagandhi, and Anti-Flag have not only produced numbers of albums filled with political call-to-action lyrics, but also have been on the forefront of organizing a global youth movement. The lyrical content of groups like Rage Against the Machine, Anti-Flag, Propagandhi, Intro5pect, Against all Authority, Thrice, Bouncing Souls, and others have addressed issues of racism, poverty, injustice, George Bush, the war in Iraq, U.S.-Mexico relations, labor politics, and rampant militarism. Contrasting the glib sexual lyricism of more mainstream pop acts, contemporary punk rock lyrics are educational, motivating, and often profound.

Given the content of their lyrics, it is not surprising that all of the aforementioned punk groups have also at some time or another been involved in political and community activism. They play benefits (for children's rights or medical services for the poor), run shelters, and most have been actively involved in promoting voter registration among youth. For example, in 2004, the organization Punk Voter organized a series of concerts called Rock Against Bush to raise awareness about the importance of the youth vote and offer voter registration. Another punk rock Web site, punkvoter.com offers online voter registration and educational materials regarding President Bush's presidential record, the global repercussions of Bush's actions in response to 9/11, and information on both candidates for the 2004 election. Punk Voter supports coalition building, education, registration and mobilization of young voters. Their aim is to unite youth, promote activism, and work for political change. Based on the response to Rock Against Bush in terms of concert attendance and sales of the compilation CDs, the politics of modern-day punk rock resonates strongly with contemporary youth. Indeed, many of the punk bands affiliated with Punk Voter or Bands Against Bush—an organization whose tagline is "your apathy is their victory"—have information on their individual Web sites regarding the Bush administration and ways to take action for social change. Listeners are encouraged to talk politics on online message boards, connect with other bands and organizations in the movement. For example, the group Bouncing Souls has a "Letters from Iraq" feature where soldiers weigh in on the reality of the war. The group Rage Against the Machine features their "Freedom Fighter of the Month." These are just two examples of the politically active content of contemporary punk rock—created for and by youth whom most adults would label as loud, unruly, and ignorant. Further disproving these stereotypical ideas and supporting the power of punk, the group Anti-Flag articulates a very clear message regarding the connection between punk and activism—showing themselves to be leaders in this necessary movement.

Although punk rock has always been "angry" and counterculture, contemporary punk rock is not only angry, but also political and highly educational.

Punk rockers are using their voices to take back the future they perceive as stolen from them by corrupt politicians, greedy businessman, and an apathetic, materialistic public. Of course, political music is not solely the domain of today's alternative rockers. Folk music and hip hop have long-offered a political education to their listeners. One brilliant example of all aesthetic genres coming together to counteract the war machine and work for peace is the AWOL project of the War Resisters League. Through art, music, poetry, and prose young artists involved in this project seek to raise consciousness and unite voices.

A perusal of alternative youth media demonstrates that (a) there is in fact a global youth culture, (b) it is thriving through music and the Internet—global communications, and (c) it is firmly focused on political and social change through supporting youth voice. Punks existence clearly demonstrates that life on the margin is ideally situated for stirring things up, that being marginalized is an ideal way to raise awareness, that music is an important motivating and educational factor, and that politics as usual does not have to be the case.

Resources
Books

Ardizzone, L. (2001). Getting' their word out: Youth peace-builders of New York City. Unpublished doctoral dissertation, Columbia University, Teachers College.

Bhabha, H. (1994). *The location of culture*. London: Routledge.

hooks, b. (1994). *Teaching to transgress: Education as the practice of freedom*. New York: Routledge.

———. (1990). *Yearning: Race, gender and cultural politics*. Boston: South End Press.

Kett, J. F. (1977). *Rites of passage: Adolescence in America 1790 to the present.* New York: Basic Books.

Willis, P. (1990). *Common culture*. Milton Keyner: Open University Press.

Web Sites

A-F Gateway. (n.d.). Anti-Flag. Retrieved September 8, 2005 from http://www.anti-flag.com

Bands against Bush. (n.d.). Bands against Bush—Your apathy is their victory. Retrieved September 8, 2005 from http://www.bandsagainstbush.org

MFA. (2003). Music for America. Retrieved September 8, 2005 from http://www.musicforamerica.org

Punk Voter. (2003). Punk Voter. Retrieved September 8, 2005 from http://www.punkvoter.com

Rage against the machine. (n.d.). Rage against the machine. Retrieved September 8, 2005 from http://www.ratm.com

War resisters league. (1923). War resisters league. Retrieved September 8, 2005 from http://www.warresisters.org

The End

Patrick (P–Phatz) Cucuta

Screams of war, poverty stricken streets,
Hospitals over filled, different gangs, same beef
The school systems in shambles, they chain us from our ankles,
Since our ancestors were left here to hang; die
Up high and dangle,
In the skies fly the Angel
The Angel of life
Come and save us, take my soul and fly high
Up high away
Away from it all
Past the stars, into the light
Break the stereotype,
In this society where death is quick
But you fight for your life
The system's critical, this government gives minimal
The people drains the earth of its minerals
But when the universe moves forward
And the Galaxy starts to progress
The Torch will pass and the future will be set
From now until the end, soon to hold the pen
To the next one
The next man
To save us from the end.

TEACHING AND LEARNING IN AND OUT OF SCHOOL

The Reasons I Teach

Earl Mitchell

I teach because I love what I do and possess the ability to expose the truth.
I teach to connect our community ties and help to erase all the painful lies.
I teach to give my students a chance, how to be proactive and take a stand.
I teach with all my heart and soul, I teach them how to reach their goals.
I teach what no one dares to touch, I teach because the system sucks.
I teach because the most satisfying thing to me
is past students coming home with college degrees.
I teach because there's nothing better in life than planting spiritual seeds,
and watching your students grow into beautiful tress
among all the chaos in touch city streets.
I teach even when people don't listen,
because they hate to hear the truth and feel conviction.
(By the way, there's a genocide in Africa, please tell the UN).
I teach about the South and West Indies,
even though I was born in Brooklyn
and raised on Roosevelt streets.
I teach because good mentors worked with me,
and giving back to the hood is my responsibility.
I teach because Jesus gave me the passion to help change lives,
and told me to hurry up son, they're running out of time.
I teach all the things I never learned,
I teach because Rodney took that beaten' and LA burned.
I teach what I feel is true, I teach urban youth, but I can also teach you.
I teach my story, not history, because standardized exams are not fair to me,
not when you expect the same results with savage inequalities.
I teach about forty acres and a mule,
and racists are unhappy people who are confused.
I teach because the media sells lies, and Maya wrote poems about how to rise.
I teach because drugs affect the whole community,
I've watched crack tear apart many families.
I teach because kids I tried to help are locked up North,
and I'm tired of single mothers crying in court.
I thought about all the reasons I teach and I must conclude, in the end,
I teach because God called me to.

We're Humans Too…

Shelley Persaud

My school has become the jail
Where we, the prisoners, the students stay
Where we're supposed to "Learn"
Where security guards and police are always searching for guns
You won't find anything
Maybe drugs from those 'wannabe' thugs
But not from the majority/ Because we're not stupid kids
Guns are not school tools
We live life happily and freely but not like fools
Don't judge us before you know us/ That's discrimination in my view
We won't be like you when you were going to school
We're a new generation
Maybe more 'loose' but definitely not fools
Don't treat us as criminals
Barking orders and expecting us to think it's required.
There maybe a few rotten apples in the bunch
But the rest are still good, so give us some trust.
We're humans too/ Just like you
So when you bellow at a student again
Think back at this poem/ And remember, we're humans
We're like you
We make mistakes and learn from them
We're not dumb enough to do the same thing again and again
We're humans too/ Just like you!

THE POWER OF RAP AS A FORM OF LITERACY

Priya Parmar

Today's youth live in a media-saturated society where *all* of its forms (television, commercials/advertisements, film, print, magazines, newspapers, billboards, radio, and popular music) play a vital role in the shaping of their identities, cultural values, and social practices. In this mass-produced, mass-consuming age of postwar capitalism, it is unthinkable and even foolish to ignore the powerful influence of popular culture on young people. Many studies support the belief that mass media is the primary influence on educating our youth, even more so than our schools. If this is the case, then why isn't the critical study of media, or critical media literacy, more prevalent in the U.S. educational system as they are in other countries such as Canada?

Students who are able to deconstruct media messages are able to recognize, question, and critically analyze its historical, cultural, social, political, and economic implications. Therefore, students are better able to understand why certain races, cultures, genders, and classes are misrepresented and underrepresented; why media is constructed the way it is; who benefits from such representations and who does not; whose point of view media is constructed from, and, more importantly, what actions can be taken to dispel stereotypes, misrepresentations, biases, and distortions.

The ultimate goal of such analysis is to create awareness and consciousness, thus leading youth to engage in social activism, and ultimately change. This typed of study is referred to as critical media literacy. Critical media literacy can be integrated into the existing curriculum and across all disciplines, ranging from the elementary to the high school level. One example of critical media literacy is deconstructing popular music such as rap lyrics found in hip hop culture. It should be noted that hip hop culture comprises four original elements: (1) graffiti art, also referred to as "graf writing"; (2) DJing ("deejaying"), also referred to as "turntabling"; (3) MCing ("emceeing"), also referred to as "rhyming" or "rapping"; and (4) b-boying, a gendered reference to the style of hip hop dance, commonly referred to as "breakin" and "break-dancing," which was also popularized by "b-girls" from its inception. For the purpose of this essay, I will be focusing specifically on the element of MCing or what is created from it: rap lyrics. It is important to understand that rap is a form of literacy that helps make available the various relations and experiences that exist between the learners and their world. In other words, the traditional forms of literacy, such as reading and writing, must be reexamined. Literacy must be viewed as much more than simply the ability to read and write the printed word; it must be opened up and expanded to embrace all forms of literacy. Rap is just one of these "alternative" or "unofficial" forms of literacy whose examination and study produce discourses that are central to a radical and actively interventionist theory of literacy.

The study of rap music using an inter-disciplinary, trans-disciplinary, and counter-disciplinary approach, known as cultural studies, allows educators and students to challenge and move beyond traditional mainstream ideologies. By critically examining and deconstructing the lyrical content of rap, educators and students open the doors for a transformative dialogue to occur, and confront the most neglected text: "culture." This form of pedagogy views students as active and critical agents of social change. Students who engage in this active, critical approach can use rap music as an empowering, liberating text that they can analyze, interpret, and challenge, based on their own knowledge and cultural experience.

Approaching the study of rap in such a fashion allows students to appropriate their own experiences, voices, and histories into the classroom, thus making knowledge more meaningful and critical. Due to the invalidation that many marginalized youth experience in school, the validation and legitimization of students' personal experiences, voices, and histories through the critical examination of rap music ultimately empowers and emancipates them.

In my own education, rap lyrics had never been discussed in the classroom, probably because of the "negative" associations with it. Rap lyrics that tend to be over-publicized by the media include lyrics that expresses misogynist, homophobic, and sexually explicit viewpoints. Conscientious or political MC's such as KRS-One and others (Public Enemy, Mos Def, Common, and The Roots) are merely dismissed as being too controversial, simply because the black cultural politics they articulate in their lyrics describe the harsh realities of social and economic suffering never before told from their perspective. These MC's are viewed as controversial essentially because they are the voice of social critique and criticism, which is precisely why the media and distribution centers have chosen not to focus much attention on them.

It can be argued that these controversial MC's are reflective of what Antonio Gramsci refers to as "organic cultural intellectuals." These "hip hop nationalists" represent the voice of the urban poor, exposing the everyday struggles of working-class blacks through lyrical expressions. Hip hop culture and rap music have thus become the cultural emblem for America's young black urban youth. Through both its lyrical and musical foregrounding of "blackness," and its aesthetic heterogeneity, rap confronts the unquestioned logic of a master narrative, thus making outsiders uncomfortable with many of the messages produced. Rap music is just one of many critical literacies that educators can use in curriculum to help youth examine the social, political, and cultural inequalities in their lives. Towards this end, administrators, teachers, parents, and students must learn not to condemn hip hop culture and its rap music. Instead, they must challenge hip hop culture to rise to its best potential.

Students from all racial, ethnic, and class backgrounds can benefit from rap music by using cultural studies approach. For the students whose only exposure to black urban life is through mass media representations, rap music can be used as a tool to help dispel stereotypes and false perceptions of black culture, hence helping students understand the struggles of everyday life for working-class blacks. As a result, the unfamiliar becomes familiar. For students who actually live the experiences described in rap lyrics, the examination of rap in itself is an empowering, meaningful, and legitimizing form of pedagogy. When individuals reflect on and understand the conditions under which they are oppressed, they are empowered to take control of their lives and create change. In a traditional, technocratically operated classroom, such knowledge, experiences, and voices are marginalized and remain virtually silenced. On the other hand, in a critical, transformative, democratic classroom, individuals' knowledge, experiences, and voices are celebrated and validated, thus creating an inclusionary environment where all voices and perspectives are heard.

In addition, rap lyrics can also be used as a tool to help the dominant class understand its position compared to others who are different. Many rap lyrics make this difference painfully clear and problematize this system of racial difference whereby blacks (and other minority groups) are marginalized, silenced, and excluded from the cultural dialogue, and where "whiteness" is assumed to be the norm. The overwhelming representation and study of white, middle-class, Anglo-Saxon males in traditional, mainstream education tends to privilege members of this group, and to devalue or denigrate the knowledge, histories, and experiences of other groups.

The traditional teacher-oriented, Western dominated ideology, which has been practiced in U.S. schools since their beginning, continues to dominate

529

the educational system. Although some progressive change has occurred, educational reform, specifically, a critical and emancipatory reform that empowers students ultimately takes time. However, an empowering education is readily attainable in individual classrooms if students can challenge, critique, and question the syllabus, texts, and materials given to them. Like any reform movement, change occurs in small, gradual steps. Thus, students who develop critical thinking and inquiry skills as described in the field of cultural studies and critical pedagogy, students are ultimately engaged in a democratic process of education that includes social activism.

In order to create and foster an empowering, democratic, and inclusive education, we as educators must practice a pedagogy filled with hope and possibility. Such a pedagogy includes the subjugated knowledge of students traditionally marginalized by mainstream, dominant ideologies. The addition of subjugated knowledge, as well as the inclusion of students' voices, histories, and experiences, opens the door for a transformative pedagogy that places race, class, and gender, as well as relevant social, cultural, political, and economic issues at the forefront of the curriculum. Ultimately, through this kind of pedagogy, these issues will resonate throughout the curriculum, transforming the traditional curriculum into one that is associated with cultural studies and critical pedagogy.

Regardless of one's pedagogical beliefs, the schools' primary goal is to aid in the construction of knowledge. Students, teachers, and parents living in today's postmodern society must learn to interact within the many dimensions of social reality. Consequently, we must accept the diverse forms of literacy that consume and make up the lives of youth, learning to adapt to this change and transform it into our own pedagogy. In doing so, we must teach critical thinking and inquiry skills that enable students to create strong, empowering identities and to form relationships with persons and communities different from them. Ultimately, for students to truly become empowered, the concept of empowerment must be seen as a *philosophy* of education and not just as a strategy to increase academic success.

Resources
Books

Alverman, D., Moon, J., & Hagood, M. (1999). *Popular culture in the classroom: Teaching and researching critical media literacy.* Chicago: National Reading Conference.

Aronowitz, S., & Giroux, H. (1993). *Education still under siege* (2nd ed.). Westport CT: Bergin & Garvey.

Kincheloe, J., & Steinberg, S. (Eds.). (1998). *Unauthorized methods: Strategies for critical teaching.* New York: Routledge.

Ross, A., & Rose, T. (Eds.). (1994). *Microphone fiends: Youth music and youth culture.* New York: Routledge.

Article
Best, S., & Kellner, D. (1999). Rap, black rage, and racial difference. *Enculturation*, 2 (2), 1–20.

HIP HOP AND EDUCATION

Rob Haworth, Joseph Carroll-Miranda, and Eric Alvarez

We want to foster the notion that hip hop has played a central role in the daily lives of youth and has been, in large part, commodified into the popular mainstream culture, which has dismantled many of its grassroots and underground origins. Within this commodification we want to demonstrate the need to support and develop the underground hip hop movement that has been so prevalent in working to integrate this culture into the public schools. We also feel it necessary to argue that hip hop can also be utilized within the classroom in order to create more democratic spaces that support youth culture and the lived realties of students.

In order to discuss hip hop and education we have decided to work within a dialogue format that adheres to a flow of ideas, rather than a traditional essay. The dialogue is between a new elementary education teacher (Eric Alvarez) who is also a hip hop DJ, and two doctoral students from New Mexico State University (Rob Haworth and Joseph Carroll-Miranda), who both have written about hip hop and education in other publications as well as worked with the hip hop scene within their respected communities.

HISTORY 101: LESSONS FROM THE CRADLE

Rob: Before we begin to discuss this idea of hip hop and education I believe it is important to get a brief socio-historical background so we can get a foundational sense of how it all came to be.

Eric: Well, the first thing we need to recognize is that we are not speaking of hip hop in terms of a genre but rather as a culture. And I don't want to break it down as KRS-One's individual elements of hip hop but put more emphasis on the lived realities of the youth that are involved in the culture. By this I mean the day-to-day experiences of the youth. It encompasses everything we do in our lives, the way we talk, the way we walk, the way we dress, the way we understand . . . what do you think?

Joseph: Yeah, hip hop culture is everything. It is more than just "this" or "that." It is how we view and understand the world. It is how we feel when we see the "popo creepin" on the "low-low." It is how we say what we feel and we feel what we say. It is in short, a way of life. How we understand everything around us is influenced and engendered from hip hop culture. That is why I think that "keepin it real" is not only lacking in hip hop but is also lacking in education. So, that is what hip hop has to add to all of this. It is an attitude and a way of seeing, doing, and breaking down things all around us. What you gotta say to that?

Eric: It is funny that you say that 'cause "keepin it real" is not only a cliché in hip hop, but has also become a common cliché in education. Looking at the educational system as a whole, it has not been "keepin it real" in bringing youth experiences into the classroom.

Rob: As a person who works with pre-service teachers you are able to start breaking down these notions of what is "real" in the daily lives of those who live in hip hop culture. With pre-service teachers we can recognize these young people's lived realities. Bringing hip hop into the classroom is bringing those voices into the classroom. When I was teaching high school the teachers would say "those f***ing students" this and that, and I would say, "who the f*** are you to critique youth and youth culture without understanding their reality." It all came down to the teacher's stereotypes of hip hop culture as gangsta thugs and drug dealers. In this sense youth culture is an effective strategy to teach and deconstruct stereotypes, as well as, decriminalize youth and the culture they embrace.

Eric: The interesting thing with hip hop is that when you are bound to a music that is seen as incriminating you are continually resisting these negative notions that hip hop is "slinging," dealing, or doing something criminal. You have a predominantly black and Latino element in hip hop, and they are always associated with informal economy and crime. That is why we have to differentiate "industry" hip hop and underground hip hop. This is precisely a way to undermine the general understanding of hip hop and the negative drug and crime stereotypes that are related to the culture. But there is a completely different element in terms of culture that is more positive and interested in the preserving of the life of youth within underground hip hop. And what is underground now used to be referred to as conscious hip hop, like when you had the Native Tongues that talked about emancipation, Afro-centricity, and the state of the disenfranchised. But now it is not referred to as conscious, but rather underground. In that time conscious hip hop was "industry" hip hop. There was no differentiation between the two.

Joseph: Totally man, you see when collectives such as Zulu Nation and Rocksteady Crew came about it was a venue for urban youth in NYC to channel the rage and frustration from the stigma of being who you were or who you were seen as. Society deemed you as one thing and here, as a culture, you were something else. You had creative forms of expressing your anger, about how things around you are f***ed up, like racism, poverty, and simultaneously wanting to go out and have fun and a good time. Many of the lyrics back in the day broke down what was happening in the inner city of NYC. This history is what has kept the "true" hip hop or underground hip hop alive. It is about taking care of your own while creating spaces to do all of this.

Rob: From what you were saying about education and creating spaces, it is important that we start looking at how those lived realities reflect our own classrooms. Bringing that socio-historical element into our classroom creates a space where shared experiences can exist. That way we can begin to co-create curriculum based on those understandings and shared experiences. So ideally the classroom reflects the experiences of the youth. Right?

HISTORY 501: DA LESSONS BECOME CURRICULUM

Eric: I think especially now we can see collectives within the hip hop communities that are starting to establish and develop a connection between education and the youth culture of hip hop. We are talking about artists like J-Live and a few others on his labels who are themselves public school teachers. You have Boots Riley and the Coup who are working in classrooms in the Bay Area. KRS-One, promoting his organization Temple of Hip Hop. Compilations like the *Funky Precedents I & II* have come together so the proceeds go toward education. Then you have individuals working within legislation to bring money into schools rather than prisons.

Rob: Russell Simmons came out and said, "Mayor Bloomberg you better not be putting money into prisons but rather into education." And we had mainstream artist like P. Diddy and others voicing their opinions, and then obviously you have organizations such as Inner City Struggle and Schools Not Jails.

Eric: Yeah, in fact P. Diddy has a nonprofit organization that helps to educate the youth in his community where Sista Souljah has developed the curriculum that she designed around the culture of hip hop.

Joseph: In fact NYC is "cracking" as we speak. Their second annual hip hop and education summit is happening in November 2004. The collective H2ED is tight! They are developing curriculum that utilizes hip hop culture. I mean, it is not teaching the youth multiplication tables using hip hop beats. It is utilizing the elements of hip hop as a lived reality and experience which then becomes the center of the curriculum. This becomes a real alternative to the traditional Eurocentric curriculum that we all have been force-fed. This collective (H2ED) is off the hook and I think it is giving inspiration to us as crazy fukas wanting to do the same thing in the boogie down borderlands. Que No?

Rob: In terms of the borderlands and working with pre-service teachers, we have been discussing and actually making it a part of the curriculum to bring in music and culture as a method of teaching.

Eric: I think as a pre-service teacher, I'm able to see firsthand the lack of understanding that is so endemic among my peers. Just in the way they attribute hip hop to negative stereotypes and the embodiment of criminal activity. And then, once the culture is presented in the classroom and the lyrics are broken down, they're hit with the reality of the culture. They begin to see that there's a completely different aspect than the perspective they're seeing on MTV. I mean, to break all of this down to them so they can understand the reality and stop and think "hmm, why *do* all of these minorities seem so resistant toward authority" or . . . I mean, why are suburban white kids latching on so tightly to Eminem? The bottom line is that these kids found someone that they can relate to. This is a lived experience that we, as teachers, need to bring to the table.

Rob: It is basically demanding the critical multicultural lens that hip hop has brought to the table.

Joseph: No doubt, down here in the borderlands most of the youth are way into hip hop. With the boom of Mexican hip hop that is becoming more and more prevalent from Cypress Hill to Delinquent Habits and from Akwid to Ozomatli, they are all stating that it is "ok" to be proud of being a Mexican or Chicanismo. We need to stand in support of youth that are proud of their roots and heritage and counter the language of the dominant culture that is stigmatizing youth as the root of many social problems. I mean picture a day without Mexicans . . . what do you think would happen down here. The language phenomenon is also something that is present within hip hop down here. Let's look at Spanglish. For many of the youth in this area, this is a lived reality educators need to deal with. Bringing their experience to the forefront of the educational experience rather than the remarks like "keep it up and you will end up in jail or with a s****y job the rest of your life" can seriously change the dynamics as far as the alarming dropout rates among Latinos in the United States.

Rob: California is definitely a bastion of racist policies, like the English only movement and Propositions 187 and 227, which have set a precedent nationwide where your language, particularly Spanish, is something that is being left out.

Joseph: In fact, under the current No Child Left Behind (NCLB) second-language learners have three years to learn English. They then are forced to adapt and insert themselves within the rest of the group. If not then "oh well, they never wanted to learn anyways." This is flat out crazy!

Rob: We can relate this to Oakland and the whole issue of Ebonics. Again the same racist policies occur.

Eric: You can't stress enough that from its roots, this has been a black and Latin culture and their languages have been targeted in schools. This is another example of separating identities in schools so they can become part of the dominant culture.

Joseph: I've kicked it with some youth down here that have expressed why they feel so out of place in schools. Their feeling is that if only their experience could be seen as relevant to the classroom setting, then they could begin to find a space within schools.

Eric: We have to create a balance within the school systems where hip hop does not just substitute old whitey's curriculum, but rather creates a space where multiple lived experiences become the center of curriculum design and implementation.

Joseph: What you just said is at the heart of the matter of creating serious educational alternatives that have to begin in the Teacher Education Program (TEP) and pre-service programs. They need to be exposed to other lived realities than their own. Hip Hop culture is an excellent way to start seeing things in a different light. I mean hip hop is so spread out world wide. Most commercials and ads on corporate television have hip hop beats and twists to them. Educators have to tap into not only the elements of the "industry" hip hop culture but the conscious and underground history that is alive and kicking all over the world. Using these cultural elements can teach all of us how to do things in a different and refreshing way.

Rob: I would add that hip hop culture transcends national and international borders. Now you have hip hoppers in Asia that can relate and express their experiences to someone in New York. By utilizing technology we are now able to create awareness where once there was none. Instead of trading tapes, music is traded via the Internet so that youth are sharing their experiences across international borders.

Joseph: Hell yeah, now it's not West Coast, East Coast, and the "dirty south" but a serious global phenomenon where the roots of hip hop culture are being re-experienced in other parts of the world. For example, in Colombia they have a hip hop movement that since its beginning has been fully political and deals with issues of social justice, imperialism, and drug wars. Also, Algerians are de-colonizing France with their hip hop culture with bands such as Gnawa. The possibilities are endless. The only limitation nowadays is a lack of imagination and a pea-minded brain.

FUTURE 701: DA LESSONS WON'T STOP 'CAUSE THEY CAN'T STOP.

Eric: Unfortunately, the mainstream curriculum developers *are* those pea-minded individuals who rejoice over standardization and NCLB. This is where the technologies that Rob mentioned earlier are going to play a big role. Now we are able to create de-centralized communities of educators who are redefining socialist and anarchist educational systems. With a global hip hop culture, we can all redefine what curriculum is and should be as well as autonomous methods and pedagogical practices that adhere to different parts of the world. This is so youth experiences, such as those within hip hop culture, can become one of the multiple lifelines of the whole educational experience.

Joseph: What is extremely important in this process is that we evoke the social justice essence within hip hop culture. Our own liberation will ensure a more collective emancipation. We have to carry on the legacies of the Zulu Nation, Public Enemy, Talib Kweli, Common, Mos-Def, Dead Prez, The Coup, and Raptivism as well as the political legacy of the Young Lords, Black Panther Party, and Brown Berets. Bringing this historical foundation to the classroom and its notions of knowledge of self, is a serious part of hip hop's emancipatory culture. This general framework of hip hop culture has the potential to co-create relationships with cutting edge critical pedagogy, critical multicultural education, and critical race theory. The big problem is that the academy, just like public schools, does not deem hip hop culture as a worthy subject within education. This is definitely changing and is also why we are doing what we are doing. Just like other academics, teachers, and collectives in different parts of the world, we are creating spaces by any means necessary.

Rob: We also have the example of the Urban Dreams project in Oakland, hip hop and social justice through the *Coup* and H2ED that brings to life many aspects of hip hop culture. As educators we need to shift our own indoctrination and prejudices and realize the possibilities of a youth-centered classroom.

Joseph: Hell yeah, H2ED and Urban Dreams initiatives have to be both local and global!!!

Eric: If the focus of education is youth, then the youth need to be involved or at least represented in the development of curriculum. Isn't that the rhyme and reason for us in utilizing the notions of H2ED? Youth and communities can co-create the curriculum they are going to be engaging in. You dig? It's not only the spoken part of the culture that we are talking about, but bringing together other parts of the culture that need to be integrated into the school system. So now let's look back at those elements of hip hop culture that KRS-One defined. We need to find a way of incorporating not only what is said through the writing element, MCing, but through the other elements as well. We must bridge the gap between understandings, representations, and misrepresentations. So, in looking at language, we could incorporate emancipatory lyrics into the curriculum. It would be a good idea to teach not only European art history but also urban art. We should not only teach classical dance, but urban dance and its elements as well. We should not only focus on fixed elements, but tap into the expressions of hip hop culture. Their worldview and way of life would then be present in their educational experience instead of being constantly demonized. Let's teach Shakespeare using Tupac, let's teach art using *TATS Crew*, let's teach dance using *Rocksteady Crew*, and let's teach poetry. . . . YOU PICK THE ARTIST!!!

Joseph: No doubt. . . .

Rob: Peace. . . .

Joseph, Rob, Eric: to be continued? Sure Nuf.

Resources

Books

Daspit, T. (2000). Rap pedagogies: "Bring(ing) the noise" of "knowledge born on the microphone" to radical education. In J. A. Weaver & T. Daspit (Eds.). *Popular culture and critical pedagogy: Reading, constructing, connecting* (pp. 163–182). New York: Garland Publishing.

Dimitriadis, G. (2001). *Performing identity/performing culture: Hip hop as text, pedagogy, and lived practice.* New York: Peter Lang.

Forman, M. (2002). *The 'hood comes first: Race, space, and place in rap and hip-hop.* Middletown, CT: Wesleyan University Press.

Kitwana, B. (2002). *The hip hop generation: Young blacks and the crisis in African American culture.* New York: Basic Civitas Books.

Mahiri, J. (1998). *Shooting for excellence: African American youth culture in New Century schools.* New York: Teachers College Press.

Mclaren, P. (1999). Gansta pedagogy and ghettocentricity: The hip-hop nation as counterpublic sphere. In C. McCarthy, G. Hudak, S. Miklaucic, & Saukko (Eds.), *Sound identities: Popular music and the cultural politics of education.* New York: Peter Lang.

Morrell, E., & Duncan-Andrade, J. M. R. (2002). *Promoting academic literacy with urban youth through engaging hip hop culture.* Urbana, IL: National Council of Teachers of English.

Web Sites

H2ED. (2004). Hip hop education: Empowerment through education! Retrieved August 10, 2004 from http://www.h2ed.net

Inner City Struggle. (2002, February). Schools not jails. Retrieved July 18, 2004 from http:\www.innercitystruggle.org

Temple of Hip Hop. (2003). Retrieved July 19, 2004 from http://www.templeofhiphop.org

TRANSFORMATIONS THROUGH HIP HOP

Mary Stone Hanley

"You know how we do" is a phrase often spoken in the spaces where hip hop is at play: the radios, clubs, recreation centers, and street corners where young people play with words and culture. The "we" implies a community and culture; "you know" implies shared meaning; and "do" conveys a sense of action. In other words, young people involved with hip hop seem to be about something, and doing it everywhere. From rural, suburban, and urban areas in the United States to clubs and studios in Europe and Asia young people have developed a culture of pleasure and critique based on Afrocentric rhythms and a centuries-long tradition of music as a vehicle for the liberation of consciousness. This essay explores the verbal music of hip hop that is called rap and the ways it transforms consciousness.

The aesthetics of rap as it emerges in the context of the African diasporic cultures is formed by three main sources: music, poetry, and orality. Music is fundamental to cultures of the African diaspora. This fact is a legacy from African traditions where music was integral to every activity in a person's life from birth to death. Musical forms reveal the ways that music is rooted in the culture. The call and response pattern, an activity in which everyone participates, is a manifestation of the communal nature of black music and Afrocentric cultures. African and African American music emphasizes improvisation and interaction, which is a way of being in the African tradition, and may be a factor in the resiliency of the people of the African Diaspora. Malone points out that the ability to retain inner values while reshaping the framework is an aspect of both African-centered music and life. *You know how we do!*

In order to gain some understanding of hip hop culture I interviewed ten MCs and two DJs and observed twelve open mics, where MCs rapped and spoken word poets performed their work. The MC is the wordsmith who uses words and rhythms to convey ideas. The DJ is a musician whose beats set the rhythmic background for the MCs and other musicians. I have attended four hip hop workshops in elementary and high schools where both DJs and MCs taught the students about the arts and forms of hip hop. I have worked with nine high school students as they critiqued the culture of hip hop and developed and performed in an open mic for their peers, parents, and community members. Through my research I have come to understand that rap performers transform the world in the give and take of the dialogic public space of artistry.

You know how we do!

Hip hop is at its essence dialogic. Bruner says that we learn a lot about the world and ourselves in dialogue with others. Rap is more than the dialogue of an "I think, therefore I am" Enlightenment head trip. The dialogic of rap is more like when a jazz musician plays his horn all up and down your spine until you've just got to say, "Alright now! Play that, my brother!"—and he does! Rap is like being in a black Baptist church when the pastor's voice crescendos, and people all around clap and call back, "Amen!" Some of the congregation cannot sit still and have to get up and move to release and receive the passion. These are the roots of rap, a musical form that is Afrocentric and dialogic, or perhaps Afrocentrically dialogic.

You know how we do!

The discourse of rap is about the integration of mind, body, and the intuitive spirit that is creativity, which is why if the beats are good and the audience is "feeling it," it doesn't matter if they only catch a phrase or two of what the MC says. In fact, the word "feeling" permeates the culture of hip hop. You often hear, "I feel you," or "I ain't feelin' you," or "you feelin' me?" The cognitive, affective, and intuitive have to connect to make sense of the dialectic of mind and body in the hip hop experience. After all, it is a form of music—and *you know how we do!*

This is not to negate the importance of thought in rap and spoken word, the nonmusical poetry of hip hop. A good MC has to be knowledgeable about the world and about hip hop itself. They have to be able to ignite thoughts, feelings, and respect in their audiences, when the listeners do hear the words above the music. What the audiences respect most about an MC is the ability to create a powerful metaphor, a turn of phrase, the ability to speak to power about oppression, or to out think an opponent. In order to do so MCs have to know something about people, places, concepts, and issues. The MCs I interviewed all said that they had to read, read, read, watch, listen, and dialogue with others in order to have something to say about the world. Thus, MCs, like other artists, are researchers.

Also, like other artists, the MC is engaged in a process that involves agency, the power to transform—the medium, the word, and the world. *You know how we do.* Eisner describes the process of the artist as perception, conceptualization, expression, and transformation. Perception is the act of giving meaning to what our senses convey. Conceptualization is the work of coalescing ideas and feelings into deeper, more complex understanding. Expression is the struggle with the concepts and the medium to speak meaning and to transform the medium, self, and the audience. Agency in the work of the MC has the power to disrupt the media and popular representations of young people, but particularly young black men. I observed the use of hip hop to teach in workshops in schools and communities and experienced a rupture in the geology of racism when whites *and* people of color had to overcome their fear of the angry and "dangerous" young black male. They were forced to release their notion of his intellectual inferiority when the black MC commands language, written or improvisational, becoming a wordsmith and the dialogic teacher who instructs about culture, form, and concepts.

You know how we do!

In one of the school workshops I attended, a young black man—let's call him George—a senior in one of the last-chance high schools where mostly poor black youth are put when, for better or worse, they refuse to conform, is involved in a session on the history and poetry of hip hop. George's skin is dark, dark chocolate brown, so close to black that you can hardly tell where his face stops and his black do-rag begins. He smirks and chews on a toothpick and swaggers in his sagging baggy pants. He has the scent of one who is nervous when caged. The leader of the workshop, MC Tight, is a young adult African American male who is also an MC. He lists ten attributes of poetry on the blackboard: simile, metaphor, imagery, alliteration, assonance, consonance, onomatopoeia, meter, rhythm, rhyme scheme. He asks if any of the participants know the meaning of the words. George smirks, chews on his toothpick, and volunteers the meaning of each of the terms. When it is his turn to perform George gets up, and freestyles, an improvisational form of word play. His thoughts come in similes, metaphors, and images that speak about being black, racism, injustice, George Bush, war, and a "rotten education" in rhyme and rhythm. The audience of mostly white teachers and students from the high school with the demographics of a predominately uppe- middle-class population was astounded. They applauded vigorously, and George took the toothpick from his mouth and smiled—a real smile.

You know how we do!

Moved by the experience, a graduate student in education at a local university, a former kindergarten teacher, a sweet and caring woman—we'll call her Sue Ann—was so impressed by George that she wanted to tell him so. But she was afraid. She saw him as a big black male who chews on toothpicks, wears a do-rag, and talks about white people and racism. She carried all of the deep-seated implications of that representation. She was scared, but she was so impressed that she pulled in her fears and went to him. She told him how wonderful she thought his poetry was. His response? He spontaneously hugged her. Sue Ann continued and told him how impressed she was with his skill in performance, and he hugged her again. The shadow that is the young "dangerous" black male showed her some love and appreciation. The one she feared was a human being who was eager to connect. The next day I saw Sue Ann at the university, and she told me about her experience and transformation. She had learned so much that day, about hip hop, about young black men, but just as importantly, about herself and her assumptions. The next day when I visited his high school I saw George and told him where his diamonds had fallen and how he had transformed his audience; he smiled again. He had had no idea of what his artistry and humanity had created. He, too, was transformed in that moment.

In the case of George and Sue Ann, hip hop had been a bridge of transformation between black and white, between young and old, between educated and undereducated, between male and female, between student and teacher, and between racism and classism—dominating and internalized. Herein is a consequence of the dialogic nature of hip hop. Through this art form, in spite of the ways that music industry moguls manipulate images and messages to reproduce the status quo of racist representations of young black people, hip hop used in communities and schools can create a public space where agency, and ruptures, and the rapture of transformation can free the mind so that the rest can follow.

You know how we do!

Resources

Books

Bruner, J. (1996). *The culture of education.* Cambridge, MA: Harvard
   University Press.

Malone, J. (1996). *Steppin' on the blues: The visible rhythms of African American
   dance.* Urbana: University of Illinois Press.

Article

Eisner, E. (1980). Artistic thinking, human intelligence and the mission of
   the school. *The High School Journal,* 63 (8), 326–334.

I WRITE FOR THAT SHY LITTLE GIRL: SPOKEN WORD'S POWER TO DOCUMENT

Shiv Desai and Tyson Marsh

In *The Evolution of Deficit Thinking: Educational Thought and Practice,* Richard Valencia discusses several models for school failure among low-socio-economic status (SES) minority students. Valencia unveils the roots of deficit thinking in his book and how it continues to exist even today. For example, in the past some scholars have stated that minority students were inferior because of their genes; other scholars blamed parents for not instilling proper moral values. Still other scholars have blamed minority students' home languages and the fact that they do not want to be part of the "melting pot." Finally, some scholars do not blame minority students or their parents, but blame the inequality in society.

A major weakness in all these models is that student perseverance, resolve, and the agency of home culture is often ignored. For example, scholars look at students' home language as a deficit as opposed to a language that is rich in history, full of nuances, and a positive part of identity. In addition, scholars do not affirm that students having pride in their home culture can create academic achievement. Finally, economic, cultural, and political systems do oppress minority students; however, it does not account for the ways student create their own spaces to express themselves and protest against oppression.

We see spoken word poetry (performance poetry) as an example of student resiliency and student agency because in writing and performing poems, students make sense of the world they live in. Students are able to inform teachers and peers of their struggles, triumphs, and determination. Moreover, through their spoken word, students have an avenue to express themselves and reflect on their conditions. We believe that through spoken word students are able to challenge concepts of deficit thinking and fight for social justice.

LAX HIGH SCHOOL AND THE PEACE CLASS

Situated approximately two miles from Los Angeles International Airport, LAX High School serves a predominantly Latino and black, low-income community. Located within walking distance from the city courthouse, the campus takes up half a city block and is closed in from the streets by the walls of the main school building and a large chain-link fence. Through our work with the PEACE class (Political Education, Art and Critical Expression), an after-school spoken word poetry club, we have witnessed how students use their poetry to speak to the realities of racism, classism, sexism, heterosexism, and other forms of oppression. We have seen how students develop a critical consciousness and commitment to social justice through reading, writing, and sharing poetry. In addition, the spoken word poetry the students create is not just for critical expression but also for critical reflection. Students are able to find their inner soul and let it out by performing their poetry.

An example of students engaging in social justice through their poetry occurred when one of our high school students informed us about a spoken word slam (a two round contest judged on a scale of 1 to 10) where youth between the ages of thirteen and nineteen from the Los Angeles area could participate. The winners of the slam would represent the Leimert Park Youth Speaks Team. Youth Speaks is an organization that promotes poetry and creative writing in schools and every year it holds an annual National Youth Speaks Contest for youth around the country to compete in a national spoken word poetry slam.

This student, who is struggling in school, found out the details of the event and made plans with us to get there. In addition, this student was able to inform his peers and motivated a few of them to join him in this educational event, sacrificing work and social activities. He and his peers were extremely excited and nervous to share their spoken word poetry that they had worked so hard to create.

The young spoken word poets bared their souls in their performances, in which they discussed issues that affected them most personally. One African American female performer compared the war in Iraq to a premature birth, and an African American male performer imagined he was a young boy in Iraq fighting for his freedom. Another African American male performer discussed the potential of his people to rise up and overcome all challenges, whereas a different African American female performer wrote a letter to the president asking why he stole the election, why we are at war, and why so many people do not have health care. A white female performer recited a poem that discussed body image and self-esteem and challenged sexist norms, while a white male performer narrated a poem in which he traveled back in time to stop the atrocities of segregation, slavery, the crusades, and the crucifixion of Jesus. In all these poems, students from diverse backgrounds acted as activists through their poetry and were able to articulate their experiences for the world to hear. Moreover, students challenged notions of deficit thinking mentioned earlier by utilizing their home language, identity, and culture as a source for inspiration, knowledge, and agency.

BACK TO THE PEACE CLASS

As we set up the classroom to better facilitate dialogue, the students slowly trickle in and as they enter the classroom they exchange hugs and hellos. We begin every classroom by having students "check-in," which means each student shares what is going on in their lives. Sometimes students have nothing to say; at other times students share deep, personal issues. Recently, students shared their concerns about the race riots between black and Latino high school students that were occurring throughout Los Angeles. The students informed us that a similar problem occurs at LAX High School every Cinco de Mayo, a Mexican holiday. Students began to share how some of them were victims of this racial violence and how most of them now refuse to come to school on this day. This particular check-in time led us to have an in-depth discussion on the causes of why such riots occur. Our black students stated several reasons why there was tension between blacks and Latinos.

One chief reason was the idea of superiority due to skin color and culture. Kareem, who seldom loses his cool, passionately stated, "They think we're inferior because we are darker! That's why when they see a group of us they run away like we tryin' to mug them!" Evan, a usually jovial young woman, exclaimed, "We just don't get each other's cultures." Our Latino students responded with similar ideas, but soft-spoken Juan also stated, "Some Latino students get upset on Cinco de Mayo because they feel Latinos only get a day, while blacks get a whole month. It's not fair!" Dave, who is always joking but today very serious, explained, "Some blacks make fun of us because we don't speak English or they make fun of our accent." Through this honest dialogue, students were provided with an opportunity to share what they felt deep inside their guts. This discussion allowed some frustrations to be let out while students moved closer to understanding each other. The next step was to write and begin the healing process. We asked students to create a poem where the black and Latino students who participated in riots were in a room together. What would they say to them?

Dre, a popular African American student, wrote a poem about a Latino and black man sitting together in a boat that was sinking. Instead of figuring out a solution, the men argued and bickered until they both drowned. Kareem wrote a poem about how the two groups are equal and share a similar culture and history. Juan discussed in his poem how the problem did not occur until high school and how in elementary school everyone played with each other. Evan articulated in her poem that instead of fighting with each other we need to attack a system that uses race to divide us. Lilly, a spirited Latina girl, wrote the following:

Kids killing kids, one after another,
In groups of kids they call their brothers
so much stealing and countless rape
Girls bound with ropes and silenced with tape
Mothers left crying for their little girls
The ones they remember with ribbons and curls
A precious life that cannot be replaced
A simple life that cannot be retraced
Why can't someone take a stand
To stop the awful destructive band
Stop all the violence, suffering and pain
So no more lives will be taken in vain
Why can't someone stop them all

So our children can grow up healthy and tall

The poem does not directly describe the racial riots, but describes brutal aspects of violence in general. Given the fact that death is ever present in our students' lives, Lilly wants students to stop being desensitized about violence. Her poem begs students to think twice about their actions because if they die, then it is the family who suffers most, not them. The poem is filled with vivid imagery such as, "bound with ropes and silenced with tape" and "remember with ribbons and curls." She paints a picture of a world where little girls are not safe and so called "brothers" force you to kill. Lilly states to students that "life cannot be replaced" and "cannot be retraced." Once it is gone, it vanishes like a person blowing out a flame. She begs at the end of her poem for "someone" to stop the violence created by students. However, that "someone" is really us (peers, educators, and community members) who need to unite and promote peace in our communities.

CONCLUSION

Students are concerned with creating a safer, better world. Students are aware of the troubles that concern our world and have ideas on improving it. Many of our students utilize their poetry as a form of protest against an unjust world. In this final poem, Dana, a shy African American girl, discusses why she writes.

"I write"
I write for those who cannot
I write for those which we've lost
I write for that shy little girl
That girl with a story to tell
About her views of the world.
I write for that boy who becomes a man
Without a man
I write from the soul
I write for that child
That crys every night
I write for my people,
My heart, my sanity.
I write to set my heart, mind,
Body and soul free
I write for those who didn't believe in me
I write for those who challenged me
I write for the pain they caused me…
I write so I don't have to struggle
And for those who did
I write to stop discrimination and segregation
Although many think we don't go through this
Anymore, because we are no longer in visible chains
I write to inspire those who need inspiration and motivation
I write so people could stop seeing things in black and white,
although everything in the world today is in color.

Dana writes to challenge those people who prejudge her and to free her mind, body, and soul. She writes for those who are oppressed and for those who have not yet found their voice. She writes for those who are most marginalized and who are the most vulnerable. Most importantly, she writes to inspire and motivate people to see diverse views, ideas, and beliefs. Throughout her poem, Dana describes folks that she views in her daily life: the little girl, the fatherless boy, the ones she lost, the whimpering child, the oppressors, and the oppressed. Dana also describes how she writes to inform those who are blind to the travesties she witnesses in her community. Finally, Dana's poem becomes a social justice text that fights for a better world.

We have witnessed through our students' spoken word poetry that students have a vision of a socially just, equitable world. Students, through their poetry, document the various predicaments and dire conditions that exist in their community. Our students become agents of change through their spoken word poetry and educate adults on what we are doing wrong and where we keep messing up. Through spoken word poetry, students become educators, shamans, and activists. As a result, our students create powerful poetry that challenges deficit thinking about low-SES minority students.

Resources

Books

Algarin, M., & Holman, B. (Eds.). (1994). *Aloud: Voices from the Nuyorican Poets' Café*. New York: Henry Holt & Co./Owl Books.

Angelsey, Z. (Ed.). (1999). *Listen Up!: Spoken word poetry*. New York: Ballantine Books.

Eleveld, M. (Ed.). (2003). *The spoken word revolution: Slam, hip hop & the poetry of a new generation*. Naperville, IL: Sourcebooks.

Mex Glazner, G. (Ed.). (2000). *Poetry slam: The competitive art of performance poetry*. San Francisco: Manic D. Press.

Reyes Rivera, L. (2001). *Bum rush the page: A def poetry jam*. New York: Random House.

YOUTH-LED RESEARCH

Rebecca L. Carver and Jonathon London

Youth-led research is a practice in which youth have primary responsibility and authority for identifying a research topic, question, and design, and then collecting information, analyzing the data, and documenting and reporting the findings and implications of their work. A driving force behind youth-led research is the belief that because youth have unique access to both their own and their peers' experiences, their voices should be privileged when exploring, interpreting, and documenting their own culture.

Because youth-led research is typically a collaborative effort, and usually involves adults who support youth by facilitating their project management and providing expertise regarding research methodology and/or the topic of concern, youth-led research can also refer to youth engagement in leadership roles during some but not all phases of a research project. The critical feature of youth participation in this collaborative research is that youth have a genuine voice and role in planning and implementing the process rather than solely taking direction from adults.

Youth-led research is typically focused on issues that are of immediate concern to young people, and that affect their well-being. Therefore it is a process in which youth play critical roles in directing the development, implementation, and application of efforts to critically assess and improve situations relating to the issues, institutions, and communities that affect their lives. Youth-led research helps young people and their adult allies grapple with pressing social issues and formulate well-researched strategies for action or advocacy on their own behalf.

Youth-led research represents a bridge between positive youth development and participatory action research. Principles of positive youth development are applied to action research while principles of action research are implemented with youth as key participants. From the theory and practice of youth development come the notions that youth are both valuable resources and works in progress (as opposed to potential adults whose identities are defined by their deficits, problems, or the risks that they face). Positive youth development also places value on youth leadership and yet recognizes the importance of creating contexts with supports and opportunities for youth to develop and express their potential. Also from the field of positive youth development come theory and practice of youth action, civic engagement, and, more recently, youth organizing, with attention to youth as social change agents in communities and institutions (such as schools).

Youth-led research extends the more participatory dimensions of the professional and academic fields of research to include youth as researchers/evaluators. Such practices reflect the valuing of local knowledge and the researcher's proximity to research subjects, and contrasts a view that truth can only be found at an objective distance. From the perspective of participatory research, research about youth could have no better researchers than youth themselves. Principal inspirations in participatory research include the popular education of Miles Horton and the Highlander Center, the notion of *conscienceiçao* (developing critical awareness and agency) from Brazilian educator Paulo Freire, and feminist and postcolonial critiques of the power inherent in the act of research. These foundational sources have influenced the practices of researchers who have trained and coached youth ethnographers. Notions of empowerment evaluation and participatory health assessment are defining a new branch of the evaluation field that focuses on the participant and the community from which they come as a means to realize social change and self-determination, as opposed to being a means to merely produce research reports.

Together, positive youth development and participatory action research define a region of theory and practice that values both the insights from the informational *products* of inquiry by engaging youth in critical inquiry, and the empowerment *processes* experienced by its participants as a result of developing and applying new analytical and communication skills. Youth-led research also seeks to benefit the broader community through the development of new leaders and through the actions taken to improve the issues identified in the research.

By engaging youth as leaders in learning communities that are conducting research on issues related to youth culture, youth-led research responds to the needs of youth to interpret and communicate their own experiences and those of their peers. In Paolo Freire's words "To exist humanely is to name the world, to change it." Youth-led research, when coupled with youth organizing, service-learning, and other modes of social action, can help young people build and actualize their capacity to name and change the world.

Youth have access to varying amounts of authority at various stages in youth-led research projects depending on the particular circumstances in which they are invited or take the initiative to become involved. The extent to which youth assume leadership roles in a research process can be thought of as having to do with both the phases of research in which the youth participate, and the amount of authority they have during these phases of the project. A youth-led research team may be exclusively comprised of youth, while another research team may have youth working in leadership roles alongside adults who consistently demonstrate that they value youth expertise and perspective. Either situation can support positive youth development while engaging youth as participants of action research.

BENEFITS OF YOUTH-LED RESEARCH

Youth-led research can be understood as having three major beneficiaries: the youth researchers, the organizations and communities that sponsor youth-led research, and the research itself.

Benefits for youth researchers include both youth experiences of agency, belonging, and empowerment and youth development of competence including skills, knowledge, and the application of both to community change. These outcomes can include the following.

- Sense of empowerment and efficacy (self as producer of knowledge and change agent)
- Sense of belonging and responsibility (to research team, to community)
- Sense of positive cultural and historical identity
- Connection to relevant community organizations and social movements
- Group leadership capacities and ability to collaborate with peers and adults
- Development of critical thinking skills
- Development of public communication skills
- Practice at data collection and analysis
- Practice in presenting research findings
- Exercise of creative expression (arts, media) skills
- Development of action planning and organizing skills
- Development of project management and production skills

- Construction of community and content area knowledge (project-specific)
- Understanding of root causes of factors effecting their lives and communities
- Development of a more critical political awareness
- Understanding of possible solutions to community problems
- Deeper understanding of community issues stemming from growth in appreciation of multiple perspectives
- Greater connection to community members and organizations
- Value and awareness of possible applications for research, evaluation, and planning in their lives and communities

Communities and organizations that sponsor youth-led research can build their own capacity through the following potential outcomes.

- Systems to utilize the youth-generated data for program, organizational, and community improvement
- Responsiveness to youth perspectives and leadership
- Increased inclusion of historically less-engaged youth
- Ability to infuse youth in an ongoing way into leadership of organization, community, and campaign
- Ability to employ youth-led research as a tool for critical inquiry to inform organizational improvement, youth leadership, community change, and other organizational goals on a sustainable basis
- Connections to other social movement organizations and resources to support implementation of youth action plans

Finally, the quality of data and analysis itself can be improved through the practices of youth-led research, for example, in the following ways:

- Research questions are focused on local youth experience and needs
- Data collection instruments (surveys, interview questions, and so on) are "youth-friendly" in format and language, and accessible to young people
- Researcher-subject relationships are more likely to be characterized by trust and respect because of the peer-to-peer quality.
- Data analysis and interpretation informed by experts in local youth culture
- Findings focus organizational change on youth experience and youth needs
- Creative reporting, which speaks to broad youth and community audiences
- Development of a more insightful and useful body of knowledge on youth culture

PURPOSES AND METHODS OF YOUTH-LED RESEARCH

One example of the purposes and methods of youth-led research comes from Sacramento, California, where the 4-H Youth Development Advisor of the University of California Cooperative Extension convened a team of youth and adult researchers to evaluate the implementation of a 4-H program called Youth Experiencing Science (YES). YES was a teen-taught, after-school, hands-on science program that had operated at 19 sites and served 2,384 elementary school children between September 1997, and June 2001. The evaluation was intended to serve both as a measure of accountability for the program funder, and as a means to improve the program. This project highlights methods and facilitation of research that engages both youth and adults in leadership roles, as well as some benefits to participants and the organization sponsoring the research.

Through a facilitated process, teen teachers, their volunteer adult coaches, and program staff conducted the evaluation. They selected two research questions: What is the impact of the curriculum on the children who participate in the after school programs? And what is the impact of the program on the teenagers who teach in the program? The group went through a process of identifying key stakeholders, program outcome goals of importance to these stakeholders, specific objectives within each goal area, and multiple sources of information that would evidence whether the program objectives that they thought were of greatest importance were being met. They went on to develop and then use data collection instruments for formal observations, performance assessments, surveying participants, and conducting focus group interviews with different stakeholder groups. Teen evaluators worked closely with adult partners on all aspects of research design, data collection, and analysis. The evaluation produced findings regarding the program's impact on teens, the program's impact on children, and the program delivery.

Facilitating the group process of youth and adult researchers shares a set of challenges with the task of facilitating any type of empowerment evaluation: It can be difficult to structure opportunities for all members to share their ideas and be effectively heard when members of the group have diverse educational backgrounds, personal experiences, concerns, interests, and talents. While youth had expertise with respect to the experiences of teen-teachers and privileged access to data on that topic, adults had privileged access to the perspectives of program staff who worked with the teen teachers. While adults were more practiced at talking with the parents of children in the program, teens were practiced at assessing the children's knowledge about the material they were teaching. The starting points for team members varied from having no prior evaluation experience and less than a high school education to having a master's degree and prior experience conducting program evaluations. Yet, youth and adults alike learned together about research methodology including concepts (e.g., triangulation and inter-rater reliability) and their application. Together, they made decisions about what data to collect, how to collect it, how to interpret findings, and what conclusions could be drawn. Both qualitative and quantitative methods were used. The final report was written by two adults and reviewed by the team.

The evaluation served its purpose of satisfying the funding agent and supplying program staff with a document that both validates their work and provides recommendations for program improvement. The team reported that they experienced personal growth, knowledge gain, and skill development through their evaluation work. In addition, team members reported changing their program delivery practices in response to what they learned from the evaluation (before the report was even written).

As the youth researchers involved in this project were also teen teachers of a hands-on science curriculum, they latched onto the science of evaluation. The teenagers began to see themselves as scientists—making observations, organizing and comparing information, communicating their findings—undergoing the same process they encouraged in the children they taught.

COMMUNITY IMPACTS OF YOUTH-LED RESEARCH

A youth-led neighborhood needs assessment project in the South of Market neighborhood of San Francisco can illustrate the power and potential of youth-led research to impact communities. Once a vibrant low-income neighborhood populated largely by a range of immigrants and merchant marines, South of Market (SOMA) in San Francisco had become the site of heated conflicts over its redevelopment and gentrification starting in the 1960s through the present. Concerned that an authentic youth voice was missing from the debates and decisions over future planning in the neighborhood, a collaborative of local youth serving organizations called SOYAC (Serving Our Youth and Community) secured funding from the San Francisco Redevelopment Authority for a youth-led community needs assessment. The project facilitator described the purpose of the project by noting, "I have worked in the neighborhood for almost five years and found it difficult to find any documentation of current youth needs and trends in the South of Market neighborhood. I knew that it was crucial that the youth voice and needs be documented so that the rest of the city would finally believe that there are children and youth in SOMA who demand a higher quality of life."

Youth in Focus, a nonprofit organization that trains underrepresented youth and adult allies in youth-led action research, evaluation, and planning, provided technical assistance for the project. Over the course of four months, a seven-member team of high school students calling itself the "Social Investigators" designed, administered, analyzed, and reported out the results of a survey on youth experiences and aspirations for the SOMA neighborhood. Based on their data, The SOYAC Social Investigators produced a detailed written report and video called "Realism."

The team used these products to advocate for SOMA youth neighborhood development and investment priorities to the San Francisco Board of Supervisors, the Redevelopment Agency, neighborhood networks, and funders. For example, SOYAC used the youth-led needs assessment as a basis for a collaborative campaign to pressure the local movie theater to offer low-priced youth tickets as a way to create more accessible youth-spaces in the neighborhood. One youth activist described this as an effort to push the movie theater to "stop displacing youth of color" through high prices and aggressive anti-loitering practices. The youth also screened their *Realism* video for the San Francisco Department of Park and Recreation to inform the design of a new neighborhood park that would respond to the needs and interests of young people. Through its research, evaluation, and creative final products, the SOYAC Youth Collective was able to give a voice to the perspectives of young people in a neighborhood that has historically been shaped by outside commercial and political forces.

Resources

Books

Adams, F., with Horton, M. (1975). *Unearthing seeds of fire: The idea of Highlander*. Winston Salem, NC: John F. Blair Publisher.

Connell, J. P., & Gambone, M. A. (1999). *Youth development in community settings: A community action framework*. Toms River, NJ: Community Action for Youth Project.

Eccles, J., & Appleton Gootman, J. (Eds.). (2002). *Community programs to promote youth development*. National Research Council and Institute of Medicine. Washington DC: National Academy Press.

Fetterman, D. M. (2001). *Foundations of empowerment evaluation*. Thousand Oaks, CA: Sage Publications.

Freire, P. (1970). *Pedagogy of the oppressed*. New York: Seabrook Press.

Ginwright, S., & James, T. (2002). From assets to agents of social change: Social justice, organizing, and youth development. *New Directions in Youth, 96*, 27–46.

Harte, R. (1997). *Children's participation: The theory and practice of involving young citizens in community development and environmental care*. New York: Earthscan.

Irby, M., Ferber, T., & Pittman, K., with Tolman, J., & Yohalem, N. (2001). *Youth action: Youth contributing to communities, communities supporting youth*. Community & Youth Development Series, Vol. 6. Takoma Park, MD: The Forum for Youth Investment, International Youth Foundation.

John Gardner Center for Youth and their Communities, Stanford University. (2002). *Youth engaged in leadership & learning (YELL): Handbook for supporting community youth researchers*. Stanford, CA: John W. Gardner Center.

Sydlo, S. J., et al. (2000). *Participatory action research curriculum for empowering youth*. Hartford, CT: The Institute for Community Research.

Youth in Focus. (2002). *Youth REP step by step: An introduction to youth-led research and evaluation*. Oakland, CA: Youth In Focus.

Articles

London, J., & Chabrán, M. (2004, Spring). Action research and social justice: Exploring the connections. *Practicing Anthropology*. Society for Applied Anthropology, Special Issue edited by M. Berg & J. Schensul. *Youth Action Research*, 28 (2), 45–50.

London, J., Zimmerman, K., & Erbstein, N. (2003, Summer). Youth-led research, evaluation and planning as youth, organizational, and community development. *New Directions in Evaluation*, special edition edited by K. Sabo on youth-led evaluation. *American Evaluation Association*, 98, 33–45.

Matysik, G. J. (2000). Involving adolescents in participatory research. *Community Youth Development*, (1), 6–10.

Zimmerman, K., & London, J. (2003, Spring). Getting to go: Building organizational capacity to engage in youth-led research, evaluation and planning. *CYD Journal: Community Youth Development*, special edition Youth Engagement in Community Evaluation Research edited by *B.* Chekoway & L. Goodyear, 4 (1), 20–25.

A MEETING OF MINDS

Shula Klinger

In this entry, we invite you to join us in the Attic. It is part of our school, the Greater Vancouver Distance Education School, but it is not a course. We learn in this space, but it's not a classroom. You can collect credit for the work you do, but it's not mandatory. You can attend without being there and you can chat without speaking. You are online. You are a writer, a reader, an avid consumer of words, a creator of fictions, and a sharer of ideas.

The Attic was created in June 2003 for readers and writers to congregate. Although hosted in the same space as a school's online courses, it was offered as a club. I expected that students would post work-in-progress and finished writing and offer each other constructive feedback. I hoped for a positive, generous environment. I hoped that the conversation would develop some momentum and that writers would feel comfortable sharing work. I opened the doors and explained to our school counselors what I hoped to do. And then I waited.

On entering the Attic for the first time, you are asked the following question: "If this space were real, what kind of chair would you bring?" This exercise serves several purposes. It gives us something to read; it lets you know that your work here is creative, since the chair need not be real; it reminds us that in this virtual space, the table is infinitely large and there is always room for everyone; finally, it gives us an opportunity to describe something about ourselves—since we can neither see nor hear each other—without actually describing our *real* selves.

The Attickers—for this is how members are known—are in Grades 8 through 12. The members are the students, myself, one member of staff at the school, and one parent who can read but not post messages. The members have shared poetry, fiction, a PowerPoint presentation, music clips, original song lyrics, audio recordings, digital artwork, drawings, and photography. We talk via group discussions, a pager, school email, MSN, and private email accounts. Between June 2003 and mid-July 2004, over 3,300 postings appeared. Over 140 of them contributed directly to this chapter. According to Molly, a relative newcomer, the Attic could be characterized as a group of "intelligent and extremely talented writers . . . whose words and wisdom I will not soon forget."

Between June and July 2004, we talked about youth culture to generate material for this chapter. I wanted to know how the members of our community perceived it, and their contributions to it. Was it connected to the "real" world of youth culture, and if so, how? I started with two questions: (1) What is youth culture? (2) Is the Attic part of it? From there, the conversation grew and spread branches in many different directions. By July 5, thirty-five separate questions had been posted or raised implicitly. Several were brought up by other Attickers. One poem, one rant, and two pieces of artwork were also shared.

WHAT IS "YOUTH CULTURE"?

The replies to these questions varied and we came back to them many times. Definitions of "youth" started literally, from "under 19" to "between 9 and 12" and moved into more abstract concepts based on one's attitudes and approach to life. The connections between youth, maturity, and social awareness were all discussed.

Katie commented ironically on the definitions of youth: "According to movie stubs, there is no such thing as youth. You go from being a child to an adult with no transition." She agreed that a person's youth depends on their outlook:

I think it depends on your level of maturity. Not the fact that you know what sex and drugs are, but the fact that you know what the dangers are in doing, or using them. Some kids think that they are as mature as a teenager, but in actuality, they obviously don't know what teenage hood / young adult living is like.

Molly gave some examples. She said that there are "many definitions [of youth culture]. I guess the average North American youth culture right now is the rap, gangster type; but. . . there's also the skateboarding type. Although those two seem to be the big cultures right now, there are many more types."

Anja agreed that "being a youth is much more mental than it is physical." She went on: "you shouldn't be turning to a mirror to decide whether you're a youth or an adult." Following another conversation, Molly returned to these questions. In the end, she agreed with Elisha, Anja, and Katie that there is much in youth culture that is unsettling, calling it "a vicious, back-stabbing world." Molly talked about

. . . a very confused society, strongly lacking in morals and direction. The stupidity of many youths astounds me. They give no thought to their future, only trying to see how many girls they can get, or how many boys they can get to notice them. I know this may sound harsh and of course it does not apply to all youth but there is a group, one which I used to know well, who spend their whole lives drinking, smoking, and basically wasting their minds. I personally never took part in this group, but I have many friends who have.

Toward the end of our conversation, Katie characterized youth culture as a period in which we do "stupid, irresponsible things . . . you never really wanted to do," as a result of peer pressure. Anja referred to it humorously as "a loathsome beast" compared to the environment we were in.

Anja took up the theme of confusion later on. Gradually, youth culture was being described as a period of decision-making amidst many conflicting ideas, finding labels to stick on people, on our relationships, experiences, and perceptions of the world. According to Elisha, many of these labels are based on superficiality:

We tend to judge each other on things like clothing, speech, musical taste, the list goes on and on . . . the color of your eye-shadow, whether your mascara's clumping . . . *oh my gosh? Did that girl just say*

persnickety? Like oh my gosh, what does that mean? She must be a freak.
Freak.

BELONGING AND "FITTING IN"

In defining "youth culture" (a label in itself), I came to see that the notion of "belonging" affected all the other labels and pressures we experience as youth. In order to determine whether or not you fit in, you have to know what *fitting in* means. In thinking about how one "fits in," we talked about the elements Elisha mentioned above, as well as the language we use. Sammi said she wouldn't "fit"

> because my dress is so eccentric (Thank you Jenn, for that LOVELY word) and I listen to all types of music, but no rap. . . . A bit of the stuff that Jenn has played for us . . . . [Thank you again Jenn, for opening my mind up a bit more then it was before (my mind is getting so stretched and opened, it's going to rip)]

Molly said that she "sort of" fit in, by virtue of her clothes, but like Katie, Jenn was firm about her position:

> I don't really subscribe to the mainstream idea of what's popular or cool. . . . If I like stuff that's popular, I'm not afraid to admit it I like it because it appeals to me, not because someone tells me to. And if I like something that isn't popular, well, the same thing applies.

As the Attickers made clear, many people who are in the age *defined by* "youth" *don't* feel part of "youth culture." In a private exchange, I asked Felicia about the element of belonging. She replied,

> I think loneliness is a big theme in youth culture. Everyone wants to feel like they're a part of something. That people care, and accept them for who they are. But the thing about growing up is you're constantly changing, things don't stay the same.

Like Elisha, Anja didn't think her language use placed her in the heart of youth culture, either. Asked where teen slang came from, she replied: "I have no idea. This could be (A) because I'm not exactly smack dab right in the middle of the social scene or (B) because I don't pay enough attention."

Like the question of "do we fit?" the question of how adults treat young people was soon addressed: "A *youth* may, unfortunately, to some, automatically be associated with immaturity, especially nowadays. There are devastating amounts of stereotyping lately against teenagers." (Anja) We continued talking about human frailty, about our desire to generalize, to find categories and labels for everything we do and are. Anja went on to argue that it's sad that it should be surprising that most teenagers are opinionated, bright, and INDIVIDUAL. I know a lot of "youths" who almost see their ages as a character flaw! They feel that when people (mainly those older than them) learn their age, they don't take what they say seriously and don't respect their thoughts and ideas as much as they would respect an "adult's" ideas.

The boundaries between youth and adulthood cannot be ignored. According to Katie, Jenn, and Anja, discrimination against young people reminds them of these boundaries all the time. Jenn told us about "a sign in a dollar store I pass on the way to the post office. It says: No More Than Two Teenagers At A Time." In reply, I asked, "If the Attic had a door and you could hang a sign on it, what would it say?" Sammi responded with a multicolored poem

DAYDREAMERS WATCH FOR THE JAILGUARDS
LOOK OUT FOR THE DOOR
SCREAM FOR HELP WITH YOUR CHAIR
DAYDREAMERS AT WORK
SHHH.... LOUD NOISES AHEAD
SERIOUS DEBATES THIS WAY
NO PASSING, UNLESS A CREATIVE MIND LURKS
REMEMBER: I FORGET
DON'T FORGET YOUR CUP(S) AND PLATE(S)
DON'T FORGET!

WHAT DID YOU SAY?

The second round of questions I asked were based on my own responses. I was thinking about culture as a recipe and wondering what the ingredients would be. As we have seen language use came up early on. What kinds of language are used in the Attic? Molly said that she didn't use "like" in the Attic "because I always think about what I'm typing. I think we don't really use slang in the Attic because we have better ways of expressing ourselves with more sophisticated words." Andrea agreed that certain kinds of language use are fitting in certain kinds of environments:

I think the Attic is slang-free [for the most part] because (1) I don't think people should type in slang, unless you're on MSN or the likes, of course, because then when you come to write actual important things like reports or essays you fall back on your writing habits. And (2) because like Molly said, there are better ways to express oneself. Especially when you have time to really think about what you are going to say, unlike speech.

I answered Andrea's thoughtful posting with an ironic comment on my British passport:

Hello there, Miss Andrea! *pushes delicately painted cup across table*
As you can see, I am following Miss Molly's posting about our extraordinary sophistication and have brought us some Early Grey tea. . .

crooks little finger and sips tea delicately

I wondered aloud, "What would happen to someone who wanted to use gangsta rap-style language in the Attic? What kind of reception would they get?" Andrea told me that they'd be "received very cordially" and Molly agreed, in spite of her skepticism about "finding any Charles-Dickens-reading, poetry-writing gangstas out there." So far, it seems that while there are certain customs for communication in the Attic, as in any culture, the way we speak doesn't necessarily mean that we will be judged—or labeled—for it.

In a "typing rampage," Sammi continued the thread, contemplating the Attic's boundaries. "I don't think that we have a type of person thingy that you have to be in order to be in the Attic . . . of course, you would have to be a dreamer, a writer, a friendly face, an EXCELLENT baker ~that's a biggy, right there!~ " She closed with an ironic wink, "Maybe I should start writing up a nice formal page on 'The Guidelines' hahaha. . . ."

On the subject of "fitting in" with teen slang, Jenn said that she doesn't use much "traditional" slang. However, she said that she uses Internet slang and gave us a lesson in Internet irony. "For example, 1337: some people who talk with that actually think it's cool, while others use 1337 to mock people like that." She gave an example from "a post I made below: '(xkyuz muh 1337 5p33l< plz!!!! lolololol)' The 1337 was added to make fun of its use. . . . Look ma, I'm dissecting my speech!"

Molly told us about an article she'd read describing "how the hip hop industry is used to sell and promote shoes, clothing, drinks, to youth." I found this idea of "buying culture" interesting, and replied by offering "brand new, shiny, Attic brand, platform sneakers with added bounce!" I wondered what everyone thought about advertising the Attic. If someone weren't a member, could they be part of our community simply by buying a pair of shoes and a logo?

Jenn claimed to have grabbed a pair right away, prancing around in her shiny new Attic brand platform runners. Sammi did, too, but the jury is still out on whether or not the Attic should be advertised. Like Anja, Katie said, "I respect people who have their own individuality over those who run with the pack. . . . I don't like being a puppet, nor do I like being a walking billboard." This idea of hanging signs and attaching labels to ourselves returned time and again.

ARE WE COOL YET?

Our conversation drifted from the language we use, the clothes we wear and whether or not we "fit in," to a collective pondering of what it means to be "cool." From the emerging discussion, it was clear that *cool*, like beauty, is a subjective thing. Sammi argued that "you're only cool if you think you are cool . . . if other people think we are dorks . . . then we are . . . to them . . . but I think that we are cool . . . so we are." Molly added, "We know we're cool, but we don't really care if other people think we're cool. But the people who think they're so cool, they *do care* if other people think they're cool, which makes them not cool. Anyone get what I'm saying?"

But what *is* "cool"? Molly said that "cool is being in that top group, the good-looking, popular group that everyone else is afraid of (not the right word for us, but the right one for a majority of people). . . . We're not in the group because we're cool. We're here because we all love reading and writing."

Next, I asked the Attickers: "How much is "body image" a part of youth culture? Who tells us what is a "good" way to look and what isn't?" The answers were unambiguous and mixed the topic of "body image" with "fashion statements." Everyone agreed that "body image has a lot to do with youth culture" (Sammi). Likewise, all of the comments about body image argued that this was unfortunate, if not ridiculous. From Sammi again, "people shouldn't focus so much on what people look like, but what their attitude and personality is . . . you shouldn't have to go as far as almost killing yourself to look good."

According to Andrea, the pressure to conform comes from the media: "The media has made youth culture so they will use this to manipulate kids into what is most profitable for them. Body image falls under that category, as Sammi already stated, because they earn thousands, if not millions, every single year from these all these 'things' to make you achieve THE look." Sammi added that fashion is purely subjective and that our peers exert a great deal of pressure on us. Andrea built on Sammi's comments with this: "There is a huge abyss between what should be and what is. Who *should* tell us how to look? Ourselves and the doctor. Who *does*? The media."

We then moved on to the question of body image in the Attic. Sammi thought that it "is a personality thing . . . because a lot of us haven't met each other in person." Andrea continued, "I don't really think about it. I concentrate on what they have to say instead. I find it better that way because then you drop the clichés and actually meet the person." This was the point where the title of this chapter came to me: we're enjoying a meeting of minds without actually meeting in person.

Molly and Katie joined the conversation, arguing that "Body image is probably the biggest part of youth culture. It seems to affect everything; what clothing you wear, who you hang out with, and especially your self confidence level." (Molly). This is where she pointed to the first significant difference between life inside the Attic and life in the world: "One of the greatest things about the Attic is, no one judges anyone else. Everyone can speak their minds freely, wear whatever they want, basically just be themselves. I agree with Sammi. Even if we do meet another Atticker, it just adds a friendly face to the post."

Katie's contribution to the "body image" theme was a colorful oration, building on and summarizing the themes and contradictions raised so far: peer pressure, conformity and the media, and interior and exterior beauty.

> **Body image** and **the media** fit together like **milk and cookies**, although, according to the media, you <u>shouldn't eat cookies</u>, because they will make you **fat**. I, personally am so tired of MTV, and magazines, and TV saying that there is only **one kind of beatiful**. <u>**Barbie** *is what beauty is*</u>. There are little girls who don't think they are pretty because they have *brown hair*. I have a number of friends who have *starved themselves* to become **thin**(ner) just so that **boys** will "date" them. So many people are so **shallow**. They don't "like" each other for **wonderful personalities**, or their **beliefs**, or for **being smart**, or even a **nice, compassionate** person. They "like" each other for their **looks**, the **clothes** they wear, and even the **people who they hang** around with. How is it that "we" as a people are *<u>controlled</u>* by the clothes other people are wearing on TV? **How is it that half the population of girls in 1 school have the same jackets, the same pants, and the same color hair?** (*and its not natural?*) I am **not trying** to generalize people, but its very hard not to, when I walk down the street and <u>every guy I see is wearing pants 20 sizes too big</u>, and <u>girls wearing the same jacket 20 sizes too small</u>.

> I know it's become a **cliché**, but Britney Spears and Christina Aguliara (?) have become **role models** for 6 and 7 year olds, and it has become okay for these little girls to look up to these "women" who are wearing **skimpy little pieces of clothing** (if you can even call them that) and now they want to wear them too.

> The media has so much control over teenagers, and even adults, its **unbelievable**. Over the last few years everyone has decided to **become the same**. The media is breeding robots and the "robots" don't realize that they are just falling under a spell called "fashion".

Anja followed with a powerful, 700-word posting. In it, she raises the themes of democracy, diversity, tolerance, and free speech:

> There is a common characteristic in everyone I look up to . . . they don't fit in with the tight standards of the world. They break through some invisible veil and take our breath away. While the rest of us try to live within the confines of some 'comfort zone' we can barely even identify, they do the opposite. These one-in-a-million people work to

expand our minds instead of clench them into perfectly round molds, they WANT to make us question our morals, sharpen our senses. . . . To me, people like this, journalists, activists, poets, actors, singers, doctors, gymnasts (ANYONE) are as invaluable as they are diverse . . . they refuse to settle into the old "only human" niche . . . they rise above and get as close as ever to conquering the world.

Sadly, some of these extraordinary folk (who are really only their own kind of ordinary) are sometimes rejected . . . out of fear, pure and simple. It's somehow atrocious to see someone carefully breaking the rules or pushing a sort of change. It stupefies the public . . . which in turn stupefies me because since when did speaking our minds become a heinous act? Nowadays . . . it's more of a lost art than anything else. That fact alone should be shocking. . . . Worst of all, when someone tries to rekindle the "lost art," it's perceived as a vulgar act of irrelevant revenge or aggression . . . leading to violence, hate and well, sometimes lawsuits. Shouldn't this foul reaction be more "appalling" than a person merely stating a rare opinion? Not in today's world . . . a "rare" opinion seems to be a warped representation of an "un-acceptable" opinion, or a "disgustingly offensive" opinion just because it's not the majority.

No wonder some of the youth of today are totally confused. How can we form opinions (I mean HONEST ones) when there is pressure leaking in from all sides?

Enter, the Attic.

There is such a . . . harmony here. And it's plain to see that we all have different opinions, different personalities and probably one of the few similarities between each and every one of us is a love of all things creative. And somehow, any contradictory thoughts or outlooks... are accepted and taken into consideration . . . with a little imagination on the side. That, to me, is how Attic culture is different from youth culture in general. There is no pressure here . . . heh, it's actually such a warm and flexible place that even bad spellers like myself aren't forced to use spell check! This is a place of encouragement . . . instead of judgment.

The Attic . . . is such an . . . easy . . . place to be a part of. You're allowed to be yourself. You're allowed to be as random and odd as you see fit (thank god for that!) . . . and this, for lack of a better word (s), "absence of constrictions" makes for one of the most comfortable atmospheres I've ever been in. It's a little bizarre, since no two of us "picture" the Attic the same . . . to some it's a meeting room in the physical sense, to others a lazy, somewhat messy, place and to others a warm haven overflowing with chairs and books.

Elisha responded generously with "Wow. . . . I thoroughly enjoyed that post. You're very articulate." She replied in detail, bringing us back to the topic of teen language use with a comment on human frailty:

> *There is such a . . . harmony here.* That's very true. There is very little dissent among the ranks here. Generally speaking, everybody seems to get along just fine. Part of that, naturally, is because . . . we aren't encouraged to discuss topics which could arouse heated debate or opinion. Everybody has expectations that they judge people by. Some of us try to harbor as few expectations as possible, but as human beings bias is an inevitability. . . .

> Here in the Attic we have a primary goal, a focus, something which unites us all and when we come here we are all immediately on a level playing field of sorts, if you consider the fact that we all enjoy the written word, that we're all in correspondence, and that we all wanted to commune with other people sharing those same qualities. The difference between the Attic and the youth culture of the "outside world" is that in here we all know at least one intrinsic thing about each other, and that is that we have, as Anja said so beautifully: "a love of all things creative."

> In the "outside world" media and society play an enormous part in the collective expectations of today's youth and in turn that affects how we judge people in our first impressions. Take for instance the changing trends in fashion. The way really long scarves have gone in and out of fashion like THAT [snaps fingers], the way thongs seem to have acquired more staying power -much to my chagrin-, the way blonde will probably forever be in, and yet forever be considered an attribute engendering a lack of intelligence. And that's just appearance . . . having been out of the traditional school system for two years . . . I realize that two teenagers could have an entire conversation in front of me and I would have NO idea what they're talking about.

While I was soaking up this wonderful writing and the unexpected directions our conversation had taken, I asked "Does a love of 'all things creative' make a person more tolerant? Is there a connection between creativity, open-mindedness, and a lack of judgment?" Elisha replied, continuing her thoughts on tolerance and human frailty:

> I would have to say yes. I think it has to do with priorities. People who are creatively inclined are often consumed by it. When people place a

lot of emphasis on art they're obviously placing less emphasis somewhere else, ie: popularity. I think, however, that people are doomed to judge others, that's just a fact, it's how we deal with the judgment afterwards. Some people keep their judgments and find reasons to enforce them, others discard their judgments and accept the person.

SCHOOL, HOME, AND CREATIVE FREEDOM

Since food is one element of many cultures, I asked the members what they thought of our own, food-oriented culture. Here, we have shared virtual cookies, homemade lemonade, hot chocolate, tea, and non-alcoholic fruit punch. Jenn explained, "it has everything to do with the friendly, easygoing atmosphere we have going here. . . . The Attic is a very warm, homey place ... so we reflect that with our actions. We can't give each other real refreshments, so virtual ones have to suffice. Speaking of which, does anyone want some iced coffee? It's very good."

Nodding "I'd love some," I asked how the Attic could be "warm and homey" when it is part of a school? *Or is it?* Sammi replied immediately with, "I don't ever think 'this is a link off of my school page. . . . '" Jenn's response was a strong one:

The Attic? *School?!!* Perish the thought! It may be located in D2L, and Shula may be a GVDES staff member, but. . . . Despite evidence to the contrary, I can't think of it as part of school. It isn't. School is traditionally a place where they try to cram info into your heads, give you horrible deadlines, and you have no freedom, creative or otherwise.

The Attic, on the other hand, is where dreams are born. Actually, I think it's more like the place where dreamers run wild. I think that since we're all writers, and people who enjoy reading, we can just relax and have a good time. We can have serious discussions like this, be all-out silly, or somewhere in between. We're perfect company for each other. The Attic is our Muse.

In my imagination, I had always seen the Attic as a place—never a personification. I appreciated the change of metaphor.

Later, in a discussion outside the Attic, Jenn kindly teased a new student who had addressed me as "Ms. Klinger." She pointed out that unlike teachers in public schools, I use my first name. This particular label shows that my role and that of a teacher are quite different. Later on, Anja argued that "this is outside school, completely separate from the stress of new modules, missing books, late homework, and the like. There are no due dates, no pressures." She went on:

Moderators hold a completely different kind of authority than teachers. I've known teachers who have been beyond supportive in school and distance education (ESPECIALLY distance education). . . . Nevertheless, it's almost as if they're wearing a sign over their heads that says "teacher." I haven't really pinned ANYTHING over Shula's head.

This posting reminded me of her earlier comment, in which she said she didn't like labels of any kind; of Katie's posting, where she argued that "it is extremely cynical to generalize and put 'us' all in a package"; and of Jenn and Sammi's comments about signs warning groups of teenagers to enter stores separately. It made me wonder if—apart from the preoccupation with body image—this act of labelling ideas and relationships and storing them in different boxes was *the* main element in one's experience of "youth culture." Anja continued,

In a community like the Attic it does not feel like "school." While [teachers] can be as helpful and welcoming as a moderator/club leader, etc, they will always obviously be concerned with education. A moderator's job is to make the students feel comfortable rather than mail them their report cards on time.

This is where Jenn jumped in to explain her metaphor for the Attic, the Muse:

I've never been able to visualize the Attic as a room. A place, yes, but not a room. Sometimes I'll "climb up the Attic stairs carrying a hoard of books," and other times I'll "hide behind a bookself," but none of that is actually what's there (here?). I was going to put "real," but I didn't think that was an appropriate word to use—it would be like saying that the Attic doesn't actually exist.

The notion of the Attic is fluid—it changes to suits our purposes, and then that idea disappears into the abyss when we're through with it . . . There's no other way that we could be sipping lemonade on lawn-chairs one minute, be in space the next, and before we know it, back sitting on our cozy chairs beside the fire. A fantastical place like the Attic cannot be a single static room.

Toward the end, I asked the Attickers if they had conversations about youth culture with others. Andrea said she tried to, but "most of my friends aren't the kind of people you can talk to about these things." Molly said she had, but while her peers didn't always act according to the beliefs they professed to hold, the Attickers were sincere and serious:

Everyone is honest and acts like themselves. I know that none of you are going to say something and then contradict yourself right away. I say this with such assurance because, even though I've never met any of you, I know that you . . . have strong morals and opinions that you won't change just because someone else says they're not "cool" or the "in" thing.

CONCLUSION

The conversation was a marvelous way to find out how the Attic was perceived by its members and how it fitted in with the other aspects of their lives; if indeed, it was separate from everything else or connected in some way, in spite of being online, disembodied and quite different from other school activities online. The Attickers considered our space to be homey but more formal than a chat environment (where slang might be used). Here, they could enjoy semi-anonymous online communication, an environment where one's age does not show or can be concealed (Anja).

I learned a lot about what was important to our small community and what values we hold. Strength of character and the ability to form one's own opinions seemed to top the list. Clearly, we were hanging together without any conflicts breaking out, so it was wonderful to hear from our members on how they thought this had come to be. I also had a chance to think through some big questions myself:

I know that I could picture you, the real you, when I type a posting to you but I don't. In my mind's eye I picture your messages and the fonts / colors / symbols you use. . . . I imagine your sense of humour and your puns; your writing style / imagery; some of the things you claim to be doing (like hiding behind furniture or playing with water pistols) but I hardly ever think of you all as physical beings.

So we hung out, enjoyed some fictitious drinks, and talked about issues that more than one contributor said they felt "very strongly" about. I found the exchanges inspiring and a wonderful education for next year. I certainly have a much better sense of what matters to our members and how clearly they think about and articulate their beliefs and principles. I learned how one can shift and stretch the metaphorical walls we inhabit. I know that I cannot impose specific conversation topics on future members, but I can definitely promote the atmosphere that our current members have created.

How do we characterize the "atmosphere"? This conversation brought out some powerful contradictions in the culture we consider to be that of "youth": first and foremost, the pressure to conform vs. the freedom to create; the obsession with the body vs. the body-less environment of the Attic; diversity and tolerance vs. judgment; belonging vs. exclusion; room to dream vs. the constraints of public education; resiliency vs. vulnerability in the face of powerful peer pressure.

I have been overwhelmed by the intellect, eloquence, and heart in this place. Disembodied or not, online or "real": however you define it, this Attic has come to be a place of true inspiration, a meeting of minds for those who would ask questions; inquisitive, creative spirits who are always looking for the right word to match the thought and the people with whom they can share them. I learned that the Attic's name is a room with a roof but it's also a Muse, a mythical person (Jenn) and a correspondence (Elisha). It's a place we inhabit but it's also a being that inspires us, whom we have created with our conversation. Next year, who knows what it will become. Let's wait and see.

Note

This chapter was made possible by the amazing participation of: Felicia D'Amato, Molly Henry, Katie Huie, Sammi Ingram, Jennifer Kendall, Caitlin Lahue, Anja Miskin, Andrea Pantoja, and Elisha Smirfitt.

THE AESTHETIC DIMENSION OF YOUTH CULTURE EDUCATION

Leila E. Villaverde

"Aesthetics," to some, is an outdated term, a concept used to discuss the elite value of the arts. Aesthetics is the branch of philosophy that traditionally explores and defines beauty, specifically investigating cultural artifacts that appeal to the senses. Yet if repositioned or defined as a way of knowing about all that encompasses the visual and creative decisions and recognitions we engage in daily, the term "aesthetics" creates a transformative dimension in youth culture education. This essay explores aesthetics as a framework for understanding the desire to express the self through the arts, music, fashion, body art, books, magazines, demeanor, attitudes, and activities, as well as using aesthetics to understand visual culture and visual literacy.

Of most interest for the twenty-first century is the study of beauty and pleasure across cultures. Cultures define the arts and aesthetics differently, ranging from distinct theories outside of everyday living to complete integration into the way of life. Exploring a multicultural aesthetics provides greater opportunities for youth to relate and connect to the arts, visual culture, image, text, sound, dance, and experiences where they deepen the meaning-making process as their identities are crafted and negotiated. In true postmodern fashion, youth today sample bits, pieces, and symbols of history, contemporize them, and seek connections to a past that will hopefully afford some clarity to the present. Why not cross cultural borders in search for connections, similarities, and struggles through what it is like for young people to define and exercise who they are in the world?

MARKING THE SELF SELF-EXPRESSION

Why do we crave individuality, or desire to stand out, be special, or be unique, in order to fit in or feel accepted? How does the self become the canvas for many creative or artistic ideas, a playground to express how we feel, who we are, what we are into, what we believe, want to exhibit or conceal? We develop a particular aesthetic or style as we craft our own identities. Seldom do we think of these decisions as aesthetic ones or choices informed by the principles of art and design. Yet day after day we make choices and exert our preference of what looks better or feels better or is more appropriate for a specific event or context. We are an aesthetic people, inundated by the visual, sensual, auditory, and kinesthetic, nonetheless we are in constant denial of this unless we adopt an artistic inclination from early on. Youth culture is no different, with one exception; aesthetic decisions seem to mark very specific temporal boundaries of the self. Youth undergo great experimentation to be "different" or exert equal commitment to be the "same." Voice is articulated in all sorts of visual, textual, and sonic literacies. What is worn and how, what music is on ipods, what books are in backpacks or pockets, what language or lingo is used provides connective tissue to a larger culture that cuts across age and ambivalence of youth and young adulthood.

The self is an agent armed with a mirror, an agent in the sense that he or she is active, interacting in the multiple contexts one negotiates daily (school, family, friends, work, recreation, and so on), sometimes undercover or in the open, with a mirror as an instrument of both recognition and reflection pointing to youth's precarious public/social role, representing the future and past simultaneously. Youth often remind adults of who they used to be or how they were when they were young, inciting both pleasurable nostalgia—even melancholy—and fear and trepidation that youth are bound to repeat similar mistakes. The mirror is used in two ways, as a reflective surface that transplants adults into the past also deterring adults from seeing youth for who they are, not who the adult used to be. The mirror can also be used by youth as an instrument for recognition both for the self and others. They can instigate a reality check (of sorts) for adults and they can explore or affirm parts of who they are. In other words the mirror is a productive tool for dealing with the space between being a child and an adult. As an agent the self is an active participant in, and creator of, the surrounding environment; thus self-expression is not a leisure activity but necessary in the construction of identity.

Self-expression is the only way in which to explore what makes us who we are, a fruitful method to do research, and to be socially engaged. Expression is a performance of voice, intellect, and emotion, consequently essential in the quality of human life; thus the process is equally important to the product, result, or outcome. The ability to express one's thoughts, ideas, emotions, or curiosities works as the impetus for inquiry, critical questioning, and awareness. Instead of pathologizing self-expression, a tenet within youth culture education is to use it as an educational space for deepening the learning experience and engaging the student in a quality meaning-making process. Self-expression then has richer purposes than just self-referential ones, no longer is self-expression couched within abstract individualism, but rather within a social, historical, and political consciousness. In search for styles or things to appropriate from previous eras, youth increase their sense of ownership and understanding by contextualizing their inquiries and knowledge of these times in history, movements, or subcultures as they make present and future aesthetic choices. Self-expression is but an attempt to connect, to be part of something larger than the self, in the here and now. Seldom is this type of expression regarded with such research potential, yet it seems logical to use an existent curiosity and practice to augment youth's agency. Identity does not have to be defined by the acquisition of external material, but rather recognized through a process of introspection that produces a certain being awake to the self, other, and society.

VISUAL CULTURE AND VISUAL LITERACY

Visual culture is a term used to encompass not only traditional definitions of what is considered art, but also imagery created through any media including excluded art forms and groups. Visual culture provides a more generic descriptor for the pervasive use of imagery in many cultures and provides a way to discuss that, which is not labeled as art, yet indicates the existence of creativity and aesthetic considerations. It explores the ways in which our lives are influenced by exposure to, contact with, consumption of visual imagery and seeks to develop a critical awareness of its functions and implications. The United States is saturated with visual information, consequently it is important to study the practices, phenomena, belief systems, norms, literacy, and mores of its visual culture.

In addition visual images create a language and developing a visual literacy establishes the ability to understand and produce visual communications. Being fluent in visual literacy becomes extremely useful for navigating the visual codes in our culture. Through this literacy youth add to the ways in which they may already analyze and define art, music, fashion, books, magazines, zines, Web sites, comic books, performances, movies, and experiences. Of additional importance is what youth can learn from these visual encounters, in what ways, investigating their perceptions and interpretations. Visual literacy is the language through which visual culture is politicized, is historical, and individual identity is constructed or contested. Visual information can serve as an interdisciplinary site inviting research, critical inquiry, and multiple, often opposing perspectives. Throughout history elements of visual culture have represented the public consciousness and the countercultural voice of a time, group, and geographic location, therefore visual culture can be a prime conduit for curiosities, questions, and possibilities. Sometimes the familiar, mundane, or taken for granted can present new ways to communicate, judge, and respond to the world or immediate location.

PRACTICES OF LOOKING

How we look and what we look at, matters. When we look we code and decode the information we perceive and interpret. We actively evaluate our surrounding and make instant decisions on what will sustain our attention, what we will comment on, what will upset us or cheer us up. Yet this is only based upon what we can actually process in the few seconds available in our minds to register and process the information around us. To develop the ways we see and to raise our consciousness about what we see and why increases what we may be sensitive to and therefore transforms our ways of knowing.

Our environment influences and constructs the methods and practices of looking. The advertisements, magazines, billboards, posters, and architecture all arrange their audience in particular positions. These visual artifacts are created to speak to, engage, persuade, or inform us. Our gaze (the way we look, the direction we look, the perspective we take in looking) is thus formed by the intents and expectations of the cultural artifacts that surround us on a daily basis as we go to school, to work, to meet our friends, to shop, to the movies, to museums, to catch the train or subway or bus, to drive or ride, and so on. The advertisements, public service billboards and posters, and signs position us in specific ways in order to structure how we relate to the information presented. Simultaneously we look back, we modify our gaze as a result of our own perceptions of the world, subsequently debunking the unidirectional superhighway of consumption. The gaze, our look, how we engage by seeing is multidirectional and can both consume or reject, agree or disagree, condone or resist. In actuality we have greater say so over what we choose to respond to, act upon, be involved with, care about, and look at. Our lives are so inundated by visual elements that many times we overlook all the information because we are simply overwhelmed. The pervasiveness of the visual does not automatically translate into accessibility, creating the need to produce a way of knowing distinctive to the twenty-first century, one where the development of a visual literacy is prioritized, one that researches the obvious, implied, excluded, and possible.

CROSS-CULTURAL AESTHETICS

In offering different ways to define aesthetics, and particularly searching for perspectives that offer new methodologies for analyzing visual culture, I turn to both Navajo and Japanese aesthetics. Both offer a much more integrated approach to understanding the impact and significance of the visual arts, and aesthetics in daily life.

Navajo aesthetics focuses on the holistic experience, on being aware of one's surrounding, reflecting on nature, and letting one's perception influence the external world. The objective is to "to walk (live) in beauty." "Navajos conceive thought to be an active and effective force that can influence the material and spiritual worlds." The importance is placed on the concept of balance, given that any entity encompasses juxtapositions at any given point, which produces the continuous evolution and movement necessary reflective of the natural tempo of life. This perspective acknowledges interaction as a prime factor in the construction of identity and meaning. We benefit from being in relationships with people, culture, places, ideas, and value systems. Any entity needs other entities to survive. If we deepen our awareness and understanding of how we relate and connect to other things and people from day to day, we grow more keenly aware of those things we take for granted as we create routines. We may then regard beauty as an oddity or as so pervasive or relative that it loses meaning. Seldom do we interrogate where the odd, forthright, courageous is just as engaging and becoming, but may not be defined as "beautiful" by the majority of people experiencing or viewing it. An obvious and common example is when people affirm, "there is beauty in the grotesque." Whether one can readily agree or not is irrelevant, the point is what the Navajos believe: Beauty is not about the external representation, but the internal substance, and it is about the greater purpose of that experience, object, or person in the whole system of life. The appreciation for life, death, and everything in between shifts the perception from attending to an end product to instead carefully examining the process.

Japanese aesthetics regards the art in life, in the everyday. It is believed a person can only transcend the material or disingenuous trappings of the world by replacing passions and consciousness with an intuitive and spontaneous acceptance of the universe. This acceptance cannot be absent of critical analysis and reflection, without it you run the risk of over romanti-cizing the universe and your place in it. Yet the implication of this aesthetic is the conditional suspension of rash, reactionary, unprocessed judgment. It cautions us to the myriad of ways in which we can jump to conclusions or judgments about what is correct, appropriate, desired, expected, accepted, or not. In addition, central to Japanese aesthetics is *wabi-sabi*, a significant type of beauty or artfulness that celebrates the rustic, simple, overlooked, irregular minor details of everyday life. It privileges the disorder and flux, sees them as inevitable, and allows order and stability to develop from within as opposed to from without. Other juxtapositions, such as being and vitality, unity and diversity, face-to-face encounters, and stillness are neces-sary, similar to Navajo aesthetics, for the sustenance of any system.

Both of these aesthetic perspectives offer great possibility in rethink-ing not only how we define aesthetics, but also, more importantly, how youth can use them to make life and culture more meaningful. For youth this requires a more significant engagement with who they are, with who others are, with their surroundings, and with ways of think-ing, as opposed to the often superficial, perpetual sampling of a multi-tude of experiences and interests. The aesthetic choices youth make in their lives, in regards to friends, lifestyles, and their search for belong-ing can be qualitatively furthered and appreciated through our compre-hension of visual culture, visual literacies, practices of looking, and cross-cultural perspectives.

Resources

Anderson, R. L. (2004). *Calliope's sisters: A comparative study of philosophies of art* (2nd ed.). Upper Saddle River, NJ: Pearson Publishing.

Sturken, M., & Cartwright, L. (2002). *Practices of looking: An introduction to visual culture*. New York: Oxford Press.

PUNK PERFORMANCES AT LIBERTY HIGH SCHOOL

Rebecca Skulnick

While research projects have studied the influence of popular culture on mainstream public schools, less research has focused on the influence of popular culture in anti-mainstream communities such as the youth in the hippie movement of the past and goth movement of the present. I spent one school year engaging with the youth culture of Liberty High School, aiming to understand how students respond to popular culture in a school of students who might, in a public school, be considered outsiders. This essay investigates not only how students were able to relate to popular culture, but how this particular school's physical and intellectual spaces enabled students to critique, rather than simply consume, popular culture.

SETTING: LIBERTY HIGH SCHOOL

Before identifying how spaces were created so that students could resist popular culture's influences, it is important to understand the uniqueness of Liberty High School. Liberty maintains its status as an independent, rather than public, school in order to, ultimately, avoid the restrictions placed on schools by the standardized testing movement. However, this independent school runs more like a socialist institution than a private school: The students are the janitors and cooks, parents volunteer to act as maintenance people and electricians, and the school's funding efforts come from the grant-writing efforts of curricular specialists. In fact, the school operates on a sliding-scale tuition, and many families who cannot pay full tuition work for the school or barter their services.

Approximately 15 percent of the students are full-tuition students. At the high school, a selection of students is founded on a premise of plurality. Students and teachers make up an interview team devoted to finding students who would best fulfill and be fulfilled by the strengths and weaknesses of Liberty.

In addition, because Liberty is a "First Amendment School" students are afforded more freedom than their public school peers and there is no dress code. In fact, rather than establishing rules in order to contain conduct, students and teachers negotiate rules with each other. Teachers and students are called by their first names and the school ethos calls for each to treat each other like equally important members of the Liberty community.

As a subcultural community, Liberty students make up a community of marginalized students who reject the influences of popular culture. However, Liberty students still live in the greater society of the United States, and their rejection of popular culture is still indebted to the major tenets of popular culture: beauty, technology, and consumerism. Gans, an American Studies scholar on popular culture, argues that the younger the audience, the more free they are to consumer culture as "omnivores," ravishing everything within their grasp whether it seems worthy of their attention or not. However, he also argues that popular culture gives youth culture alternative choices of behavior, and therefore allows, rather than disallows, for personal freedom. The paradox of these two statements reflects the irony that, while the Liberty School allows its students freedoms, its students still seem compelled to imitate each other's style. Much like the fictionalized academy for mutants in the popular film *X-Men*, Liberty is a school that actively opposes the consumption of popular culture and informs an alternative myth based on difference from the majority. Liberty is like Xaviar Academy of *X-Men* in that it provides students a place to be different and thrive in this difference. However, since the marker of a mutant is much more blatant than the marker of "alternative," Liberty students must prove their allegiance to being different both to each other and to themselves.

ELLA ON PUNK AND CONSUMERISM

As part of a kindergarten through twelfth-grade school system, the students at Liberty learned "style" from those who came before them: the punks of the 1980s, the students who were seniors when Ella, the young woman whom I most closely worked with for this essay, was still in grade school. The current students at Liberty may design their own sense of style and activities based on contemporary influences, but they concede that the fashions at Liberty were influenced by, as Ella explains, "the high school before us . . . so we had all the robust, expressive 1980s punksters in the school. We had one guy who had a huge Mohawk with spikes so that's what influenced us." Liberty students' relationship to popular culture has been influenced by its former students and current musical icons: the punks who dressed and acted radically in order to perform a political message, and the current musicians who defy corporate lifestyles and consumerism. While most of the current students do not listen to punk music or follow traditional punk ethics, as a collective whole, Liberty High School students observe two basic punk tenants: a need to define themselves as different from mainstream adolescents, and, in an effort to distinguish themselves, a general aversion to consumer trends featured around mainstream adolescent culture.

ELLA ON CLASSROOM SPACES THAT DEFY POPULAR CULTURE

In an effort to describe Liberty students' reactions with and against popular culture, I will, in this section, focus my analysis on a particular classroom event. One day Tim, one of the students' favorite teachers at Liberty, made an announcement in a potent whisper to Ella's class: "One-third of the world is teenagers. If you don't think that's tremendous political power?—'I'm Hollywood! I want your money!'—Vampires sucking your blood." Anti-consumerist commentary runs rampant throughout Liberty's various "monitors" and gazes: The school is sponsoring the making of a straw bale house in order to create a mechanism that conserves energy and is cost-efficient; Liberty events are sponsored by local businesses and organic food stores and restaurants; teachers and students cultivate a school garden and actively recycle cans; the only vending machine in the school sells organic juices. It is precisely those visual markers that youth take seriously, such as clothing, which I took seriously in my efforts to understand Liberty's youth culture.

ADVERTISING

One of the assignments in Tim's class was to create a collage of yourself using magazine articles. The students search through magazines and show each other pictures. When a picture of Barbie is revealed, a conversation ensues that dramatizes the difference between the mainstream—those who wear high heels—and the marginalized—those Liberty-type individuals who have "flat feet" and can stand on their own.

Tim: Barbie can't stand on her own.

Ella: Well, the wheelchair Barbie has flat feet because she wears tennis shoes.

Linda: Teenage Barbie has flat feet!

Eric: That's because she's poor.

The Ella and Eric tag-team wit that most fully epitomizes the humor and intelligence of The Liberty students.

A symbol of 1980s consumerism, Barbie is the toy some punks played with quite seriously just before cutting and dying her hair and piercing her head with clothespins. In fact, according to her father, when Ella received "Prom Barbie" as a four-year-old, complete with crown and feather boa, she immediately cut off its hair, removed its clothes, and used a rope to hang Barbie, by her neck, to the kitchen chair. At twelve, Ella decided to do her junior high project on Barbie, featuring wheelchair Barbie. Ella's four-year-old, twelve-year-old, and sixteen-year-old stances on Barbie show her development from a dramatic child, to an inquisitive and political pre-teen, to a witty and sardonic teenager. As one of the many visual advertisements chosen to discuss during the class activity, Ella's interest in wheelchair Barbie illustrates not only her awareness of consumer culture, but also her ability to discuss various topics with the mainstream and yet also speak to the anti-mainstream.

REMEMBERING SEPTEMBER 11

Perhaps Ella maintains her ability to speak to both cultures through her sense of humor. In fact, satire is highly lauded in Liberty and punk culture.

On September 30, three weeks after the anniversary of 9/11, students finally present parts of their visual notebooks to the class. The first Liberty student presented her 9/11 tribute page with proper Liberty sarcasm: "This is the American flag. I like this because my flag says 'Made in China.'" Ella, the next presenter, maintains the ironic savvy of these "punk" Liberty adolescents; she introduces her second page of the album, entitled "9/11," saying, "That's the tattoo from Captain America. I like the symbolism." It is interesting that neither student fully explained why Captain America and the "Made in China" American Flag were funny and neither student had to explain: Liberty students' disdain for corporate capitalism and imperialism is an intrinsic part of their collective identity. In addition, this classroom's focus on deconstructing popular cultural images and icons allowed for students to better express their own questions concerning mainstream media. Even so, because collectively students seem to agree on their dissent and reinforce each others' efforts to critique, rather than support, popular culture, The Liberty High School students maintain a subculture in which the mainstream voice still reigns.

DRESS

Dress and fashion is a way for teens to communicate who they are to the outside world without speaking. In her study of jock and burnout culture in a Detroit high school, Eckert explains, "Clothing is a particularly powerful social marker because it is regularly renewed and never separated from the individual in public situations. Just about every component of external clothing has indexical or symbolic value in the category system." As in traditional punk culture, Liberty students show off their anti-consumer philosophy through dress. In fact, at Liberty there is no dress code, though one student confessed that she saw a student come to school with a "F*** Censorship" shirt on and the faculty made her put a piece of duck tape over it. In the fall semester of 2003, Liberty students could take a creation course on making clothes, bags, and compact disc cases out of duck tape and many walked around the school with duck tape purses and belts. In this way, Liberty fashion replicates that of the original punks: "Punk reproduced the entire sartorial history of post-war working-class youth cultures in 'cut up' form, combining elements which had originally belonged to completely different epochs . . . all kept 'in place' and 'out of time' by the spectacular adhesives: the safety pins and plastic clothes pegs . . . distorted reflections of all the major post-war subcultures."

Because of the lack of dress code and the faculty support of creative expression, it is impossible to not notice the way students dress at the Liberty School. Twelve-year-old students wear black T-shirts, skirts, fishnet stockings, and combat boots with permanent marker sketchings on their arms stating: "I Hate Avril" (meaning Avril Lavigne). In fact, the entrance of the Liberty School is decorated with a large sheet of white paper on which students may write what they wish—from political messages to impulses. One of the largest sketches shows the words: Avril = Britney + Tie. Most of the younger students at Liberty are forceful about their abhorrence of Avril Lavigne, the pretend punkster who hails from Canada, her homeland being the only "cool" thing about this teen idol. While Avril may not be a part of mainstream teen culture, she is a commodity and therefore, not cool. It is not enough for students to write or speak their distaste for Avril—they mark it on their bodies. Dress, politics, and music are intrinsically connected.

While the expression "Avril is okay because Canada is cool" may express some Liberty students' disdain for United States policy, Liberty students' repulsion of Abercrombie and Fitch runs rampant. During a lunch at a local taco restaurant, Mary and Lucy explained to me why they did not like Abercrombie and Fitch: "Janis used to wear a lot of Abercrombie and Fitch, and we just told her not to wear it because there were a couple of shirts that Asian people had a huge problem with and . . . we just told her it was what we thought . . . We weren't like you can't wear it." "Who is 'we'"? I asked them. "A lot of people," they replied. Another student asserts a similar message, without overt political overtones, when she responds to the question, "Is there any pressure to dress a certain way at Liberty?" "No, actually people are going to look at you kind-of funny if you come in dressed like a public school kid . . . they aren't going to say anything about it, they aren't going to judge you for it." Finally, Ella expressed her disdain for Abercrombie & Fitch, in that, "Most people here aren't shapely enough to wear Abercrombie and Fitch [and] feel the pressure to look a certain way. I mean, being raised in this country, I have, but in this school I have never felt any pressure from anyone else to look any other way." In fact, the clothing company Abercrombie & Fitch's ad agency told *Women's Wear Daily* that "'teens love sexy bodies and they're more conscious of that than ever. . . .'" While Ella was not aware of the company's overt marketing strategy, she certainly felt its effects and named its influence.

ORIGINALITY

My participants did not agree on whether there is or is not an implicit dress code at Liberty, and all but one felt as though they were able to wear whatever they wanted Even so, one particular idea ran consistently throughout the interviews and was best expressed in Ella's interview when she was trying to explain what bothered her about some people: "It's like, people show who they really are and then who they want to be. So that's just the image they want to send other people." I was particularly interested in Ella's distinction between form and content and that there might be something essential to someone's character. The idea that a person can create a unique expression of self, completely separate from outside influence, was expressed by all of my participants.

In discussing punk culture and students' rejection of the mainstream, Ella explained, "The whole idea of punk is originality." The conversation continued as follows:

Rebecca: What is the definition of original?

Ella: I don't know. It's hard. Original is different than like just a stereotype cause that's what it's like, they are opposites. . . . I think it has to do with why, the reason behind the things you do, not necessarily what you do. If you see a pair of shoes, and you really like them because there's something about them that's who you are and who you want to be so you get them, even though you didn't create them or anything, it's still original. If you see a pair of shoes or see someone wearing a pair of shoes, and you want to be just like that person, you're not coming up with some image of yourself that's only you, that's original. You want to do something that someone else is doing.

Rebecca: What if you are walking around and you see someone's pair of shoes and you're like, those are cool! And then you say, "Where did you get those?" That's different than going to a shop and thinking those are cool?

Ella: No, no, no! It's not like that. Because you could see someone and think, those are cool for me but if you just idealize that person and just want to be that, it's not something personal that you want to express, it's something you want to join, that's when it's not original. That's the big thing with punk. I mean, it starts out and it's about expressing things and it becomes a fad so it's not even about expressing things it's about dressing like you're trying to express things and that's really hypocritical and kind of funny.

Ella and her clothes and her mockery of the other kids who aren't original—who, according to Ella's definition of originality, want to copy other people's sense of style. However, Ella purchases her clothes at Hot Topic, the mall punk store, and participates in popular culture. While trying to understand her concept of original, I realized that this originality is like Ella, a part of the anti-mainstream, but also able to converse with the mainstream—she is bilingual in this way and quite subversive. She recognizes that she lives within a world that supports unhealthy body images but locates her world within a subculture that supports "original" body images—any expression that comes from the self. Does it matter if that self is, perhaps unconsciously, influenced by popular culture?

CONCLUSION

Because popular culture reflects the myths of mainstream America, it functions as a legal and political context for private culture by defining the boundaries within which permissible behavior and thought may occur. Popular culture saturates youth media and lifestyle, including schools. From Whittle's sponsorship of *Channel One* to Pepsi and Coke rallying to put only their vending machines in particular school districts, public schools implicitly support consumerism. Just because schools make use of "free" textbook covers that ask "Got Milk?" with Tyra Banks clad in a bikini and milk mustache, is not to say that many public schools do not try to resist overtly supporting corporate consumerism.

Most schools do not lend their students spaces to challenge popular culture because, perhaps, their homecoming courts, proms, and football teams uphold the myth of "adolescent" as innocent and attractive rather than complex and conflicted. If schools are being rewarded for replicating the archetype, why would they want to create spaces that might challenge this image? However, creating such spaces is critical in helping students sustain a sense of critical thinking. This essay emphasized how a school can create critical spaces in which adolescents may respond to popular culture, thereby enabling adolescents to question popular assumptions supported in media and popular culture. What is more, this essay suggests that adolescents not only consume popular culture and behave like the mythic "adolescent," but they also are powerful enough to inform representations of adolescent culture, and find their way into this encyclopedia.

Resources
Books
Eckert, P. (1989). *Jocks & burnouts: Social categories and identity in the high school*. New York: Teachers College Press.
Finders, M. (1997). *Just girls: Hidden literacies and life in junior high*. New York: Teachers College Press.
Gans, H. (1999). *Popular culture and high culture: An analysis and evaluation of taste*. New York: Basic Books.
Hebdige, D. (1979). *Subculture: The meaning of style*. New York: Routledge.
Lesko, N. (2001). *Act your age!: A cultural construction of adolescence*. New York: Routledge.
Quart, A. (2003). *Branded: The buying and selling of teenagers*. New York: Basic Books.
Web Site
The Association for Supervision and Curriculum Development (ASCD). (2004, September). Retrieved September 27, 2004 from http://www.firstamendmentschools.org

Movie

Arad, A., DeSanto, T., Shuler Donner, L., Singer, B., & Winter, R. (Producers). Singer, B. (Director). (2003). *X2: X Men united*. [Motion picture]. United States: 20th Century Fox.

REFUGEE YOUTH: AT HOME, IN SCHOOL, IN THE COMMUNITY

Elizabeth Quintero

Teachers and students around the world have been facing stark challenges that seem to only become more complex as the months proceed. On the one hand, all over the Middle East, the Balkans, and into Africa, successive generations have handed down a legacy of loss, desperation, and betrayal to their children. The political and economic conditions affect all aspects of education. On the other hand, economic globalization—with all its disadvantages and advantages—has uprooted families and brought people together in previously unpredictable circumstances. Refugees in their adolescent years are often in the most difficult of all situations.

The events of the last decade have not only opened borders across the world, but also pointed out that we in the human service professions have urgent responsibilities to newcomers to our communities. We have a responsibility to learn from them about the newcomers' history and their cultures. Our cultural, human roots are no longer neatly contained within borders. Stories are the nearest we can get to experience as we tell of our experiences. Some say that the act of our telling our stories seems linked with the act of making meaning, an inevitable part of life in a postmodern world. This process only becomes problematic when its influence on thinking and learning goes unnoticed or is ignored. This is as true for adolescents as it is for adults or younger children.

COMPLICATIONS IN THE HOME

Today no region or continent lacks refugees. Often these people are caught between danger at home and loss of identity in a strange land. Millions have fled their homes in fear and seek safety in strange societies where they may be isolated, different, and often impoverished. The new refugees are different from refugees in the past in that the new refugees are culturally and ethnically vastly different from their hosts. They often come from countries that are in a different stage of development than that of the host country. They are likely to lack relatives and other potential forms of support in their country of resettlement. These are reasons that schools and agencies assisting refugees in daily life and in resettlement need as much information as possible about them in order to be supportive.

It is important for host communities not to dismiss the reality of these newcomers. We must consistently try to reduce the distance between ourselves and the reality of the oppressed. We must be passionate about gaining the knowledge of the histories, strengths, and needs of the refugees.

Power and access to all types of knowledge, resources, and education are huge issues. Increasing numbers of refugees and immigrants are living in communities that are new to them. There is often an emphasis on maintaining cultural identity and native language within a pluralistic society, but this is difficult because there are increasing inequities, socially, economically, and culturally. Across the world, issues that combine history and culture, traditions, and attempts at new understandings of current and future society are complex and difficult.

These complexities were vividly seen in the experiences of Ali, a young man, age fourteen, from Somalia. He is the son of a Somali woman, and was born in the midst of the horror of war in that country in 1985. His mother was told that he died during the birth. She did not know that after traveling with the family of his father through some of the underground refugee camps and networks, he was brought to the United States to live with a relative who was a United States legal resident in Texas in the early 1990s. When Ali was brought to her door one night and left, his mother was fleeing an abusive relationship, dealing with post-traumatic stress syndrome, and struggling with parenting a three-year-old and a two-year-old in refugee housing in a small city in the Midwest. There was very little explanation for either the boy or his mother.

By this time, Ali spoke English well, and was adept at observing his peers in terms of behavior, dress, slang and joking, and playing soccer. He looked most closely like his African American neighbors, but he had such a different history that there were some disconnects in terms of his interpersonal relationships and his language. Which language from rap songs could be repeated over and over again, loudly, on the soccer field? Which comments were okay to make in groups of peers one doesn't know very well? What about talking with adults? Needless to say, living with a strictly Muslim mother who had not developed a relationship with him from birth caused conflicts. Almost everything he said and every gesture he made at home was considered disrespectful. After several family "blow-ups" he left. He was apprehended and temporarily lived with a social worker/soccer coach who acted as a temporary foster parent. After two attempts to rejoin his mother and her two younger children, he was sent back to Texas to the relative who had not wanted him. This would be tough for any adolescent, but it is devastating for a man with Ali's history.

PERSONAL HISTORY, LITERACY, AND SCHOOLING

What does personal history mean when studying literacy? In the particular case of new refugees and immigrant students, this issue becomes huge. The Hmong refugees who came to the United States in the 1990s had had little or no formal education or access to English instruction. Some were pre-literate. The Hmong culture is historically an oral culture; this was the first generation of Hmong who were using printed materials as a way to learn.

One school district's approach to building upon community and cultural strengths shows possible ways to use diverse learners' strengths and serve their needs. In 1997, in an urban school district in Minnesota, there were 7,537 students classified as Limited English Proficiency (LEP), with the majority (71 percent) speaking Hmong. To address the specific needs of children learning English as a second language, an innovative transitional bilingual/whole language program was developed. This program, supported by Title VII funding, spanned a two-year period, and its effectiveness was evaluated at the end of its second year.

The overarching philosophy of the school district is that every student can learn. It is a special challenge to provide opportunities for success for children who come to school with limited English proficiency and, in some cases, with minimal formal education. The goal of this bilingual program was to provide opportunities for success through the presentation of concepts and the development of skills in a language that they fully understand, and in a manner sensitive to the cultural values and behavioral patterns with which they are familiar. In other words to address the question of: What does personal history mean when studying literacy?

Evaluators documented a strong educational program that values bilingual, multilingual students' language process and sociolinguistic skills and the resulting interpretations of their worlds. The program supported the sociocultural relationship between family, community, and child and especially applauded the contributions of caring, active parents.

Some aspects of the evaluation directly show the important ways schools can support refugee youth in the schools. For example, during the project evaluation, every parent interviewed in the experimental group was happy that the students were being taught to read and write Hmong and were being encouraged to speak Hmong for part of their day, every day, at school. A few comments in the parents' words reflected these thoughts (translated from Hmong):

- My daughter speaks both Hmong and English to me, but I am happy to see that the Hmong language has been taught in the public school systems. Yes, I am happy. It will be useful to her and she will have a sense of culture.

- All persons in the home speak Hmong. Their writing and reading of Hmong is fair but progressing. I am only happy for them because it can only help them to read and write Hmong.

The parents also acknowledged wanting their children to study and learn English. They commented:

- They both are very enthusiastic about their work and I am sure their English skills are great. But they speak only Hmong in the home. They can speak fine to Americans.
- Learning English is good for job to help their future.

As a parent so poignantly said: "School is the only thing that no one can take away from them (an education)."

One of the students, Mai, was born in a refugee camp for Hmong people fleeing Laos. She spent three years in the camp in Thailand and then came to a city in the Midwest. Through the struggles of her dedicated parents, the links made with social service, Headstart, and school personal, and her own strengths, creativity, and intelligence she became a successful student. She excelled in high school and received a scholarship to attend university. She is currently in a teacher education program and student teaching, and is set to graduate in May. She is very happy with her career and she has good friends who are "American." She still lives with her parents, who are wildly proud of her, but who also worry because of the necessity for her to "have a foot in both cultures." She is twenty-two years old. This is much too old for a traditional Hmong man to take her for his wife. She is determined to keep her connections to the large Hmong community, but it is difficult. She sees women her age who have four children already. She loves children and wants her own some day. She understands modern medicine in the United States society. Yet, she has great respect for shaman healing in her community. So, being bilingual and bicultural has its advantages and disadvantages.

OUTSIDE SCHOOL: COMMUNITY WORK

A unique museum project in London, England gives refugee and immigrant students opportunities to use their histories and languages to help educate their new communities about the world. In Spitalfields, East London, is 19 Princelet Street, which is an old house serving as a living monument to London's refugees.

The house was built in 1719 and was originally home to a Huguenot family of silk weavers who had fled persecution in France. Later, other immigrant families from Ireland, and Jewish families from Eastern Europe lived in the house.

It was a Jew and a Muslim who first happened upon the house and recognized it as a building that could help to communicate to new generations something about the history of immigration in east London. They led a project to have it opened as a museum. The building is run by volunteers.

The museum celebrates cultural diversity in London but is also very sober about the sadness and turmoil caused by leaving your own home and confronting a hostile environment. The exhibition gives a hard-hitting message about the real lives of immigrants and the need for racial tolerance. It has become a place for school visits of students from neighboring schools. Many of the students themselves are immigrants and refugees from Bangaladesh, Pakistan, Bosnia, and Sudan.

Nafja has been volunteering at the museum since it opened two years ago. She came to England three years ago and told Susan, the museum director, that she was afraid that she would be an old woman before she learned English. Now, at age fourteen she is an articulate speaker for the museum, for refugees, and most specifically for her family and community. She leads tours at the museum, she has been interviewed by the BBC, and she reads mystery novels by American writers. She is in high school now and she told this author that she is studying hard because she will go to law school at Oxford and become a lawyer who specializes in immigration law.

Nafja is on hand when many of the school groups come to the "Suitcases and Sanctuary" exhibit. The exhibit is interactive in an old-fashioned way. There are suitcases to be opened, cards to be filled in, and luggage tags to write on. There are boxes to look in and poetry and art to touch. There are suitcases full of paper boats, newspapers, stamps, and potatoes. Videos and posters provide visual stimuli while voices from the past crackle through telephone receivers and hidden speakers in the synagogue's old toilet. Hasib Abdul, age eleven, said, "It reflects the past and present, where old and new are neighbors." Nafja is doing her part for herself, her family, the school students, and visitors. We have a lot to learn from her and other refugee youth.

Resources

Ali, M. (2003). *Brick lane*. London: Doubleday.

Clandinin, J. D., & Connelly, F. M. (1994). *Handbook of qualitative research*. London: Sage Publications.

Fadiman, A. (1998). *The spirit catches you and you fall down: A Hmong child, her American doctors, and the collision of two cultures*. New York: Farrar, Straus and Giroux.

Freire, P. (1998). *Pedagogy of freedom: Ethics, democracy, and civic courage*. New York: Rowman & Littlefield.

Pipher, M. (2002). *The middle of everywhere: The world's refugees come to our town*. New York: Harcourt.

Quintero, E., & Rummel, M. (2003). *Becoming a teacher in the new society: Bringing communities and classrooms together*. New York: Peter Lang.

IDENTITY FORMATION AND ACADEMIC ACHIEVEMENT "PIECED" TOGETHER

Ruthann Mayes-Elma

Have you ever thought about how your academic achievement is affected by your identity? Probably not, but I on the other hand have. As a fifth-grade teacher I have often questioned whether there is any correlation between identity and academic achievement—and if there is, what is it—which is why I decided to conduct this qualitative research study. As with any study it is essential to describe the setting and the participants in which the research was conducted, as these factors are highly correlated with the study's findings.

INQUIRY SETTING

Klein Intermediate School (KIS), a three-year (grades fourth through sixth), affluent public school in southwestern Ohio, is the site of this study. This school consists of 1,249 students between the ages of eight and thirteen. All of the 1,249 students are from the surrounding area and either walk, ride the bus, or have their parents drop them off at school. Of the students that attend Klein Intermediate, 90.5 percent are European American, 4.0 percent are Asian American, 3.0 percent are African American, 0.9 percent are Hispanic, and the remaining 1.6 percent of the student population are defined as "Other." As with many schools that have a predominantly European American student population, the teacher population mimics that of the students. At KIS there are 70 teachers; 97 percent European American and 3 percent African American.

This school is considered an upper-middle-class school. The parents, mothers especially, of this school are very active in PTO, which provides special luncheons throughout the year to its teachers, a beginning of the year and end of the year "celebration" to thank the teachers, and a prayer chain that prays for the district's teachers every week. Parents also volunteer to grade papers every week, laminate, make copies, and are room mothers/fathers for their child's classroom. Since a majority of the mothers are full-time stay-at-home moms they also spend a lot of time calling the teachers about grade changes. According to one teacher, "There are a lot of positives to having parental support, but there are also a lot of negatives. It's a double edged sword."

The building itself is kept in pristine condition both on the inside and out. Klein Intermediate was built in 1999 and then added on to in 2001, with plans to add another building to the "campus" beginning in the fall of 2004. The buildings that make up this "campus" are set up with each wing in pod formation. This pod formation is supposed to support a community feel. Since the school is so big and has such a large amount of students, the designers wanted to build a school that was large enough to accommodate all the students, but small enough to foster community. Each pod has twelve classrooms in a circle with windows looking out into the middle of the circle, which is deemed the community area. Teachers and students alike do feel a sense of community within their pod.

INFORMANTS

The informants I selected for this study fit into two categories: students and parents. I chose some of the participants randomly; others were chosen because of teacher's recommendations; some others voluntarily approached me to be included in the study.

The nine parents who participated consisted of six European American females, one European American male, one African American female, and one Asian American female. The fifty-eight students who participated consisted of fifty-two European Americans, three Asian Americans, two African Americans, and one Indian American. Of the fifty-eight students, thirty-two were female and the remaining twenty-six were male. The students were in fifth grade and all participated voluntarily in the study.

DATA GATHERING (INTERVIEWS AND SURVEYS)

The data gathered in this study was obtained through interviews and surveys. I started each interview with a general question, "Can you tell me about how you see yourself?" This often sparked more conversation than I initially thought it would. The order in which the sequence of questions asked changed in each interview, but the questions primarily remained the same, expect in a few cases. On average I spent about 30 minutes with each parent interviewed and 20 minutes with each student interviewed. Some interviews lasted a little longer because of the amount of information the participant was willing to provide.

DATA ANALYSIS

Identity

As I began looking for themes as I analyzed my data I found two common themes among student's identity: the "traditional" group and the "deviant" group. Before I get to that though, I feel it necessary to define identity as I will be using it. Many theorists have found identity to be a key component of culture.[1] I agree with these theorists, and define identity as becoming aware of oneself as a person, expressing one's uniqueness, and expressing one's commonalities. Adams stated that identity is an internalized, self-regulated system that requires the individual to make a distinction between the inner self and the outer social world.[2] Children derive a sense of who they are from the definitions others supply them with, the roles they fill, and the media as a whole. This is not to say that children have no choice in their own identity, they do indeed have choices. Although identity is socially constructed, children do have the choice, whether they consciously recognize the choices or not, to accept what society is telling them or to become something other than what society is telling them to be.[3]

Identity is a construct that has been examined by many researchers, across a wide range of disciplines. Depending on who you read, there are two basic definitions of identity. The first of these is the "authentic self,"[4] but for the purposes of this paper the second definition of the social construction of identity will be the focus. This definition emphasizes the importance of acknowledging the ways in which identity is shaped by society, and the ways in which one's identity is embedded within the larger social context. Socialization has a significant impact upon who you are and how you see yourself. Parents, peers, friends, acquaintances, and strangers are just a few of the individuals who shape your identity, not to mention the institutional influences upon identity which include media, church, and school.[5] These institutions convey powerful messages about who one should be, and who one currently is. However, social construction does not treat the individual as passively accepting these institutional messages about identity; rather, the individual actively constructs an identity, and accepts, challenges and constructs in his/her own way the messages received from institutions, cultures, and other people.

As the participants of this study actively constructed their own identity two distinct groups emerged: the "norm" and the "deviant." The students in the group that identified themselves as "normal" used words and phrases to describe themselves such as: "social," "fun-loving," "caring what others think," "afraid," "try to look my best," "caring about grades," "into the same stuff as everyone else," and "just like everyone else." In these interviews and surveys there seemed to me to be a big need to fit in. The students were constantly asking me what others had said, which of course I could not tell them. Many of the "normal" students seemed very rote in their responses; sometimes it just didn't seem genuine. They were very uncomfortable; moving around a lot in their chairs, twisting their hair, and playing with their hands. One girl even admitted that she was nervous. When I asked her why she replied, "I don't know. It's just weird talking about me." At the end of many different interviews I had to reassure the students that I wouldn't tell anyone what they had told me.

On the other hand, the students that identified themselves as "different," which I deemed as "deviant," seemed very genuine and relaxed with their responses. These students were very laid back, didn't seem to care what others had said, and very open with their feelings. These individuals describes themselves as: "sensitive," "not caring what others think," "not into sports," "feelings hurt in the past," and "happy." Not one of these students acted nervous or told me that they felt nervous. The "deviant" group's interviews were longer than the "norm" group, which was due to the fact that the "deviant" group opened up much more and added more details to their answers/conversations. What I found most interesting about the "deviant" group was that a majority of them stated that they didn't care what others thought of them. When I asked them why, I found the fifth-grade students very grown-up in their answer of, "Why should I?" Wow! If only more of us could have that attitude! Why worry so much about what others think? If you are happy, then why fall victim to others' cynicism? I am so amazed at how grown-up and secure the students less than half my age are and what great attitudes they have. I find it very amazing that these students are not the "norm," but instead the "deviant" ones. They certainly are "deviant"; I wish all of us could be so lucky.

Achievement

It is interesting to find that all of the students termed "deviant" were different than their "normal" peers in a positive way, thus "deviant" in this study became a positive; whereas in the general society most people would see "deviant" as negative. The "deviant" students were happier, had more self-esteem, were more self-reliant, and more content with themselves and the world around them. I know I have my Ph.D. in curriculum and not in psychology, but the "deviant" students seemed to be mentally healthier individuals than their "normal" counterparts. These students were less concerned with fitting in to a prescribed mold, which left more time for them to concentrate and direct their attention elsewhere, which might have been to their academic performance. Those that were termed "normal" all discussed, whether in length or not, how they tried to fit in with others at school and in their classes, which might have left less time and energy to concentrate on academics.

After interviewing and surveying the students about their identity it was very interesting to look at their grades from the past year. All of the students took four subjects continuously throughout the year: math, science, social studies (which was American history), and language arts. They also took five "special" subjects (as they were termed) intermittently through-out the year, which I did not focus upon: technology, health, gym, music, and art. As I focused on each student's final grade in all three trimesters I found a much wider range for the "normal" students than for those termed "deviant." The grade range for the "normal" students ranged all the way from A's to F's; whereas the "deviant" student's grades ranged from A's to C's. The "deviant" students also had many more A's as final grades than did the "normal" students. This was very consistent with what the students told me about their grades in the interviews.

The "normal" students described their academic achievement as: "poor," "not good," "good," "pretty good," or "just like everyone else," but the most frequently used adjective was "okay." Whereas the "deviant" students described their academic performance in much the same way, they also used adjectives to describe their grades that the "normal" students did not, such as: "adequate," "excellent," and "not as good as they could be." I found this "not as good as they could be" interesting since the lowest grade earned was a C, and most earned A's. Even though few of the "deviant" students described their performance as "excellent" or "good," most described it with less than positive or mediocre adjectives. I was surprised to find the "normal" students had a much more positive attitude toward their perfor-mance than did the "deviant" students, especially considering the "normal" students had lower grades on the average than the "deviant" students.

So as it turns out, the "deviant" students that had a much greater self-concept had a much lower concept of their academic performance as com-pared to their "normal" counterparts. The "deviant" students were much harder on themselves academically, yet more accepting of themselves as people; whereas the "normal" students were the opposite.

CONCLUSION

It is always difficult talking with people, much less children, about such personal issues as identity. Many of the students were very open and honest with me about their feelings, about their constant need to "fit in." Some of the students told me about instances when they hadn't "fit in" with the other students with such devastation that I as a researcher found it absolutely intriguing, but I as a person wanted to wrap my arms around them and tell them that they didn't need to "fit in" because maybe what they were trying to fit into wasn't worth it. Which brings me to an interesting question I began thinking about when analyzing the data; do any of these students at any one time think about if what they are trying to fit into is really worth fitting into or if it is in their best interest in the long run to fit into this group? None of the students talked with me about questioning themselves on the topic of "fitting in," instead it was discussed by the "normal" students as a given, something they had to do, not something up for debate. Through my research I found that there is a direct correlation between identity and achievement, but have the students put the two together? In their own way, have they questioned the structure put into place by society? Are they happy with the decisions that they think they have no other choice in? I guess I just found my next research endeavor!

Notes

1 See Bosworth, 1999; Druxes, 1994; hooks, 2000; May, 1992; Paechter, 2001; and Shotter, 1998.
2 See Adams, 1992.
3 See Adams, 1992; Belenky, Clinchy, Goldberger, & Tarule, 1997.
4 See Erikson, 1975.
5 See Butler, 1999; Kilbourne, 1999; Lippa, 2002; Lorber, 1994; Sadker & Sadker, 1994; and Walker, 1999.

References

Adams, G. R. (1992). Introduction and overview. In G. R. Adams, T. P. Gullotta, & R. Montemayor (Eds.), *Adolescent identity formation* (pp. 1–8). Newbury Park, CA: Sage Publications.

Belenky, M. F., Clincy, B. M., Goldberger, H. R., & Tarule, J. M. (1997). *Women's ways of knowing: The development of self, voice, and mind* (10th ann. ed.). New York: Basic Books.

Bosworth, M. (1999). *Engendering resistance: Agency and power in women's prisons.* Hampshire, England: Ashgate Publishing.

Butter, J. (1999). *Gender trouble: Feminism and the subversion of identity* (10th ann. ed.). New York: Routledge.

Druxes, H. (1996). *Resisting bodies: The negotiation of female agency in twentieth-century women's fiction.* Detroit, MI: Wayne State University Press.

Erikson, E. H. (1975). Once more the inner space. In *Life history and the Historical Moment.* New York: Norton.

hooks, b. (2000). *Feminism is for everybody: Passionate politics.* Cambridge, MA: South End Press.

Kilbourne, J. (1999). *Can't buy my love: How advertising changes the way we think and feel.* New York: Simon & Schuster.

Lippa, R. A. (2002). *Gender, nature, and nurture.* Mahwah, NJ: Lawrence Erlbaum.

Lorber, J. (1994). *Paradoxes of gender.* New Haven, CT: Yale University Press.

Paechter, C. (2001). Using poststructuralist ideas in gender theory and research. In B. Francis & C. Skelton (Eds.), *Investigating gender: Contemporary perspectives in education* (pp. 41–51). Philadelphia: Open University Press.

Sadker, M., & Sadker, D. (1994). *Failing at fairness: How America's schools cheat girls.* New York: Charles Scribner's Sons.

Shotter, J. (1998). Agency and identity: A relational approach. In A. Campbell & S. Muncer (Eds.), *The social child* (pp. 271–291). East Sussex, UK: Psychology Press.

Walker, A. J. (1999). Gender and family relationships. In M. B. Sussman, S. K. Steinmetz, & G. W. Peterson (Eds.). *Handbook of marriage and the family* (2nd ed.) (pp. 439–474). New York: Plenum Press.

The Beauty Incident

Carolina Mancuso

Not all high schools offer thorough and interesting social studies classes, perhaps excepting occasional in-depth discussions of world events, such as the recent tsunami disaster. Adolescents might feel they have nothing to say about such horrible occurrences, especially because many have relied on their experiences during 9/11; or they may be able to express their feelings only through fearfulness, groans, and feigned disinterest. Though high school teachers may attempt to offer engaging history and social studies lessons at times like these, they may also feel uncomfortable addressing hot topics like racism, sexism, and socioeconomic status. Whether the issues arise during classes or outside the classroom and the school, teachers may also not be familiar with conflict resolution practices and may feel unclear about their own positions and unwilling to risk offending students or finding ways to support certain views as well.

At the same time, neither teenagers nor their parents may seek newscasts through newspapers and electronic media in busy households. Parents may feel as unprepared as teachers, unable to find enough time to discuss controversial news items with their adolescents, or feel they would stumble through their own inability to probe explaining complex issues. Likewise, adolescents may hide their opinions from their parents.

However, teenagers do have strong opinions about what is going on in the world, opinions that are held deeply and personally. When they are unsure of what they believe, they may resist being criticized. Nonetheless, many of them spend much of their free time maneuvering through risky territory, for example, and puzzling how to find a path through frustrating information. Even when parents are open and willing to help their teens evaluate various opinions, adolescents' thoughts are most often shaped through the media.

There are schools, however, in which teachers are prepared to use strategies referred to as "critical pedagogy," "critical literacy," and "media literacy," approaches first introduced by Paulo Freire and John Dewey. Teachers experienced with such methods possess the potential to open the door for adolescents to examine and understand how they take in and analyze their own popular culture that they confront each day. Such interests include designer clothing, often way beyond prices adolescents can manage or get their parents to manage; ever-rising costs of teenage music and film as well as new technologies, again beyond the cost young people or parents can bear; their fanzines, publications of subculture, that by themselves carry a great deal of youth culture. Unfortunately, a number of teenagers also find themselves seeking drugs and other verboten items of interest on the streets. All of this identity-forming culture can pose problems for teenagers who struggle to find a sense of self and create identities that can keep them from the undertow of a continual media-blitz. Where and how do they find themselves in that whirlpool? How much do they feel at ease accepting what they hear and see, and how much of their values do they already reject?

SATELLITE ACADEMY: A BRIEF DESCRIPTION

During the past year, students in an alternative high school in New York City agreed to become part of a research project grounded in media literacy with two of their teachers and a professor from Brooklyn College City University of New York (CUNY). The setting was one of four Satellite schools in New York City: Forsyth Street, Manhattan; Jamaica, Queens; 34th Street; and a new Bronx school. All are alternative high schools, the first founded at Forsyth Street in 1979. It is a vital and diverse community of learners devoted to transforming young minds and lives through education, nurturing self-determination, hope, and confidence. Satellite Academy on Forsyth Street provides two hundred students who have opted out of larger traditional high schools with the opportunity to complete their education in a smaller and collaborative learning community. The school offers the second chance they deserve. For example, each student becomes a member of a family group, forming small communities within the larger community of the school. Students meet in their family groups four times a week. It is there that they can share difficulties, and give and get help from their teacher and their peers. Through working autobiographically and within a curriculum called Learning to Learn, students find ways to begin to examine their beliefs and assumptions with the context of adolescent culture. Much of that work has to do with how students understand issues involving media literacy. Not only were the family groups excellent environments, but also the Satellite schools had the engaging and interesting social studies and history classes.

A RESEARCH PROJECT: "THE BEAUTY INCIDENT" COMES TO SATELLITE

In the first episode—"The Beauty Incident"—that had caused the elementary school to struggle to understand what had happened, the adolescents interpreted what they had learned during the role-playing and the videotaping. While in a class, Tanya P., a new student from Russia who had been accepted in the school, was teased in an eighth grade art class about her feelings about black people. Someone told her that a black student wanted to be her boyfriend, but she told the students that she didn't see any "beauty" in black people. What she was purported to have said circulated throughout the school, causing students to become concerned about what Tanya said and what appeared to be a lack of intervention on the part of teachers and administrators in the northeastern elementary school.

Students there were upset because it appeared that none of the teachers were trying to help Tanya change her racist attitudes. When students learned that she was Russian, they began to talk about how the Russian students who enrolled in the school were often arrogant and unfriendly. They also noticed the ways in which the Russian students dressed and conducted themselves, habits that kept them from fitting in with the rest of the school.

As the incident spread around the school, professionals in conflict resolution came to the school and interviewed the students in groups or individually talked with them regarding what happened in the art class and since. The students felt that the principles that the school had held had broken down. Some students, seeing Tanya at the pizza parlor at lunch hour, became agitated toward her and threw pizza at her. Following that episode, Tanya wrote an essay about her beliefs and what she had learned studying the Nazis as a student in Russia. The conflict resolution group returned at intervals to interview students and teachers, and found that the residue of the "Beauty Incident" remained in the elementary school.

A RESEARCH PROJECT: "THE BEAUTY INCIDENT" IN FAMILY GROUP ONE

The Satellite schools have also had a long-term relationship with Facing History and Ourselves, a national organization for social studies and the humanities. When the research project was described as part of Facing History, the students were even more eager to be involved in it. The project, titled "The Beauty Incident," a case study by Facing History, documented a critical episode of bias in an elementary school in a Northeastern city. Family groups proved to be the most opportune environments for the students to engage in "The Beauty Incident." The first family group of these urban high school students began by analyzing their definitions of beauty and interpreting a case study focused on beauty, race, and gender. They also examined their own attitudes on beauty, self-image, race, gender, and influences from popular youth culture.

Next, reading the verbatim words of the elementary students, they enthusiastically took on roles and videotaped the script. Following their analysis, volunteers conducted a collaborative curriculum project from their interpretation of the student and presented the lessons in a middle school. The Facing History staff interviewed various eighth graders (some witnesses to the original incident, some not) as well as teachers and administrators in order to assist in helping the school better understand what had happened. The case study was quite long, so it was revised to approximately a third, so that the students at Satellite could take on the roles, acting as teachers and interviewers, while other students videotaped the play script.

The teachers at Satellite worked with the researcher to explain the preliminary aspects of the project so that the students could understand what they needed to do. First of all, the students sat in a circle listening to what the project was about, that is, the content of the case study, asking questions, and sharing what they thought about "beauty" in general and about themselves and their friends. They were given a sheet of paper with pre-test "sentence stems" left blank so they could fill in their ideas about beauty. Then they did a "gallery walk," responding to the sentence stems and those of their peers on poster paper that was mounted on the walls of the classroom. Students walked around adding thoughts to the posters with markers.

Many students wrote about beauty as a byproduct of confidence and self-esteem. A few resorted to media literacy values, but for the most part, those were read later. Surprisingly, many of the students wrote about their parents teaching them about beauty and how to think about it. For the most part, they took a mature point of view, even with a lot of time spent on grooming and new clothes and so on. Many said they did not want to "try to look like someone else"; felt that a good personality and mentality was important, including respect for themselves and for others. The young women wanted to be sure that their boyfriends would respect them and maintain a positive attitude toward them.

Following the "gallery walk," students read aloud a story written by a young teenager whose mother called her "ugly." The discussion then stimulated other students to tell how well or how insultingly their parents treat them and how they felt when it happened. After reading through the script revised from the case study, a session was devoted to having the students take roles and videotape the script. In an additional session, we asked them to address the content issues of the case study. Many of them considered how things might be different if some of the students in the elementary school where the Beauty Incident took place took it upon themselves to discuss stereotyping or discrimination. They brought out excellent ways to help racist people understand how cruel such attitudes can be. Many of them expressed a willingness to try to help the person purge racist attitudes.

A RESEARCH PROJECT: "THE BEAUTY INCIDENT" SATELLITE VOLUNTEERS MAKE A LESSON PLAN WITH THEIR TEACHERS TO BRING THE PROJECT TO A LOCAL NEW YORK CITY ELEMENTARY SCHOOL

Before the project began, the students had been told that after the video-taping of the script and the analysis of the incident, there would be an additional phase of the research in which the Satellite students could volunteer to work with their teachers to become mentors in co-creating a lesson plan to bring the project into a local elementary school. The final phase of the project was unique in its objective of engaging teachers and their students in curriculum planning. Visiting a local elementary school, that final piece was also videotaped, asking the younger children to write and read their thoughts about the incident and the content. The significance of the project lay in its use of critical literacy skills to analyze a case study, its impetus to engage high school students in constructing curriculum with their teachers, a highly unusual occurrence in the classroom, and its potential for those students to mentor others—elementary students—who would, also under the tutelage of the adolescents, analyze the incident.

A RESEARCH PROJECT: "THE BEAUTY INCIDENT" IN FAMILY GROUP TWO

The project in Family Group Two unfolded like Family Group One. When Group Two was finished, two students volunteered to go to the local elementary school; however, they decided not to after all. Two Family Group One students created a lesson plan with their teacher and the researcher and videotaped a session in the elementary school, using the lesson plan they conducted by themselves.

Resources
Books

Dewey, J. (1975/1909). *Moral principles in education.* [Preface by Sidney Hook.] Carbondale: Southern Illinois University Press.

Facing History and Ourselves. (2002). *The beauty incident: A school-based case study for examining issues of race, culture and membership.* Boston: FHAO.

Fishman, S. M., & McCarthy, L. (1998). *John Dewey and the challenge of classroom practice.* New York: Teachers Community Press.

Flinders, D. J., & Thornton, S. J. (Eds.). (1997). *The curriculum studies reader.* New York: Routledge.

Gardner, H. (1983). *Frames of mind: The theory of multiple intelligences.* New York: Basic Books.

Goleman, D. (1995). *Emotional intelligence.* New York: Bantam.

Kohn, A. (1996). *Beyond discipline: From compliance to community.* Alexandria, VA: ASCD.

Lantieri, L., & Patti, J. (1996). *Waging peace in our schools.* Boston: Beacon.

McLaren, P. (2003). *Life in schools: An introduction to critical pedagogy of popular culture: Literacy development among urban youth* (4th ed.). Boston: Allyn and Bacon.

Schon, D. A. (1983). *The reflective practitioner: How professionals think in action.* New York: Basic Books.

Shor, I., & Pari, C. (Eds.). (1999). *Critical literacy in action: Writing words, changing worlds.* Portsmouth, NH: Heinemann Boynton Cook.

Stock, P. L. (1995). *The dialogic curriculum: Teaching and learning in a multicultural society.* Portsmouth, NH: Boynton/Cook.

Yagelski, R. P. (2000). *Literacy matters: Writing and reading the social self.* New York: Teachers Community Press.

Articles

Morrell, E. (2002, September). Toward a critical pedagogy of popular culture: Literacy development among urban youth. *Journal of Adolescent & Adult Literacy, 46* (1), 72–77.

Rogers, R. (2002, May). "That's what you're here for, you're suppose to tell us": Teaching and learning critical literacy. *Journal of Adolescent & Adult Literacy, 45* (8), 772–787.

ENGLISH AND U.S. CULTURE

Jungkang Kim

Socialization of Korean youth in the era of globalization can be defined as a process in which Korean youth engage in constructing their identity in relation to the global society in which English has become a powerful medium of international communication. As English has become an important medium of international business, politics, education, culture, and communication, the language carries a significant meaning for Korean youth, and its presence is vividly felt in their education, social, and cultural activities. In Korean society English is associated with globalization, prosperity, modernization, and power; therefore, English language education is highly promoted and forcefully encouraged among Korean youth via the national foreign language policy that requires English education in elementary school through high school. In college knowledge of the English language is more valued than that of their academic major. The current language education policy and high demand for English reflects the global spread of English and the increase in

English speakers in non-native English speaking countries. The worldwide expansion of English is manifest in various aspects of the lives of those who are in contact with English, and it has raised concerns regarding the impact of English on their national language and identity. In such a complex and conflicting social reality, the journey of Korean youth in the construction of identity is a big challenge for them. They are socialized into their national culture as Koreans while becoming socialized into the global society and culture through learning English. The focus of this essay is to learn how Korean youth develop a sense of identity in the given social reality where two cultures and languages represent conflicting values and cause identity conflicts.

MEDIA AND ENGLISH LANGUAGE EDUCATION

English language education in Korea takes place in various social contexts such as education institutes, social organizations, and cultural activities. The contemporary era of information and technology provides Korean learners of English with better access to information and resources for learning English via a variety of channels such as the Internet, newspapers, magazines, television, movies, and radio. The media, therefore, has made its way into the core of English language education in Korea rapidly, and it has had great impact on various domains of education. Due to its easy and quick accessibility to any necessary information and source, learners and teachers find mass media useful and attractive resources for learning English.

Language as a carrier as well as a product of culture plays a significant role in the construction of one's identity. People who are using or speaking a language tend to develop attitudes toward the language in association with its culture. Therefore, when there is an influence of another language on one language community, one's identity as a member of the community is liable to change. English as a medium of international communication has rapidly expanded in the postwar period, and it has been widely used in South Korea due to the contact with the English language since the end of World War II. In South Korea, education receives the highest status in society, and therefore school plays an important role in the socialization of young Koreans. Currently, English as the primary foreign language in the school curriculum is viewed as an essential means to social and economic upward mobility. Those who are knowledgeable and fluent in English have an advantage in academic and career opportunities. Therefore, one's ability to use English in both written and spoken forms can be directly associated with the individual's position in society. However, as the media has become a very popular way for Korean youth to learn English due to its convenience, efficacy, and accessibility, many concerns regarding its impact on their identity have been raised. The prevalence of the media, as well as other forms of cultural products such as printed materials, music, and fashion, has raised concerns among Korean people with regards to its role in the transmission of cultures from English-speaking nations. Through the exportation of cultural products from native English-speaking nations to non-native English nations, the social and cultural knowledge and values of the former are transmitted to the latter. Among all the cultural forms, television and movies have become a major channel for cultural exportation and the widespread use of English.

One classroom that I observed in a foreign language institute in South Korea showed how the power of English is present and exercised on a daily basis by using the media for learning English. Various American television programs were repeatedly played in every class, and students were filling in the blanks on their worksheets as they were watching American TV programs such as talk shows, news, sitcoms, and other entertainment shows. When the students were asked as to the source from which they learned about American culture, most of them selected American television programs as the biggest source. They critically addressed the role of the media in portraying certain images of American people and culture, and its impact on the attitudes and perceptions of Korean youth toward that culture and themselves, which contributes to identity conflicts. Traditional Korean values consider the family a core, essential unit to all other social groups. That is, social and cultural events are centered on family, and social relationships are built around the relationships among family members. American family values that they see on TV and in the movies tend to validate individuals and their personal interests and rights. They were skeptical of the extent to which the media portrays the real lifestyle of Americans. They expressed a great deal of admiration for the culture, but there was evidence that the images of American people and culture portrayed in the media were idealized.

American popular culture is considered to have a great impact on the ways that Korean youth act, talk, and think and the construction of their identity. Korean youth are well aware of the role of the media in shaping their perceptions and attitudes toward self and others. The Korean students in the English classroom felt that the United States is portrayed in the media as a nation of power and prosperity, which has a large impact on how Korean youth perceive and interpret messages transmitted. Culture of developed, powerful nations is perceived as "better," which puts American culture in a superior position to Korean culture. They defined Americanization of Korean youth as a mindset that reflects and promotes such perceptions and attitudes. Korean youth are conscious of the process of Americanization manifested in the various contexts of their social and cultural lives. They are concerned about the rapid change that Korean society is going through. American fashion trends, popular culture, and social activities may represent Americanization of Korean youth in a superficial way. Nevertheless, they acknowledge those material and external factors reflect the inner, mental state of Korean youth. They understand how language can play a powerful role in constructing the mind of human beings and the way they perceive the world around them. For Korean youth, English symbolizes values, beliefs, and norms of a more civilized, modernized culture. These attitudes and perceptions are vital for constructing identity in association with the English language. Therefore, English is not perceived only as a tool for communication; rather, it has become an ultimate end in itself that Korean youth are striving to achieve in their education.

IDENTITY CONFLICTS AND CONSTRUCTION

Korean youth receive mixed and confusing messages about learning English and show ambivalence in their attitudes and perception toward English. On the one hand, English represents prosperity and globalization; on the other, it is viewed as a threat to the Korean language that represents the national identity and unity of Korean people. They want to learn English, but they also resist learning the language. They feel the same way about American culture. They listen to American music, watch Hollywood movies, and are fascinated by American pop culture; however, they are concerned about the impact of Americanization on Korean culture and traditional values. Acceptance and resistance to the English language and American culture are discussed among Korean people in the national debate on the "English as an official language" movement and "Early English language education."

The conflicting attitudes of Korean youth have significant implications for both the English and Korean languages in Korean society as well as in the international community. The students I interviewed identified problems regarding the current education system and the role of parents in their children's English education. They were mostly concerned about young Korean children who are naively exposed to English and American culture, and they stressed the responsibilities of parents, teachers, and the education system. English is introduced to Korean students along with its culture. However, they are not provided with-appropriate opportunities to learn about the cultural, social, and historical contexts of the English language as it relates to Koreans. They are naively exposed to American culture as they come in contact with cultural activities via American media, which causes confusion among young Koreans and leads to a struggle between the two languages and cultures. In defining the role of English education in Korean society, however, Korean youth find the conflicts of identity and culture clash inevitable. They view it as part of the globalization in which the Korean people as a nation take part, and English is a vital factor.

Whereas the Korean language is associated with young Koreans'traditional values and culture, English becomes a place where their new identities and roles in society are constructed and defined in relation to the larger, global society. Because English is a powerful tool for social and economic success, Korean youth view the language as a privilege that they have over their previous generations. Therefore, they want to be associated and identified with the power represented by the language and the privileges available only for those who know and use the language. They are also well aware that the privilege and power are not equally accessible for all. Opportunities for learning English are not equally provided for all Korean youngsters since private foreign language schools are costly for most Korean families. More importantly, they understand that English itself does not guarantee education, social, and economic success even though it is a useful, essential tool.

They respond to such a conflicting, confusing reality of Korean society in many different, unique ways. Some are resistant to English, but favor American culture. Some are devoted to learning English, but do not want to be assimilated into American culture. There are also those whose motivation to learn English comes from their fascination with American culture. Nevertheless, they have come to learn how to reconcile the conflicts and define their own meaning of English education within the given reality. The struggle that Korean youth are experiencing in the world of conflicting values and cultures truly reflects their socialization process as members of both local and global societies. Korean youth develop a sense of identity in the learning of English by making meaning of their new learning experience and critically reflecting on the social context where their learning takes place. In the end, they search for their identity in this socialization process, not in the ways that others define for them but through creating a learning context where they ask questions, reflect on their knowledge, test new knowledge, and negotiate differences.

Resources

Books

Bok, Gu-Il. (1998). *Our national language in the era of globalization.* Seoul, South Korea: Moonhak and Giseoung Press.

Browne, Ray B., & Browne, P. (Eds.). (2001). *The guide to United States popular culture.* Bowling Green, OH: Bowling Green State University Popular Press.

Canagarajah, A. S. (1999). *Resisting linguistic imperialism in English teaching.* Oxford: Oxford University Press.

Crystal, D. (1997). *English as a global language.* Cambridge: Cambridge University Press.

Ember, M., & Ember, C. R. (Eds). (2001). *Countries and their cultures.* New York: MacMillan.

Kim, Young Myung. (2000). *I am denouncing.* Seoul, South Korea: The Hankyoreh Shinmun.

Levinson, D. (Ed.). (1991). *Encyclopedia of world cultures.* Boston: G. K. Hall.

Pennycook, A. (1994). *The cultural politics of English as an international language.* London: Longman.

Phillipson, R. (1992). *Linguistic imperialism.* Oxford: Oxford University Press.

Phillipson, R., & Skutnabb-Kangas, T. (Eds.). (1995). *Linguistic human rights: Overcoming linguistic discrimination.* New York: Mouton de Gruyter.

Pilkington, H. A., & Omel'chenko, E. (2002). *Looking west?: Cultural globalization and Russian youth culture.* University Park, PA: Penn State University Press.

Steinberg, S. R., & Kincheloe, J. L. (Eds.). (1998). *Kinderculture: The corporate construction of childhood.* Boulder, CO: Westview Press.

Articles

Francis, N., & Ryan, P. M. (1998). English as an international language of prestige: Conflicting cultural perspectives and shifting ethnolinguistic loyalties. *Anthropology & Education Quarterly, 29,* 25–43.

Giroux, H. A. (1994). Doing cultural studies: Youth and the challenge of pedagogy. *Harvard Educational Review, 64,* 278–308.

Kubota, R. (1998). Ideologies of English in Japan. *World Englishes, 17,* 295–306.

Masavisut, N., Sukwiwat, M., & Wongmontha, S. (1986). The power of the English language in Thai media. *World Englishes, 5,* 197–207.

McDonogh, G. W., Gregg, R., & Wong, C. H. (Eds.). (2001). *Encyclopedia of contemporary American culture.* New York: Routledge.

McKay, S. L. (2000). Teaching English as an international language: Implications for cultural materials in the classroom. *TESOL Journal, 9,* 7–11.

Norton, Bonnie. (1997). Language, identity, and the ownership of English. *TESOL Quarterly, 31,* 409–429.

Pakir, A. (1999). Connecting with English in the context of internationalisation. *TESOL Quarterly, 33,* 103–114.

Pulcini, V. (1997). Attitudes toward the spread of English in Italy. *World Englishes, 16,* 77–85.

Ramanathan, V. (1999). English is here to stay: A critical look at institutional and educational practices in India. *TESOL Quarterly, 33,* 211–230.

FRENCH IMMERSION STUDENTS IN CANADA

Josée Makropoulos

Student participation in French immersion programs across Canada has led to the emergence of a bilingual youth culture, which has been largely seen as a national success story and has served as an example for numerous countries where second language instruction is promoted. In the Canadian context, immersion programs are geared toward English-speaking students so they can develop functional levels of bilingualism by acquiring French as their second official language. Unlike other bilingual programs, the immersion approach introduces French for the instruction of academic subjects and as the main medium of communication for teacher-student and student-student interactions. In the past forty years, immersion programs have attracted diverse student groups, who see this bilingual education option as meaning different things in the Canadian context.

When the first immersion program was introduced in Canada in 1965, it was designed for Anglophone students in Quebec who came from families where neither one of their parents spoke or understood much French. Until then, a large portion of the private industry in the predominantly Francophone province was controlled by the Anglophone middle and upper middle classes, who had been able to maintain English as the convention of language choice in the workplace and during inter-group interactions. However, times were changing during the Quiet Revolution of the sixties, as the French language gained political and economic clout in the midst of the mobilization of the Francophone majority of Quebec. Several Anglophone parents subsequently wanted to provide their children the opportunity to develop functional levels of bilingualism in order to secure their social position. This was, however, not an easy task at the time, since French schools were not geared toward Anglophones and existing French second-language programs did not teach students how to effectively communicate. Intent on finding a solution, a group of parents from the suburbs of Montreal worked closely with Professor Lambert and his associates at McGill University to achieve the feat of implementing an experimental kindergarten French immersion class for their children.

The popularity of the St. Lambert French immersion experiment led to the introduction of similar programs in various regions of Quebec and Ontario. Soon after, the French immersion phenomenon became intimately linked to the promotion of an officially bilingual Canadian culture. Indeed, the federal government passed the Official Languages Act in 1969, which granted English and French equal status as the official languages of the country. The Canadian government also set up the Official Languages in Education Program (OLEP), whose payment formulas to provincial and territorial governments helped make the French immersion option a viable education alternative for thousands of young Canadians. Newly formed associations, such as Canadian Parents for French (CPF), also helped promote French second-language education opportunities.

By the early eighties, French immersion programs had spread from coast to coast in the country, and were accessible on a voluntary basis in one of three entry points. The early entry point is offered from the onset of kindergarten to primary students, who learn at least 50 percent of the time in French. The late entry point typically begins after the completion of the regular English primary program, where intermediate students are immersed for about three quarters of the day in French in grades seven and eight. A less common option is the middle entry point, which is offered by some elementary schools in grades three or four, where students spend about half of the day taking classes in French. Students who begin these three entry points are usually integrated in the same French immersion classes during their secondary education from grades nine to twelve.

The nationwide expansion of French immersion was accompanied by a vast production of research that showcased the benefits of the program for English-speaking youth. At first, studies helped dispel parental fears about bilingualism by demonstrating that immersion students did not suffer from intellectual confusion or mental deficiencies. It was demonstrated that French immersion instruction posed no risk to the maintenance of English as a first language, and it allowed students to reach high levels of proficiency in French. Some studies also showed that immersion students were more likely to excel in academic subjects than youth in regular programs. According to some theorists, the main reason why French immersion students were doing so well in the program was related to the cognitive benefits of learning a second language in an additive bilingual context.

Sociological research conducted in a northern Ontario community in the early eighties, however, raised skepticism about the culture of immersion student achievement. As empirical evidence revealed that the gross family income of early immersion students was significantly higher than the community norm, it was argued that student success in immersion had more to do with social class bias than the merits of the program. Other studies conducted elsewhere in Canada indicate that middle-class values play a determining role in the parental selection of the early immersion option, but that social class bias is significantly less pronounced among students enrolled in the late French immersion program. Nevertheless, recent research shows that late immersion selection rests primarily on a recommendation system, which recruits many students from lower socioeconomic backgrounds who are academically oriented and perform well in school.

Many students from lower socioeconomic backgrounds who get recommended to the late immersion program come from immigrant families, which include many visible minority youth who speak a heritage language other than English or French. Their delayed entry into the late immersion track can be voluntary because some immigrant parents find their children will be better off focusing on learning English at the primary level before focusing on French. However, many immigrant parents involuntarily end up sending their children to regular English programs because they lack the information and resources to do otherwise. In contrast, immigrant families who enroll their children in the early immersion track are quite knowledgeable about the merits of a bilingual education in spite of the fact that many have a modest income. Quite a few of these immigrant parents benefit from cultural ties to French, or had immigrated to Quebec prior to settling elsewhere in the country. Nevertheless, immigrant families who choose the early and late French immersion typically see this bilingual program as a means for their children to make it in the Canadian context and to succeed in a multilingual global economy.

Although Canadian French immersion programs are geared toward students in the English majority, an emerging body of literature indicates that minority Francophone participation has been an ongoing phenomenon since the early seventies. Back then, several minority Francophone parents found themselves obliged to send their children to early immersion program when French schools were not available in their predominantly English-speaking communities. This situation significantly improved with the passing of Section 23 of the Canadian Charter of Rights and Freedoms in 1982, which guarantees the right to minority French instruction in Canada. Nevertheless, some French parents from various socioeconomic backgrounds who are eligible to send their children to minority French schools continue to choose immersion programs instead. Recent ethnographic research indicates that early immersion programs are predominantly selected by linguistically mixed couples, which are composed of an eligible Francophone parent and a non-eligible parent who speaks English or a heritage language as their native tongue. These families essentially find that early immersion suits their bilingual family needs to a greater extent than French minority schools. The late immersion option is chosen by a smaller number of Francophone parents, whose children previously attended regular English programs or had received French instruction in the province of Quebec or elsewhere in Canada. When faced with the reality that their children were experiencing the consequences of French loss, the Francophone members in these families often believe that late immersion can help teenagers keep their link to the French language.

Another issue that has gained recent attention is the phenomenon of French immersion attrition. Demographic data indicates that immersion enrollment rates are highest at the elementary and intermediate levels, and that overall student participation decreases starting at grade nine in the secondary level. Hence, the vast majority of Canadian students who begin French immersion end up dropping out of the program before graduating from high school. The attrition rates are especially high among early immersion students, whereas students who are recommended to late immersion are more likely to stick with the program in high school. Preliminary findings also suggest that boys are more inclined to leave the immersion program than girls. When girls do drop out, they are also more likely than boys to pursue their French second-language studies in a less advanced program, such as in extended or core French classes. Nevertheless, all students who are not academically inclined are at a high risk of dropping out of immersion programs.

In spite of these challenges, the French immersion phenomenon is largely seen as a successful program that has effectively promoted a bilingual culture in the Canadian context. Demographic data indicates that immersion programs have played a central role in the unprecedented growth in the number of young English Canadians who can now speak French. Research also shows positive attitudes and high levels of support for the official languages among younger Canadians as compared to the older generations. As the federal government passed the Canadian Action Plan for Official Languages in 2003, it seems very likely that French immersion students will continue to play a vital role in safeguarding the official bilingual character of Canadian society in the twenty-first century.

Resources

Books

Churchill, S. (1998). *Official languages in Canada: Changing the language landscape.* Quebec: Canadian Heritage, Government of Canada.

Mannavarayan, J.-M. (2002). *The French immersion debate. French for all or all for French?* Calgary: Detselig Enterprises Ltd.

Lapkin, S. (Ed.). (1998). *French second language education in Canada: Empirical studies.* Toronto: University of Toronto Press.

Makropoulos, J. (Forthcoming). *A Canadian story about French immersion stayers and leavers in an Ottawa high school.* Unpublished doctoral thesis, University of Toronto.

Rebuffot, J. (1993). *Le Point sur . . . l'immersion au Canada.* Anjou, Canada: Centre èducatif et culturel.

Articles

Dagenais, D., & Day, E. (1999). Home language of trilingual children in French immersion. *Canadian Modern Language Review/La revue canadienne des langues vivantes,* 56, 99–123.

Heller, M. (1990). French immersion in Canada: A model for Switzerland? *Multilingua,* 9, (1), 67–86.

Olson, P., & Burns, G. (1983). Politics, class and happenstance: French immersion in a Canadian context. *Interchange,* 14, 1–16.

POP FICTION AND LITERACY

Grant Wilson and Peter Pericles Trifonas

Pop fiction has had an often ignominious reputation, from the penny dreadful of the Victorian Age, to the pulps of the 1930s and 1940s, to the dime novels and "airport books" of the modern day. This particular breed of "lowbrow" literature has often been the poor cousin of the modern novel. Often relegated to the paperback racks of 7-Elevens and decorated with embarrassing cover art that seems to be inspired by adolescent male fantasies, popular fiction has often been looked down upon as unsuitable material to be teaching in a high school. Yet within the various genres that litter the field of pop fiction there are several works that are not only worthwhile, but also relevant.

Popular culture was co-opted by the elite long ago. From Andy Warhol's first portrait of Marilyn Monroe to the London Philharmonic performing with The Who, popular culture and its power as an economic force seems to have rendered much of the snobbishness about "pop" obsolete. Universities offer courses on Madonna, and postmodern theory states that the works of Walt Disney are of equal value to those of William Shakespeare. Yet the intrinsic value of popular fiction as part of the reading list in high schools seems to be discounted. Perhaps because of the seeming power of the canon of Western literature, many educators feel that only "serious" novels need to be studied. Granted, certain works in the current curriculum are timeless. To replace Shakespeare with Stephen King would not only deprive students of narratives of incredible depth and historical and artistic significance, it would not engage them for very long. Although King's work can find a place in the classroom, its constant presence on the television, movie screen and best-seller list can also render it banal. However, genres such as horror or science fiction can lead to broader themes and areas of discussion that can speak to students in a language they are familiar with.

Although the "classic" genre of pop fiction covers science fiction and fantasy, it can also be applied to other genres such as cyberpunk, the detective story, and the modern horror story. Rather than looking only at the relative merits of the one genre, an argument can be made that all these forms of popular fiction have certain elements in common, beginning with a desire to tell a story and to entertain.

The educational uses of popular fiction are in the possibilities of relating the real world experiences of youth to the visions of a possible world depicted by the novels. For example, the image of the Utopian/Distopian future in science fiction and fantasy can provoke philosophical reflection and critical thought about the human condition and the future of humanity. The type of reading that popular fiction promotes develops a critical cultural literacy because it uses themes that are relevant to students, drawn from the relative freedom of the fiction of the imagination. Rather than looking at the realism of the modern novel and the constraints imposed by time and space, science fiction allows students to address issues imaginatively and build on their own references instead of the references implied by authorial ownership. As Bruce Sterling wrote in the preface to fellow cyberpunk writer William Gibson's short story collection *Burning Chrome*:

> Science fiction writers . . . are wise fools who can leap, caper, utter
> prophecies. . . . We can play with Big Ideas because the garish motley
> of our pulp origins makes us seem harmless . . . yet our ideas perme-
> ate the culture, bubbling along invisibly, like background radiation.

In short, the freedom from being taken seriously by the canon gives the
genre freedom to explore difficult and controversial subjects. Utopian/
Distopian literature is about human futures and encounters with other
human and non-human sentient beings that broach questions of responsibility and difference, or the self and the other. For example, William Gibson's
Johnny Mnemonic, (a courier whose memory has been voluntarily altered to
transmit data and then forget it is carrying important data in his head that
has been stolen from the Yakuza) can lead to an examination of the relative
dangers of new technologies and the ethical debates of bioengineering and
enhancement. Science fiction and fantasy are a means of introducing critical
discourse on recognizable issues to youth in a form that is readily accessible
within popular culture.

Popular fiction expands notions of critical literacy that have been marginalized by a narrow view of cultural literacy demarcated as lists of
canonical authors, great books, and timeless insights. If we truly live in a
postmodern world, than the teaching of the classics doesn't necessarily
imply that it is done with the traditional list of authors and timelines. Relevance to students' lives and connections to their worlds still have to be
made, whether in Elsinore or on Mars. Critical inquiry doesn't have to be
pushed aside. That said, the use of science fiction and fantasy as vehicles
for critical speculation are probably easier to implement than examining
the gender roles in *The Great Gatsby.* Popular fiction doesn't yet have the
baggage of critical analysis and the weight of a position in the Great Western Canon to affect its interpretations, although the medium of popular
fiction does address issues that affect and are relevant to students.

For example, there is a need to address the role of women writers in
speculative fiction and the need to teach their works. As Jane Donawerth
states, "Women have participated vigorously in the writing of science fiction throughout its two hundred year history, and many have written with
adolescent readers as their audiences." Beginning with Mary Shelley's
Frankenstein, or The Modern Prometheus (1818), which "was the first novel to
center on a problem of science," women have influenced and shaped the
types of stories written in the genre that has only in our century been called
"science fiction." As the genre has developed, women writers are highlighted in their ups and downs to succeed in the marketplace of popular
fiction. For example, Donawerth posits an interesting theory on the relatively fallow period for women writers in the 1930s and the disappearance
of women science fiction writers:

I think that editorial policy, or simply civic pressure on the women, kept their stories from earning money that could go, instead, to a man supporting a family during the Depression . . . the idea that women did not belong in science fiction became entrenched.

The times changed along with women's greater cultural roles so that by the 1960s women writers participated in introducing "stylistic experimentation" and a development of "less conservative themes such as sex, drugs, and critiques of war, imperialism, and the misuse of the ecosystem." In short, as the Civil Rights Movement and the rights of women evolved, so did their contribution to the genre.

Teaching science fiction written by women is a way of introducing students, particularly female students, to professions not traditionally considered suitable for women (sciences, engineering, technology-based professions). There is a glaring disparity in the number of females to males in these careers due to issues of overt discrimination, the lack of encouragement female students receive to pursue these professions, and teaching strategies that are not inviting to female students. Women science fiction writers can provide a welcome alternative to preconceived notions in certain scientific professions. Teaching women writers provides a counterbalance to these issues that cause girls' lack of interest in science. This counterbalance will serve to introduce students, male and female, to

worlds in which men and women participate equally in scientific discovery; role models in the portrayals of women scientists; and a mode of arousing interest in science, through literature, that is traditionally more congenial to female students.

By teaching only men as models, female students receive negatively enforced messages not only about who is qualified to write (males), but also about how women are portrayed in science fiction and popular culture. According to Donawerth, "male science fiction writers are notorious for neglecting to picture women and children in their world or for stereotyping the females they include." This is another counterbalance that allows female students to explore their own voice. In addition, the unrestricted parameters of speculative fiction (the "What If?" factor) let female students emphasize their uniqueness and distinct voice in popular culture. This voice provides "a growing awareness of important contemporary issues, such as changes in gender roles [and] the importance of empathy and communication" as an alternative to "aggression, for resolving human problems." Finally, paraphrasing from another writer on women and science fiction, Donawerth concludes that "women writers draw upon the subversive, satirical and iconoclastic" in science fiction to offer "freedom . . . from the constraints of realism" and "a means of exploring the myriad ways in which we are constructed as women."

Science fiction and the popular fiction genres can be an effective tool for teaching beyond the curriculum, reaching into areas of deeper meaning that raise the level of youth consciousness and their awareness of real world issues that the themes of these books engage: in particular the teaching of values. As James Prothero notes, the teaching of fantastic literature is a misunderstood genre that is "not serious and is therefore, for kids." This contemporary prejudice is part of "the post-industrial move towards realism" and neglects the mythic elements that fantastic literature connects to our own psyche.

Citing an interview with Joseph Campbell, Prothero sees the genre as "present day forms of Mythology and really should be taught as such." He goes on to state

> I think that most readers and critics stumble over the superficial unreality of the tales. Such works cannot be criticized on a realistic level. Our post-industrial indoctrination has taught us that anything not a courtroom or laboratory fact is a lie. This is why "myth" has become synonymous with "falsehood", a meaning not previously attached to the word.

Prothero sees myth as a way of teaching "meaning, not by realistic logical exposition, but rather by imagination and metaphor." As such it can be an antidote to the loss of meaning in modern culture, a culture that has grown too reliant on the acquisition of knowledge solely through reason. This reliance teaches facts and tends to forget about meaningful context in an author-based approach to teaching cultural literacy. When Donawerth speaks of the need to create meaningful contexts for female students in a male-dominant field, she is also advocating an understanding that goes beyond the simple knowledge-based, rote memorization strategies. The need for context, then, is to allow students to find deeper meaning based on their own experiences and on themes that are relevant. As Prothero sees it, the lack of contextual meaning "has been a fragmentation of culture and a loss of community . . . the post-industrial assumption that humankind needs only cold, hard facts and scientific reason is culturally disastrous and psychologically naive." From these contexts come values, values that students will be able to see as vibrant and part of their broader culture. By approaching value-based themes and premise-based stories that engage the students' imaginations, values can be taught not only in some civic-minded exercise, but also as a means of introducing ritual and initiation, two things that writers such as Joseph Campbell and Mircea Eliade have noted are becoming sadly absent in our modern age. These rituals and initiation practices help to give a world cultural meaning and to enforce our notions of our interconnectedness. Their absence leads to a greater alienation and a disconnect between people. The mythic elements of speculative fiction, the invitation for the reader to suspend disbelief, offers a freedom for students to increase their levels of understanding about the real world via the imagination. Our teaching of values can only be enhanced when reality is addressed via the signposts marking the imaginative field of popular culture and its fictions as well. Popular fiction can open avenues to the discussion of complex themes and controversial topics that are important to youth. Challenges to the literary and cultural canon should inform the teaching of youth, as well as a willingness to focus on the *why* and the *what* of the stories we know, understand, and take for granted as topoi of cultural truth and value.

Resources

Book

Gibson, W. (1987). *Burning Chrome*. New York: Ace Books.

Articles

Cox, M. (1990). Engendering critical literacy through science fiction and fantasy. *English Journal*, 79 (3), 35–37.

Donawerth, J. (1990). Teaching science fiction by women. *English Journal*, 79 (3), 39–45.

Prothero, J. (1990). Fantasy, science fiction, and the teaching of values. *English Journal*, 79 (3), 32–34.

YOUTH CULTURE AND CREATIVE LITERACY

Pam Joyce

The TLC, which stands for "Transdiciplinary Literacy Curriculum," is a program that is one of the most effective alternative methods for contemporary-educators to use in dealing with the youth culture of the twenty-first century. Its practice of incorporating everyday life into educational lessons occurs within a simple sequence of three steps: Phase #1—The Lesson Palate (preparation/assessment phase), which helps to acquaint the teacher with the specific needs of the students; Phase #2—The Verbal Connector Prompt (connector/engagement phase), which encourages natural verbal participation of each student; and, Phase #3—The "Triple Z Technique" (3ZT) (lift/platform phase), which lifts the spirit and academic level of each

Paved Footsteps (only twenty sumthin' days)

Maureen A. McKeever

Realizing how short a month to appreciate
African American history
Is a bittersweet thing to see
Only twenty sumthin' days to really acknowledge
How much the African American community has done for society
As I observe the young generations of African Americans
Some seem to take disinterest in learning about their identity
Not realizing how African American leaders and inventors
Reshaped the environment
Paving footsteps for others to cross upon
No matter what the circumstances may be
I try hard to learn so much
Only twenty sumthin' days isn't enough
I need a lifetime to acknowledge
How so many devices and essentials wouldn't be here without their courage
I'm not trying to sound racist
But no matter what month you're represented
Just remember we need more than twenty sumthin' days
We need a lifetime
Let's not forget it.

student and provides a platform for continued growth. Each phase provides a scaffold to the next phase and provides scaffolds within the phase.

This approach is designed to interest and advance children of all ages and levels, as well as combat America's growing problem and legacy of minority underachievement. Using TLC's techniques for exploring personal creativity in addition to overall growth, learning disadvantages can be ultimately undone, and students who would otherwise be lost in the system, yet who do have the raw materials needed to master reading and writing varied text, are instead able to reach their maximum potentials in literacy.

Back-tracking through educational history uncovers numerous failed attempts at creating positive spaces for specific student populations. Today, as in the past, space seems to more often be created for the negative and not the positive through highly unrealistic student or teacher demands that cannot possibly be met under existing conditions. These presently poor learning conditions must change drastically in order for nurturing educational environments to flourish rather than flounder. As suggested by James Allen, students' minds may be likened to a garden that needs to be intellectually cultivated or allowed to run wild. He also notes that whether this metaphorical garden is cultivated or neglected by its gardeners—or in this case, teachers—it must and will bring forth. Therefore, useful seeds must be planted in students, or we will all reap what we sow and an abundance of weed seeds will fall therein, continuing to produce a kind of renegade, misguided vegetation posing as students. Essentially, what society and academia choose to feed into students will eventually become the buds of either positive or negative "floweration." Students will then spit back what was given to them, and if we cannot put anything productive in, we will not receive the rewards of a successful harvest. It is important to remember that children often live up to the expectations placed on them, and we will not see equal achievement in our schools, in the workplace, and in American society until we expect the same level of accomplishment from all students and offer them the same opportunities to learn as well.

Unfortunately, so far as today's American youth culture is concerned, there has yet to be across-the-board successful harvest. Instead, the legacy of disservice to underachieving students—especially to a percentage of minority students—has been both consciously and unconsciously embraced and thus perpetuated by the American educational system in many schools across the country. This kind of pattern is never easily broken. Even when productive, innovative, and creative teaching is taking place, it is difficult for underachieving students to shed the stigma of being sentenced to lower-level classes year after year. Moreover, the effect of this injustice under the ever-watchful and judgmental eye of higher achieving students is just as damaging in terms of developing a dominant group who is culturally insensitive as the damage from politicians and mindless educators.

Noting the process of seemingly nondemocratic practices of student education across America, it is believed by a number of researchers, such as Mehan (1993), that schools steer children toward certain roles in life and that schools teach children of different ethnic and socioeconomic classes to cultivate the social skills that will ultimately be most important in surviving or succeeding at their anticipated levels in school as well as later in the workforce. This outlook or present reality in the end only serves to limit everybody involved. Thus, the need for more open curriculum opportunities, especially in those classes purposely geared toward underachieving minority students, is both evident and prevalent.

In an attempt to create this new perspective, the "No Child Left Behind" slogan has become the mantra of the day. This document, which carries varied vacillating implications about equity and its relation to the distribution of knowledge, basically means that all students will be proficient in all content-area classes at specific intervals of their education. But this has not always been the case, and surely the educational system does a disservice to students when these beliefs are espoused in print or articulated randomly and then subsequently not upheld. In this way, on the surface, educational equality sometimes presents an image of caring and interest in all students, although in practice the concept only benefits the hegemonic student population. Consequently, the disparity in the practice of this educational policy has resulted in a grave disservice to a selected group of students, most often low-income, Hispanic, and black students, as well as a subtler disturbance affecting the rest of the student population. Maxim Greene (1995) contends that the cycle of predictability must be constantly questioned and challenged to avoid the danger of habit swathing everything and swallowing any hint of an opening possibility. Along these same lines of thought and in light of the current state of affairs in the educational system, it would seem apparent that implementing transformative alternatives rather than piecemeal incremental change would be considered change moving toward the best interest of the students. This overdue new perspective can take form through curriculum such as the TLC.

The "achievement gap" in some ways relates to curriculum because it refers to an academic achievement chasm between minority and nonminority students most typically identified by standardized test scores. Many educators believe the educational system and a myriad of internal and external variables, such as race, culture, geographic location, politics and economics, to name a few, have had an influence on the crippling problem of minority youth underachievement. This problem has been perpetuated by society in multiple ways, one of which is the unequal distribution of knowledge sharing in the educational system. Too often, however, under-education is portrayed as solely a black problem and not a national one. Farai Chideya (1995) writes that in general, Americans are not learning the basic skills they need. In fact, she notes, a 1993 study documented by the U.S. Department of Education and the Educational Testing Service found that half of American adults of all races are either illiterate or have minimal reading and math skills. The gnawing question remains: What are the roots of this disparity? Chideya asks if the passing down of family income, status, educational background, and work opportunities form the basis for continuing success. One caveat to those who equate educational achievement with intelligence contends that American dropouts include not only slow children but also gifted children who become bored and sometimes rebellious. Thus, it appears that all students need much more TLC.

A familiar battle, closing the achievement gap has been a recurring problem for a significant period of time in educational history. Suggestions for closing or narrowing the achievement gap have been addressed both in the past and in the present. Some solutions for closing the gap, however, are embedded within our curriculum but have inadvertently been disguised in the current system. Solutions are intertwined and entangled inside the educational bureaucracy, searching constantly for a means to surface. Fortunately, change comes when one can go beneath the layers and unearth the hidden potential that all students have to offer. In this day and age, teachers must be mindful that they have the power to formulate lessons based on students' lives, and multilevel interventions through curriculum can be explored and then implemented in order for underachieving students to at least begin to acknowledge their hidden potentials and be lifted to higher levels of achievement. After working with labeled "gap students" for over fifteen years, I decided to pool my knowledge and sort through the multiple theories related to student underachievement. Subsequently, from the overabundance of information an alternative strategy for teaching literacy skills emerged, which I call TLC.

Originating from the need for students and educators to become more involved in the learning process, TLC was generated from the silent messages of students labeled as underachievers but who, in contrast, exhibited a zest for learning while simultaneously demonstrating a repressed ability to achieve. Through TLC, these students who have the raw materials needed to succeed academically are then able to reach their maximum potential. Hence, the birth of TLC opens a world of possibilities for students. This world of possibilities needs to be opened and expanded for all students, especially those who seem to be stuck in an educational rut.

Teachers have to be the master puzzle solvers to fit the pieces together in the world of possibilities in order to inspire and motivate the youth of today. Building this kind of experience with all the right components is certainly challenging, but not impossible. Narrative, informational, persuasive, and everyday reading texts are essential for the construction of knowledge because they are encountered on a daily basis in our society. The influx of these particular texts in our lives makes it imperative that students be brought into that reality and exposed to these texts in natural settings and with regularity. If students are allowed to see how the world fits into their reality, they will embrace new information and continue to add new discoveries to their existing knowledge. Through this new reality they will see their potential and be able to give back the manifestations of their potential to the world.

While traveling along these new, undefined terrains of reality, students sometimes need additional support systems beyond what traditional schooling has to offer because of the vast increase in information and the ever-growing sophistication of technology. It thus becomes apparent that the age-old phrase "It takes a village to raise a child" is still valid and important. In the classroom TLC is a part of the "village." It is a literacy strategy with a human component that is reflected in the participatory, reflective, and interactive nature of the technique, and it is committed to providing literacy skills for all students to reach their highest potential.

TLC is an academic technique "dedicated to the enhancement of literacy," based on the theory that all children can learn to appreciate and understand the value of the printed word and experience positive feelings about the multiple aspects of literacy. It is a learning strategy that assists teachers with planning lessons and writing real-world curricula that reaches all students in various disciplines and in flexible time periods. The innovative lessons, which involve information sharing, are co-constructed with students and therefore, are constantly changing and flexible in nature. Students evolve from a three-phase network in which the 3ZT is the third and culminating phase. Students who participate in the phase #3, 3ZT lesson, can expect to enhance their literacy skills, critical thinking skills, and their appreciation for reading and writing.

The flexibility of the 3ZT includes the time involved for each lesson, the lesson content, and specific directions that allow students to experience sequence in a more natural manner as opposed to "out of context" drill and skill procedures most students can not relate to, much less learn from. In addition, students are more prepared for various testing situations in the classroom and on national levels, they join in conversation more readily, their self-esteem is raised due to transformative incremental achievements, and apparent academic advancements, they learn how to take personal ownership in the learning process, and they become involved in lesson planning from beginning to end. The 3ZT framework offers a viable option for underachieving students to experience valid feelings about achievement. It involves the use of the following:

- Metacognition—when students explore thoughts about their own thinking and the factors that influence thinking
- Schema—when students reflect on the underlying framework of their past experiences and attempt to find connections with information presented in class

- Scaffolding—when students' skills are elevated by means of supportive efforts from the teacher and classroom peers
- Student ownership of learning—when students are encouraged to participate in planning what they learn and implementing parts of the lesson
- Student's choice of curriculum materials based on real-world resources—when students creatively interject and negotiate materials used for lessons covered in class

PHASE 1

Lesson and curriculum planning using the Transdisciplinary Literacy Curriculum is an art that evolves in phase #1 from three initial sensory aspects, intuition, regenerative insights, and creativity.

- *Intuition* involves the ability of an educator to see within the soul of a student and determine what makes her receptive to receiving, interpreting, and producing information.
- *Regenerative Insight* involves the ability to continuously generate ideas and topics that students can relate to on a variety of levels.
- *Creativity* involves the ability of an educator to keep the spark in teaching while beckoning for enthusiastic student response. The push for nontraditional type creativity stems from the premise that if teachers can get creatively passionate about what they teach their enthusiasm will hopefully in time spread to their students.

When intuition, regenerative insights, and creativity are involved in the process of learning, the result is students who are able to transfer information received into something they can relate to on a daily basis in all aspects of their lives.

The Lesson Palate (Preparation/Assessment Phase)

TLC lesson planning begins with the Lesson Palate, which supplies the tools and the outline for creativity. The creation of a lesson by a teacher is similar to the creation of a piece of art by an artist who follows a sequential progression with space for flexibility, which ultimately leads to the creation of a masterpiece. The teacher is immersed in the creation of the lesson, similar to an artist who loves her craft and is totally immersed in the creation of an artistic piece. The teacher artist is involved in the process in an experiential way. The Lesson Palate is where the lesson begins to take shape. The palate is diversified only because it has to appeal and inspire the multiple intelligences and multiple dimensions of all students. It basically captures the beginnings of the creative process in steps #1 to #6. It is the first step of an action plan for closing the achievement gap and/or addressing student underachievement.

The *Lesson Palate* #1 to #6 encompasses the following:

1 An understanding or focus for what needs to be taught. The understanding evolves from the student's needs combined with the required curriculum of the school. Taking these two factors into consideration, the basic question is what life lessons/skills do we need to impart to students? There are many tools provided for the answer to that question. The required curriculum of a school district, the state curriculum requirements, and/or the perceived student's academic needs are usually combined and provides the direction for the life lesson/skill that is taught.

2 Teacher knowledge of the students. Knowledge about the individual students is a necessary step because the teacher needs to know how to deliver the life lesson/skill of the day to each student.

3 Use of the environment. If educators are constantly on the alert, the environment talks to them and invites interaction and personal creativity. The environment has instructional materials and cognitive tools to offer and they should be used.

4 Visually enticing lessons. The visual aspect of lesson planning can include computer graphics, clip art, or a mixture of fonts but the main idea is that it should be appealing to the students.

5 A life lesson/skill that is relevant. One that must be presented in "real time" and incorporated in lessons. The impact should enable students to make connections and transfer their skills.

6 Ideas for student made materials. Students enjoy being involved in choosing innovative materials for instruction and teachers can use the ideas to enhance the appeal of lessons.

PHASE 2

The Verbal Connector Prompt (Connector/Engagement Phase)

The Verbal Connector Prompt (VCP) is where speaking becomes a priority. The VCP is the spoken introductory part of the lesson and oral discourse is significant in planting the seed of the lesson especially for underachieving students. The value of speech is maximized in the VCP because first students have to explore schema pertaining to the discussion topic and then verbalize what they know with the teacher's assistance when necessary. It is important because it helps students to connect the subject matter with real life through informal verbal interaction. The VCP required for each lesson helps to ease the student into the lesson and create a level of comfort in the classroom. A successful VCP is based on first completing all the steps from 1 to 6 in the Lesson Palate and then utilizing that information to assist in the formulation of an interesting VCP. In the VCP, the teacher must relate the lesson to an anecdote, personal experience, something happening in the world, community, or a student experience. The role of the teacher in this case is to prompt and nurture the students to share their information in an open and safe environment. This procedure helps students relate personal significance to the lesson and assume immediate participation in the lesson with confidence and without apprehension.

Phase 2 helps to direct students toward positive progressive movements and connects life experiences while promoting the enhancement of literacy skills.

PHASE 3

The "Triple Z Technique" (3ZT) (Lift and Platform Phase)

The lesson creation process ends with the use of the 3ZT. The use of a template (see lesson samples) is suggested in order to ensure that the lesson is fine-tuned and crafted to include all necessary elements for a well-rounded lesson. 3ZT is based on the theory that all children can learn to appreciate and understand the value of the printed word, acquire useful literacy skills, and experience positive feelings about the multiple aspects of literacy. Students who participate in the 3ZT can expect to enhance their literacy skills, critical thinking skills, and recover and/or uncover an appreciation for reading and writing. Narrative, informational, persuasive, and everyday reading texts are core components of literacy encountered on a daily basis in society and essential for the construction of basic knowledge. The influx of these particular texts in our lives makes it imperative that students gradually step into that reality by regular exposure in natural settings. If students are allowed to see how the world fits into their reality, they will embrace new information, and continue to add new information to their existing knowledge. When the world fits into the student's reality then the teacher has managed to access information that is familiar to the student and incorporate it into instructional lessons. In this world of lived reality students immediately connect with the information from a common point and through this new reality they see their potential and are able to give back the manifestations of their potentials to the world.

3ZT requires a minor change in curriculum orientation, and, as Joe Kincheloe advocates, this is not extremely difficult to accomplish if teachers are aware of the need for change. The minor change required is simply to incorporate the 3ZT into the existing or new subject matter. The technique provides the teacher with all the components of a well-rounded lesson. The 3ZT is a rigorous multi-step instructional process, which allows for flexibility in lesson/curriculum design. It monitors and paces the flow of information received and produced by students during a lesson by scaffolding information from the first Z to the third Z and by determining what skills reading, writing, speaking or listening/viewing should be used in a particular step (one, two, or three) of the lesson. In light of the variability of the lesson content the 3ZT affords enough flexibility within the template to address the needs of each individual as well as the group.

Lessons, which involve information sharing, are co-constructed with students therefore they are changing and flexible in nature. The 3ZT calls for collaborative efforts, which build learning experiences that, take place in partnership as well as on individual levels ultimately fostering collective and individual social and intellectual growth on multiple levels. In this sense each phase and all steps scaffold information to the learner. The scaffolding aspect of 3ZT is similar to Vygotsky's Zone of Proximal Development. Here Russian Psychologist Lev Vygotsky constructed a cultural-historical psychology, on the concept of mediation. In this mediated context Vygotsky maintained that human action is not a direct response to the environment. Instead, it is mediated by culturally meaningful tools and signs that make the human being able to perform new and more conceptually difficult tasks. Collaboration with other humans creates zones of proximal development where novices learn as a result of their interaction with more experienced individuals. In the 3ZT students interact with their peers as well as the experienced teachers and the scaffolding process is known as the lift and platform. The lift and platform first incorporates scaffolding with mediated interaction, known as the lift, and secondly incorporates a self-advocacy aspect, known as the platform, that insures the possibility of lifelong learning and self-sufficiency.

The flexibility of the technique includes the time involved for each lesson, the lesson content, and specific directions that allow students to experience sequence in a more natural manner as opposed to "out of context" drill and skill procedures. There are multiple student benefits that ultimately surface with the use of the 3ZT, a few of which are listed below.

- Students are more prepared for various testing situations in the classroom and on national levels
- Students join in conversation more readily
- Student's self-esteem is raised due to incremental achievements
- Students experience apparent academic advancements
- Students become involved in lesson planning from beginning to end
- Students learn how to take personal ownership in the learning process

Each point on the letter Z represents a skill to be enhanced namely, reading, writing, speaking (core skills), and listening/viewing (magnifier skills). The core skills are always addressed in a lesson and the magnifier skills are addressed as additional support for students who need further scaffolding. Each Z phase represents a different level of information sharing. In addition one of the most intriguing aspects of the creative process is that it can be merged into existing curricula in various subject areas. It can be the basis for a lesson or used to create a supplemental lesson. It assists teachers with planning lessons and writing curricula that reach all students, in various disciplines, and in flexible time periods.

The 3ZT addresses twelve instructional areas, in three Z phases, in a thirty-minute and ninety-minute time period. There is also room for the teacher to expand the time period to better address the needs of the students. Time management and study skills are also addressed in each phase. The sessions are customized to the needs of the students, which make the learning sessions flexible yet comprehensive. Sessions incorporate summarizing learning experiences and making life connections. Culminating sessions, which occur according to teacher/student agreement, are dedicated to demonstrations of learning, which involve sharing information learned from a personal viewpoint and from building a connection with the world. The culminating sessions can be in each Z phase or in Z phase #3 only and should be discussed with students.

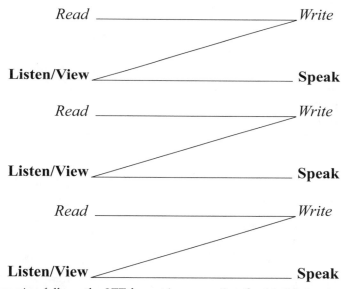

Each session follows the 3ZT format incorporating the 4 to 12 step prodecure, 4 steps in each Z phase, within a flexible time frame.

"Triple Z Technique" – This diagram shows the 3ZT 12 steps.

- Lessons can be divided into two or three days for each Z phase, based on student needs
- A listening or viewing activity can be included with reading and writing activities according to teacher's judgment of student progress
- At least one set of listening/viewing activities should be included in the three Z phase procedure

- Teachers may highlight any appropriate lesson focus that is necessary after following the various lesson planning procedures of the TLC.

VERBAL CONNECTOR PROMPT

Song Lyrics

Lesson Objective: Students will interact with the elements of persuasive reading text.

Teacher Thoughts: Music is a fun instructional pathway to get the interest of young people. There is a collection of diverse musical styles that come over the airwaves and are pumped into homes on a daily basis. Some people are moved to reminisce after a meaningful song while some are moved to dance. It doesn't matter because the basic element that practically all people have in common with music is that it does something to or for them.

Note: This model script is simply a suggestion of how to get informal discussion started in the classroom. It is not to be followed verbatim. (Grade levels may vary.)

Model Script: Main idea of the VCP is to start a discussion and to stimulate student prior knowledge about the topic.

Starter Question—Do the lyrics of a song speak to you? Students discuss

Students Discuss: Reactions they might have to your favorite songs.

Students Discuss: Do you have a favorite musical artist? Students Discuss

Lead in to Lesson:

Do you think the lyrics of a song can influence a person?

"THE TRIPLE Z TECHNIQUE"

"Z" #1 Text: Lyrics from a rap, rock, or pop song that might qualify as persuasive text can be used for this scaffolded lesson. Note: teachers may opt to white out profanities before presenting the text to the students	Read Students read the lyrics individually or in pairs	Write Students write personal interpretations of the meaning of the lyrics. Students take notes during the music video on how and in what specific ways, if at all, do the actions in the video equate to the lyrics	Listen/View Students view the music video. Students listen to the song on tape or CD. Students take turns singing the lyrics	Speak Students discuss the meaning of the lyrics in sections. Students discuss what is implied by the actions, clothing, images, props, etc. used in the music video	Strategies/Obj. Identify persuasive reading text elements (extrapolate relevant information from written text for a specific purpose). Note taking Oral expression Critical thinking skills Persuasive techniques
Time frames	10–15 minutes	10–15 minutes	10–15 minutes	10–15 minutes	40–60 min.(total)

"THE TRIPLE Z TECHNIQUE"

"Z" #2	Read Each student pair concentrates on a specific stanza of the song Each pair reads the assigned musical lines for meaning	Write Students discuss with partners and write about new findings and/or elaborate on initial findings Summarize and post on board Chart persuasive techniques used then post (whole class activity	Listen/View Students listen to pair presentations and use board postings as guides Students view and/or listen to the song and take note of the visuals used in the music video	Speak Students discuss what message or messages, if any, are sent to the youth population through the lyrics of the song. Students discuss persuasive techniques (specifically those found in the lyrics)	Strategies/Obj. Identify persuasive reading text elements Note taking Oral expression Critical thinking skills Summarizing techniques Persuasive techniques
Time frames	10-15 minutes	10-15 minutes	10-15 minutes	10-15 minutes	40-60 min. (total)
"Z" #3	Read Students access internet information about the song Share information with the class Read posted student made persuasive techniques chart	Write Develop a chart that connects aspects of the video with your life or with society Create a 2 column chart entitled Life Connection Chart or create a Venn Diagram and indicate the intersecting areas between the lyrics of the song and society	Listen/View Listen and/or view the song again to extrapolate addition insights	Speak Students discuss the difference between the auditory and visual presentation of the song Students discuss how the lyrics of the song might qualify as persuasive text Students discuss persuasive techniques and its influence on them	Strategies/Obj. Silent reading Opt: Socratic Seminar Critical thinking skills Compare and contrast Making connections Transferring information to real life situations Persuasive techniques
Time frames	10-15 minutes	10-15 minutes	10-15 minutes	10-15 minutes	40-60 min. (total)

The 3ZT can be completed in the 1st, 2nd, or 3rd time frame. The completion time depends on the teacher and the students. Excerpts from phases #1, 2, and 3 of the *song lyrics lesson* listed above can be completed in a 90 minute block class.

Resources

Chideya, F. (1995). *Don't believe the hype: Fighting cultural misinformation about African-Americans.* New York: Plume, Penguin Group, Penguin Books.

Greene, M. (1995). *Releasing the imagination: Essays on education, the arts, and social change.* San Francisco: Jossey-Bass.

Kincheloe, J. (2001). *Getting beyond the facts: Teaching social studies/social sciences in the twenty-first century.* New York: Peter Lang.

Mehan, H. (1993). Beneath the skin and between the ears: A case study in the politics of representation. In S. Chaiklin & J. Lave (Eds.), *Understanding practice: Perspectives on activity and contest* (pp. 241–268). Cambridge: Cambridge University Press.

ORGA-NIZED YOUTH SPORT AND ITS ALTER-NATIVES

Handel Kashope Wright and Tatiana V. Ryba

INTRODUCTION

This entry addresses organized youth sport and its alternatives. Rather than presenting and taking up organized youth sport as a taken-for-granted, ubiquitous phenomenon, it points to the fact that youth sport

Urban basketball

had an initial sociocultural purpose, has a history that reflects sociocultural politics, and is related to efforts at social engineering. The essay distinguishes between children's and youth's self-organized games and organized youth sport and outlines present characteristics of and trends in contemporary organized sport. Finally, it presents the rationale for the emergence and growing popularity of alternatives such as "ecosports" and "the new PE."

POPULAR CONCEPTIONS AND DEPICTIONS OF YOUTH SPORT

American popular culture in general and the film industry in particular typically portray youth sport as a rite of passage, a means of building character and self esteem, and of inculcating youth with mainstream values. In the movie *Remember The Titans,* for example, high school football players successfully face and overcome numerous physical and psychological challenges at training camp. For these young athletes, football functions as a symbolic initiation into manhood: overcoming adversity enables them to transform themselves "from boys to men." *Remember the Titans* is typical of Hollywood sport movies, the vast majority of which deal with males. The British movie, *Bend It Like Beckham,* is atypical in that it deals with a lead character that is both female and South Asian. It tells the story of Jess, an aspiring and talented soccer player who in the process of playing both pickup soccer with boys in the park and later organized soccer on a girls' team, challenges gender and race/ethnicity stereotypes, and at the end wins an athletic scholarship and the heart of her handsome young white male coach.

Whether typical Hollywood fare like *Remember the Titans* or less typical movies like *Bend it Like Beckham,* youth sport films reflect and contribute to the function of organized youth sport, namely to produce and reproduce dominant mainstream values such as individualism, self confidence, single-minded focus on one's goals, and the meritocratic notion that social status and ultimately happiness are attained through sheer individual effort.

However, while mainstream perspectives and values of white, heterosexual, middle-class values, perspectives, and representation remain dominant in organized youth sport, they are also recently being challenged by alternative youth sports which, ideally, stress participation and cooperation over competition, and sociocultural representation and contextualization over individual performance. Examples such as "ecosports" and "the new PE," have emerged as preferred alternatives to traditional youth sport for some youth and their parents who are uncomfortable with recent trends in organized sport, including an overemphasis on individualism and competitiveness, increased technologization, creeping corporatization, and pseudo-professionalization.

FROM CHILD'S PLAY TO ORGANIZED YOUTH SPORT

All through history children and youth have used their own initiative to organize and play traditional games and even develop new ones. Without the supervision of adults they have made all the decisions from whether to follow traditional rules or make up new ones to selecting team members, from meting out penalties and deciding on rewards, to determining the duration of the game. Obviously these youth organized games and activities remain a perennial and still vibrant part of youth and children's activities as evident in everything from races on the school playground to hopscotch and jump-rope on the block sidewalk, from hide-and-seek in the neighborhood to beach volleyball during the family picnic, from pick-up basketball in the neighborhood basketball courts to swimming at the local pool.

Since about the end of the nineteenth century, the games and activities organized by youth and children have been joined in an increasingly high profiled, systematic way by youth sport organized by adults. Adult organized youth sport were initially very gender specific: they were distinctly masculine in conception, motivation, and activities, designed as part of the preparation of boys for the game of life. Girls were excluded from organized sport because it was thought that physical exertion was not appropriate for the "weaker sex," that girls needed to focus on becoming mothers, caregivers, and homemakers, occupants of home and hearth, rather than robust participants in the outdoors and real workplace outside the home. Sport activities also reflected class distinctions. Middle and upper-middle-class boys were encouraged to participate in individual sports such as tennis through which they would learn self reliance, decision making, and independence; characteristics that were valuable for their assumed future as self directed entrepreneurs, military officers, and political leaders. Working class boys were restricted primarily to team sports like baseball through which they would learn to operate as part of a team, follow directions, and learn interdependence; characteristics that were valuable for their assumed future roles as factory workers, farm hands, and enlisted soldiers.

After World War II, organized youth sport programs grew dramatically in the United States. From the 1980s they attained a very high profile due to developments in society such as a dramatic increase in the number of two working parent families, a strong view of the world outside the home as dangerous, the related perceived need for virtually round the clock adult supervision of children's and youths' activities, the notion that non adult supervised youth activities led to deviant behavior, and an increased awareness of the importance of high-performance sports in popular culture. While initial problematic characteristics such as class and race distinctions, and the marginalization of girls have been ameliorated somewhat, they still persist. Despite the passage of Title IX (which mandated equal funding for male and female sports in educational institutions), for example, girls sports are still plagued by pervasive sexism (females are supposedly inferior athletes), an aesthetic panic (sport "masculinizes" girls), and homophobia (sport "lesbianizes" young women), causing a significant number of girls to eschew sport altogether or withdraw in their teens.

THE ALTERNATIVES: ECOSPORTS AND THE NEW PHYSICAL EDUCATION

Prominent sport sociologist Jay Coakley has observed that contemporary youth sport is changing in at least five significant ways. First, organized programs have become increasingly privatized. Second, organized programs increasingly emphasize the "performance ethic." Third, there has been an increase in the number of elite training facilities dedicated to producing highly skilled and specialized athletes. Fourth, parents are becoming more involved in and concerned about the level of participation and success of their children in organized youth sports. Finally, participation in "alternative sports" has increased and functions as a form of resistance to very structured, highly competitive, adult-controlled youth sports.

Many youth and their parents enthusiastically embrace and subscribe to the first three characteristics of contemporary organized youth sport that Coakley identifies and have thus contributed to the acceleration of these processes, especially as a means of developing youth into elite athletes. Other youth and their parents, however, consider these characteristics as distinctly negative, acting against those initial reasons youth are attracted to sport (to have fun, to learn skills, to socialize, and for health and fitness). For this dissenting minority, ecosports and the new PE provide a much preferable alternative.

Ecosports can be either outdoor sports such as rock climbing, hiking, kayaking, and mountain biking, or indoor sport such as martial arts and yoga. They are "nontraditional" and "alternative" sports that often involve unstructured play and no specific rules, emphasizing participants' enjoyment and fun, cooperation over competition, and process over outcome. In this sense they are a counterpoint to traditionally organized performance technosport, that is sport that is performance oriented and which is being dramatically transformed by technology (e.g. equipment, training process, and coaching method).

Another recent phenomenon is the new physical education. This is an approach to PE that emphasizes collaborative games and activities rather than competitive, performance oriented team sport. The goal is to teach children and youth the foundations of fitness, nutrition, and stress management, and to promote a lifetime of physical activity. It includes such activities and sport as jogging, weight lifting, ultimate frisbee, badminton, and archery.

CONCLUSION

While traditional organized sport remains dominant and vibrant, both the new PE and ecosports have proved very attractive to some youth precisely because they do not have a high profile, attract little media attention, and have proven relatively resistant to commodification. With these alternatives, participation is an end in and of itself. Some sport studies scholars view the growing popularity of ecosports and the new PE as a form of resistance to organized corporate sports and the commodification of technosports. Ironically, however, the growing popularity of ecosports has attracted the very factors of corporatization, media interest, and formalizing of rules many youth were trying to avoid. Because it is an overall alternative approach, the new PE still offers the most promise as an alternative to technologized and performance driven organized youth sport.

Whatever the perceived pros and cons of the various forms, sport and physical activity are on the whole highly beneficial for youth. From children's self organized play to technologized youth sport to cooperative alternatives, sport and physical activity have the overall effects of building character, self esteem, and interpersonal relationships, and contributing to the health and fitness of youth.

Resources

Coakley, J., & Donnelly, P. (Eds.). (1999). *Inside sports.* London: Routledge.

DeKnop, P., Skirstad, B., Engstrom, L.-M., & Weiss, M. (Eds.). (1996). *Worldwide trends in youth sport.* Champaign, IL: Human Kinetics.

Murphy, S. (1999). *The cheers and the tears: A healthy alternative to the dark side of youth sports today.* San Francisco: Jossey-Bass.

Ryan, J. (1995). *Little girls in pretty boxes: The making and breaking of elite gymnasts and figure skaters.* New York: Doubleday.

Sage, G. H. (1998). *Power and ideology in American sport: a critical perspective* (2nd ed.). Champaign, IL: Human Kinetics.

C.H.A.O.S.

Mary E. Weems

Chaos: The disordered state existing before the creation of the universe

Creativity   Healing   Acting out   Opening   Sharing

Facilitating the release of the imagination-intellect of young people is a communal, respectful, reciprocal learning act. The imagination and intellect are inextricably linked and operate similar to blood circulation. The imagination is the "heart" of thinking because you can't get a new idea without it and you also can't *get* or work out a new idea without the complexities of the intellect represented in this metaphor by the arteries, veins, and capillaries. For me, the thinking process is the same for all people, including artists, scientists, and scholars—it happens in a smooth flowing, inseparable process.

The number one goal of K–12 education should be to help students develop their imagination-intellects through activities that target one or more of its five components: Aesthetic appreciation, oral and written expression, aesthetic experience, dramatic performance, and social consciousness.

Say what! I mean: man/woman teach them to think like jazz music is made on the improv tip, ideas flowing in and out of the conscious/subconscious like Niles river water, moving through the mind too fast to trace, connecting, disconnecting with something you've read, or heard, or wrote down, or listened to, and most of all lived. This is why artists, and children in schools that put the arts first—do well on stupid stuff like proficiency tests, cause the arts is about working things out, jazz is about working things out, thinking is about working things out.

Miles Davis plays in the background, Billie Holiday sings, June Jordan is a background singer—improvising in heaven—a hip amen corner.

This messy, auto/ethnographic multigenre, performance text revisits this theory within the context of one middle school classroom in an inner-city school I'll call "History." It is a reconstruction of some of the important moments I had with the students, including when I was struck, like a bright star in each eye, with what can happen in the midst of so-called chaos.

The term chaos has a double meaning in this piece. It is the acronym for Creativity, Healing, Acting Out, Opening, and Sharing. Creativity refers to exercising the imagination-intellect, which, like a muscle, becomes stronger the more you use it. Healing means becoming conscious of your racial or cultural history and learning to heal from the wound of racism. Acting Out uses improvisational theater to deal with current issues in a constructive manner, and Sharing means working as a community by sharing our lived experiences through reading out loud and small group and moderated open class rap sessions.

Chaos also references the chaos of all public school districts including the bureaucracy, which is so steeped in confusion that schools are constantly being asked to do things at the last minute, to do them over, and to do them in a way that makes the school district appear in the best light, particularly in the areas of attendance and proficiency testing. The chaos of each school community is a living entity that changes each day like the weather, depending upon district administration requests, teacher/staff/student mood, curricular requirements, and extracurricular school programming.

On the other hand, in the midst of all of these layers of chaos, inside the classroom with its straight rows, identical chairs, and rules of conduct centered on silence and the so-called efficient delivery of knowledge into the empty minds of the students—the idea of disorder, of allowing students to talk throughout the class period, to lead the class discussions, and to decide how to interpret the lesson for the day is not the norm, and I'd only allowed these kinds of behaviors for short spans of time with each new group of students I encountered.

This school has a passionate principal and staff—each committed to their students. Thanks to an innovative principal who believes in the importance of having a strong cultural foundation and in the power of the arts, "History" has developed an environment grounded in culture, history, and community.

Money being oh-so-not-funny as usual, thanks in part to the wrong-headed "Massa"-oriented property tax base and W.'s "Leave no child's behind un-spanked" I had exactly five 80-minutes sessions with each group of students AND the fifth session had to be a performance reflecting what the students had learned about making the transition from child to adult during the residency.

I selected this particular school for this piece because it's where I was working when I discovered the power of constructive chaos, including how giving up as much control as possible can lead to the creation of the universe—a one-line poem.

A blue bag blows down a naked inner city street—the sky in disguise.

On all first days I focus on four things: Community building, History, Creativity, and Acting Out (improvisation) because I want to emphasize the importance of knowing your history as part of loving yourself, to see how students respond to pertinent creative writing activities designed to check their imagination-intellectual development, and Acting Out because improvisational theater is an excellent way to allow the issues we need to address around the topic (in this case Rites of Passage) to develop on the vibe of the moment.

Day One

I'm always pumped on the first day I meet with a new group of people. In this instance, I'm also a little nervous because this will be the first time I've facilitated a Rites of Passage (ROP) experience with young men only. I wonder if they'll listen to anything a woman has to say about becoming a man. I meditated to Miles's *My Funny Valentine* before I left, said a prayer to the Creator that I'd connect with the students, learn, and hopefully share something useful. The "hope" is because I always have a game plan ready, but since I live and work always in the moment, and believe in improvising based upon the vibe between me, the students, and the space—I never know exactly what's going to happen. It's kind of like having a birthday each time, not knowing what's inside the gift of a new learning community.

Since the makeshift school housed in a trailer waiting for a new school to be completed was short staffed, there was no teacher available to be in the class with me. This allowed me the freedom to have a chance to connect with the students as the only adult present, and to use the loud rap lyrics by folks like 2Pac, Nas, and Common—with the volume pumped up beyond what I usually try. Even though the students didn't know it, this would be my first experience working with all African American young men, other than the times I've spent at two Ohio penitentiaries working with adult inmates—some not much older than these eighth grade students. Pac's "I Wonder if Heaven Gotta Ghetto" plays in the background as they enter, and I'm standing just inside the door as is my custom to greet each one as they come in:

Me: Hey how you doin? Love them tight Timberlands you got on, you just get 'em? Student: Naw, but thanks. . . . Got 'em last week, who are you? Me: I'm Dr. Mary Weems and I'm here to do the Rites of Passage program with ya'll. Student: Huh? How'd I get in here, I didn't sign up for nothin'—must be in the wrong place. (He turns to leave with a wink to a friend entering right behind him—he returns a few minutes later with the teacher who'd signed him up.) Meanwhile several students have bounced in behind him checking me out, listening to Pac, asking permission to flip through my CD case which is filled with some of the most current hip hop out. Student: Dag she got the "s" here. Me: No cussin. Students: (1) Sorry, miss. (2) Man, nigga you know better, you know if the prinicipal catch you. . . . (3) How she gon' know. (4) Hey, ya'll see that movie last night with Samuel Jackson in it? (4) What SWAT? (5) Yep. . . . (Bell rings).

Once everyone was seated, I began by telling them that although I'm not a man myself, I had a wonderful grandfather, uncle, and brother as positive male role models growing up, and I'm here to share what I've learned about being a man from them. I shared that I was born and raised in the so-called hoods of Cleveland, that I am a poet, playwright, performer, and Ph.D. [*Student: What's that mean? (I explained what the Ph and then the D meant.)*] who loved working with young people, and I asked each student to either give me the story of how they got their name, or tell me about an object they carry with them all of the time.

Student: Hunh, mama got my name out of a baby name book. See her and daddy couldn't agree on a name. She wanted to name me after her grandfather "Earle." Yep Earl-E like the time I have to wake up to be on time at school. Daddy hated that name and thought people would be teasing me for the rest of my life AND that I'd have to spell it. He wanted me to be named after him, "Langston" after that Harlem Renaissance black man and mama thought that name would keep people asking me IF that's who I was named after . . . so they got a baby book, mama closed her eyes and opened it to a "boy" page and daddy closed his and put a finger down—it landed on James—that's me.

Student: One young man took out a picture of his baby brother who died from Sudden Infant Death Syndrome. "This was my brother Michael—we called him Mikey—I loved him a lot. One day mama went into his room and he was laying there on his stomach—cold. I keep this picture to remind me how important it is to love somebody." (Silence.) Me: I'm looking at him trying not to cry, and at the other young men unsure of how to respond, thinking of my own long-dead little cousin Rosalind who died this same way before the term had been coined. The moment that feels like an hour passes.

Next, I explained that I was here to help them think about the importance of making the transition from child to adult, and that since we only had a short amount of time to spend together we were going to focus on the first "rite": self-esteem. Thanks to an idea I picked up from Tony Sias, administrator of dance, drama, and theater for a school district, we started by coming together in a unity circle to begin by building positive energy between us and in the space:

> We come together
> to honor our ancestors
> and ourselves
> we will respect each other
> listen to each other
> learn from each other
> and always do our best

Alright let's get the positive vibe pumped up in here with 3 Power Claps

At first, the young men didn't want to hold hands, the macho-vibe was high, they didn't know *who* I really was—plus they were trying me like all young people do at first. But when the principal stuck her head in just in time (like we'd rehearsed it) to hear me say, "Ya'll want me to call the principal in here so she can ask you to at least try everything I'm asking you to do?" cooperation levels increased ten-fold, and we were on our way toward building an ad hoc learning community.

To get their creative attention and to share some of my poetic voice, I shared a poem about my high school experience:

> School Days
> I want every brick back.
> My school invisible as a hit-and-run
> driver pulls me through the air
> spinning like a child's top
> The chain link fence
> is an intricate ghost.
>
> I hear the sighs of friends
> who didn't make it to 40, or 30, or 20.
> They left their school spirits and diplomas in the office
> with blank names and no signatures.
>
> There are rebels in the halls, three-cornered
> hats, bell-bottoms, thigh-high mini-skirts, and tie-dyed
> shirts. I smell fish-on-Fridays, the only day
> the "we-real-cool" kids came to school.
> For 2 dollars you could get your fill of fried
> rectangles of cod, crispy fries, and day-old-cole slaw.
> The bell was always five minutes off—the sounds
> loud, slick, and predictable.

This is where wearing bobby socks, and Frankenstein
shoes, I was kissed by a marathon runner—a boy
with green hair, and a face that kept me daydreaming.

I entered those double glass doors with wet
ears, knock-knock knees, and legs long enough to take
two steps. I left with a yearbook
that didn't have my picture in it.

                                                    Mary Weems

I asked students what they thought about the poem, and responded to questions such as,

Students: "What does intricate mean?" (Me: Look it up in the dictionary over there, yeah you can do it right now.) "What are Frankenstein shoes?" (Me: They were called platform shoes, young girls wear them today, but call them stacks.) "Ms. W. did that boy 'really' have green hair?" "Do you still know him?"

I noted that whereas I usually have to teach my undergraduate students how to listen closely to poetry, and pull questions out of them like nails in an old piece of wood, these young men had listened carefully without being prompted. I talked about the importance of making the most of the K-12 school experience, by learning as much as possible, hanging with a positive circle of friends, and getting along with your teachers as much as possible, because if teachers know students care about learning most go out of their way to help young people achieve.

I pointed out that the reference to the ages of friends I'd lost over the years who'd never finished high school was a reminder to me and anyone who will read the poem of how important education is, how precious life is—and that not a moment of it should be wasted. Several young men wanted to let me know that they understood this. Most of them aspired to go to college and they'd lost someone they loved already—many of them to senseless gang violence.

I gave the young men a handout that listed eight Rites of Passage themes:

1 Love for self and others
2 Respect for self and others
3 Honor for all that God/Allah/Yahweh has made
4 Strength to soar above distractions
5 Wisdom to know what is right
6 Courage to stand up for what is right
7 Patience to take your turn
8 Pride in who you are.

We used it as a guide for a discussion about the importance of making a positive transition from child to adult:

"Shoot, I ain't respectin nobody and nothin' unless they respect me too." "Love yourself? Course I love ME—I don't know about that other stuff who you talkin' about Poetry Lady." (Me: *I'm talking about the importance of loving yourself first so it will be possible for you to love somebody else whoever that person is.*) *"I'm cool on the first two, the one I want to know about is the 'distraction' one—what does that word mean?"* (Me: *Whip out that dictionary the librarian keeps on the shelf over there, look it up and you tell me.*) *"Now, me (jumping up and down in my face as he's talking) I don't have patience—I mean NONE, what do I do about that?"* (Me: *You try your best to slow down a little, and you get a bit older, young brother, patience will come as you get tired of rushing through stuff and messin up—that old sayin' "haste makes waste" is so true.*)

Next, I passed out large pieces of white drawing paper and asked them to draw something that reflects how they see themselves as young men. I explained that this could mean drawing images of their favorite things to do, words including poems to describe them, or important people in their lives. I added that this was not about being able to draw well but rather about creating a piece that would reflect who they are. Each student was asked to share what his drawing meant. A couple of them stood out: One young man used black as his only color. He drew a huge picture of the world and this tiny, tiny, image of a stick figure with the word "me" beside it and an arrow pointing to him. Another used black, red, yellow, and blue colors to draw a basketball court, a basketball spinning on its side, a college building with the word "Moorehouse" written on it, and his small house with a picture of himself, his mama, and his little sister standing beside it.

I briefly introduced Rites of Passage rituals from all over the world. The young men were most interested in an ancient African ritual that required the male to kill a lion as one of the rites for manhood. I talked about the importance of history, and that (as Bro. George Jolly, friend and black historian says) people who don't know their history are like computers without the software. I shared the story of Charles Drew, who after developing the process for preserving blood, resigned his position as head of the National Blood Bank system during World War II because the U.S. government mandated that blood transfusions would be segregated. The students were not surprised by this revelation, but discussed at length how upsetting it was to learn that Drew died for want of a blood transfusion. Each day of the residency I shared the autobiographical information of an important black male, including Nat Turner, W. E. B. Du Bois (they already knew about Booker "Uncle Tom" Washington), Malcolm X, and Marcus Garvey.

I ended day one by having them write either their responses to "Who Am I?" or select an emotion and describe it, for example "Happiness is. . . ." What follows are short excerpts from this writing exercise:

"Happiness is a Black woman you fall in love with." "Happiness is an orange shirt against Black skin." "Anger is a Black devil after death." "Fear is a white person before freedom." "I am a Black male." "I'm a King." "I am a star." "I am a honor student." " I am a artist."

I ended by asking them to think about who their heroes are and asked them to bring a picture of that person to our next session.

Day Two (Revelation)

This morning I was so pumped about getting to History that I drove right by the street the school is located on and didn't get to the library space we were meeting in until 8 AM on the nose. By then, all of the young men were in the room and the energy met me as I quietly opened the door in words, a blast of gear in brand name colors: red, lime green, denim blue, black, yellow—Sean John, Rocawear, Tommy Hilfiger, and Phat Farm jackets, and pants, hoodies in black, blue, and gray (these I had to ask them to remove thanks to a dumb school dress policy enforced by the school district)—several pairs of Timberlands were propped up on the tables, and they were talking to each other, hitting beats on their desks, freestylin', brushing their brush waves, and waiting for me. I didn't see any photos— but I get that a lot when I ask students to bring things from home—sometimes it works—most often not.

Normally I would have immediately broken this vibe up by asking them all to sit in their seats, and be quiet long enough to establish what we were going to share for the day, but seeing the student (one of my favorites) I'll call Chico stopped me—before the students even noticed I was in the room. He was laying flat on his back on one of the tables, with one leg up in the air, listening to the beat of one of his peers, and flowin' about what it meant to be a hero, among other things—a light went off in me and I stood there taking it all in, zeroing in on separate conversations (all loud enough to hear from the doorway)—realizing that they'd already started working together in meaningful ways without me, that in the midst of what seemed like noise, young men in groups of two and three were talking about such things as what being a hero was, and "reasons" why they didn't bring the photo. I heard a lot of mamas and grandmamas names mentioned, and a couple of non-daddies discussed, along with one or two real father's, including stepfathers, some were talking about a basketball game they'd played the day before against another school—I thought about what the principal or another teacher might think if they'd walked in at that moment, and I smiled as I turned the light on and off to get their attention, knowing I was witnessing something important:

"Hey, what's your name again? Ms., Dr. Williams, I mean Weems I wanna read your 2-Pac poem you told us about yesterday." "Me too!" "Aw so—I asked first." The cacophony is cool. *Young men in a middle school that I remind myself is housed in a trailer with no gym, no lunchroom (they walk across the street to the elementary school in shifts at lunch time), no computer room. Outside the landscape is used beer bottles, scraps of paper, no grass, stomped dirt.*

We began with our unity circle. This time everyone except one young man (there's always one), Chico—who simply shifted from his back to resting on his side from his place on top of the table—cooperated.

(Me: Chico, what's up?) "Huh?" (Me: I mean why you the only young man not in the circle with me?) "Aw, man. . . ." (Me: I told you about that) "(Laughing) Yeah, okay you right, I mean Ms. Dr. Weems I don't like holdin dudes hands. . . . You know what I mean?" (Me: Yeah, but humor me—now come on.)

We continued.

Handout

(*Note*: I share it here because it may be useful, but I never got around to discussing the handout. Operating on the vibe, we moved through the 80 minutes in other directions, and I asked them to keep it in their folders for future reference.)

Suggestions for Making the Transition from Male to Man:
Male: A person of the masculine gender.
Man: An adult male who is responsible, independent, and dependable.

1. Educate yourself. Know the history of Black people including our origin on the continent of Africa, the history of slavery in the U.S., The Civil Rights Movement, The Harlem Renaissance Movement, The Black Arts Movement of the 60s, and the History of Hip Hop Culture.
2. Honor your elders.
3. Respect yourself and all others.
4. Take responsibility for your actions.
5. Connect with a male role model for advice and guidance.
6. Believe in yourself.
7. Help others in your community whenever you can.
8. Be a role model for young male children.
9. Keep your word.
10. Strive for excellence in everything you do.

I told them about my hero—my granny and how she was the first person to listen to me read my poetry, that since my mama and me didn't get along, I used to talk to granny about everything. I shared some of the good advice she'd given growing up, such as "Don't never be a follower

Cookie—always make up your own mind, even if you're wrong, get in trouble because you made the wrong decision not because somebody persuaded you to," and "In life you have to give up something to get something." I told them without my granny in my life, it would have been a real nightmare.

Next, I shared Tupac's poem "Nightmares" out loud, which begins "I pour my heart in2 this poem and look 4 the meaning of Life/the rich and powerful always prevail and the less fortunate strive through strife." I asked them if anyone brought their picture.

"Oops! nope, I forgot," dag, sho didn't, you know I left it in mama's car this mornin', etc. Me: all right ya'll I get the point—ya'll forgot. Okay then let's listen to some Nas while ya'll write and tell me about your heroes.

Excerpts: Student 1: My hero is my mother because she teaches me how to be a man. She teaches me how not to be a punk. She is my role model. Student 2: My stepfather goofy and honest, smart and silly, he takes care of me. Student 3: I don't have a hero, my daddy is a zero.

I told them that I never had a father in my life and that for a long time I got into relationships with the wrong men, mainly because I didn't have any idea what to look for in a man—no one had taught me. And although I did have positive male role models in my grandpa, brother, and uncle—it's not the same. I never talked about young men or relationships with them—they didn't think I was supposed to have any.

Next, I asked them to work in small groups on skits that had to do with their interpretations of "respect." The best skit was one about police harassment. In it, two young men were rap artists out on a Friday night riding in a gold caddy with tight Spreewell hubcaps. They were on their where to an all-white suburb to hook up with some girls who'd invited them to a party. On the way they were stopped by two white police officers who asked them to get out of the car, made them assume the position, then asked them to do some rap for them to prove they were rap artists. One young man started a beat, while the other did this incredible rap about cops harassing young black men when they should be somewhere eating a donut. The young men playing the cops who were speaking perfect white folks English and treating the young rap artists with complete disrespect—commenting on their sagging pants, their turned-back hats, and questioning whether or not their ride was stolen. The cops responded by doing their own imitation of a rap about how and why the two young men were going to jail for insulting them.

The applause at the end of the skit was long and loud, and the laughter during and after had an edge to it. These were young men who were too familiar with police harassment, and they thought their peers had captured it perfectly in the skit.

I ended by testing my ability to give up as much control as possible. I told the young men that we needed to decide what we were going to share for our final program. I asked for volunteers to (1) put a drill together using R-O-P; (2) act as an MC for the presentation, including introducing each person; and (3) select and organize music to play during their performance. I told them that I couldn't do this alone, that I was giving them most of the responsibility, and that the bar had been set high by the young women when I worked with them the previous week—it was their time to represent.

The excitement in the room was touchable. Chico volunteered to be the MC and immediately started telling people who was going to do what. Another young man had drill team experience, and he and his partner took over putting the drill together and actually started working on it immediately. A couple of students who could draw volunteered to make an ROP sign, and one young man volunteered to sing (he didn't know what yet, though). I told them all of this sounded good to me, that I wanted everyone to wear all black for the program, and that they had until Thursday (two days) to get it together because I wanted to see and hear everything they'd put together for final approval.

Day Three
(Students spend the session planning, organizing, and directing rehearsal.)

Day Four (Rehearsal)
I've never been so nervous before a final program. Thursday was almost a total disaster. Several young men had not been practicing the drill and the drill captain put them out. Turns out, though, that other young men in the class had been watching and were ready to step in and take their place. The young man who was supposed to sing didn't come to school so he was a question mark. A couple of young men who had volunteered to do their "hero" pieces were getting nervous and tried to back out. (*Me: Unh, unh, no backing out now. This is what I mean when I talk about "community" ya'll we got to have each other's backs—we don't have anybody to replace you so you've got to come through for us.*) They changed their minds. The young man who'd volunteered to do the music had his stuff together though, *and* Chico was ready with his freestyle about becoming a man. He was especially excited because he knew his mama was coming to see him. A couple of young men shared that their fathers were planning to come too.

Day Five (Showtime!)
Everybody dressed in black and arrived on time for our quick run through to prepare for our presentation today at 11:30 AM. (*Me: Ricco, you still doin' that positive freestyle for me for the final program?")* "Yeah man." (*Me: Young brother I keep tellin' you I'm not your man.*) "I mean yeah, Poetry Lady, if you want me to. . . ."

Chaos personified. Since we didn't have an auditorium or any large enough space to practice in, young men were all over the library in small groups practicing lines of poetry, or their drill, or song—it was one loud, continuous noise, kind of like I imagine the "bang" before the universe was created.

We were going to use the gym across the street in the elementary school for the program, but no one had told the gym teacher. So when we got across the street, he kept us waiting outside in the cold (the only entrance we were allowed to use to the gym) for fifteen minutes after his class had ended. Instead of getting inside with enough time to go over a few things, we walked in with the parents, the principal, and the invited students.

Chico took over immediately as MC—and I let him. I wanted to see if something powerful would continue to come out of the constructive chaos of our learning community, if what I felt when I saw Chico laying on his back that day was useful.

As we'd planned, Chico started by introducing me. I stepped up to the mike to welcome our audience and immediately dropped my binder on the floor—paper scattered everywhere. Young men started picking up papers and giving them to me, while Chico made some silly remark about "technical difficulties," which made the audience laugh. A few minutes later, I'd regrouped, told the audience that the young men were going to run the program, and taken a seat on the floor with the students.

The show was wonderful. Each young man had a copy of the program flow, and stepped up each in his turn to share. The highlight of the presentation was the "hero" pieces. When the young man read his poem about his stepfather, you could hear a rat peeing on cotton. When Chico did his flow about being a man, his mother was hollering "go on baby, get down" as if he'd just won some kind of award. The audience applauded after each and every presentation and stood up to clap at the end when the young men did their stomp-drill and original R-O-P chant.

The principal was so pleased that she complimented us on a job well done before she thanked our audience for coming and told the students to get back to school. The young man's stepfather, who'd taken an early lunch break to come and see his son's performance, stepped up to me with tears in his eyes. He told me that he had no idea his son felt that way about him—that it made him proud to be loved and respected so much.

C.H.A.O.S. in the classroom is cool. Teachers are under so much pressure to perform, to get stupid test scores up, and to do more with less, to make less mean more to students. I hope something I've shared in this piece will encourage educators to take the risk of giving up as much power and control of their classroom as possible—anything in the universe is possible.

Young Organic Intellectuals in New York City

Regina Bernard

For my parents, my brother & sister, and pre-2000 Hell's Kitchen

Who would suffice as great examples of an organic intellectual? Malcolm X, Phoolan Devi (India's "Bandit Queen"), the late Pedro Pietri, Miguel Pinero, or Hector Lavoe? What do these individuals have in common? Is it that they are all of color or dead, or both? Perhaps organic intellectualism and its death is the larger social concern of forms of intellectualism, but the elementary perspective of similarity that can be analyzed here is the fact that none of these great people received a formal education that placed them on society's map. It was not through their great academic achievements that we have learned who they are, if we have learned of them at all. Thus, the term "organic intellectualism" is defined as a form of intelligence that develops from one's environment outside of the traditional institutions that cultivate knowledge. Organic intellectualism is developed from the street, the parks, the playgrounds, the barbershops or the beauty salons, and anywhere else that helps inform one's intelligence outside of school. This essay is not intended to sound anti-intellectual by promoting learning that takes place outside of school; rather it is an analysis of what is possible in a traditional intellectual setting through the perspectives and experiences of the organic intellectual.

In elementary, junior high, high school, and, even more frightening, college, curriculums are used to determine what students should read and even write about, thus it helps to constrict what students are allowed to think about. Professors and teachers in traditional intellectual settings are often the sole creators of what one learns, but organic intellectuals help to decide what is retained. Although structure is important, it is oftentimes used as a way to constrict the minds of students, in that they are gaining one perspective of a particular topic or subject and therefore not finding a personal connection to the material. So focused on "class aims" and a "do now" enveloped in time management, students are conditioned to pack their bags even before the change of bells occurs, as teachers remind students of their "assigned" readings for the next class. By the time some students have reached the next class, their minds and concentration have shifted from one context to the next; how many times does that context place the students themselves at the center and in relation to what they have learned or read? Are these lessons that they can share among the girls and boys on their neighborhood block?

During my early years of educational training I was lucky enough to already have a love of reading prior to the intensity of the reading assignments that school demanded of me. I spent a lot of leisure time reading for non-school assignment purposes. I read everything, but I had a particular affection for Stephen King, R. L. Stine, Judy Blume, Cynthia Voigt, *Archie*, *Betty & Veronica* comic books, and other readings that did not represent me in any way. Although they did not represent me, these readings were accessible both in the school library and in young adult sections of various bookstores. Even if my imagination attempted to place me in the main character's role or setting, it wasn't possible because of the pictures on the cover of the book. Each of these books—at that time and now, still—are beautifully illustrated with white teenage girls and boys. During my post-school hours I oftentimes shopped around bookstores for texts that related more or more closely represented me. Perhaps someone in some novel looked like me, or lived in a neighborhood like I did, or did the things that me and my friends from my neighborhood did. By junior high school I had fallen into a relationship with Zora Neale Hurston, Langston Hughes, Wallace Thurman; the work of Piri Thomas and Nicholasa Mohr; and the works of Nuyorican poetry. The authors reflected something that previous books had not. They reflected images and experiences I saw in myself, and better still, they also reflected people I saw on a regular basis in my neighborhood. Being born and raised in Hell's Kitchen in the 1970s–2000s, reading became my partner because of the low-excitement levels of activities that were available to young people growing up on my block. From my window in Hell's Kitchen I watched as almost all of my girlfriends became mothers before they were old enough to vote. I watched as populations of adults developed some type of drug or alcohol problem. I was not on my stoop with my friends playing all types of games, or boy-watching, or smack-talking; instead I was reading, professionally dancing, and learning dispute resolution in after-school programs, and by the time I was fourteen I was working at the New York Public Library.

Although my experience may appear to be one that centers myself amid a picturesque gloom and doom, it was quite the opposite. The "gloom and doom" that I have described is one that society has shaped us to believe is dreary for young people. Particularly in neighborhoods of color, these behaviors and experiences, whether learned or adopted, are seen as a "crisis," which then helps to create stereotypes about us as people of color. Neighborhoods that are heavily populated by people of color are referred to as the "inner city," where learning is minimal, employment is low, and all of society's ills are running rampant in a frightening perspective of "street culture." In other words, it is not a place for a young person to grow up. For instance, anthropologist Phillipe Bourgois regards El Barrio (Spanish Harlem) as one of New York City's toughest neighborhood, one that is plagued by the use and sale of drugs, unemployment, illiteracy, and party people. For those who have no experience interacting with or living among blacks and Latinos, this text helps to scare off people from outside neighborhoods similar to the one he analyzes. To counter this idea of Puerto Rican culture being centralized around drug use and abuse, Juan Flores gives a perspective of the cultural traditions of Puerto Ricans and Nuyoricans as a people whose culture has been highly influenced by music, history, and political consciousness.

On the contrary, my neighborhood gave me enough leverage to learn the rights and wrongs of youth into adulthood. It allowed me to engage in a duality of existence, one that helped to formulate traits of both organic and traditional intellectualism. What exactly did my friends and I learn on our apartment building stoops as opposed to the corridors of our schools? I learned how to speak, read, and write Spanish fluently from my Dominican babysitter who never learned to speak English, even though that was my native language. I used Spanish on my stoop to convey messages about homework, life, and the betrayals that youth brings. Years later, in my role as a professor to hundreds of students, I have now begun to teach my mother Spanish, and take pride that I am able to converse with my undergraduate and graduate students who speak Spanish as their native language. I also used Spanish, as a child, to help serve as a child-translator for many Latino/a immigrants in my neighborhood.

Another organic lesson came from my childhood friends and me learning the truth about Santeria. We could identify santero/as by their clothing and demeanor alone. In school I was taught that Santeria was a cult that engaged in the practice of devil worship. I was also taught that Santeria's practitioners could be identified by their eyes, which rolled backwards. My organic intellectual experience taught me that practitioners did not have rolling eyeballs; in fact, the one I encountered wore glasses and many pieces of gold jewelry, never went to school but knew which candle to light for which prayer, and lived down the hall from me. Like the children she entertained in her apartment, unbeknownst to our parents, she was also an organic intellectual. Teenage girls in my apartment building were cooking extensive meals for their entire families before they hit puberty. The boys were either working on their extensive and artistic graffiti masterpieces, demonstrating a break-dancing debate, or secretly participating in recipe exchanges with the girls.

Why doesn't school reflect the personal and learned experiences of youths of color? Research has shown that teenagers are more likely to be victims and perpetrators of crimes during the three hours after school. It is obvious that these youths prefer to look to their norms and social spaces once school is over because of the lack of connection between the hours of school being in session and the hours when it is over. The traditional intellectual model of teaching and learning asks that students learn to read, write, and work through mathematical problems regardless of their backgrounds and their social situations. Although it may seem a fair request of students who do attend school, one has to also think about how students should be able or encouraged to use their organic methods of reading, writing, and working on math problems in connection to what is required of them. Some may say that after-school programs supply the remedy for this connection of organic intellectualism and traditional intellectualism. However, students have to *see* the potential in what after-school programs can offer them, and essentially have to *want* to be there. Many teens have jobs that require them to begin working directly after school, thus those students cannot partake in after-school functions. A few hours on the weekend becomes used as spare time for working youths to engage in their organic and social spaces. From this small amount of time for youths to experience themselves outside of work and school, they are forced to conform and constrict themselves in various mindsets. Homework becomes directly related to school, and school becomes directly related to going to work once school is over. In this framework youths tend to outgrow their organic intellectualism and social spaces when they are not at school or at work. If school and employment opportunities are not places where youths can offer their organic skills, experience, and ideas, what is left of the young organic intellectual? The young organic intellectual begins to shed his or her homemade intellectualism and opts for something a bit more traditional in style. For example, he or she may become embarrassed by an illiterate grandparent, rather than explore the depths of that illiteracy juxtaposed to how the grandparent cannot read but can tell time or count money.

Schools have inculcated dialogues about multiculturalism and diversity as a bridge that connects young students of color to curricula that represents them. However, no one asks the students who represent this population the simplest set of questions: Who are you? What makes you you? What do you know? What did you know before you came to school and what do you know now? Academics for many New York City youths is built on intimate relationships and friendships within the school, but when it comes to personal connections to what they are learning, oftentimes they must wait until college to experience this. I remember when I attended Norman Thomas High School, my love of reading began to grow outside of the school hours because of the impact my English teacher had on me. We read literature fit for Puritans and anyone else that was *not* of color. I longed to hear or tell my own story. I wanted so desperately to write an essay on what my friends and I did on our apartment building stoop, about how much we knew about Hell's Kitchen as opposed to the people who now live there who at that time were fearful of us when we lived there. I wanted to tell of the Laundromats, the fire escapes, the break dancing we competed to master on our block or the basement of our building. I wanted to tell my teacher that the drinking scenes in his assigned readings were viewed as social for the characters in the text; however, the reality of my neighborhood would have academicians view those same drinking scenes among people of color as alcoholism. I used my wants to ask my English teacher, "Why can't we maybe do something different but still within the requirements of the reading?" His response, "If you don't like it, you can go play in heavy traffic." I was crushed. My love for reading became resentful of ideas that did not represent any of my experiences. Out of this resentment I began to develop research skills by seeking texts that spoke directly to my experiences. At one point, my research resulted in finding nothing, so I began to write my own narrative and organic experiences in poetic forms. I refused to do his assignments after that, and I pretty much refused to attend his class altogether.

Young organic intellectualism, developed in New York City, seems to be so feared by the general public, both visitors to New York and natives. The fear seems derived from the lack of the general public being exposed to this type of knowledge expression. Academics and traditional students are used to reading of these particular places, and they may find shame in speaking out if their own neighborhood ends up on a syllabus or reading list. Many do not take the time to understand how it is that young people organize themselves and express what they know and how they have come to know it. Another example from Norman Thomas High School was the issue of "captive lunch." The high school, which is located on Park Avenue in Manhattan, is home to many corporate businesses and corporate Americans. The school population was over 90 percent students of color. For two years, we were allowed to eat our lunch outside of the building if we did not wish to eat at the school cafeteria. As New York City police officers watched our every move on the outside of the school during lunch, we still managed to digest whatever we could in our forty-five minute sprint to the nearest deli or pizzeria. When residents and businesses of the Park Avenue community began to get nervous about our presence—to them we appeared in droves—we were forced to eat lunch in the cafeteria from their time of complaint until we graduated. Imagine thousands of students in one cafeteria at the same time. The absence of our activist and political voices juxtaposed with every other social dynamic (race, age, gender, and socioeconomic status) lent itself to another birthing of the organic intellectual. Many of the "captive" lunch-eaters worked on rap songs and competed in the cafeteria to a wide audience of listeners and cafeteria employees. Other students learned how to braid each other's hair in various African styles, some wrote poetry and read it to others, and some shared tips on how to beat the system—the parental system—through the development of youth-language, also known as "gibberish," which some students spoke more fluently than their requirements of Spanish or French. Mostly, all of us were engaging in the steady development of our organic intellectual spaces. The things we could not learn from the classes before or after lunch were being constructed, taught, and memorized in the cafeteria. Those were the lessons we took back to our block for all the rest of the kids to learn.

Schools and other traditional institutions of intellectualism have failed young people in their attempt to create a bridge between the two forms of intellectual development. Instead of teaching from tools (experiences) that youth already have, traditional institutions of intellectualism have used what they *think* they know about what young people have. Take spoken word, for example. Spoken word in the Nuyorican tradition has always been about writing and reciting from what you feel and have experienced. Spoken word has now taken on the tradition of mass marketing popularity, such that it is available on HBO and beneath Broadway lights, and it is also being "taught" to many New York City youths by way of after-school organizations. How does one teach not from experience, but about experience? Is that even a concept that one can package and sell?

In self-reflecting I look back at my most memorable experiences having to do with learning something: my brother teaching me how to ride a bike, me teaching myself how to roller skate and wanting to become a "roller derby girl," my sister teaching me how to memorize lyrics to songs she would sing to me, or learning how to color-coordinate my 1970s dress code, my mother teaching me how to multiply numbers like eight and nine and tell time on a clock, my father teaching me to cross every "t" and dot every "i," and the boldness in how to ask teachers questions about lessons without fear. My grandmother teaching me the art of caring for the elderly and the constant process of self-reflection one must engage in, in order to see one's center, my "abuela" for teaching me Spanish and never having learned English herself. My family for being multicultural and engaging me in the exploration that makes me multicultural as well, so that by the time academia got hip to "multiculturalism" it was already deeply sewn into the fabrics of my life. It wasn't until graduate school that I again felt the same way about learning things the way I had previously learned them: organically and from my environment and from those who shared spaces in that environment as well. Graduate school has taught me the traditionally intellectual terminologies for words and definitions of experiences that I have always had, but never knew that organically acquiring them was an applicable concept in school.

Resources

Books

Algarín, M., & Holman, B. (1994). *Aloud: Voices from the Nuyorican Poet's Café*. New York: Henry Holt & Company, Inc.

Blume, J. (1976). *Forever*. Riverside, NJ: Simon & Schuster Adult Publishing Group.

Bourgois, P. (1996). *In search of respect: Selling crack in El Barrio*. Cambridge: Cambridge University Press.

Devi, P., Rambali P., & Cuny, M-T. (Eds.). (2003). *The bandit queen of India*. Guilford, CT: Lyons Press.

Flores, J. (2000). *From bomba to hip hop: Puerto Rican culture and identity*. New York: Columbia University Press.

Hughes, L. (1977). *The ways of white folks.* New York: Knopf Publishing Group.

Hurston, Z. N. (1990). *Their eyes were watching God.* (Edited by Henry Louis Gates). New York: HarperCollins Publishers.

Kincheloe, J., & Steinberg, S. R. (1997). *Changing multiculturalism: New times, new curriculum.* London: Open University Press.

King, S. (1985). *The shining.* New York: Doubleday and Company, Inc.

Mohr, N. (1973). *Nilda.* New York: HarperCollins Children's Books.

Pietri, P. (1984). *The masses are asses.* Maplewood, NJ: Waterfront Press.

Stine, R. L. (1990). *Wrong number* . Riverside, NJ: Simon & Schuster Children's.

Thomas, P. (1977). *Down these mean streets.* New York: Random House Inc.

————. (1980). *Stories from El Barrio.* New York: William Morrow & Company, Inc.

Thurman, W. (1999). *Infants of the spring.* New York: Random House Publishing Group.

Voigt, C. (1983). *Dicey's song.* Riverside, NJ: Simon & Schuster Children's.

X, Malcolm, & Haley, A. (1975). *The autobiography of Malcolm X.* New York: Random House Inc.

Web Sites

CBEL 182. Hip-Hop Culture and Society. (2004, September) Retrieved September 17, 2004 from http://www.cbel.com/hip-hop_culture/?order=theme&setcols=4

Department of Youth and Community Development. (2004). Retrieved September 28, 2004 from http://www.nyc.gov/html/dycd/html/services-afterschool.html

InsideSchools.org. H.S. 620 Norman Thomas High School. Retrieved October 1, 2004 from http://www.insideschools.org/fs/school_profile.php?id=972&page=2

Sanabria, I. Semblanza de Hector Lavoe El Hombre, El Artista, Y Su Vida. (1992). Retrieved October 1, 2004 from http://www.hectorlavoe.bigstep.com/generic0.html;$sessionid$L5ZDXVIAAAKYJTZENUFJPQWPER WRJPX0

Smythe, T. (2000, April). Gotham Gazette. Retrieved September 27, 2004 from http://www.gothamgazette.com/article/20010401/15/665

Vodoun and Afro-Religions Links. Retrieved October 1, 2004 from http://www.hermetics.org/afro.html

Search

Jasmine O. Kennerly

People say these are supposed to be my best years
How can that be when these schools try to intimidate you with fear?
Every day I enter this prison.
Just to get an education
What is the reason?
I come in every morning and go
Through metal detectors
And when you ask why,
They give you so many lectures.
I'm here for an education
I don't carry a knife or a gun
Coming in here is like these cops or security substitutes for whites,
See black people and think gun.
Run. What are you running for?
I'm just a teen with my head on straight.
Even though I tend to lose it on
The so-called prison line where I have to wait. Oh Damn!
I set the alarm off!
Time to go to the side
Take off your boots please, asks the security.
It's the metal in my *Tims*,
Just relax, breathe
Or maybe it's the metal in my bra,
Awww
Sorry if your feelings are hurt
But my integrity won't be dragged through dirt.
Because you're looking for us young ones
To have something you can search.

Editors' note: Tims refer to Timberland Boots

CONTRIBUTORS

ERIC ALVAREZ is an elementary school teacher in Phoenix, Arizona. His classroom work consists of negotiating curriculum with students in order to make learning meaningful to their everyday lived experiences. He continues to spin records and supports the Hip Hop Movement.

JANNIS K. ANDROUTSOPOULOS is the editor of the subproject "youth-cultural media styles" with a group of researchers who look at "language variation as communicative practice." Since summer 2003, is junior professor for medium communication at the University of Hanover. Interests of research: sociolinguistics, aspects of medium communication, youth communication, text local analysis, and orthographic variation.

LEONISA ARDIZZONE is an assistant professor at Fordham University's Graduate School of Education. A former classroom teacher, her primary research interests are all related to peace education: youth culture and peace-building, teaching peace through science, and science and spirituality.

BRIAN BAILEY is a doctoral student at the University of Rochester's Warner Graduate School of Education and Human Development. He is interested in methods of teaching with new technologies that expand traditional definitions of literacy and open up new spaces for youth agency, identity exploration, emotional expression, and critical thinking.

EFFIE BALOMENOS is an artist and illustrator, a cultural critic, as well as a teacher of visual arts. Her interest and expertise in the relationship between aesthetics and culture has found its critical expression in her art and writing. She has published in the area of aesthetics education and has illustrated a series of picture books that is being used in schools around the globe.

REGINA BERNARD was born and raised in Hell's Kitchen, New York City. She graduated with a BS in Criminal Justice from John Jay College of Criminal Justice, and an MA in African American Studies from Columbia University's graduate school of Arts and Sciences. She is currently a PhD candidate in the Urban Education department of the Graduate Center where her research is focused on New York City Organic Intellectualism. Regina teaches both black and Latino studies at Baruch College, and teacher education courses at Hunter College.

MELANIE E. L. BUSH is an assistant professor at Adelphi University. She is the author of *Breaking the Code of Good Intentions: Everyday Forms of Whiteness* and other publications, and has been active for many years in struggles for social and racial justice.

CARL BYBEE is the director of the Oregon Media Literacy Project, and an associate professor of communication studies in the School of Journalism and Communication at the University of Oregon. He continues to write, teach, speak, conduct workshops, and involve himself in the community, focusing on the role news and entertainment media play in raising our children as budding consumers and more hopefully as young citizens who understand the difference between people democracy and corporate democracy. He recently scared and inspired himself and his students by having them reread Erich Fromm's 1941 classic, *Escape From Freedom*.

FAITH BYNOE is a master's degree candidate at Long Island University. Her work focuses on life span development and engagement of youth in community building. She currently lives in Washington DC.

JOSEPH CARROLL-MIRANDA is originally from Puerto Rico. He is a doctoral candidate specializing in learning technology at New Mexico State University.

ROYMIECO A. CARTER, M.F.A. is an assistant professor of graphic design in the Art Department of the University of North Carolina at Charlotte. He teaches courses on graphic design, digital media, visual literacy and theory, and social criticism. He has written articles on graphic design education, art education, gaming, human computer interaction, and graphics computer animation.

REBECCA L. CARVER is an assistant professor in the Department of Educational Leadership and Cultural Foundations at the University of North Carolina at Greensboro. Her scholarship focuses on intersections among the topics of experiential education, youth and community development, school reform, educational policy, and qualitative research.

J. VERN CROMARTIE is a professor of sociology at Contra Costa College where he also serves as the program coordinator of the Sociology Program, and the chairperson of the Social Science Department. He is the editor of

Ithaca Work: Selected Papers and Speeches from the 10th Annual International Working Class Academics Conference.

PETER DACHILLE, JR is a freelance writer, photographer, restaurant critic, painter (walls, not canvases), an avid reader, G.O.P., and Star Wars fan. Since none of those pays well, he has a job to while away the time. Born and raised in Brooklyn, he is probably still there.

SHIV DESAI is a doctoral candidate at the UCLA Graduate School of Education in the Urban Schooling Division. He taught for five years in both Los Angeles and New York City. Shiv is interested in investigating how spoken word can assist students in engaging in critical literacy, as well as expanding the notion of hip hop in the classroom.

STACEY DUNCAN, being of sound mind, body, and spirit, engages a dynamic life variety, including the medium, the message, and the matrix. She is also student and faculty in the Language, Literacy, and Culture program at New Mexico State University.

ELENA DUQUE has a doctorate in education from the University of Barcelona in Spain. She now teaches in the Autonomous University of Aguascalientes in México. She has publications about critical pedagogy and gender education. She works on feminism, gender education, critical pedagogy, and multiculturalism.

LAWRENCE ENG is a PhD candidate in the department of Science and Technology Studies at Rensselaer Polytechnic Institute. His primary research interests include (postmodern) youth subcultures, strategies of cultural resistance involving the appropriation of technology and science, public understandings of science, and the sociology of youth violence.

ELLEN ESSICK is a faculty member in Public Health Education at UNC Greensboro. In addition to writing and presenting on feminist theory and eating disorders, she also trains public school teachers on a variety of health topics such as sexuality and the impact of poverty on teaching in the public schools.

AINHOA FLECHA is researcher at the Department of Sociological Theory, University of Barcelona. She teaches sociology of education and women in popular education. Her research interests focus on gender studies, particularly from the perspective of dialogic feminism and the inclusion of "othered women."

REBECCA A. GOLDSTEIN is an assistant professor of curriculum and teaching at Montclair State University. She is the editor of *Useful Theory* (Peter Lang 2006).

JESSE GOODMAN is professor of education and American studies at Indiana University. His primary interests include school reform, identity formation, sexuality education, western intellectual history, and teacher education. His new book is: *Reforming schools: Working within a progressive tradition during conservative times* (2006).

RHONDA HAMMER is a research scholar at the UCLA Center for the Study of Women, and a lecturer in women's studies and communications. She is the author of *Antifeminism and Family Terrorism.*

MARY STONE HANLEY is an assistant professor of arts education and multicultural education at the University of North Carolina at Chapel Hill.

DR. MYRNA HANT is a visiting scholar at the UCLA Center for the Study of Women. Her research focuses on television studies.

ROB HAWORTH is a doctoral student at New Mexico State University in the College of Education. His research focuses on anarchism and decentralized forms of decision making, youth culture, and critical multicultural social studies.

ROB HELFENBEIN is assistant professor of teacher education at Indiana University–Indianapolis. His research combines critical geography, cultural studies, and education.

KATHRYN HERR is an associate professor at Montclair State University in the College of Education and Human Services. She also edits the journal, *Youth and Society.*

LYNN M. HOFFMAN, a former middle and high school teacher and administrator, is an associate professor at Bucknell University.

WINTHROP R. HOLDER is founder of *Crossing Swords* and *Counter-Currents,* two highly acclaimed critical and creative thinking journals for high school students. For the last four years he has been facilitating ONE MIC, a monthly lunchroom symposium, and is the author of the forthcoming *Classroom Calypso: Giving Voice to the Voiceless* (Lang 2006). His students provided much of the poetry in this encyclopedia.

GLORIA E. JACOBS is an assistant professor of literacy at St. John Fisher College. She studies online literacy practices and its implications for writing instruction.

HEIKE JENß is a lecturer at the Institute of Cultural History of Textiles at Dortmund University. She has conducted ethnographic research in the interdisciplinary project "Uniforms in Motion: The Process of Uniformity in Body and Dress," and has written articles on mass-customization, identity and fashion, secondhand dress, and methodology.

PAM JOYCE is a Reading Specialist who has been in education for over twenty-five years. She is currently a doctoral student in urban education at the CUNY Graduate Center in New York City. Her new book will be out in 2006, dealing with the SSDD of schooling (Same s***, different day).

OLAF KARNIK, born 1962, lives in Cologne as a freelancing journalist and author for *Neue Zürcher Zeitung, Frankfurter Rundschau, INTRO, WDR 3, Deutschlandfunk, ARTE, Suhrkamp Verlag,* and *Kiepenheuer & Witsch.* He also works as a musician, deejays, and curates music events.

JENNIFER KELLY, University of Alberta, is the author of *Under the Gaze: Learning to be Black in White Society* and *Borrowed Identities.*

JUNGANG KIM is an assistant professor of education at Furman University and teaches in the TESOL graduate program.

JOE L. KINCHELOE is the Canada Research Chair at the McGill University Faculty of Education. He is the author of numerous books and articles about pedagogy, education and social justice, racism, class bias, sexism, issues of cognition and cultural context, and educational reform. His books include: *Teachers as Researchers, Classroom Teaching: An Introduction, Getting Beyond the Facts: Teaching Social Studies/Social Sciences in the Twenty-first Century, The Sign of the Burger: McDonald's and the Culture of Power,* and *City Kids: Understanding Them, Appreciating Them, and Teaching Them.*

SHULA KLINGER's interest in online moderation and storytelling began in 1995, when she logged into eWorld. She created and moderated the Attic—an online space for high school students—at the Vancouver School Board in June, 2003. Shula now works for the South Island Distance Education School in Victoria, BC, as a consultant in online school development.

MICHELE KNOBEL is an associate professor at Montclair State University, New Jersey, USA. She has worked within teacher education in Australia, Mexico, and the U.S., and her research interests currently focus on new literacies and new technology practices.

HEINZ-HERMANN KRÜGER holds a chair in education at the University of Halle Wittenberg in Germany and has published widely in the fields of educational theory, qualitative research methods, and youth history and ethnography. His current interests include the critical analysis of postmodernism and childhood/youth in East and West Germany.

MACHIKO KUSAHARA is a researcher in media art and theory, who has been publishing and curating in the interdisciplinary field connecting art, science, technology, culture, sociology, and history. Her recent researches are on correlation between digital media and traditional culture. She published sixteen laserdiscs on computer graphics and coauthored *Art@Science* (Springer), and *The Robot in the Garden* (MIT Press).

COLIN LANKSHEAR is a permanent Mexican resident currently working half time as professor of literacy and new technologies at James Cook

University in Cairns, Australia, and one-third time as a visiting scholar at McGill University in Montreal.

SERENA PARRIS LARRAIN is a doctoral student at Georgia Southern University. She received her master's degree in instructional technology in 2002.

PEPI LEISTYNA is an associate professor of applied linguistics graduate studies at the University of Massachusetts–Boston. His books include: *Breaking Free, Presence of Mind, Defining and Designing Multiculturalism*, and *Cultural Studies: From Theory to Action.*

ROB LINNÉ is an associate professor of English education at Adelphi University's Long Island and Lower Manhattan campuses.

RODNEY E. LIPPARD is currently the integrated library system workflow librarian at the University of North Carolina at Chapel Hill. He is also a student in the PhD program for educational leadership and cultural studies at the University of North Carolina at Greensboro where his research interest includes issues surrounding gender and sexuality.

JONATHAN LONDON is executive director of Youth In Focus. He has a doctorate in rural social science and a master's degree in city and regional planning

KEISHA McGHEE LOVE has a doctorate in counseling psychology. Her research program focuses on stepfamilies and parent–child relationships.

JOSÉE MAKROPOULOS is a doctoral candidate in the Department of Sociology and Equity Studies in Education at the University of Toronto. She also teaches on a part-time basis for the Department of Sociology and the Faculty of Education at the University of Ottawa.

CURRY MALOTT is currently assistant professor of education at Brooklyn College/CUNY and co-author of *Punk Rockers' Revolution: A Pedagogy of Race, Class, and Gender.* He is a musician and students often see him sk8ing to class along the streets of Brooklyn.

CAROLINA MANCUSO is a writer, teacher, and editor in the fields of education, theatre, the arts, and community affairs. Her short stories, essays, and articles have been published in a variety of journals, magazines, and anthologies. One of her stories won the Reed Smith Fiction Award and was nominated for the Pushcart Prize. She is completing a novel about women serfs in 13th century France

TYSON MARSH is a doctoral candidate at the UCLA Graduate School of Education in the Urban Schooling Division. He was involved in student activism at the University of Washington prior to his doctoral work. Tyson is interested in investigating how spoken word can assist students in engaging in critical literacy, as well as expanding the notion of hip hop in the classroom.

RUTHANN MAYES-ELMA is a visiting professor at Miami University of Ohio and also teaches fifth grade in Cincinnati. Her newest book is *Not Empowering: The Women of Harry Potter.*

GABRIELE MENTGES is a professor at the Institute for Art and Material Culture at the University of Dortmund. She researches art and the cultures of the world and is working in the context of the research project "Uniform in Motion: To the process of the university forming of body and clothes" (housed at the Universities of Dortmund and Frankfurt).

DEBRA MERSKIN received her doctorate at the University of Syracuse and is an associate professor in the School of Journalism & Communication at the University of Oregon.

STACEY MILLER (sj) is an assistant professor in secondary English education at Indiana University of Pennsylvania, is a published SLAM! poet, and is interested in space/time research on non-traditional teachers.

DAVID MUGGLETON was once involved in the 1970's punk rock scene, and is now senior lecturer in the sociology of sport at University College–Chichester. He has particular research interests in youth and sporting subcultures, and is the author of *Inside Subculture: The Postmodern Meaning of Style.*

KLAUS NEUMANN-BRAUN is a full professor at the University of Basel, philosophical-historical faculty. His main areas of research are: medium and communication sociology, public and prescription ion research, popular culture analysis, and method development (image analysis).

PRIYA PARMAR is an assistant professor of adolescence education at Brooklyn College–CUNY. She teaches language and literacy acquisition at the elementary and secondary levels to both undergraduate and graduate students. Her scholarly interests include critical, multiple literacies, multicultural education, youth and hip hop culture, and other contemporary issues in the field of cultural studies in which economic, political, and social justice issues are addressed. Professor Parmar's published scholarly works include "Critical Thinking and Rap Music: The Critical Pedagogy of KRS-One" in *The Encyclopedia of Critical Thinking* (Greenwood Press, Spring 2004), "Spoken Word and Hip Hop: The Power of Urban Art and Culture," a 3-part series co-authored in *Urban Education: An Encyclopedia* (Greenwood Press, Fall 2004), and "Rap Music and Oral Literacy" in *The Encyclopedia of the Social and Cultural Foundations of Education.* Professor Parmar also serves as a Hip Hop Cultural Specialist for the New York area representing The Temple of Hip Hop, an international organization promoting education and cultural awareness of the true meaning of hip hop culture, as well as advocating social and political activism on the inter/national level and in the greater New York area.

JAMES PETERSON is an assistant professor of English at Penn State University, Abington College. He is also the founder of Hip Hop Scholars, Inc., an educational consulting firm.

DAVID POVEDA is an educational and developmental psychologist. His interests are children's discourse and learning in different contexts.

CHRISTINE QUAIL is an assistant professor of communication arts at the State University of New York College at Oneonta. She is on the Steering Committee of the Union for Democratic Communications, an international media and democracy organization. Her research includes political economy of communications, cultural studies, and critical media literacy, and she is a co-author (with Kathalene A. Razzano and Loubna H. Skalli) of *Vulture Culture: The Politics and Pedagogy of Daytime Television Talkshows* (Peter Lang 2005).

ELIZABETH QUINTERO is associate professor in the Department of Teaching and Learning at NYU. Her teaching, research, and service involve working with multilingual families, students, and young children. She is the co-author of *Becoming a Teacher in the New Society: Bringing Communities and Classrooms Together* (with Mary Kay Rummel), and the author of *Problem-Posing with Multicultural Children's Literature: Developing Critical, Early Childhood Curricula*.

BIRGIT RICHARD is professor for new media at the Goethe University in Frankfurt. Her fields of specialization include: new media, aesthetics of everyday life (contemporary youth cultures, fashion, design, popular culture, and gaming: representation of women in computer games). She is editor of the *Kunstforum International Volumes* on Fashion, Time, Images of Violence, Art and Life Sciences, and Art and Magic, and founder of the Youth Culture Archive. Her current research focuses on "Uniform in Motion" which considers the topic of uniformity of body and clothing, and she is part of a team that developed and executed a major exhibition: "Coolhunters: Youth cultures between media and market" at the ZKM Karlsruhe 2005. Professor Richard is the author of many books and articles on her research subjects.

DR. ANTHONY M. ROSELLI is associate professor of education at Merrimack College, North Andover, MA. His most recent book is *Dos and Don'ts of Education Reform: Toward a Radical Remedy for Educational Failure.*

DR. TATIANA V. RYBA, University of Tennessee, conducts interdisciplinary research on the intersection of sport studies and cultural studies.

DR. AXEL SCHMIDT is an assistant at the Institute for Medium Sciences at the University of Basel. His research areas are media and communication sociology, the study of youth popular culture, and procedures of qualitative social research.

LIEN SHEN is a doctoral student in the Department of Art Education at Ohio State University, teaches a computer graphic course, and developed a group study course in the Department of Art Education: Visual and Cultural Discourse—Beyond Japanese Anime and Manga, which is offered once a year at OSU. Shen was a manga artist in Taiwan.

REBECCA SKULNICK is a doctoral student at Indiana University. She is currently writing her dissertation on how particular adolescents, those citizens who are "becoming" adults, learn not only from schooling, but also from the media's influence on their own performative identities and sociopolitical choices.

SANTIAGO SOLIS is a doctoral student at Teachers College, Columbia University. His research interest is in examining children's picture books through a crip-queer framework.

SHIRLEY R. STEINBERG is an associate professor at the McGill University Faculty of Education. She is the author and editor of numerous books and articles and co-edits several book series. The founding editor of *Taboo: The Journal of Culture and Education*, Steinberg has recently finished editing *Teen Life in Europe*. She is the editor of *Multi/Intercultural Conversations: A Reader*. With Joe Kincheloe she has edited *What You Don't Know About Schools; Kinderculture: The Corporate Construction of Childhood* and *The Miseducation of the West: How Schools and the Media Distort Our Understanding of the Islamic World*. She is co-author of *Changing Multiculturalism: New Times, New Curriculum*, and *Contextualizing Teaching* (with Joe Kincheloe). Her areas of expertise and research are in critical media literacy, social drama, and youth studies. She sends a shout-out to all her colleagues and friends in the United States who have suffered the absurdity of national "accreditation" these past years.

DREW TRAULSEN is a high school and college U.S. History teacher and graduate student from Chico, California.

PETER PERICLES TRIFONAS is a professor at OISE/University of Toronto. He has published extensively in the areas of cultural studies and philosophy. His most recent books are *Deconstructing Derrida* (with Michael Peters) and *After Literacy*.

BART VAUTOUR is a graduate student in English at Dalhousie University. His research areas include youth studies and Canadian literature.

LEILA E. VILLAVERDE is an associate professor of cultural foundations in the Department of Educational Leadership and Cultural Foundations at the University of North Carolina at Greensboro. She is also the co-director of graduate studies for the Women's and Gender Studies Program. She teaches courses on curriculum studies, gender studies, and visual literacy and aesthetics. She is the co-editor of *Dismantling White Privilege: Pedagogy, Politics, and Whiteness*, and *Rethinking Intelligence: Confronting Psychological Assumptions about Teaching and Learning*.

WENDY WALTER-BAILEY is an assistant professor of education at Franklin College. She teaches multicultural education, secondary special methods for social studies and language arts, and general education liberal arts classes dealing with culture and diversity.

MARY E. WEEMS is a poet, playwright, performer, social foundations scholar, and educational consultant. Books include: *Public Education and the Imagination-Intellect*, *I Speak from the Wound in My Mouth*, and *Poetry Power*.

GRANT WILSON teaches English and media studies. He is a critical educator who uses popular culture as a foundation for pedagogical practice.

HANDEL KASHOPE WRIGHT is the Canada Research Chair in Comparative Cultural Studies and director of the Centre for Culture, Identity, & Education at the University of British Columbia. He is the author of *A Prescience of African Cultural Studies*.

Index